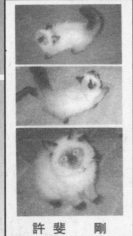

許斐　剛

Breed: Himalayan (Sealpoint) male.
Name (official name): Kahluamilk —
nickname is Kal.

He is the model of Kalpin in the
story.
This picture was taken two or
three months after he was born.
When he was brought home on
June 26th (my birthday), he could
fit in my palm. I hear kittens spend
18 hours sleeping, but Kal stays
awake for 18 hours. Even though
Kal likes to play, recently I've been
too busy and I feel bad.

Takeshi Konomi 2000

About Takeshi Konomi

Takeshi Konomi exploded onto the manga scene with the
incredible **THE PRINCE OF TENNIS**. His refined art style and
sleek character designs proved popular with **Weekly Shonen
Jump** readers and **THE PRINCE OF TENNIS** became the No. 1
sports manga in Japan almost overnight. Its cast of attrac-
tive male tennis players enticed legions of female readers
even though it was originally intended to be a boys' comic.
The manga continues to be a success and is now on its 22nd
graphic novel. A hit anime series was created, as well as
several video games and mountains of merchandise.

THE PRINCE OF TENNIS
VOL. 3
The SHONEN JUMP Manga Edition

STORY AND ART BY
TAKESHI KONOMI

English Adaptation/Gerard Jones
Translation/Joe Yamazaki
Touch-up & Lettering/Andy Ristaino
Graphics & Cover Design/Sean Lee
Editor/Michelle Pangilinan

Editor in Chief, Books/Alvin Lu
Editor in Chief, Magazines/Marc Weidenbaum
VP of Publishing Licensing/Rika Inouye
VP of Sales/Gonzalo Ferreyra
Sr. VP of Marketing/Liza Coppola
Publisher/Hyoe Narita

Printed in the U.S.A.

Published by VIZ Media, LLC
P.O. Box 77064
San Francisco, CA 94107

Shonen Jump Manga Edition
10 9 8 7 6 5 4
First printing, August 2004
Fourth printing, November 2007

PARENTAL ADVISORY
THE PRINCE OF TENNIS
is rated A and is suitable
for readers of all ages.
ratings.viz.com

THE WORLD'S
MOST POPULAR MANGA

www.viz.com

www.shonenjump.com

Shonen Jump Manga

テニスの王子様

THE PRINCE OF TENNIS

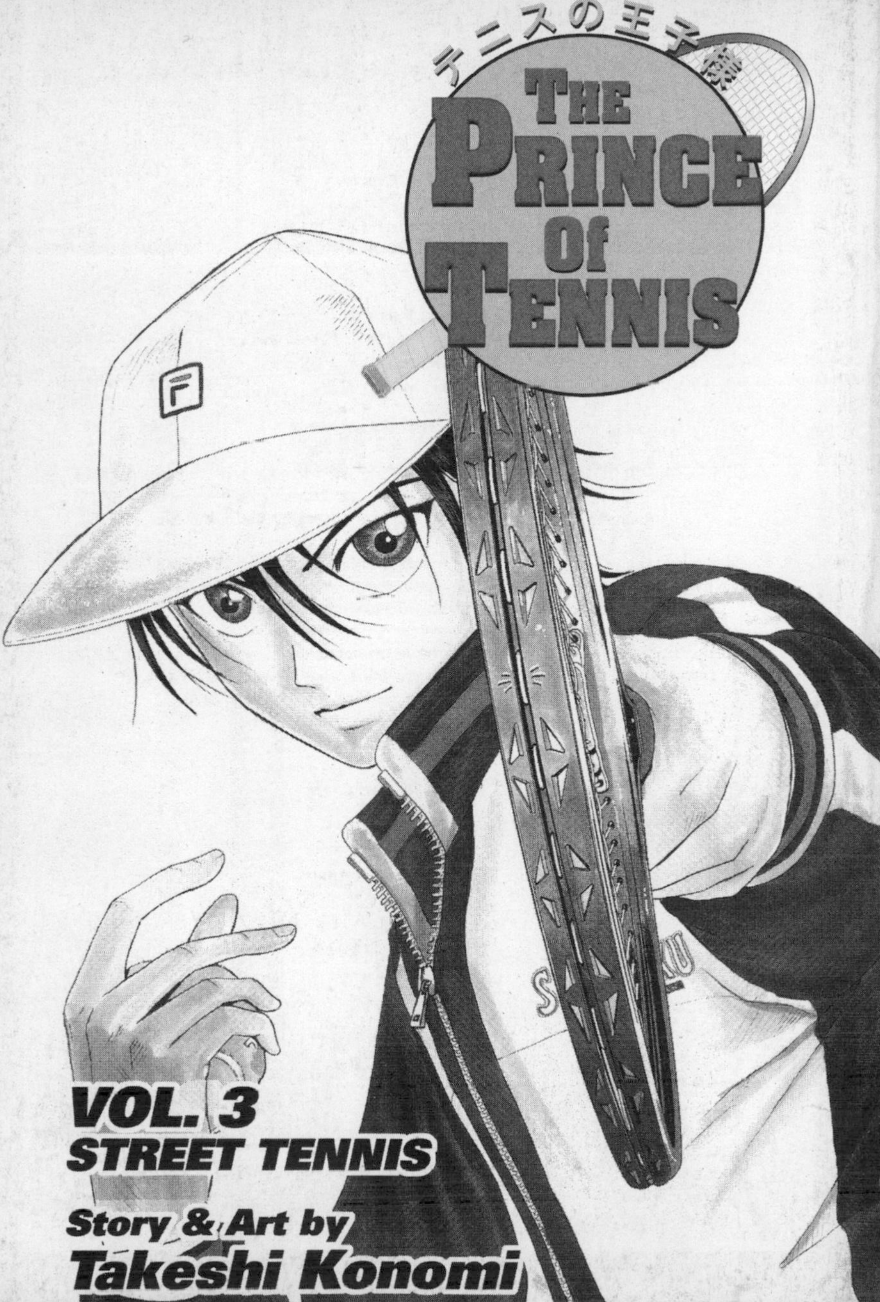

VOL. 3

STREET TENNIS

Story & Art by

Takeshi Konomi

Shusuke Fuji

Seishun Academy Tennis Team (9th Grade)

Shuichiro Oishi

Seishun Academy Tennis Team Assistant Captain (9th Grade)

Kunimitsu Tezuka

Seishun Academy Tennis Team Captain (9th Grade)

STORY & CHARACTERS

VOLUME 1 ▶ 3

Ryoma Echizen

Seishun Academy Tennis Team (7th Grade)

THE PRINCE OF TENNIS

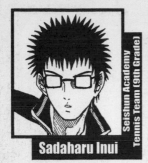

Seishun Academy
Tennis Team (9th Grade)
Eiji Kikumaru

Seishun Academy
Tennis Team (9th Grade)
Takashi Kawamura

Seishun Academy
Tennis Team (9th Grade)
Sadaharu Inui

Seishun Academy
Tennis Team (8th Grade)
Takeshi Momoshiro

Seishun Academy
Tennis Team (8th Grade)
Kaoru Kaido

Seishun Academy
Tennis Team (Coach)
Sumire Ryuzaki

RYOMA ECHIZEN, A TENNIS PRODIGY AND WINNER OF FOUR CONSECUTIVE U.S. JUNIOR TOURNAMENTS, HAS RETURNED TO JAPAN AND ENROLLED AT SEISHUN ACADEMY. HIS COOL DEMEANOR PUSHED THE BUTTONS OF A FEW MEMBERS OF THE TENNIS TEAM AND THEY SOUGHT HIM OUT— BUT NOT ONE CAME CLOSE TO HIS OVERWHELMING SKILL AND KNOWLEDGE OF THE GAME. HE'S JUST BEATEN TWO TEAM STARTERS TO EARN THE RIGHT TO PLAY IN THE DISTRICT.

Seishun Academy
Tennis Team (7th Grade)
Sakuno Ryuzaki

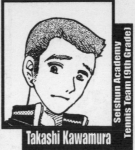

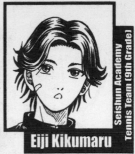

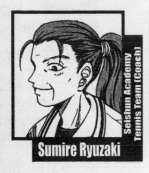

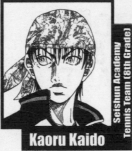

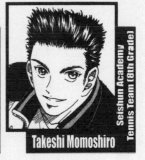

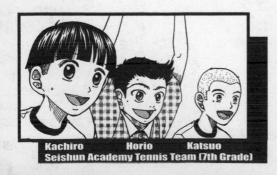

Kachiro
Horio
Katsuo
Seishun Academy Tennis Team (7th Grade)

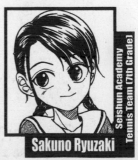

Contents

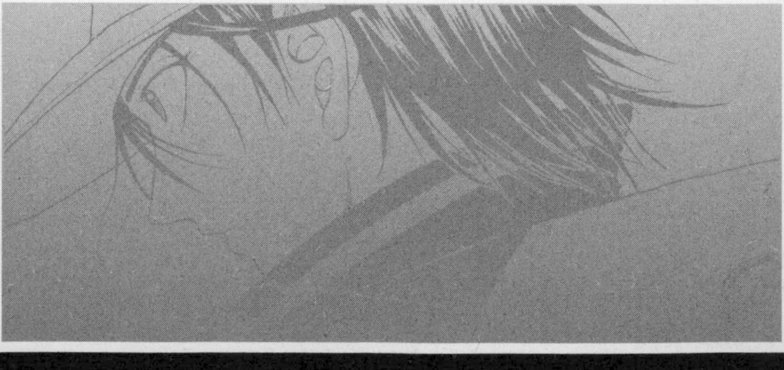

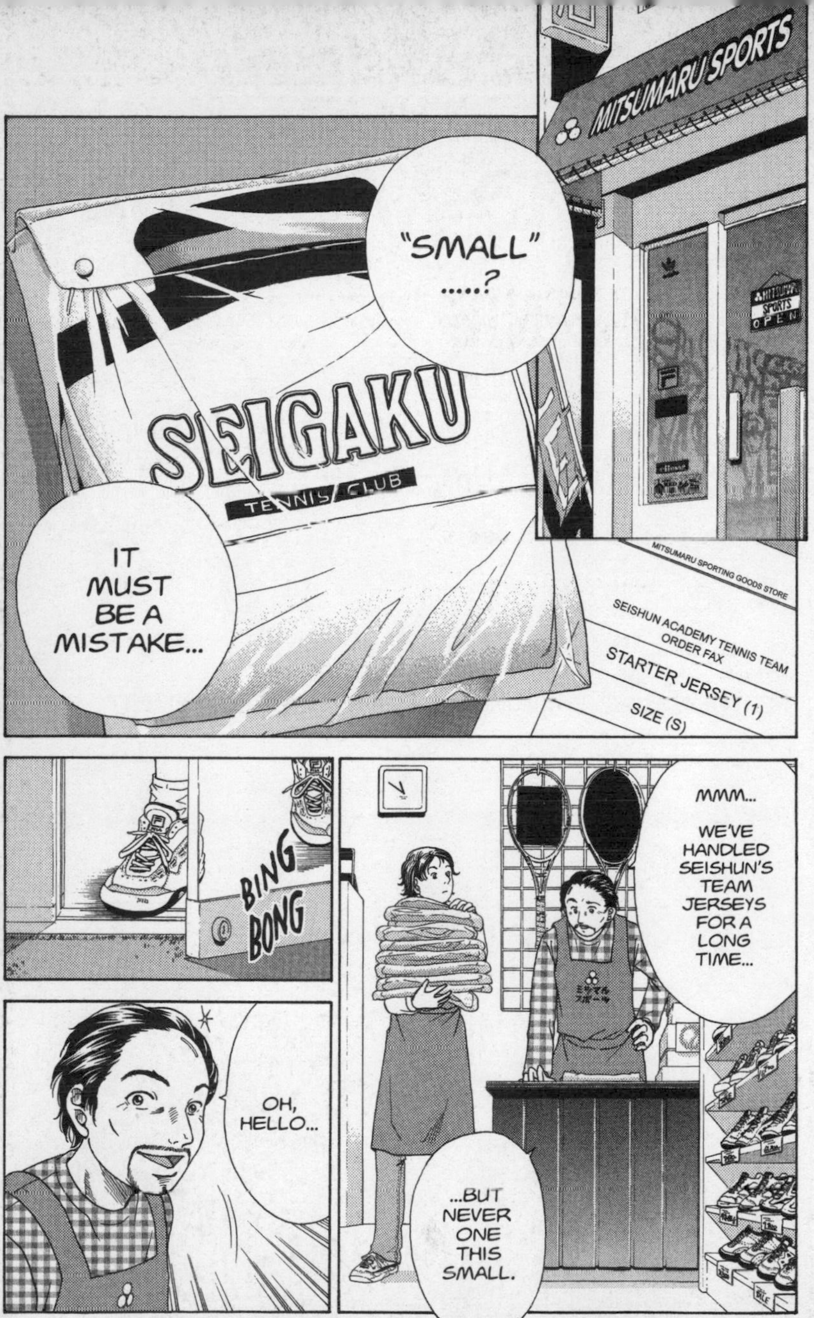
MITSUMARU SPORTS
SEIGAKU
TENNIS CLUB
"SMALL" ......?
IT MUST BE A MISTAKE...
MITSUMARU SPORTING GOODS STORE
SEISHUN ACADEMY TENNIS TEAM ORDER FAX
STARTER JERSEY (1)
SIZE (S)
MMM...
WE'VE HANDLED SEISHUN'S TEAM JERSEYS FOR A LONG TIME...
...BUT NEVER ONE THIS SMALL.
BING BONG
OH, HELLO...

GENIUS 17: WARM-UPS

GENIUS 17

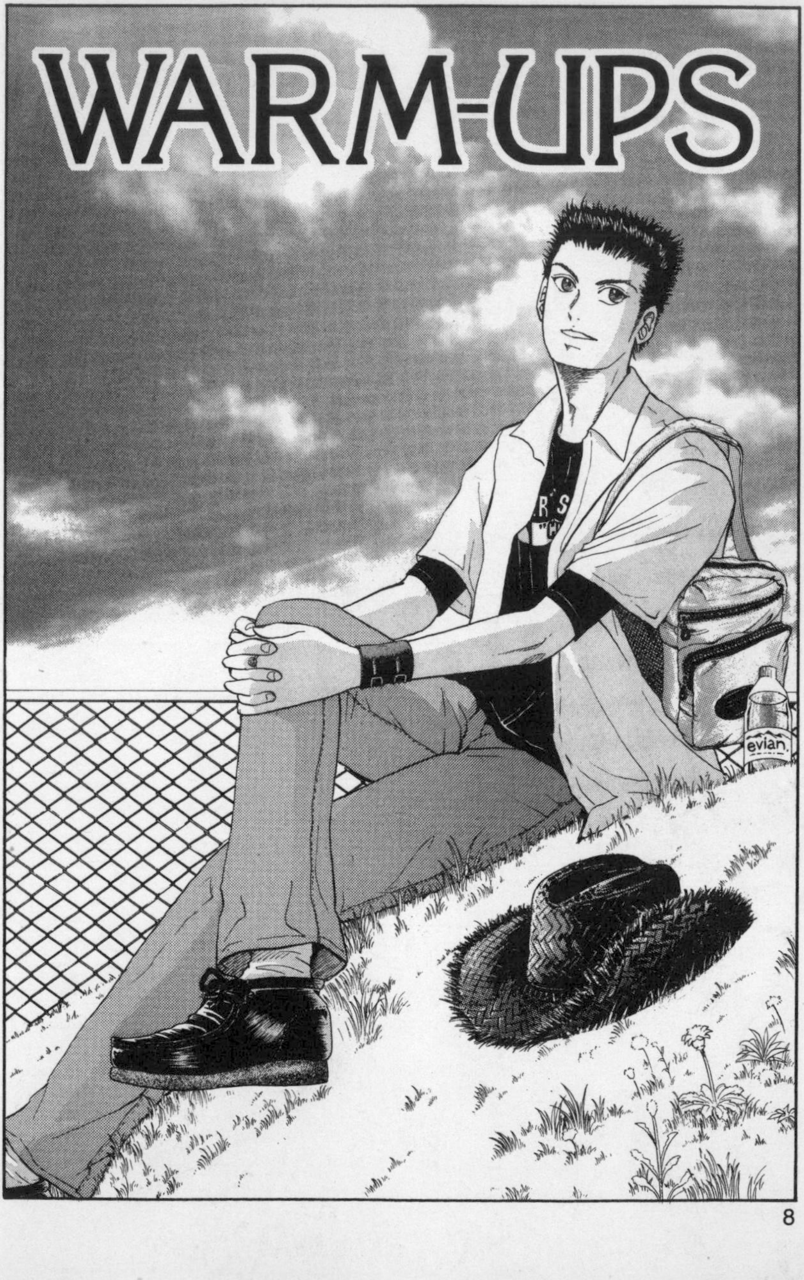
WARM-UPS
evian

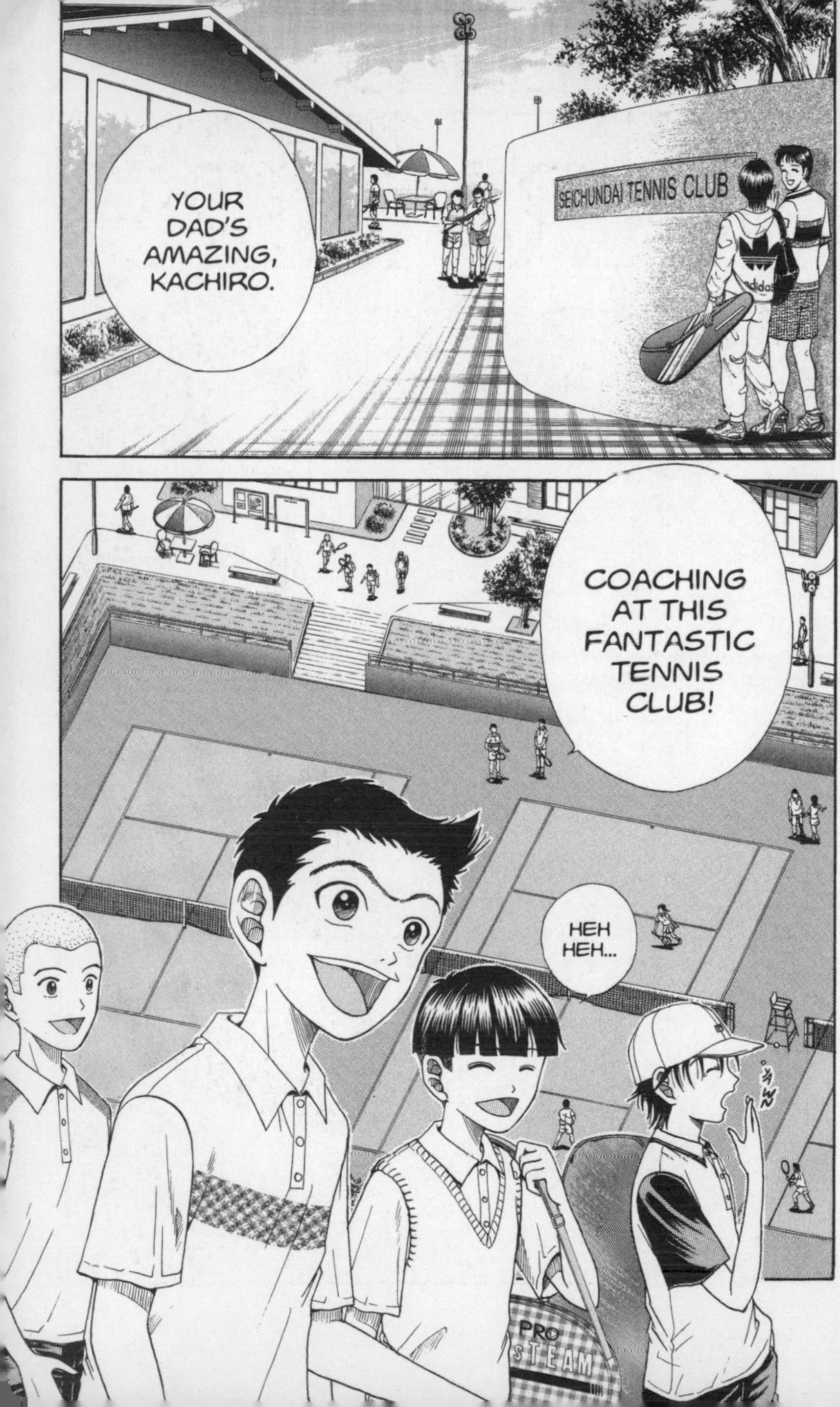
SEICHUNDAI TENNIS CLUB
YOUR DAD'S AMAZING, KACHIRO.
COACHING AT THIS FANTASTIC TENNIS CLUB!
HEH HEH...
PRO STEAM

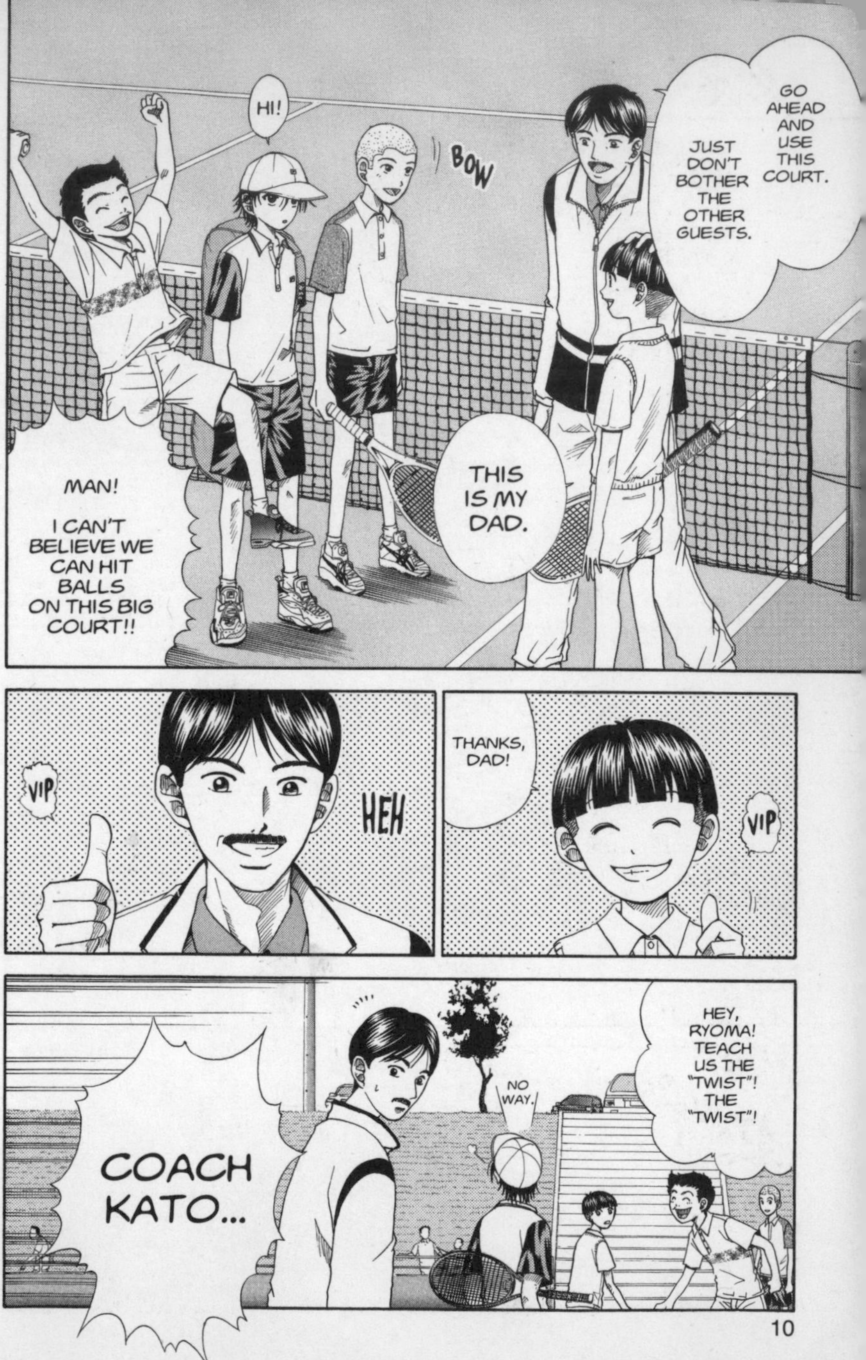

GO AHEAD AND USE THIS COURT.
JUST DON'T BOTHER THE OTHER GUESTS.
BOW
HI!
THIS IS MY DAD.
MAN!
I CAN'T BELIEVE WE CAN HIT BALLS ON THIS BIG COURT!!
THANKS, DAD!
VIP
HEH
VIP
HEY, RYOMA! TEACH US THE "TWIST"! THE "TWIST"!
NO WAY.
COACH KATO...

READ THIS WAY

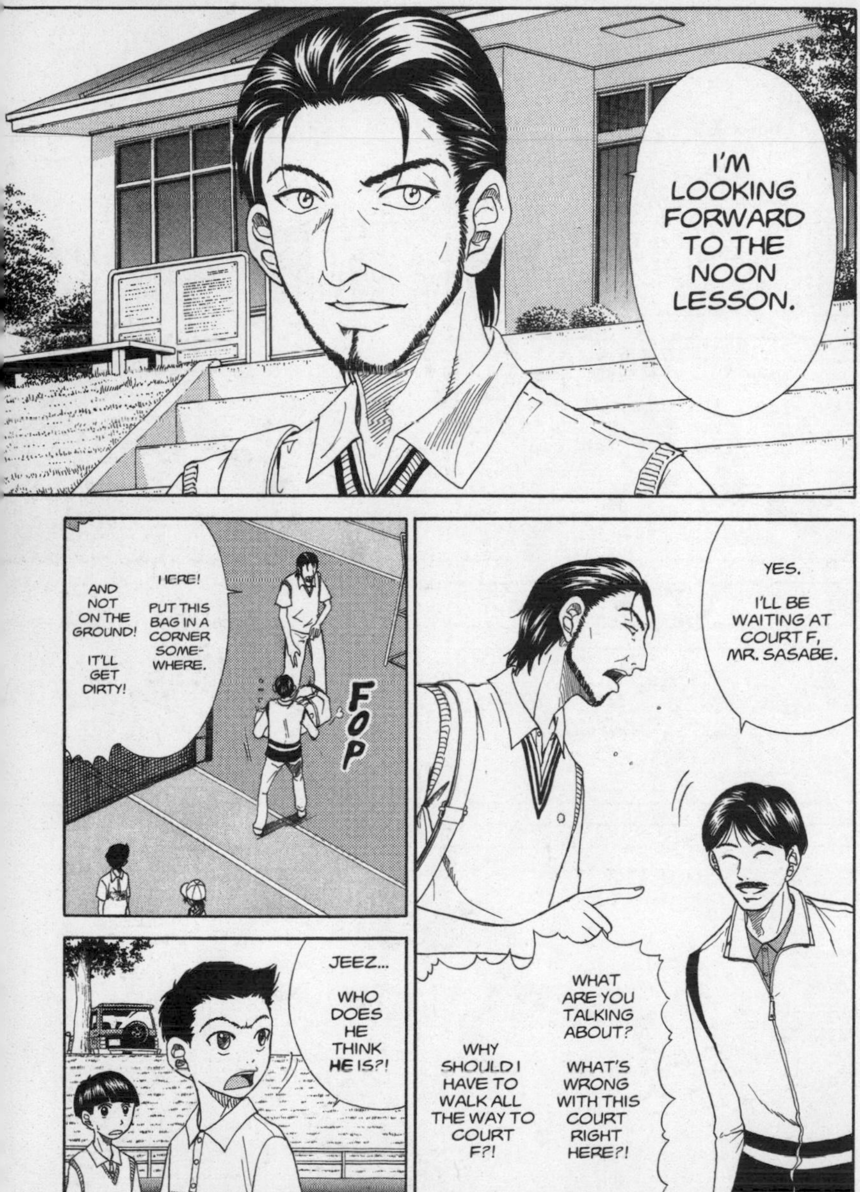
I'M LOOKING FORWARD TO THE NOON LESSON.
YES.
I'LL BE WAITING AT COURT F, MR. SASABE.
WHAT ARE YOU TALKING ABOUT?
WHAT'S WRONG WITH THIS COURT RIGHT HERE?!
WHY SHOULD I HAVE TO WALK ALL THE WAY TO COURT F?!
HERE!
PUT THIS BAG IN A CORNER SOME-WHERE.
AND NOT ON THE GROUND!
IT'LL GET DIRTY!
FOP
JEEZ...
WHO DOES HE THINK HE IS?!

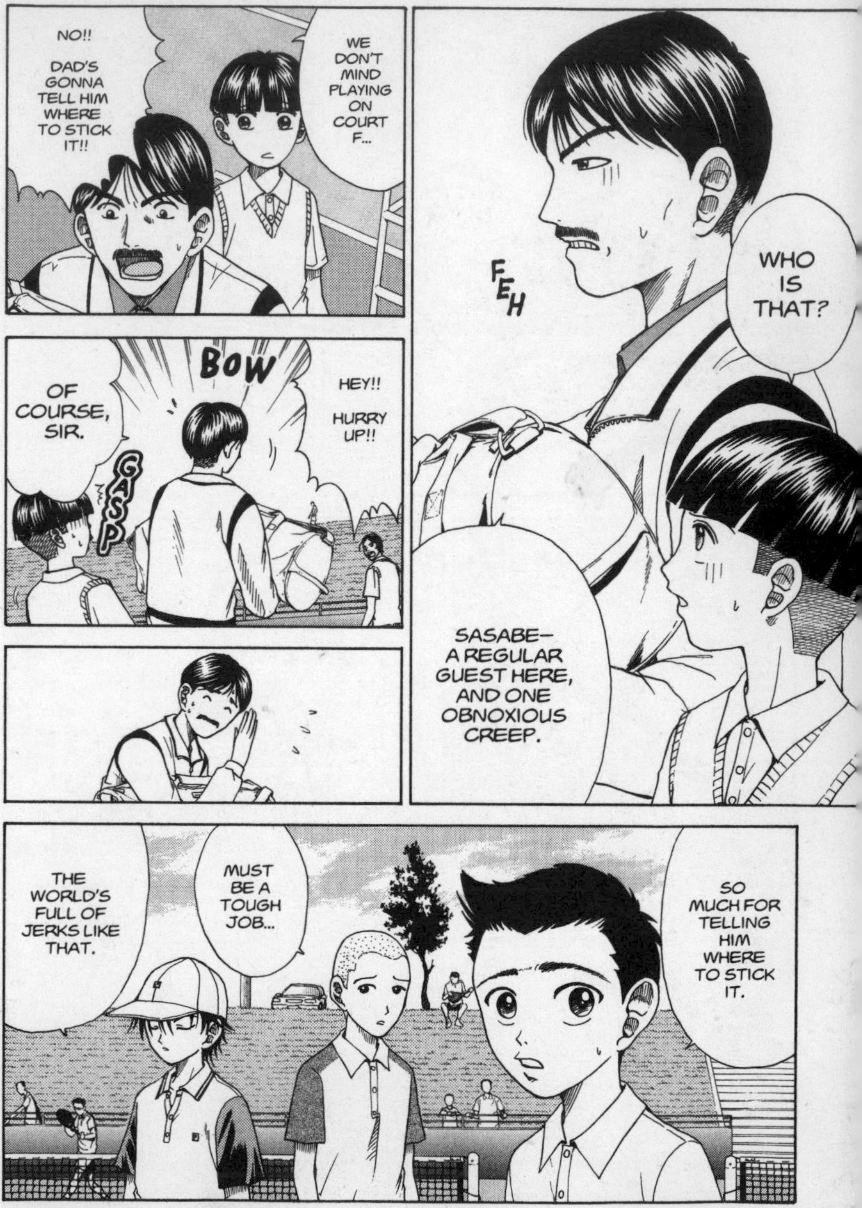
WHO IS THAT?
FEH
SASABE—A REGULAR GUEST HERE, AND ONE OBNOXIOUS CREEP.
WE DON'T MIND PLAYING ON COURT F...
NO!! DAD'S GONNA TELL HIM WHERE TO STICK IT!!
HEY!! HURRY UP!!
BOW
OF COURSE, SIR.
GASP
SO MUCH FOR TELLING HIM WHERE TO STICK IT.
MUST BE A TOUGH JOB...
THE WORLD'S FULL OF JERKS LIKE THAT.

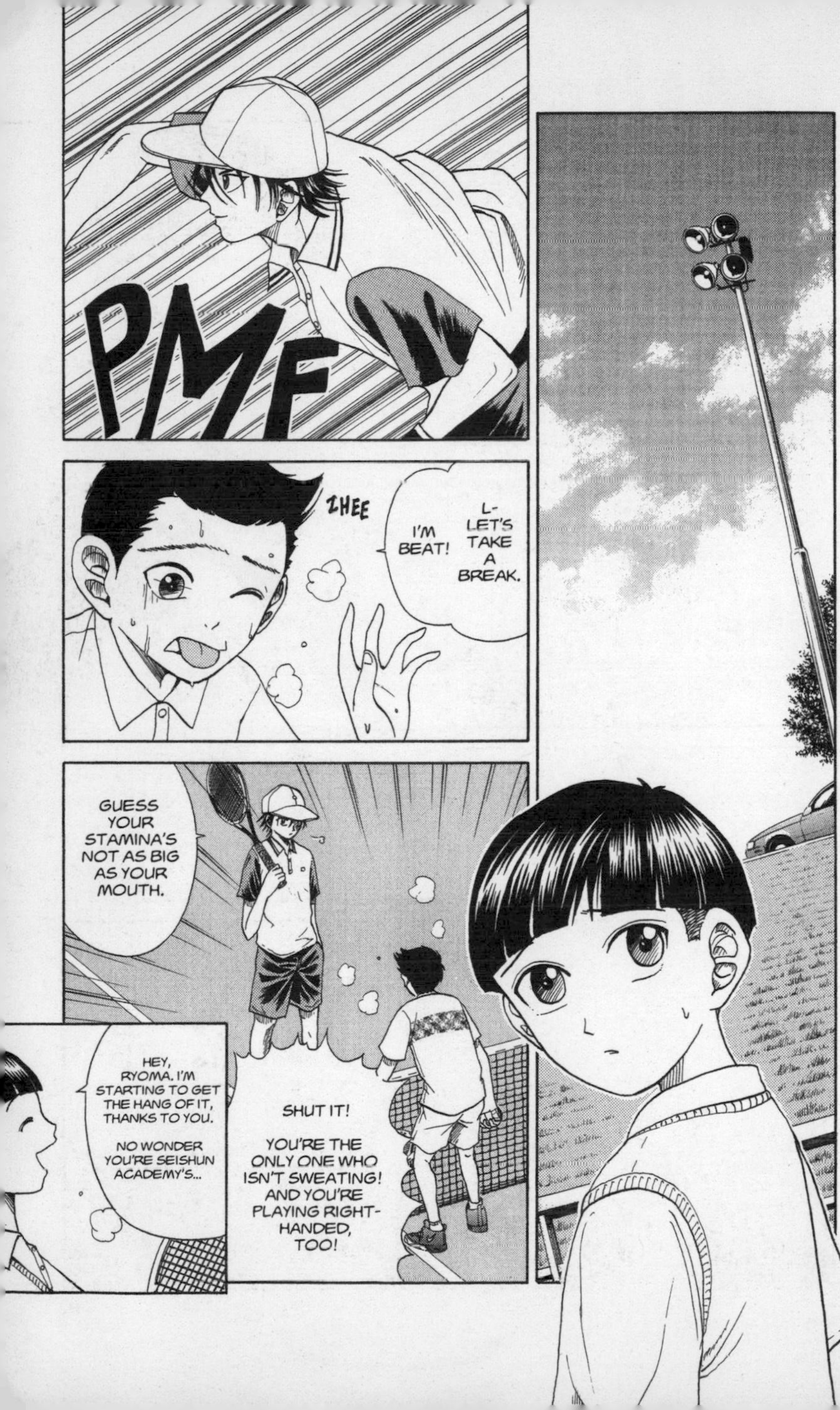
PMF
ZHEE
I'M BEAT! L-LET'S TAKE A BREAK.
GUESS YOUR STAMINA'S NOT AS BIG AS YOUR MOUTH.
SHUT IT!
YOU'RE THE ONLY ONE WHO ISN'T SWEATING! AND YOU'RE PLAYING RIGHT-HANDED, TOO!
HEY, RYOMA. I'M STARTING TO GET THE HANG OF IT, THANKS TO YOU.
NO WONDER YOU'RE SEISHUN ACADEMY'S...

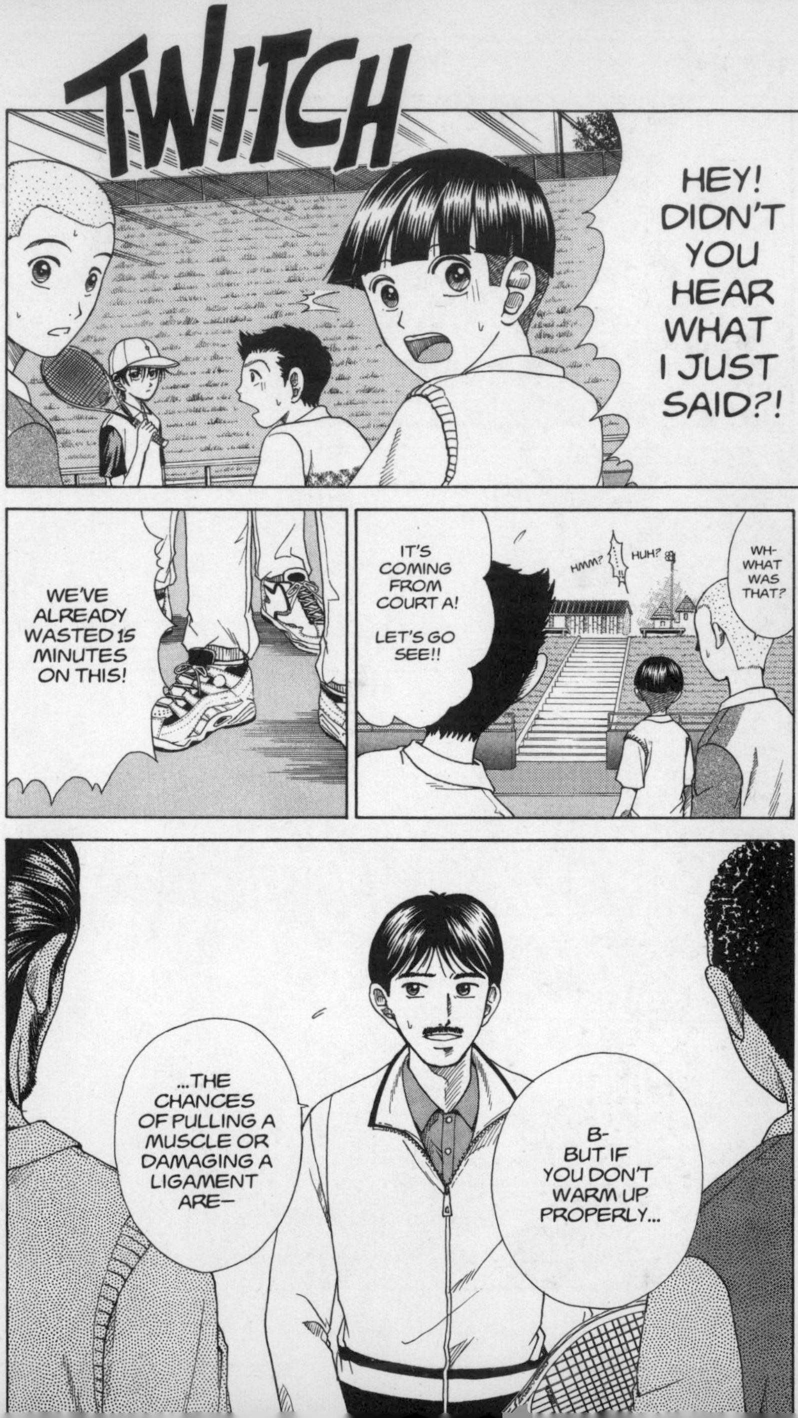

TWITCH
HEY! DIDN'T YOU HEAR WHAT I JUST SAID?!
WH- WHAT WAS THAT?
HUH?
HMM?
IT'S COMING FROM COURT A!
LET'S GO SEE!!
WE'VE ALREADY WASTED 15 MINUTES ON THIS!
B- BUT IF YOU DON'T WARM UP PROPERLY...
...THE CHANCES OF PULLING A MUSCLE OR DAMAGING A LIGAMENT ARE–

READ THIS WAY

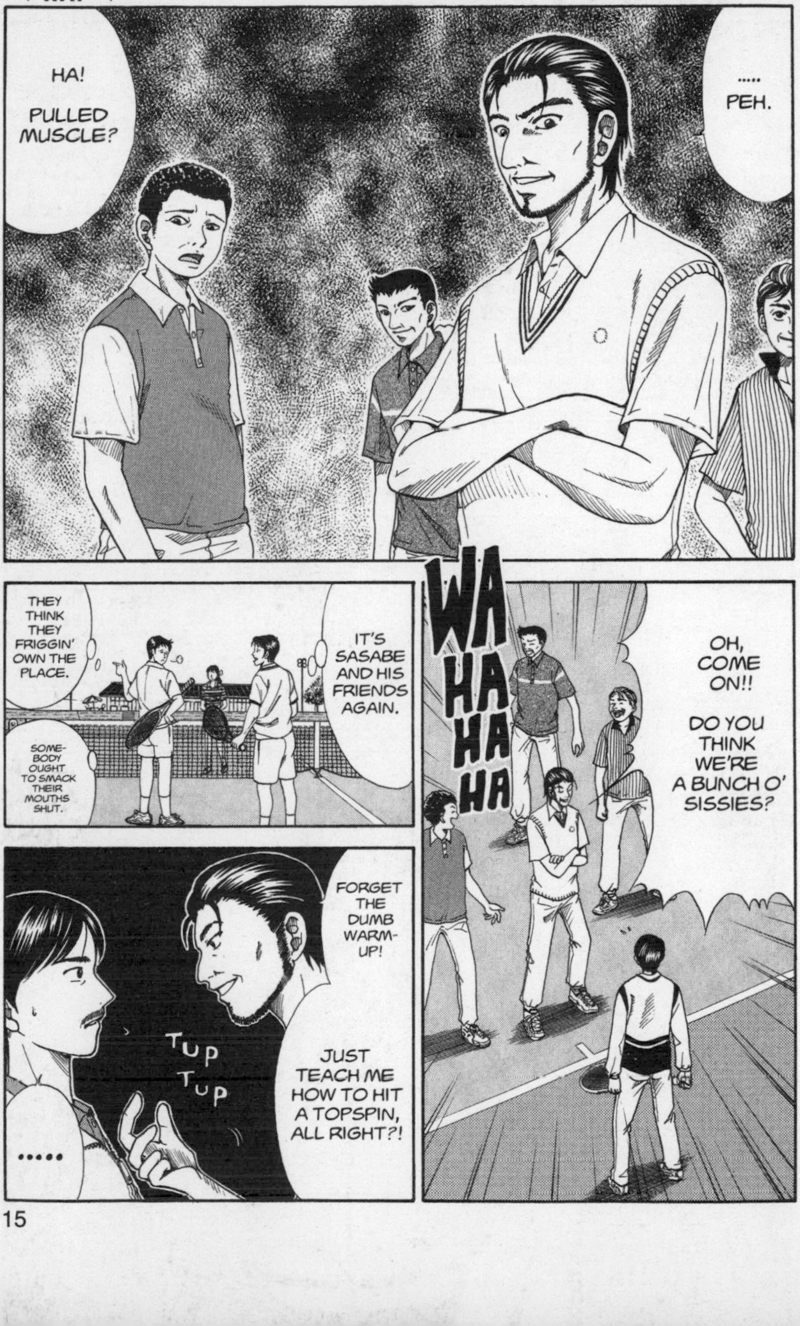
.....
PEH.
HA!
PULLED MUSCLE?
WAHAHAHAHA
OH, COME ON!!
DO YOU THINK WE'RE A BUNCH O' SISSIES?
IT'S SASABE AND HIS FRIENDS AGAIN.
THEY THINK THEY FRIGGIN' OWN THE PLACE.
SOME-BODY OUGHT TO SMACK THEIR MOUTHS SHUT.
FORGET THE DUMB WARM-UP!
JUST TEACH ME HOW TO HIT A TOPSPIN, ALL RIGHT?!
TUP TUP
.....

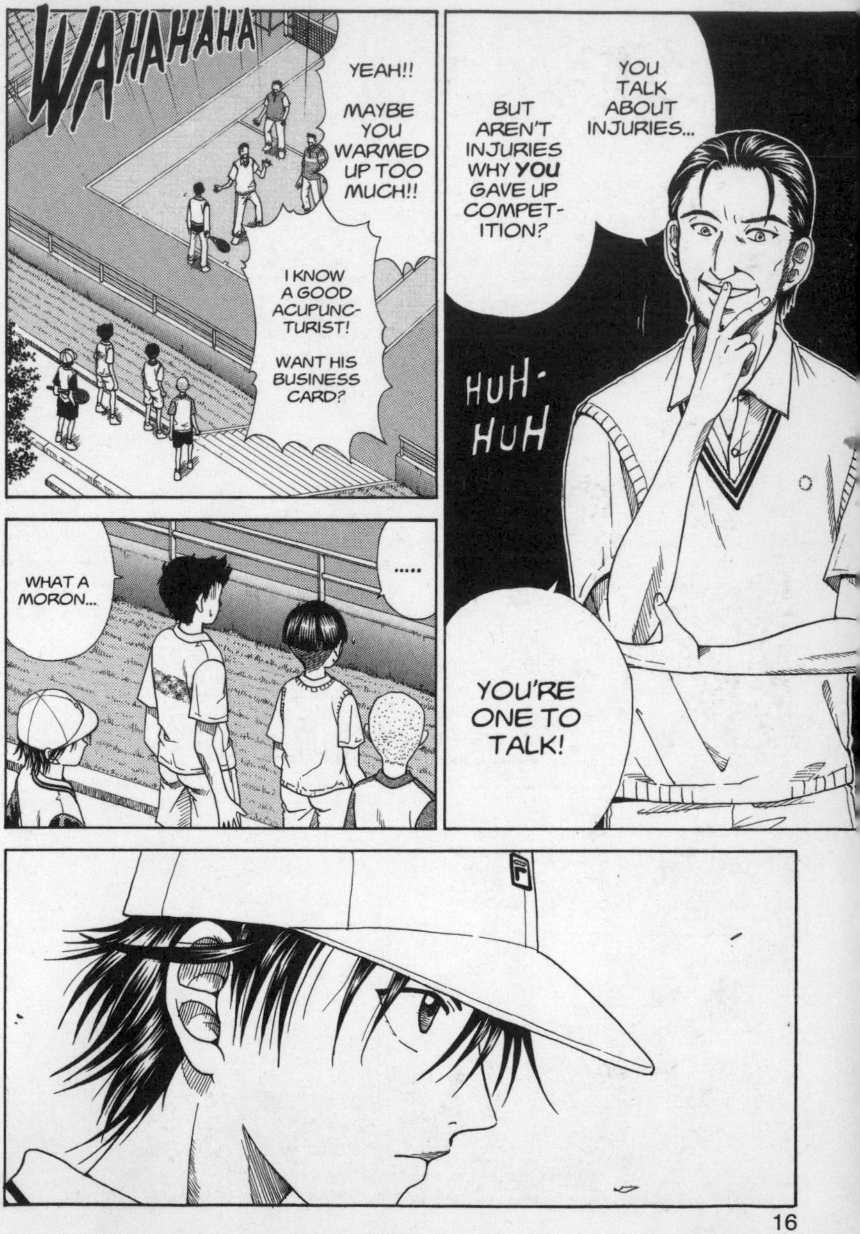
YOU TALK ABOUT INJURIES...
BUT AREN'T INJURIES WHY YOU GAVE UP COMPET-ITION?
HUH-HUH
YOU'RE ONE TO TALK!
WAHAHAHA
YEAH!!
MAYBE YOU WARMED UP TOO MUCH!!
I KNOW A GOOD ACUPUNC-TURIST!
WANT HIS BUSINESS CARD?
.....
WHAT A MORON...

READ THIS WAY

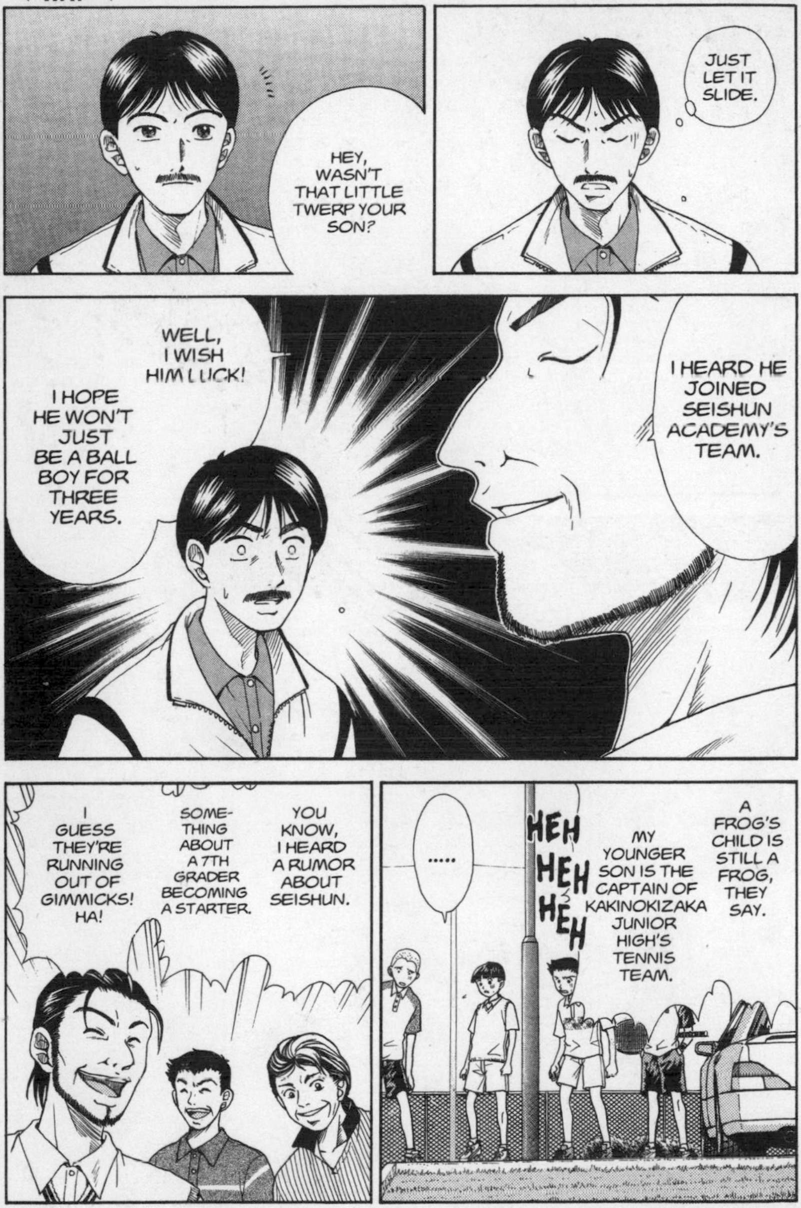

JUST LET IT SLIDE.
HEY, WASN'T THAT LITTLE TWERP YOUR SON?
I HEARD HE JOINED SEISHUN ACADEMY'S TEAM.
WELL, I WISH HIM LUCK!
I HOPE HE WON'T JUST BE A BALL BOY FOR THREE YEARS.
A FROG'S CHILD IS STILL A FROG, THEY SAY.
MY YOUNGER SON IS THE CAPTAIN OF KAKINOKIZAKA JUNIOR HIGH'S TENNIS TEAM.
HEH HEH HEH HEH
......
YOU KNOW, I HEARD A RUMOR ABOUT SEISHUN.
SOME-THING ABOUT A 7TH GRADER BECOMING A STARTER.
I GUESS THEY'RE RUNNING OUT OF GIMMICKS! HA!

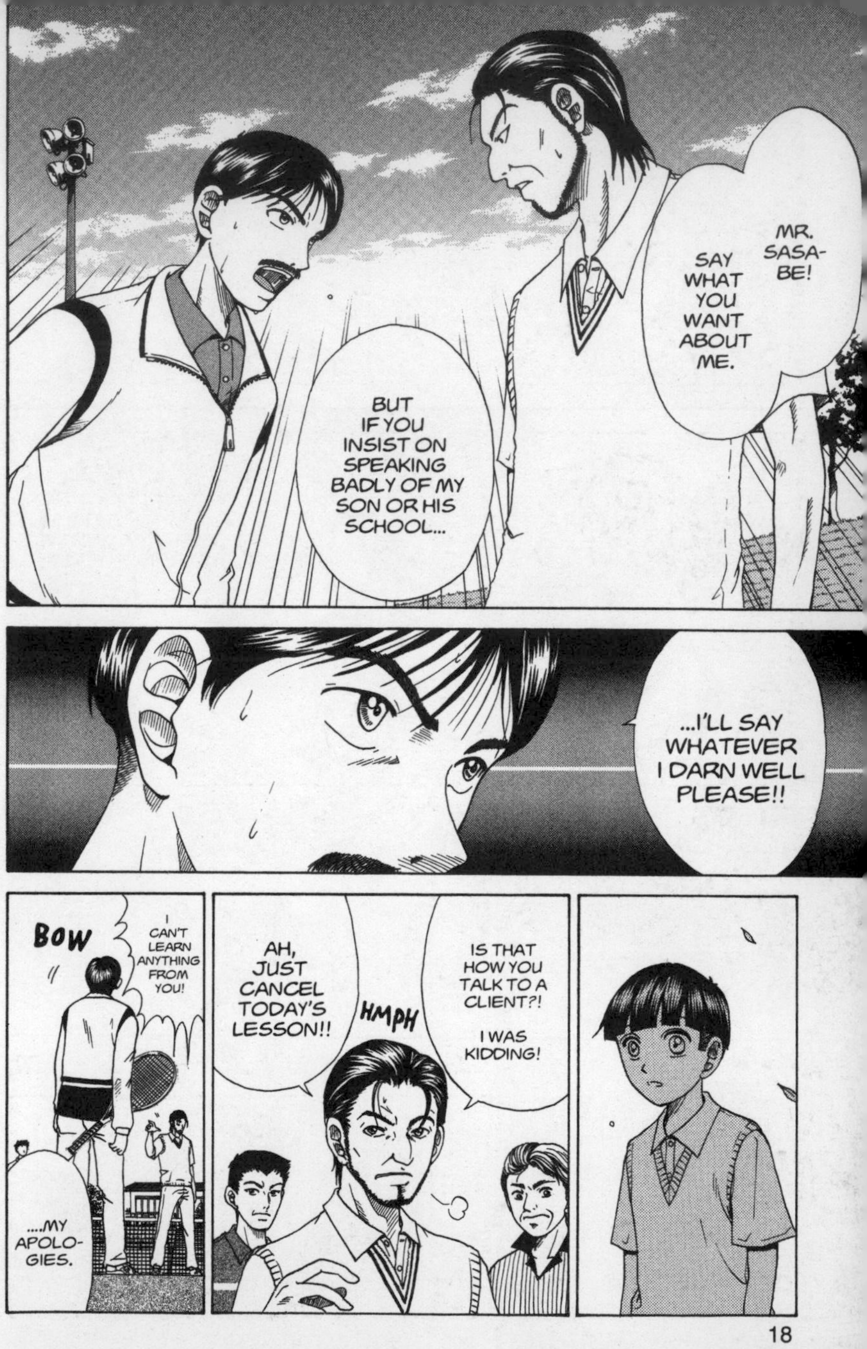
MR. SASABE! SAY WHAT YOU WANT ABOUT ME.
BUT IF YOU INSIST ON SPEAKING BADLY OF MY SON OR HIS SCHOOL...
...I'LL SAY WHATEVER I DARN WELL PLEASE!!
IS THAT HOW YOU TALK TO A CLIENT?! I WAS KIDDING!
HMPH
AH, JUST CANCEL TODAY'S LESSON!!
I CAN'T LEARN ANYTHING FROM YOU!
BOW
....MY APOLOGIES.

READ THIS WAY

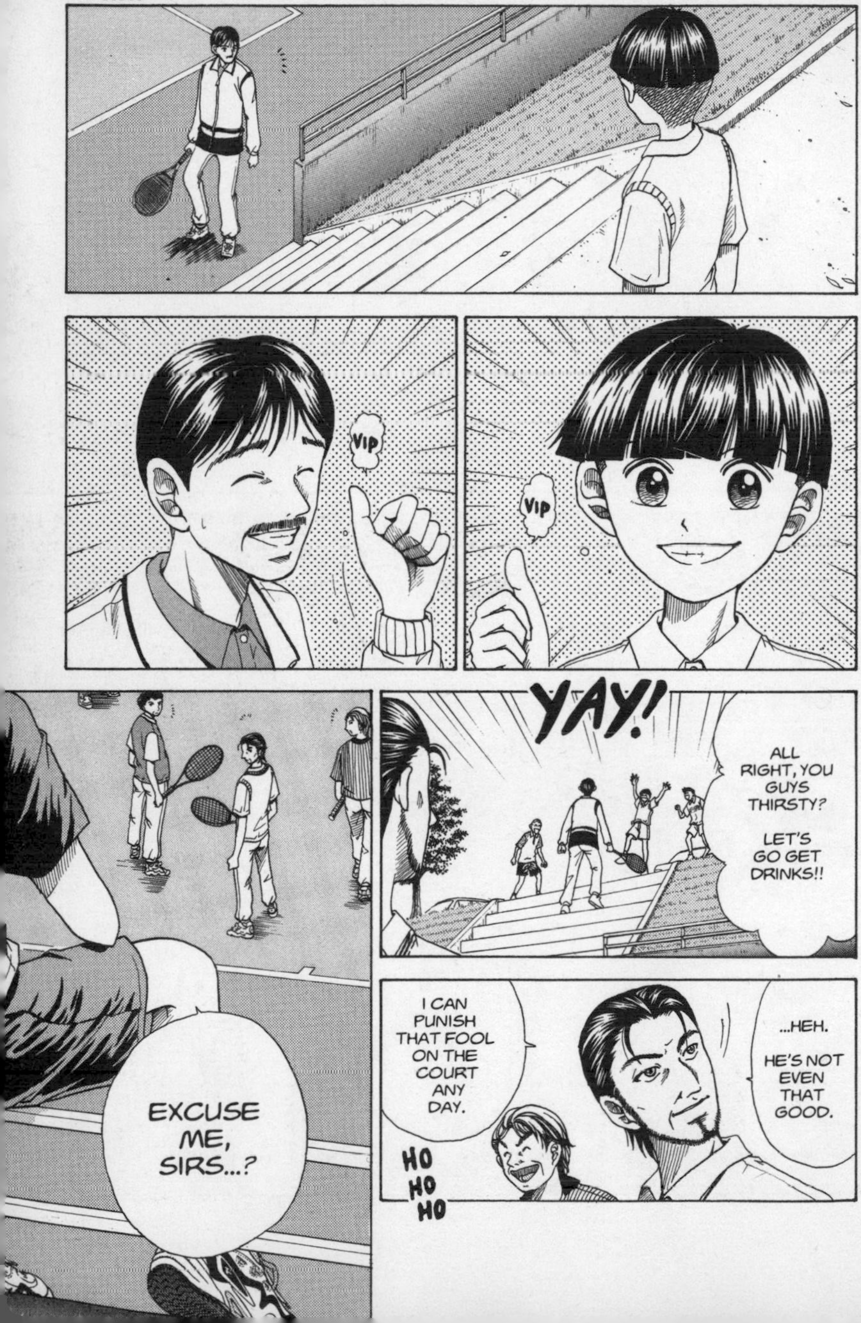
VIP
VIP
YAY!
ALL RIGHT, YOU GUYS THIRSTY?
LET'S GO GET DRINKS!!
...HEH.
HE'S NOT EVEN THAT GOOD.
I CAN PUNISH THAT FOOL ON THE COURT ANY DAY.
HO HO HO
EXCUSE ME, SIRS...?

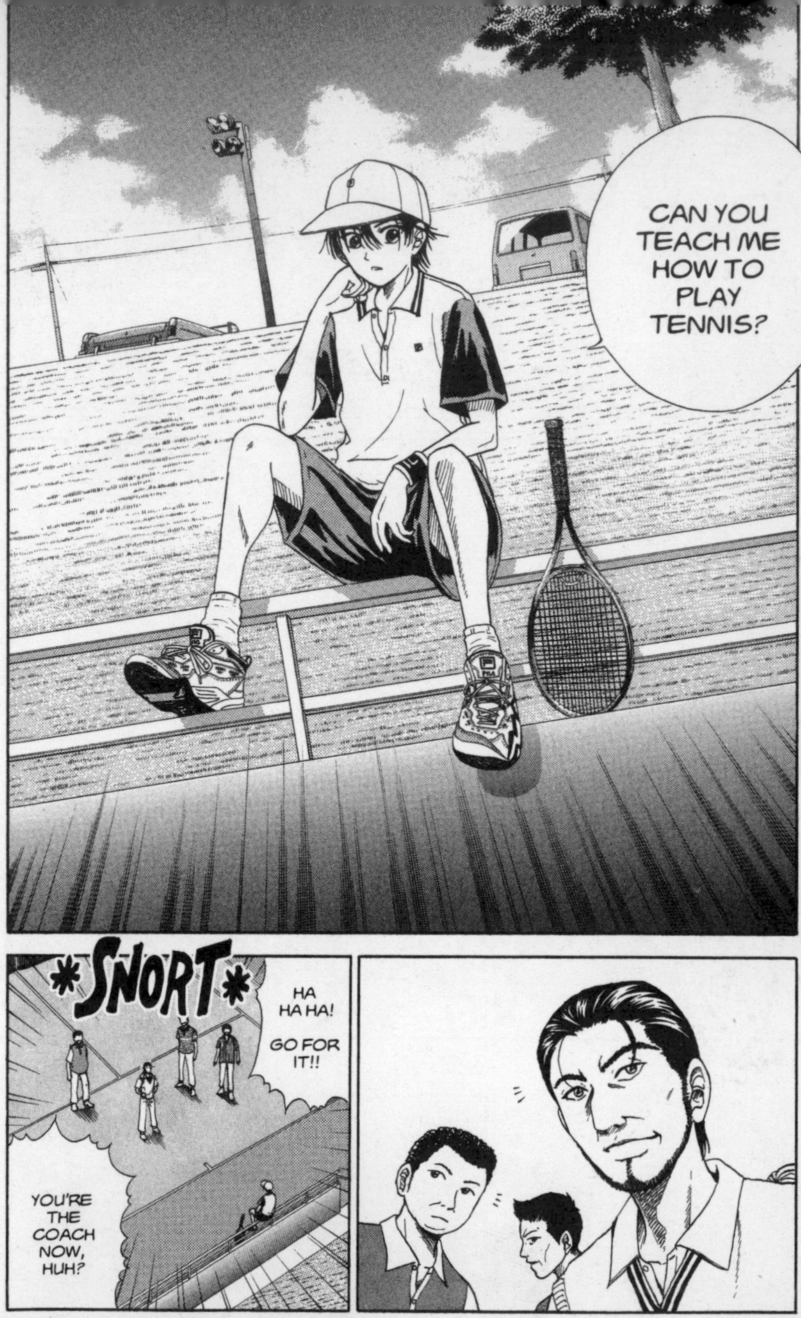
CAN YOU TEACH ME HOW TO PLAY TENNIS?
SNORT
HA HA HA!
GO FOR IT!!
YOU'RE THE COACH NOW, HUH?

READ THIS WAY

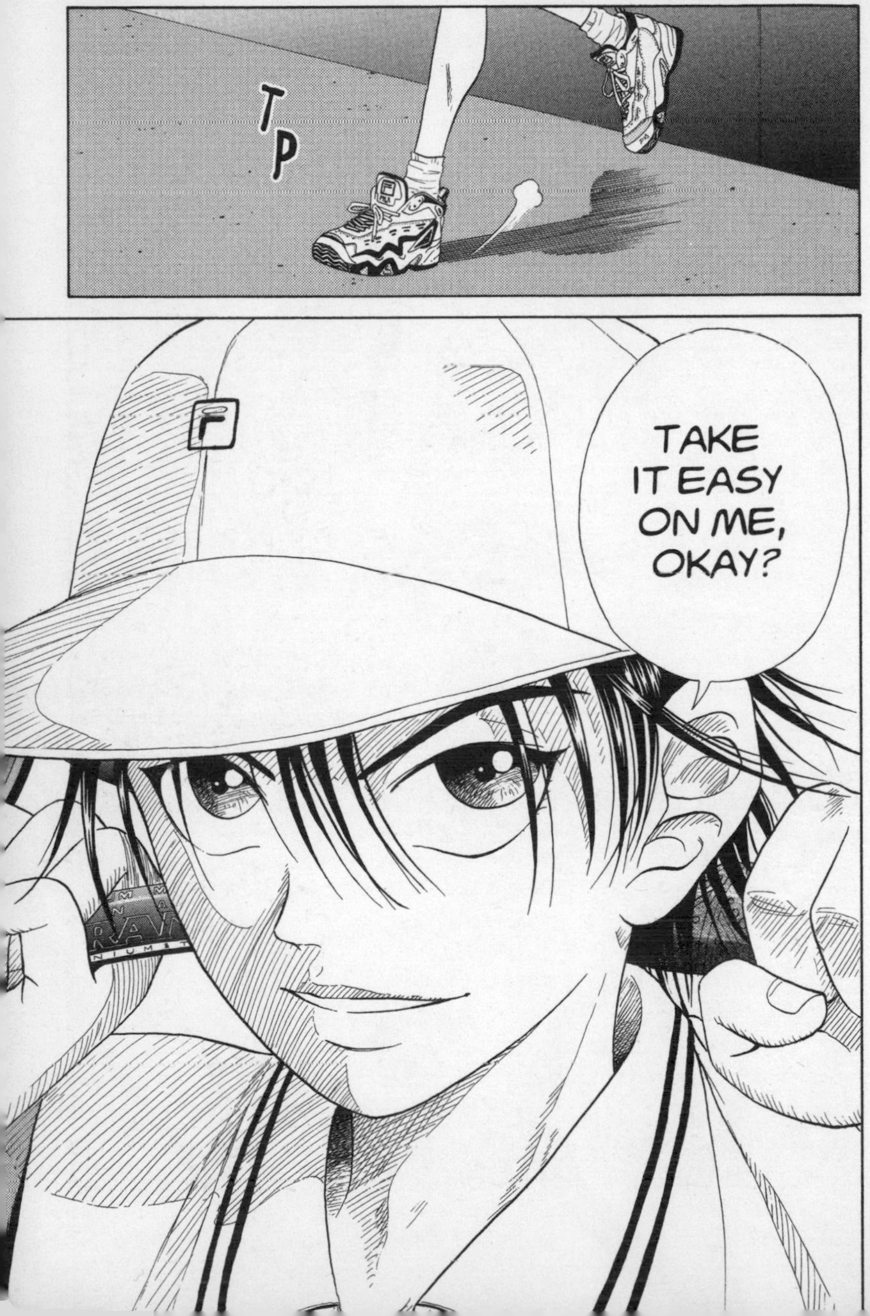
TP
TAKE IT EASY ON ME, OKAY?

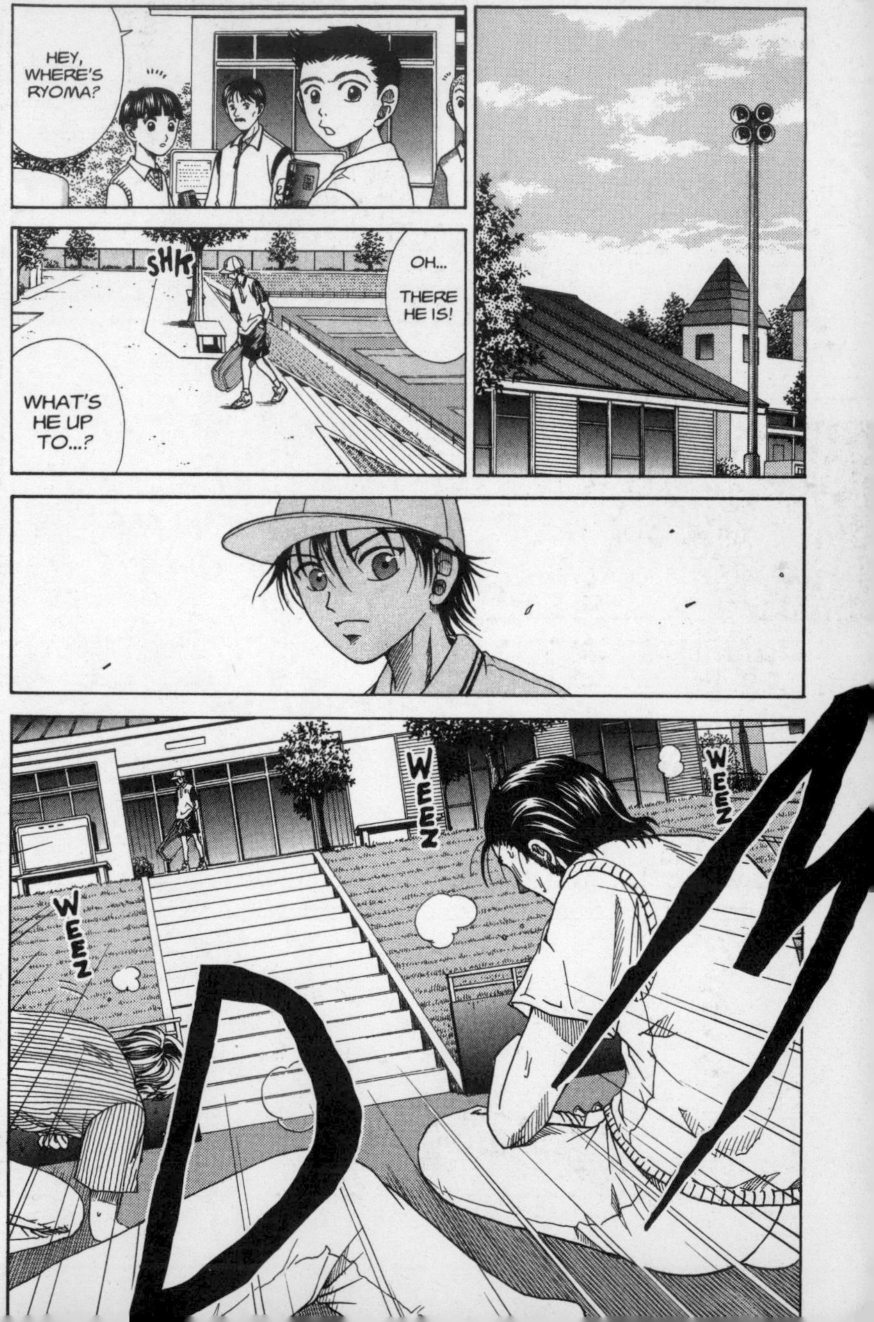
HEY, WHERE'S RYOMA?
OH... THERE HE IS!
SHK
WHAT'S HE UP TO...?
WEEZ
WEEZ
WEEZ

READ THIS WAY

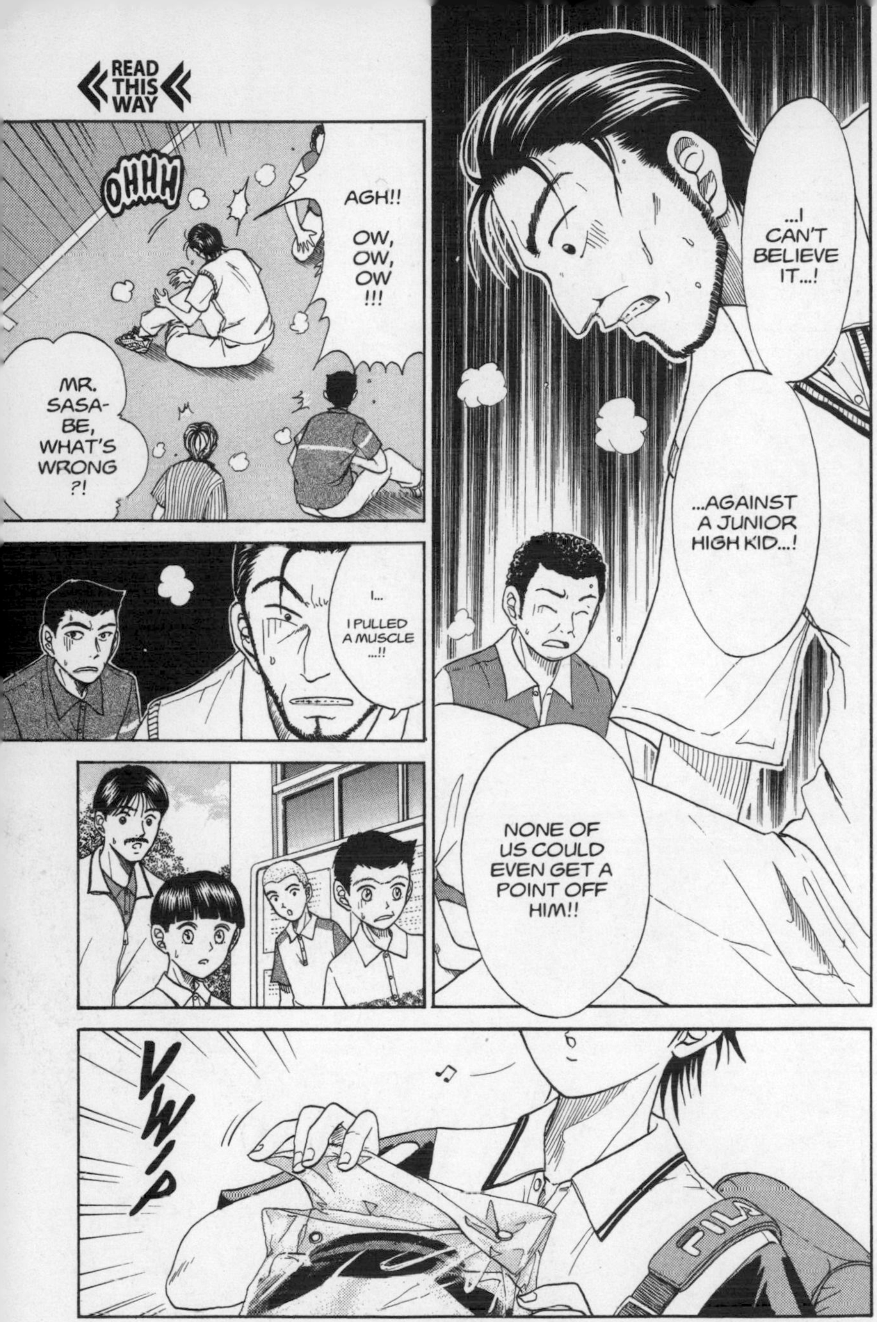

...I CAN'T BELIEVE IT...!
...AGAINST A JUNIOR HIGH KID...!
NONE OF US COULD EVEN GET A POINT OFF HIM!!
OHHH
AGH!!
OW, OW, OW!!!
MR. SASA-BE, WHAT'S WRONG?!
I... I PULLED A MUSCLE...!!
VWIP

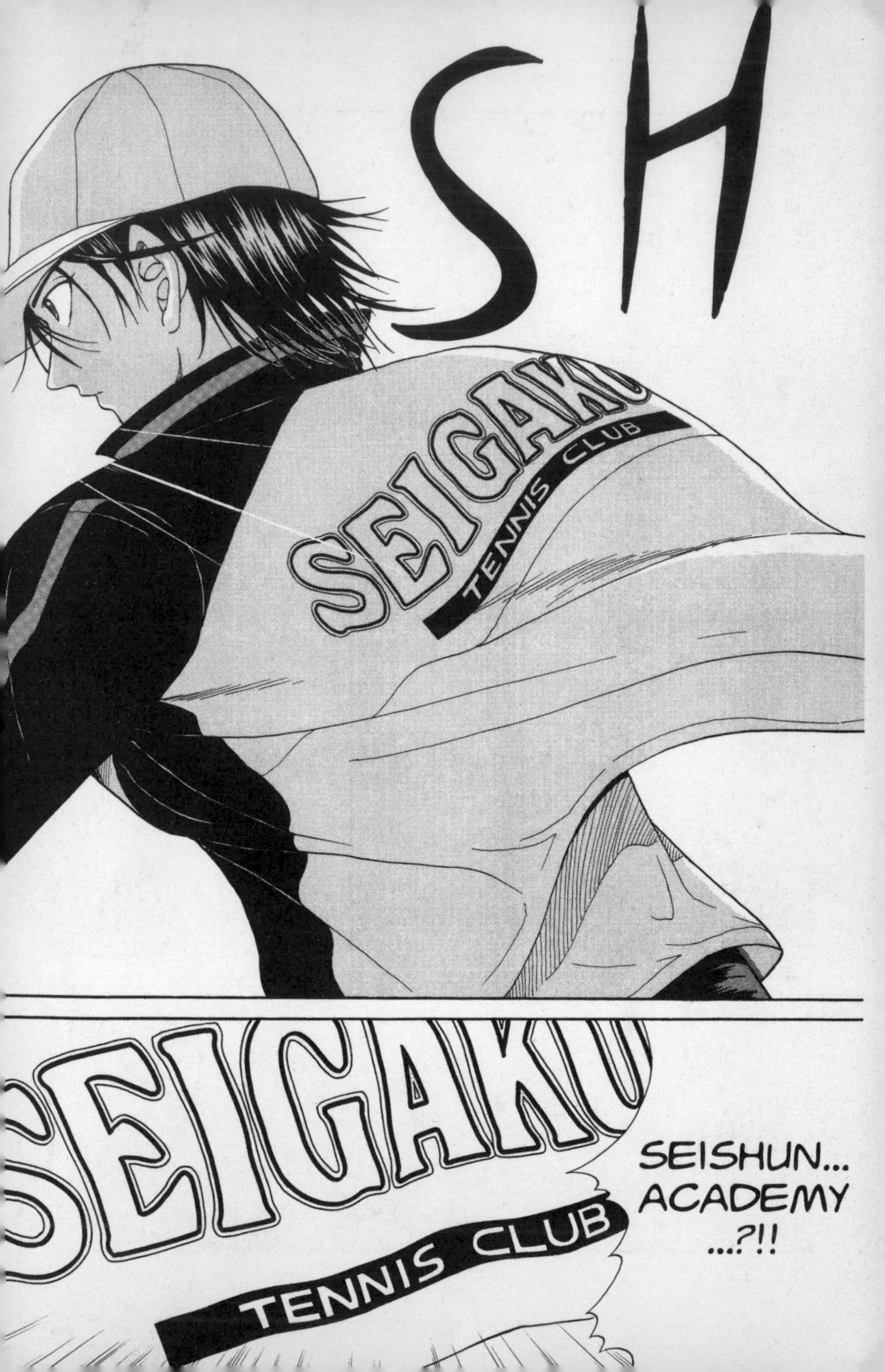
SH
SEIGAKU
TENNIS CLUB
SEIGAKU
TENNIS CLUB
SEISHUN... ACADEMY ...?!!

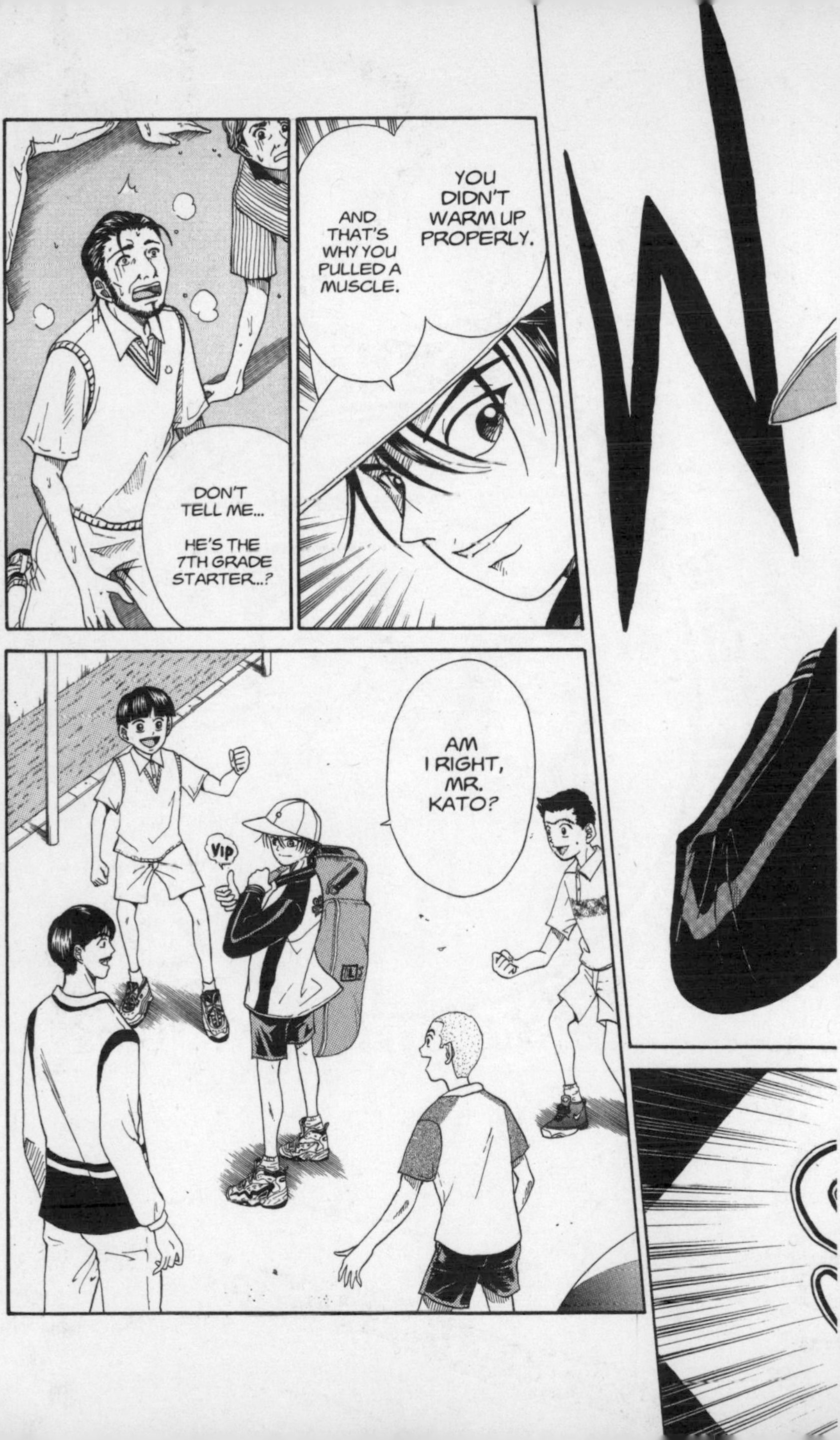
YOU DIDN'T WARM UP PROPERLY.
AND THAT'S WHY YOU PULLED A MUSCLE.
DON'T TELL ME...
HE'S THE 7TH GRADE STARTER...?
AM I RIGHT, MR. KATO?
VIP

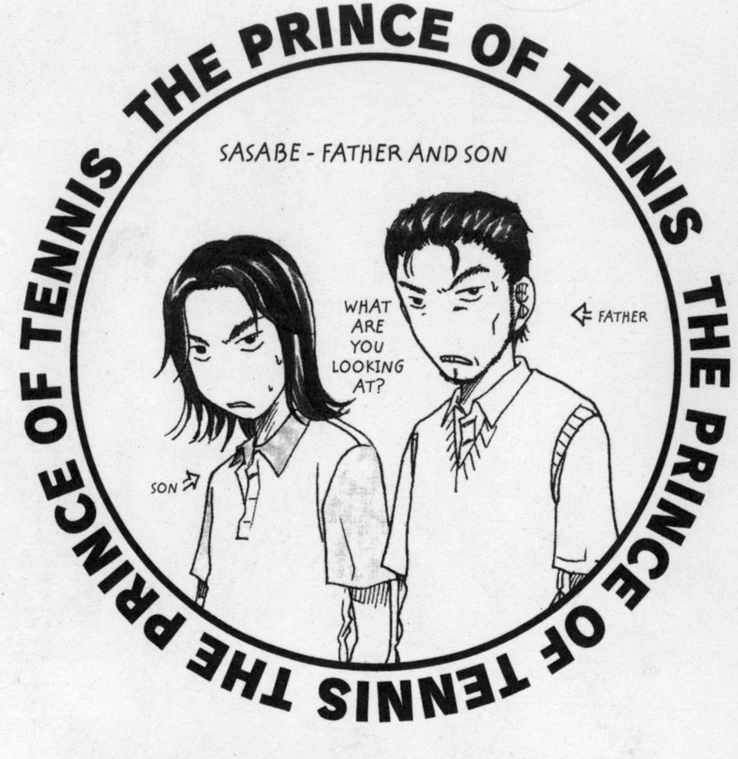
THE PRINCE OF TENNIS THE PRINCE OF TENNIS THE PRINCE OF TENNIS
SASABE - FATHER AND SON
FATHER
WHAT ARE YOU LOOKING AT?
SON

GENIUS 18:

BAD LOSERS

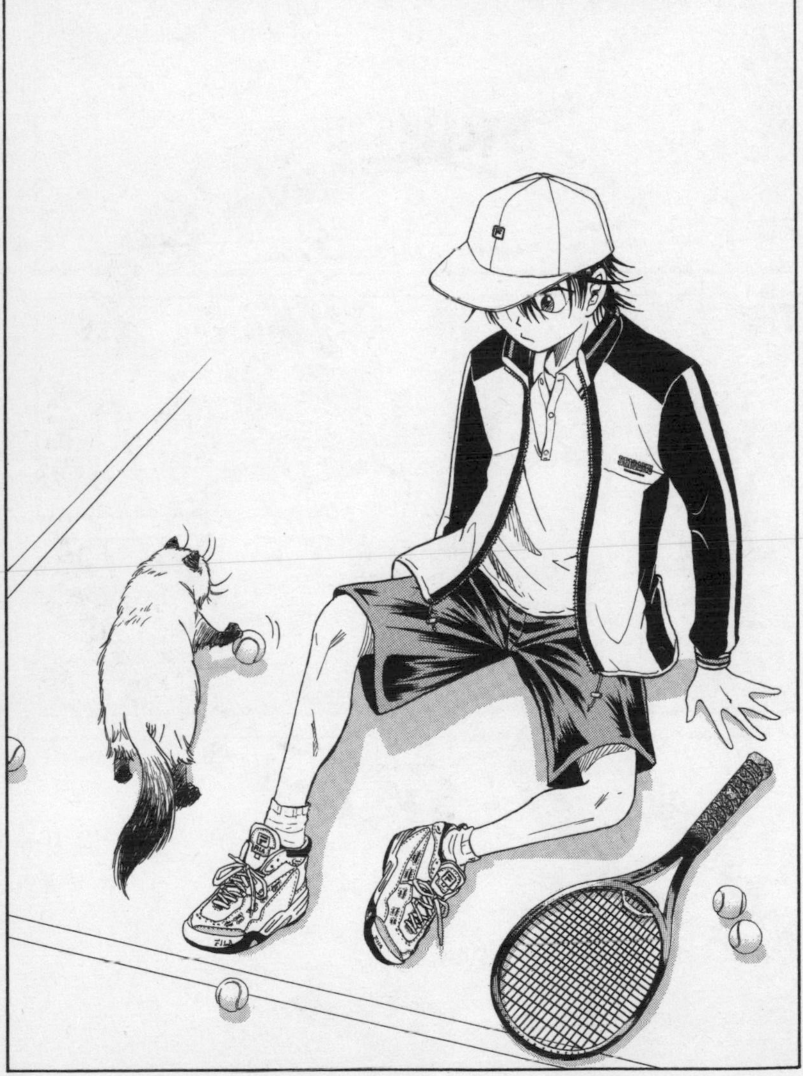

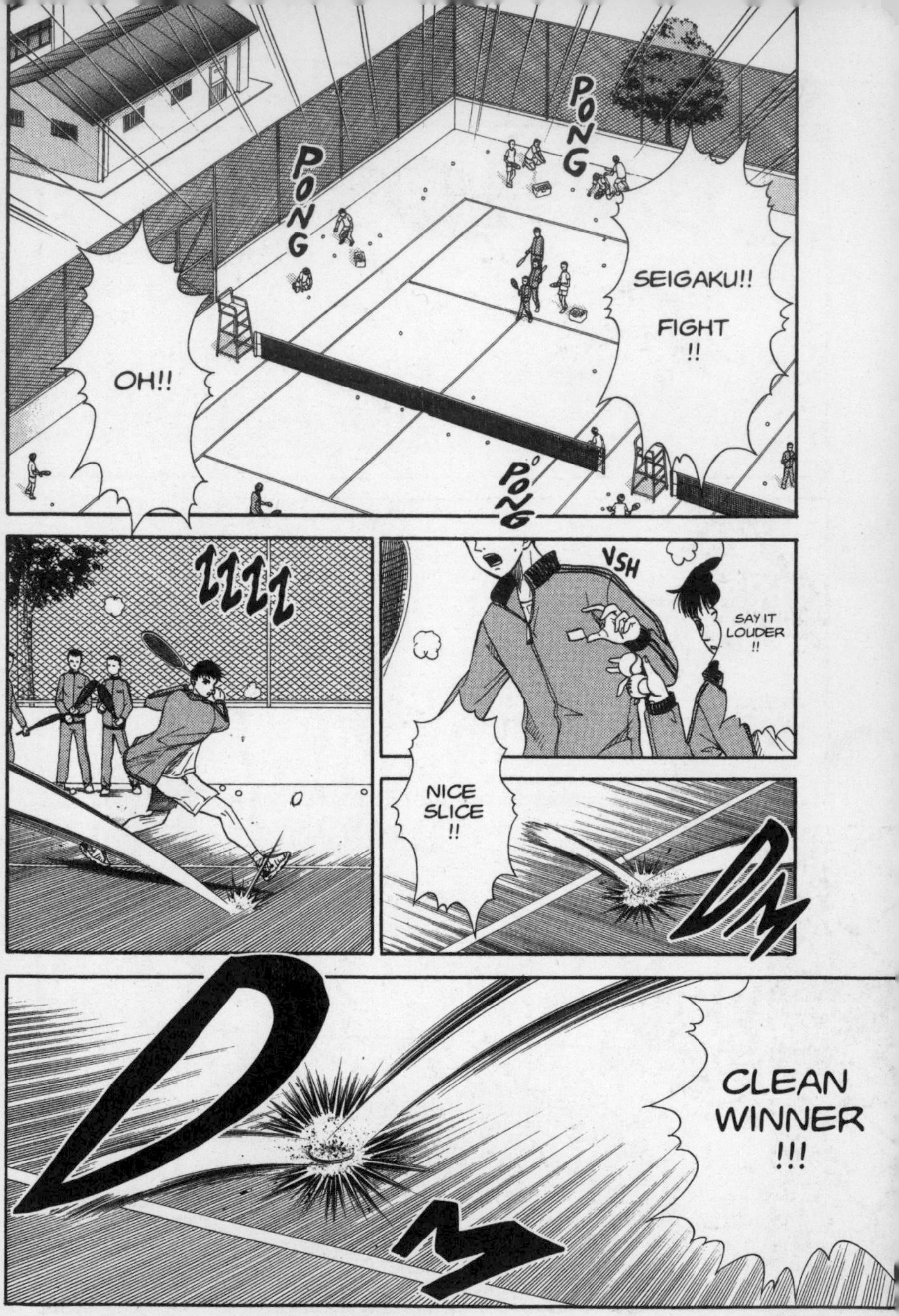

PONG
SEIGAKU!!
FIGHT !!
PONG
OH!!
PONG
SAY IT LOUDER !!
VSH
NICE SLICE !!
DM
ZZZZ
CLEAN WINNER !!!
DM

FIGHT !!

SE– I– GA– KU–

THE DISTRICT PRELIMI- NARIES ARE JUST TEN DAYS AWAY.

FEELS LIKE IT'S ALMOST HERE.

POM
PONG

NICE PASS -ING SHOT!

HEH HEH

OOOH –!!

KRI

WHAT KIND OF DRILL SHOTS ARE THOSE?

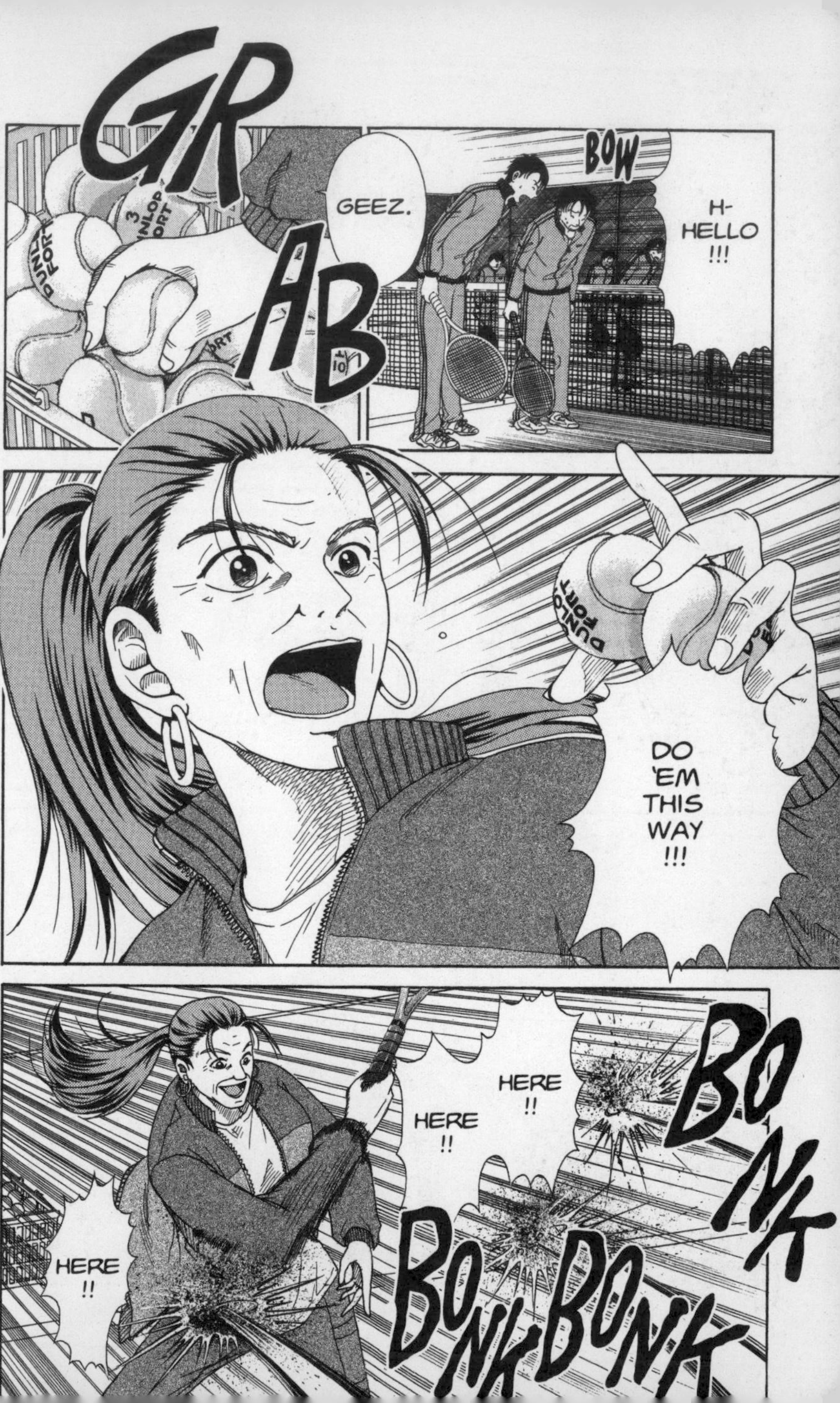
BOW
H-HELLO!!!
GRAB
GEEZ.
DO 'EM THIS WAY!!!
HERE!!
HERE!!
HERE!!
BONK
BONK
BONK

READ THIS WAY

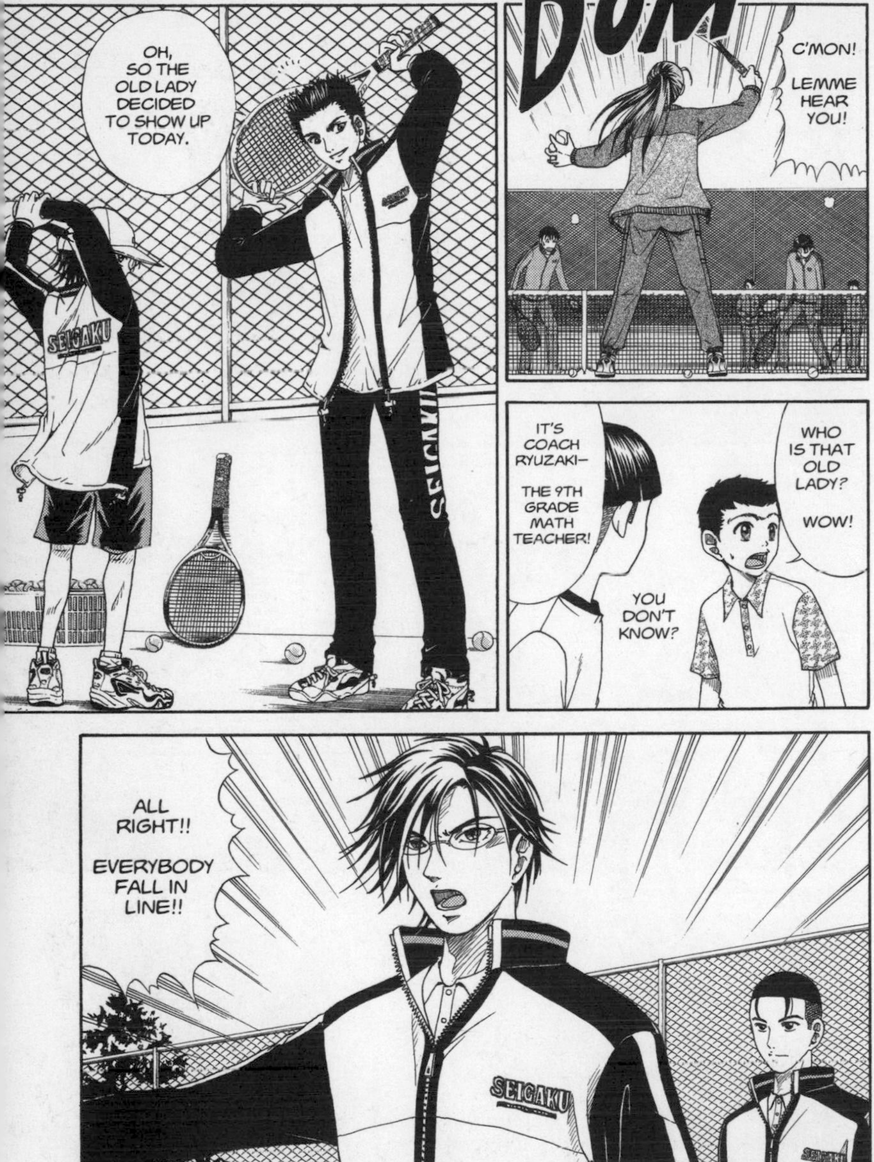

DOM
C'MON!
LEMME HEAR YOU!
WHO IS THAT OLD LADY?
WOW!
IT'S COACH RYUZAKI—
THE 9TH GRADE MATH TEACHER!
YOU DON'T KNOW?
OH, SO THE OLD LADY DECIDED TO SHOW UP TODAY.
ALL RIGHT!!
EVERYBODY FALL IN LINE!!

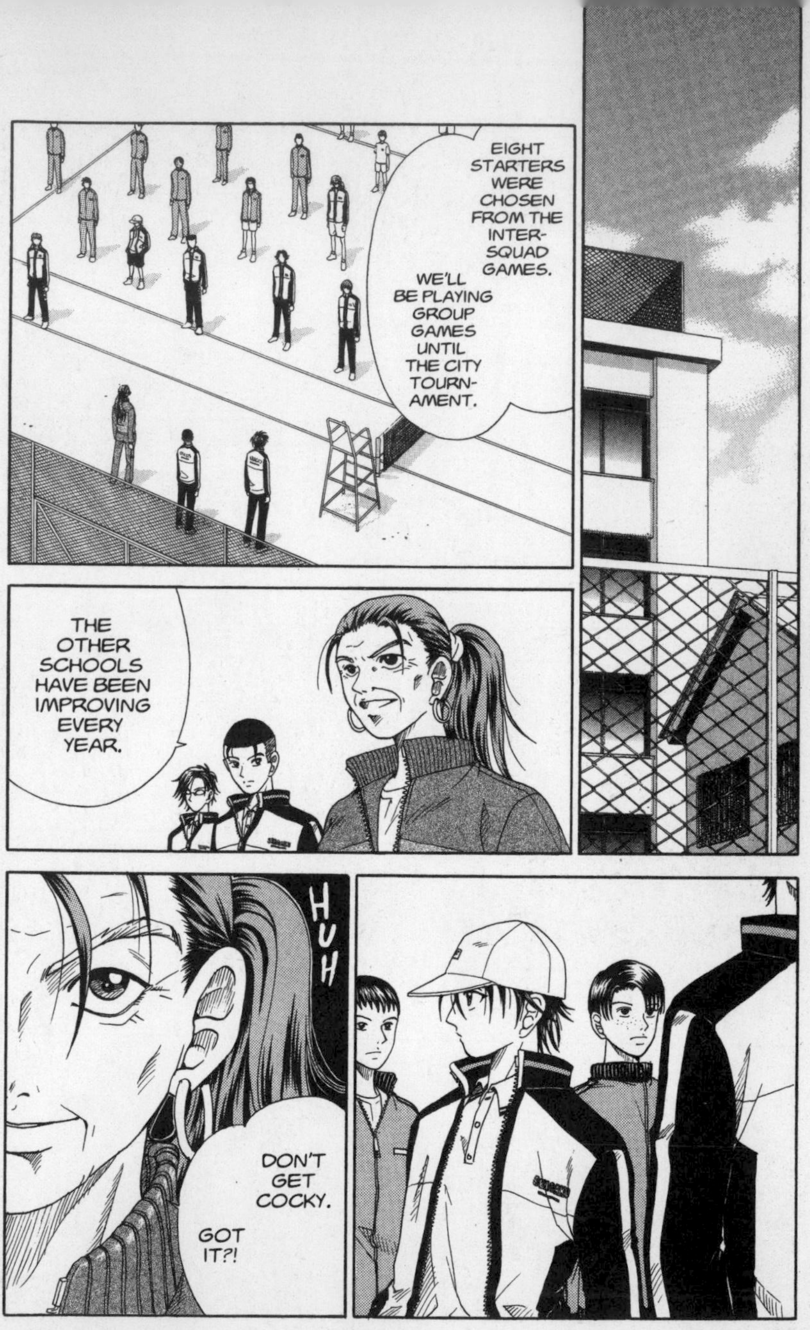
EIGHT STARTERS WERE CHOSEN FROM THE INTER-SQUAD GAMES.
WE'LL BE PLAYING GROUP GAMES UNTIL THE CITY TOURN-AMENT.
THE OTHER SCHOOLS HAVE BEEN IMPROVING EVERY YEAR.
HUH
DON'T GET COCKY.
GOT IT?!

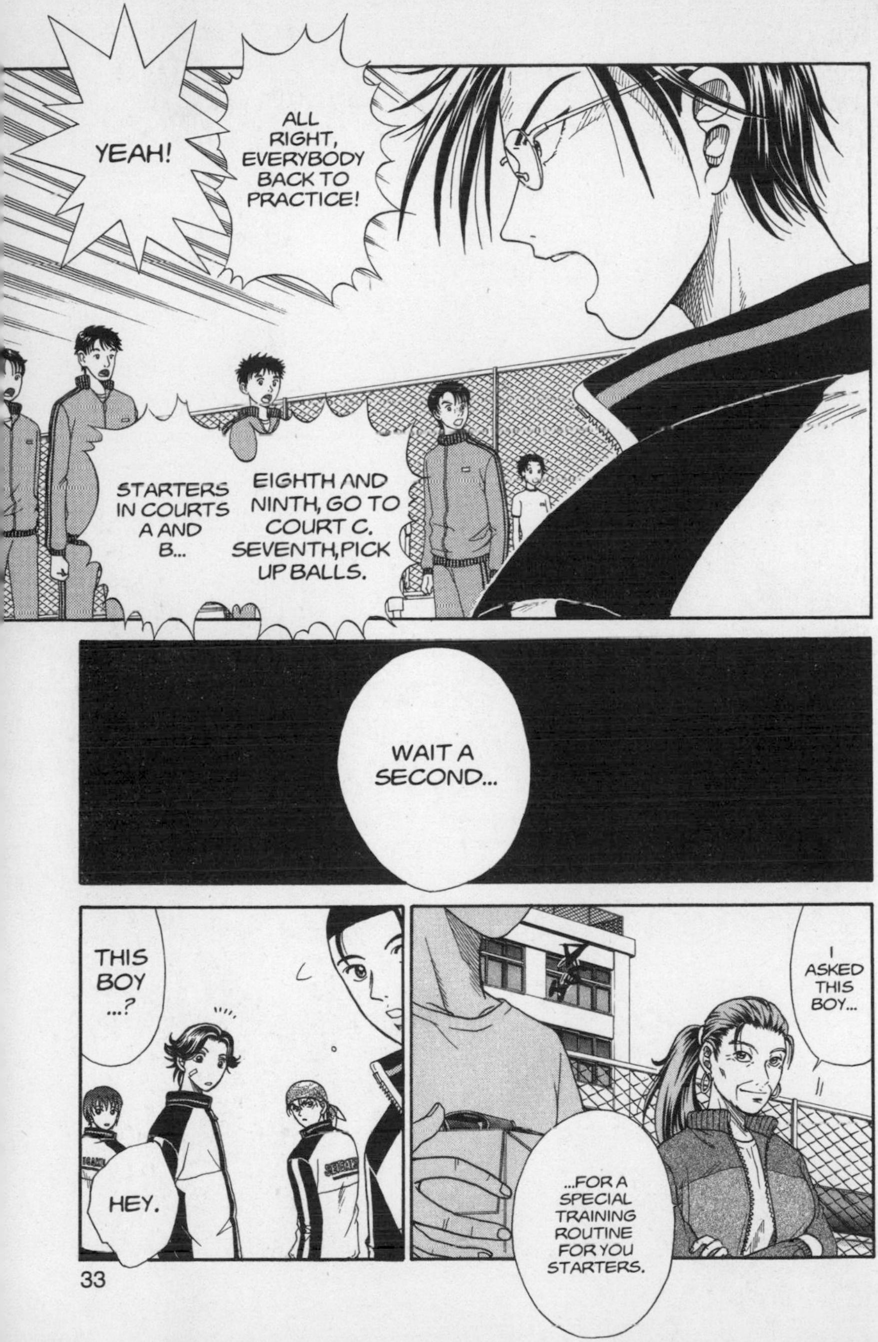
ALL RIGHT, EVERYBODY BACK TO PRACTICE!
YEAH!
STARTERS IN COURTS A AND B...
EIGHTH AND NINTH, GO TO COURT C. SEVENTH, PICK UP BALLS.
WAIT A SECOND...
I ASKED THIS BOY...
...FOR A SPECIAL TRAINING ROUTINE FOR YOU STARTERS.
THIS BOY ...?
HEY.

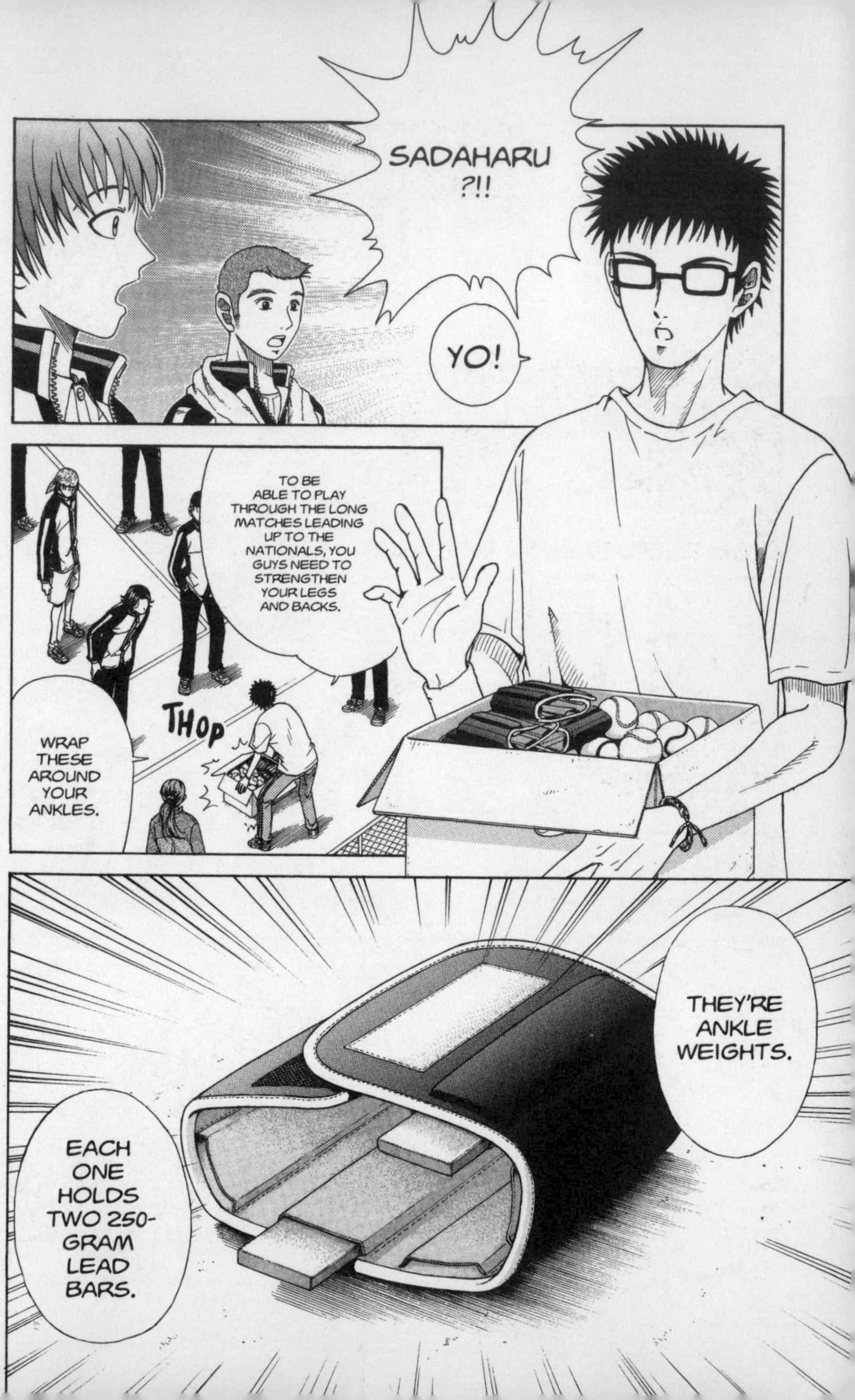
SADAHARU ?!!
YO!
TO BE ABLE TO PLAY THROUGH THE LONG MATCHES LEADING UP TO THE NATIONALS, YOU GUYS NEED TO STRENGTHEN YOUR LEGS AND BACKS.
THOP
WRAP THESE AROUND YOUR ANKLES.
THEY'RE ANKLE WEIGHTS.
EACH ONE HOLDS TWO 250-GRAM LEAD BARS.

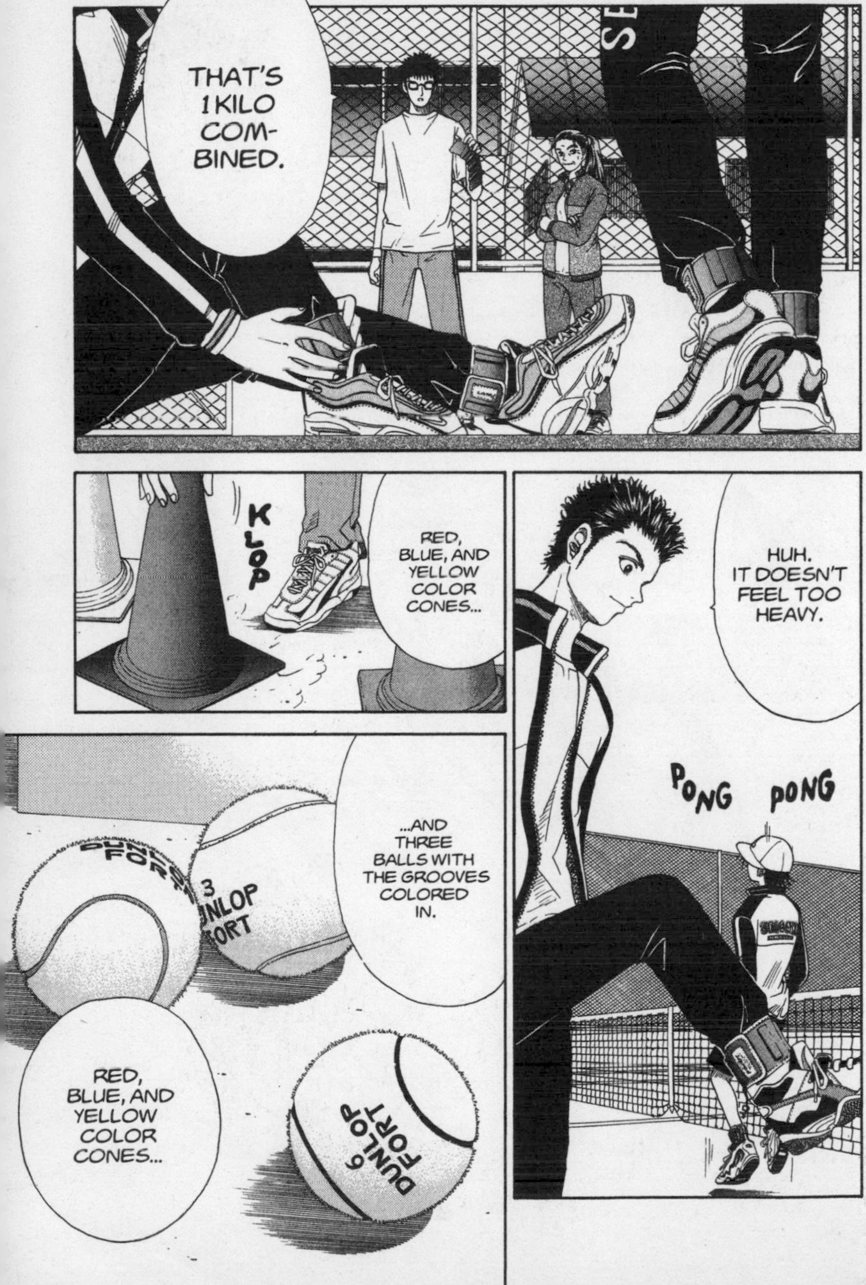
THAT'S 1 KILO COMBINED.
HUH. IT DOESN'T FEEL TOO HEAVY.
PONG PONG
KLOP
RED, BLUE, AND YELLOW COLOR CONES...
...AND THREE BALLS WITH THE GROOVES COLORED IN.
RED, BLUE, AND YELLOW COLOR CONES...
DUNLOP 6 FORT

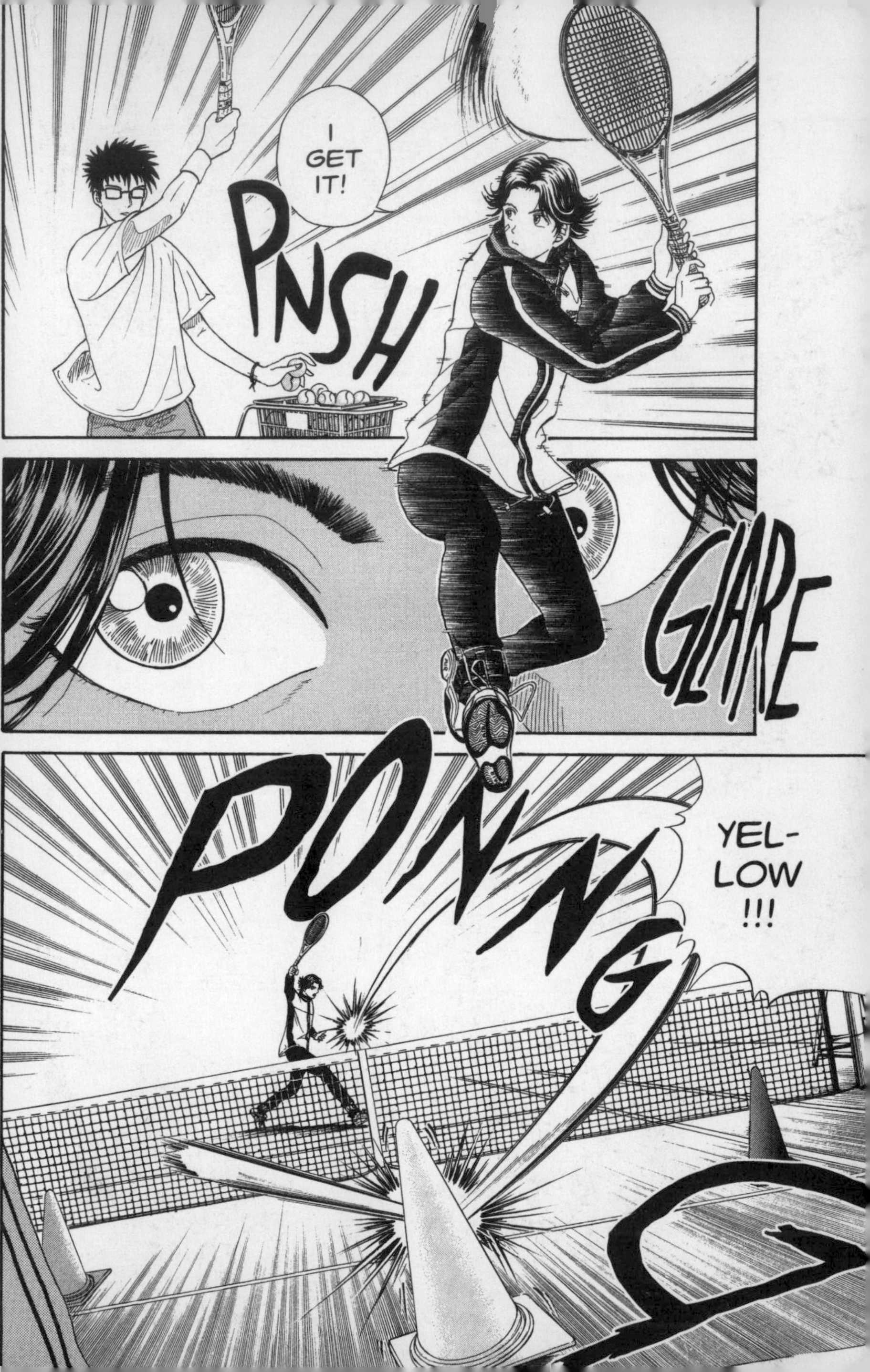
I GET IT!
PNSH
GLARE
YEL-LOW!!!
PONNG

READ THIS WAY

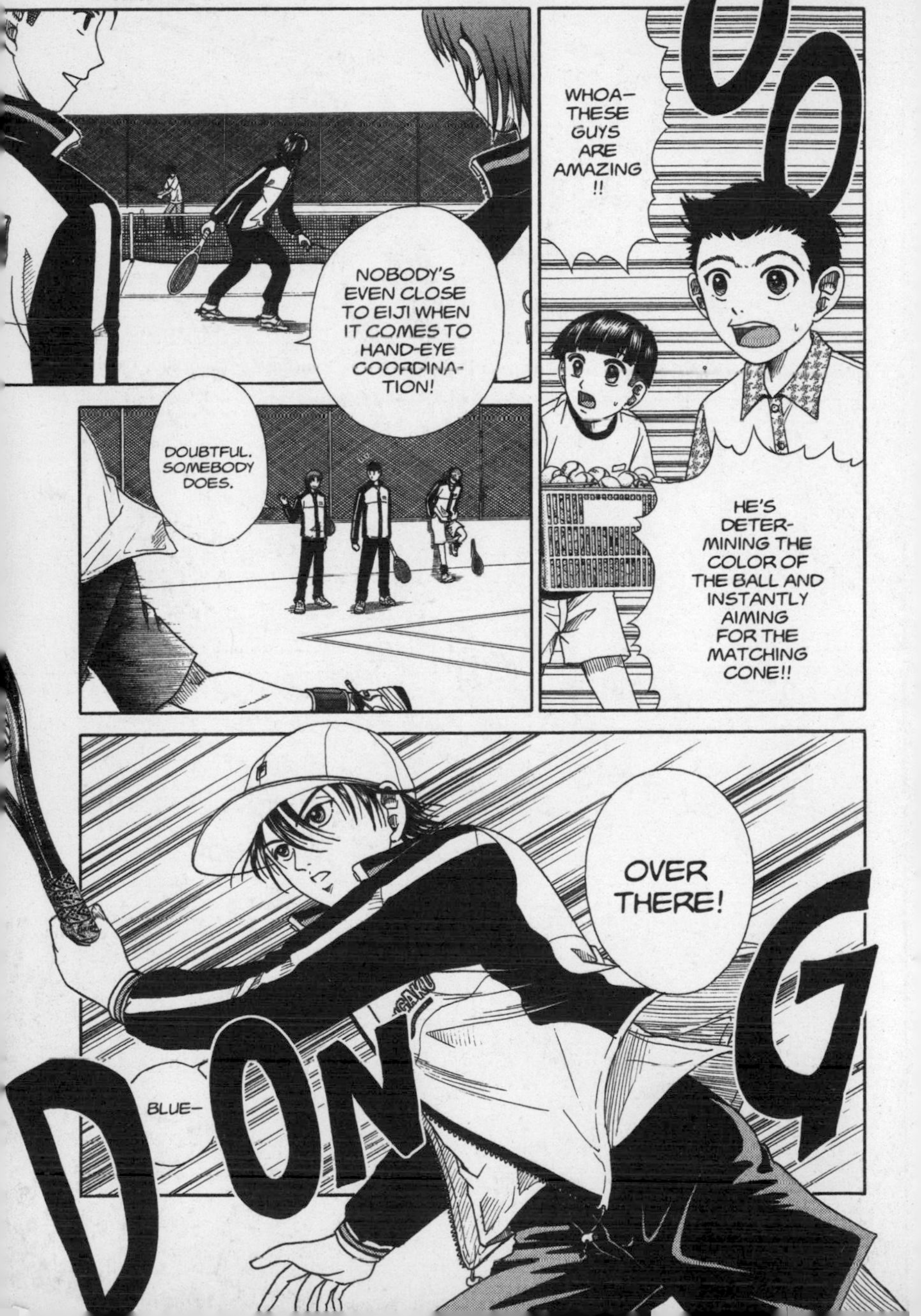
OO
WHOA— THESE GUYS ARE AMAZING !!
HE'S DETERMINING THE COLOR OF THE BALL AND INSTANTLY AIMING FOR THE MATCHING CONE!!
NOBODY'S EVEN CLOSE TO EIJI WHEN IT COMES TO HAND-EYE COORDINATION!
DOUBTFUL. SOMEBODY DOES.
OVER THERE!
BLUE—
DONG

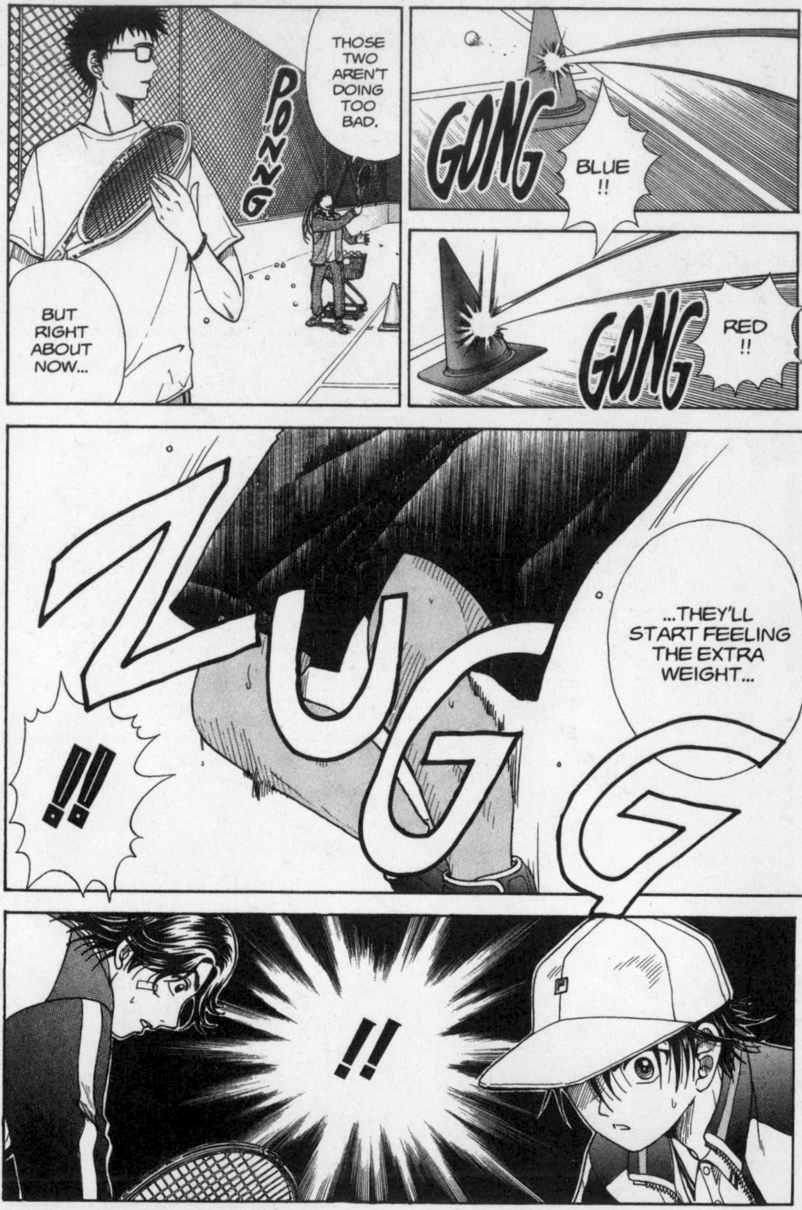
GONG
BLUE !!
GONG
RED !!
THOSE TWO AREN'T DOING TOO BAD.
PONNG
BUT RIGHT ABOUT NOW...
...THEY'LL START FEELING THE EXTRA WEIGHT...
ZUGG
!!
!!

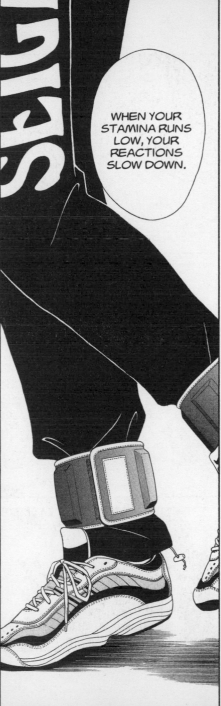

WHEN YOUR STAMINA RUNS LOW, YOUR REACTIONS SLOW DOWN.

HEY... MY LEGS FEEL HEAVY ALL OF A SUDDEN...

HMM...

THIS COULD BE TOUGH...

R-RED...

...EIJI, WASN'T THAT BLUE?

HUH? OH, NO WAY— ACK!!

THAT WASN'T FAIR, SADAHARU!!

IT WAS RED!!

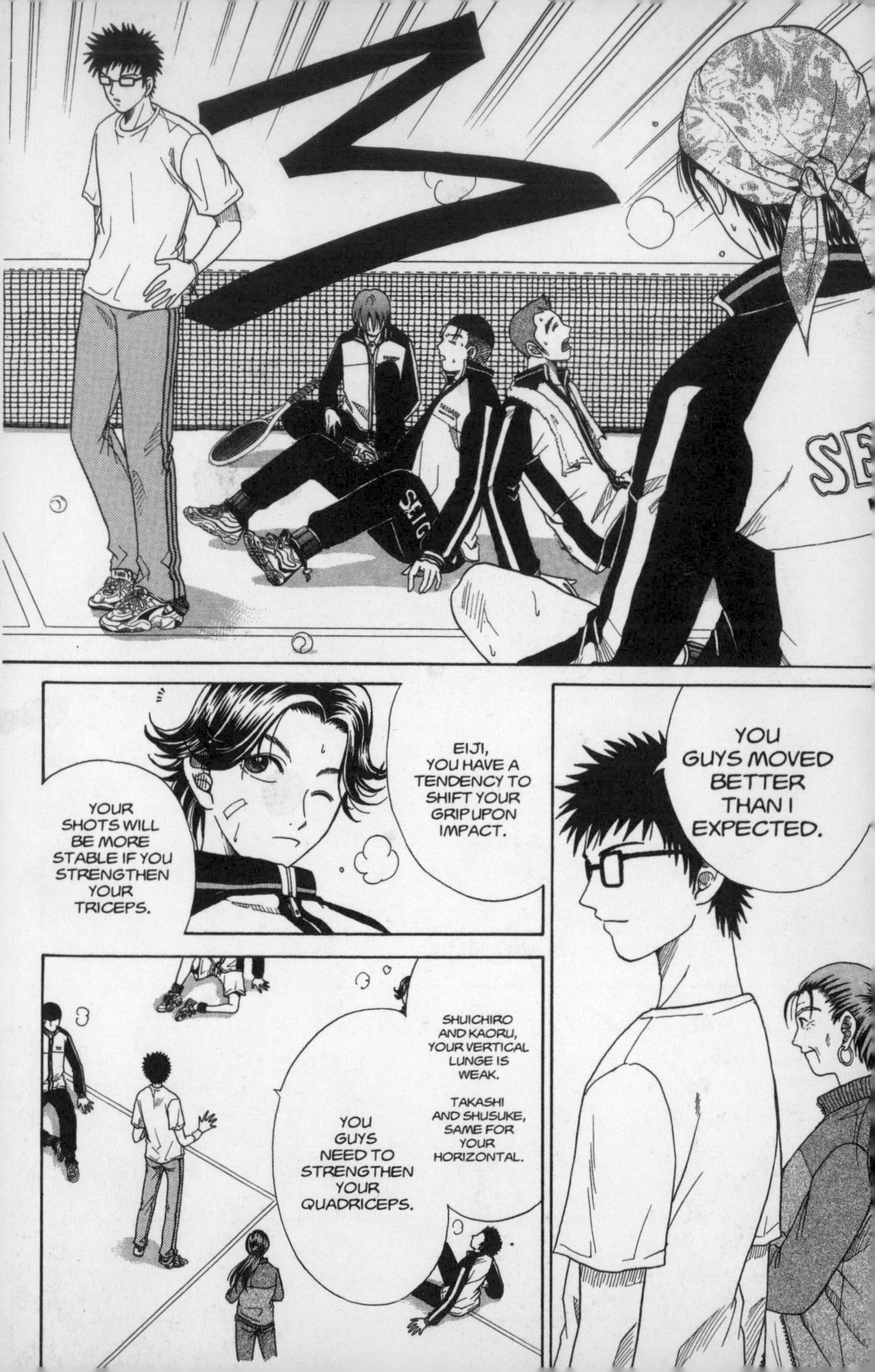
YOU GUYS MOVED BETTER THAN I EXPECTED.
EIJI, YOU HAVE A TENDENCY TO SHIFT YOUR GRIP UPON IMPACT.
YOUR SHOTS WILL BE MORE STABLE IF YOU STRENGTHEN YOUR TRICEPS.
SHUICHIRO AND KAORU, YOUR VERTICAL LUNGE IS WEAK.
TAKASHI AND SHUSUKE, SAME FOR YOUR HORIZONTAL.
YOU GUYS NEED TO STRENGTHEN YOUR QUADRICEPS.

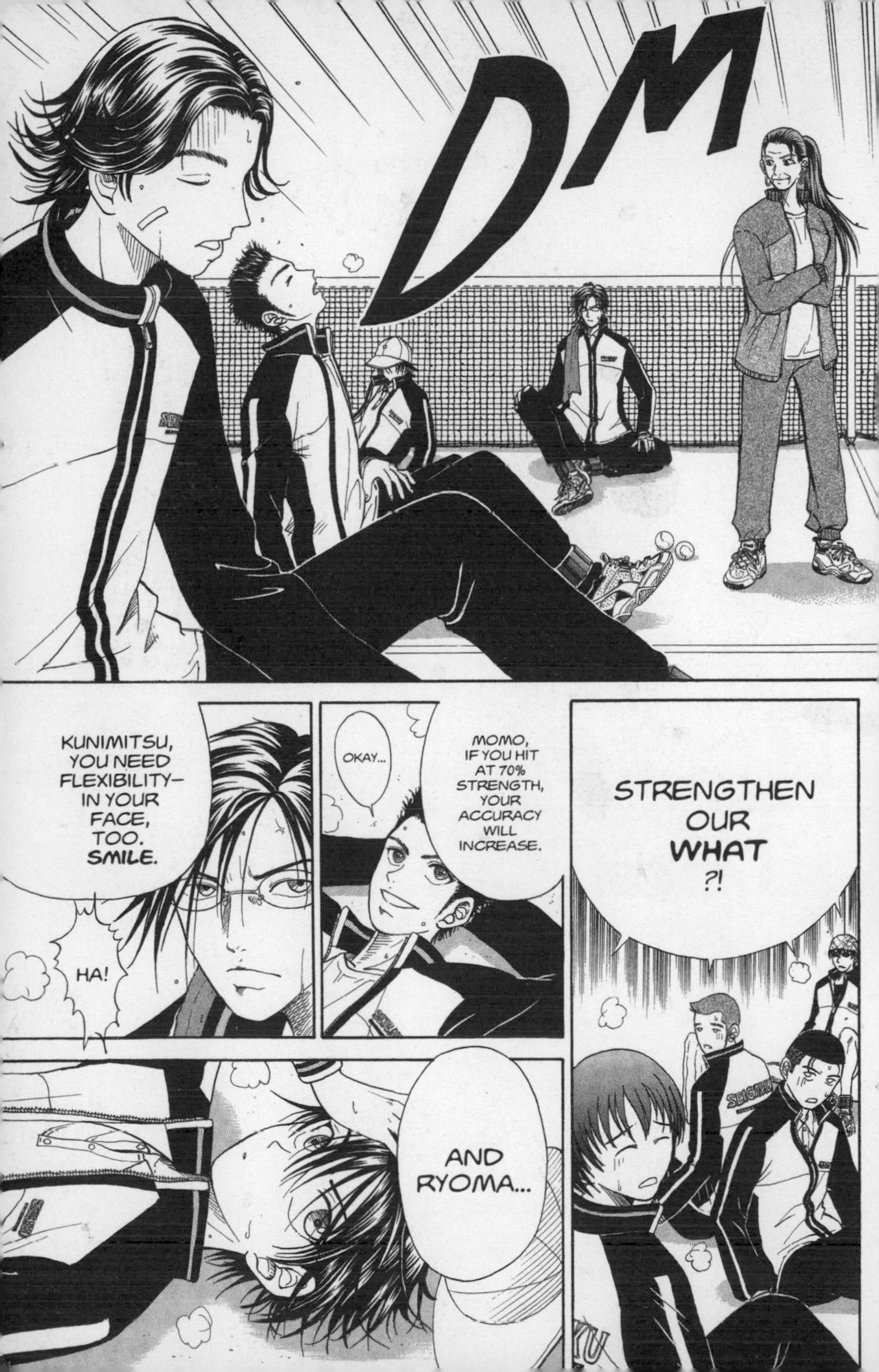

DM
STRENGTHEN OUR WHAT ?!
KU
MOMO, IF YOU HIT AT 70% STRENGTH, YOUR ACCURACY WILL INCREASE.
OKAY...
KUNIMITSU, YOU NEED FLEXIBILITY— IN YOUR FACE, TOO. SMILE.
HA!
AND RYOMA...

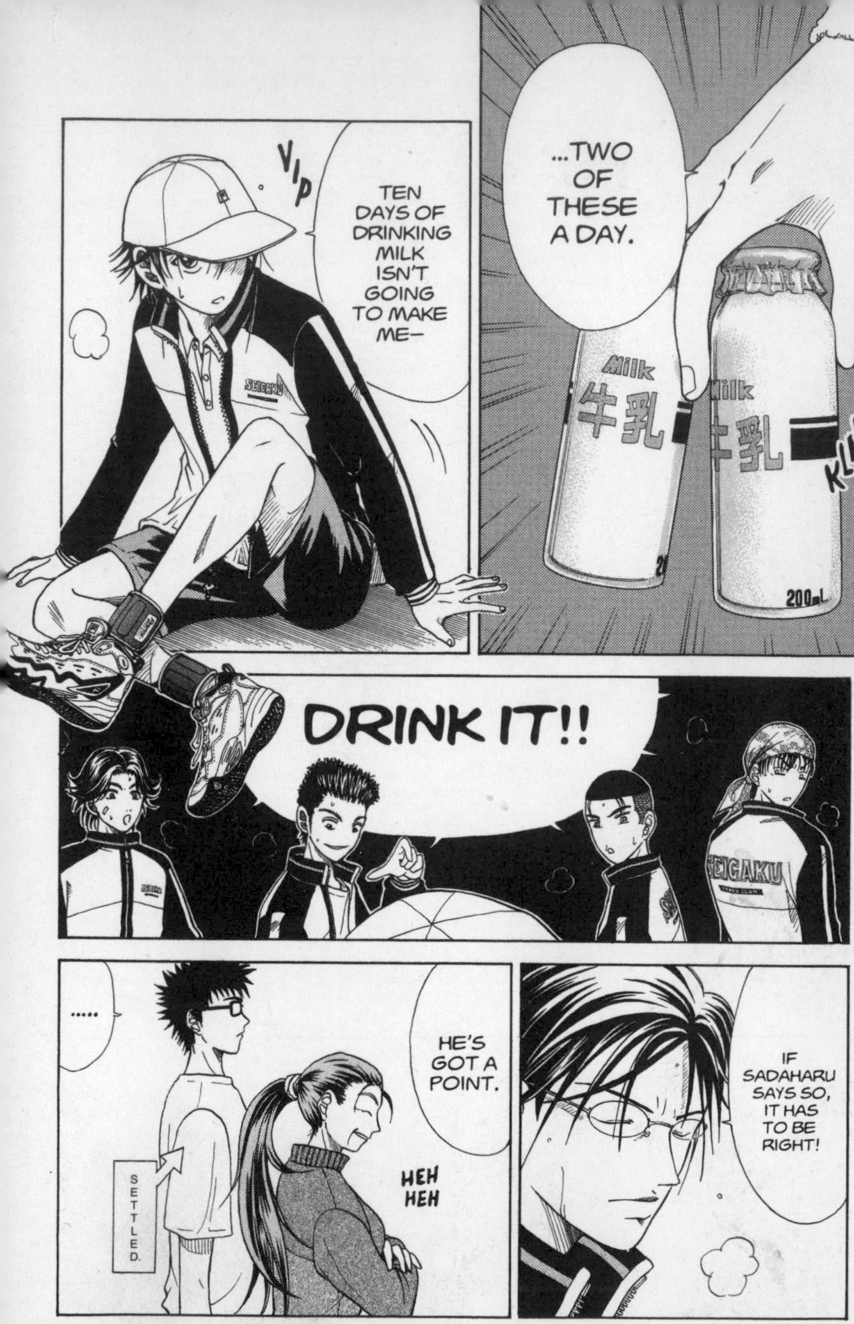
...TWO OF THESE A DAY.
Milk 牛乳
Milk 牛乳
200mL
KLINK
VIP
TEN DAYS OF DRINKING MILK ISN'T GOING TO MAKE ME-
SEIGAKU
DRINK IT!!
SEIGAKU
IF SADAHARU SAYS SO, IT HAS TO BE RIGHT!
HE'S GOT A POINT.
......
HEH HEH
SETTLED.

READ THIS WAY

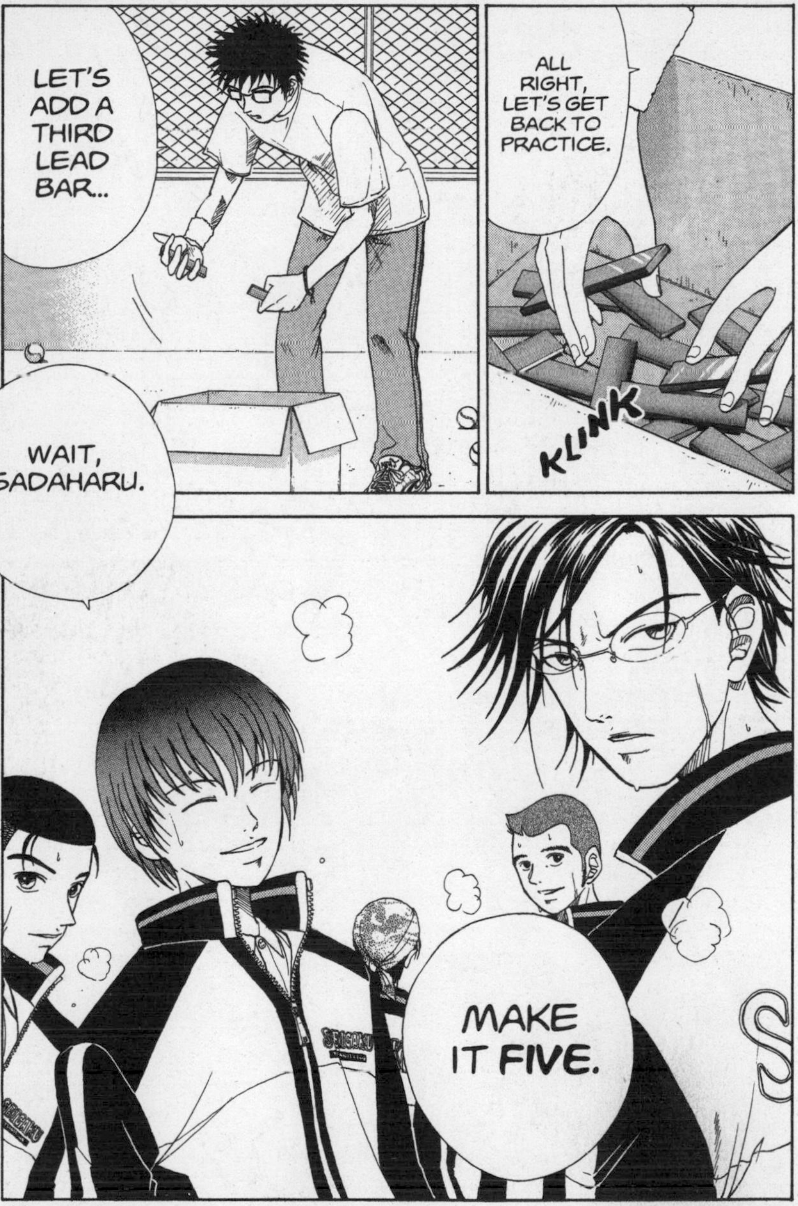
ALL RIGHT, LET'S GET BACK TO PRACTICE.
KLINK
LET'S ADD A THIRD LEAD BAR...
WAIT, SADAHARU.
MAKE IT FIVE.

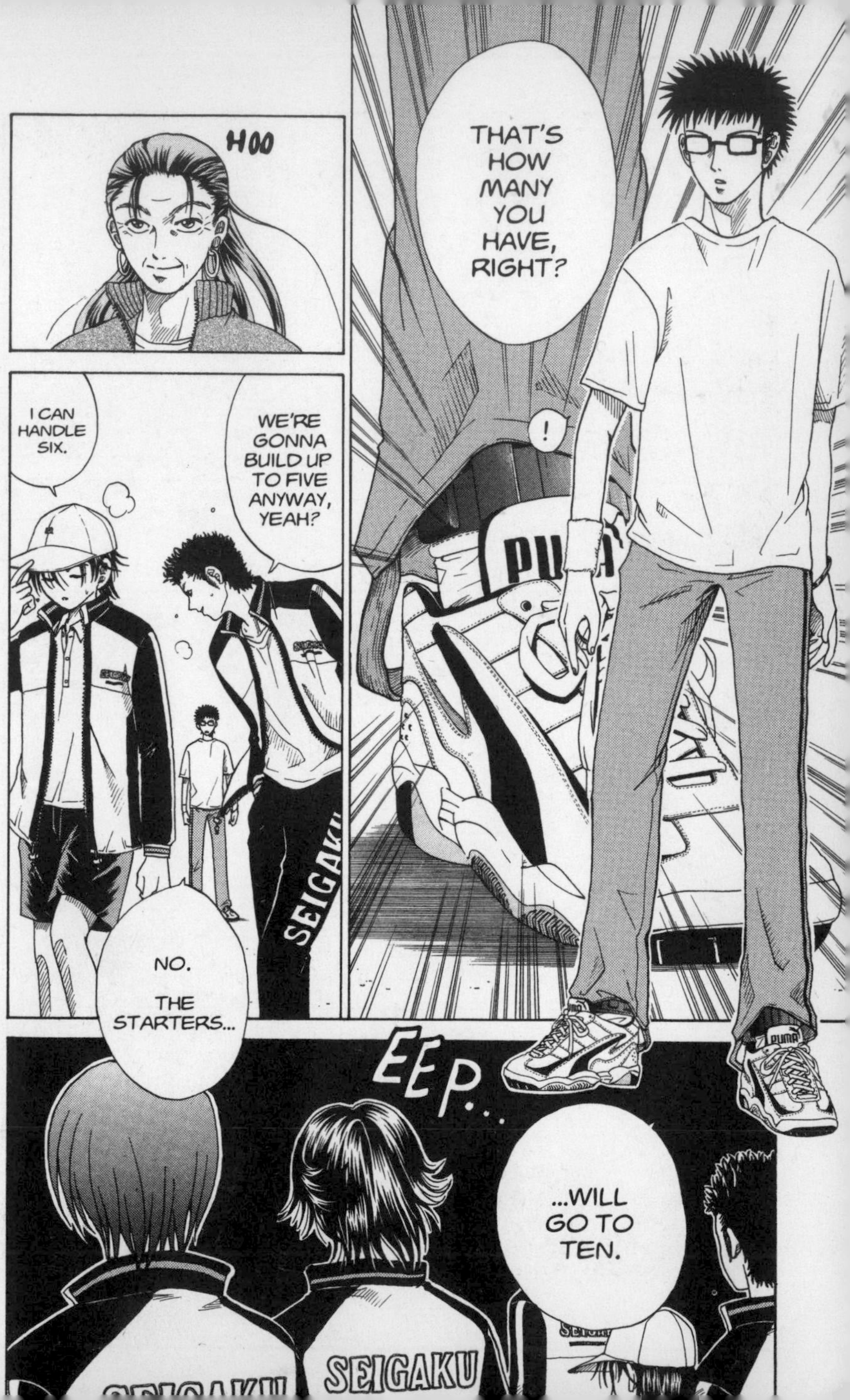
THAT'S HOW MANY YOU HAVE, RIGHT?
!
HOO
WE'RE GONNA BUILD UP TO FIVE ANYWAY, YEAH?
I CAN HANDLE SIX.
PUMA
SEIGAKU
EEP...
NO. THE STARTERS...
...WILL GO TO TEN.
SEIGAKU
SEIGAKU

READ THIS WAY

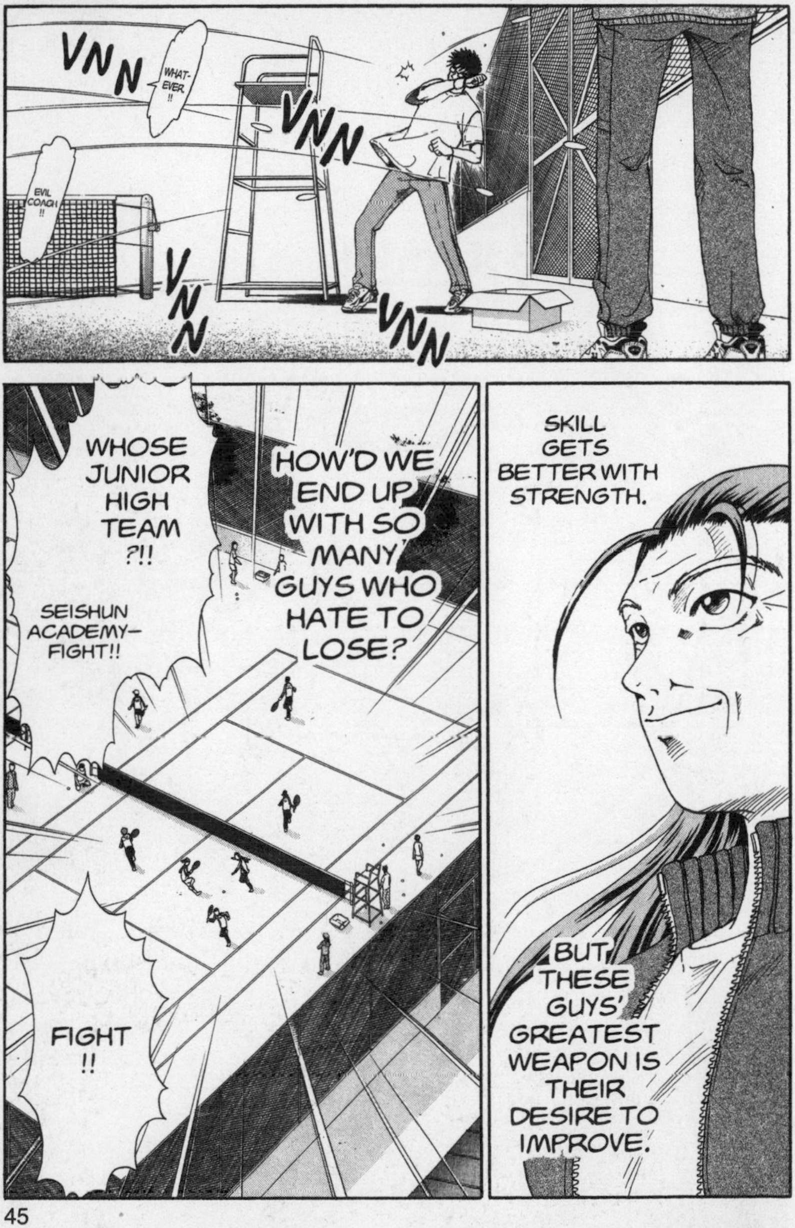
VNN
WHAT-EVER!!
VNN
VNN
EVIL COACH!!
VNN
SKILL GETS BETTER WITH STRENGTH.
BUT THESE GUYS' GREATEST WEAPON IS THEIR DESIRE TO IMPROVE.
HOW'D WE END UP WITH SO MANY GUYS WHO HATE TO LOSE?
WHOSE JUNIOR HIGH TEAM ?!!
SEISHUN ACADEMY— FIGHT!!
FIGHT !!

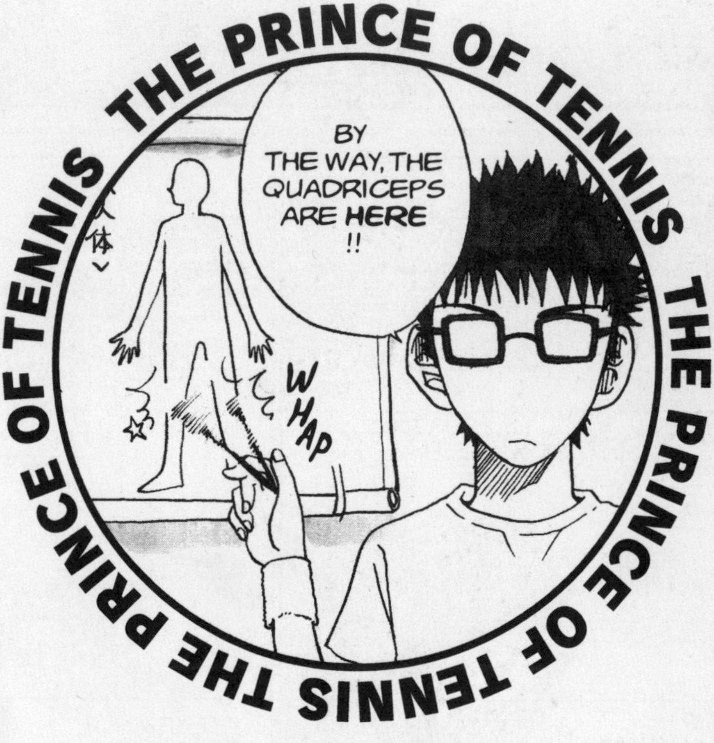
THE PRINCE OF TENNIS THE PRINCE OF TENNIS THE PRINCE OF TENNIS
BY THE WAY, THE QUADRICEPS ARE HERE !!
WHAP
人体

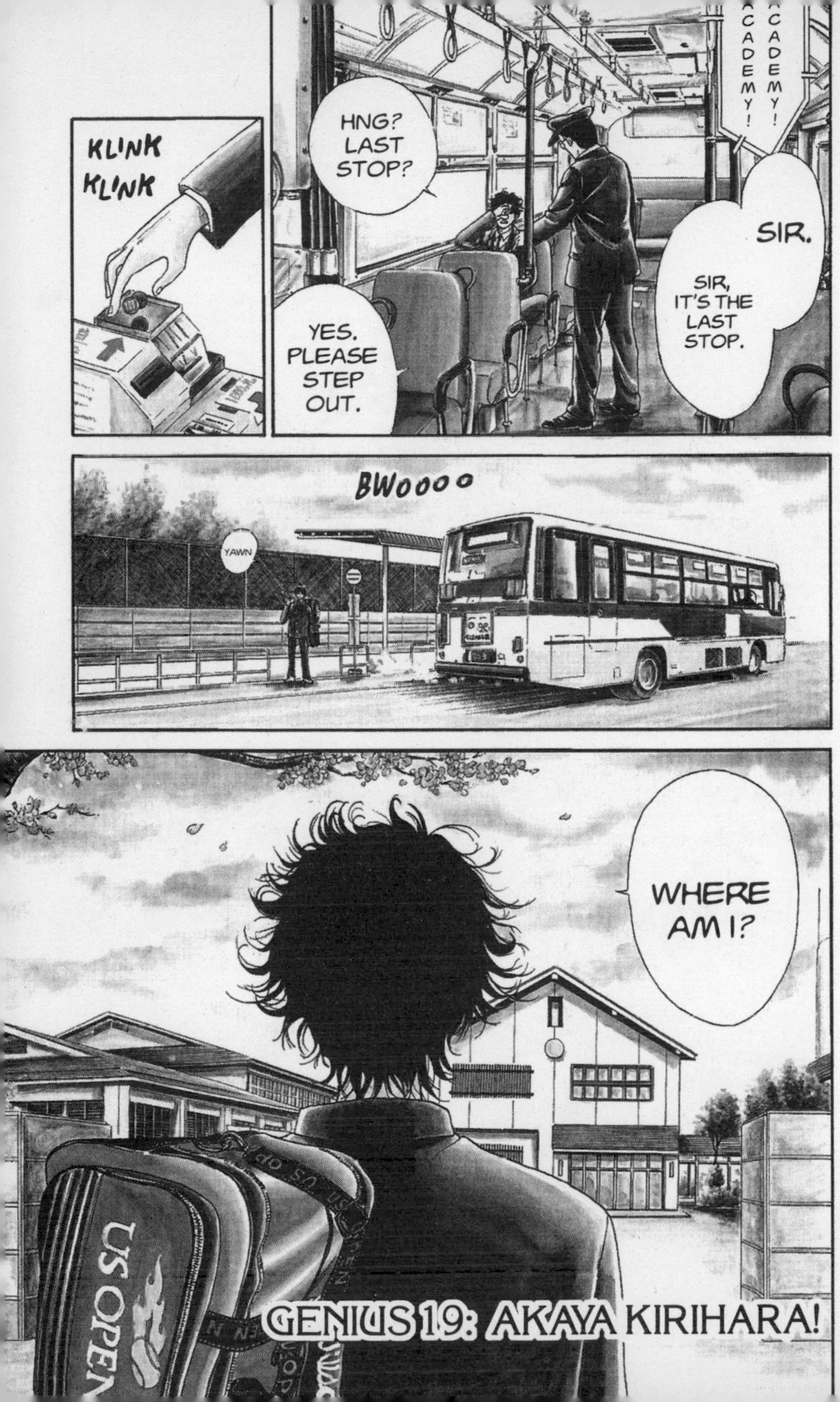
ACADEMY!
ACADEMY!
SIR.
SIR, IT'S THE LAST STOP.
HNG? LAST STOP?
YES. PLEASE STEP OUT.
KLINK KLINK
BWOOOO
YAWN
WHERE AM I?
US OPEN

GENIUS 19: AKAYA KIRIHARA!

GENIUS 19:

AKAYA KIRIHARA!

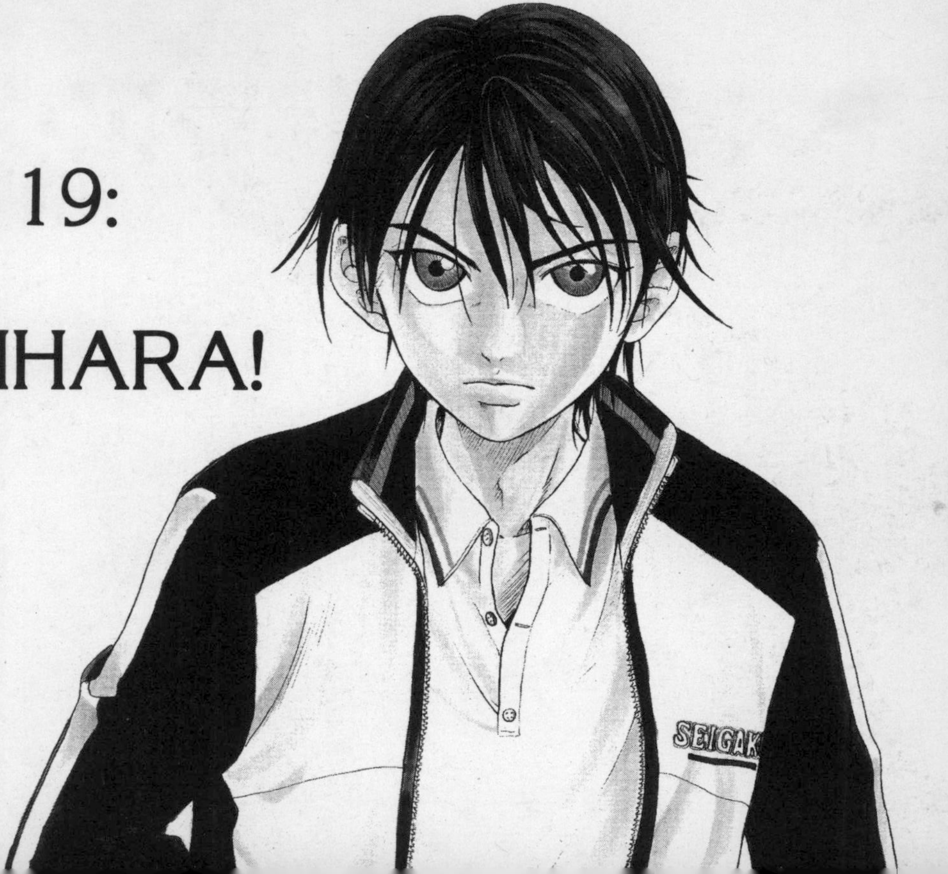
SEIGAKU

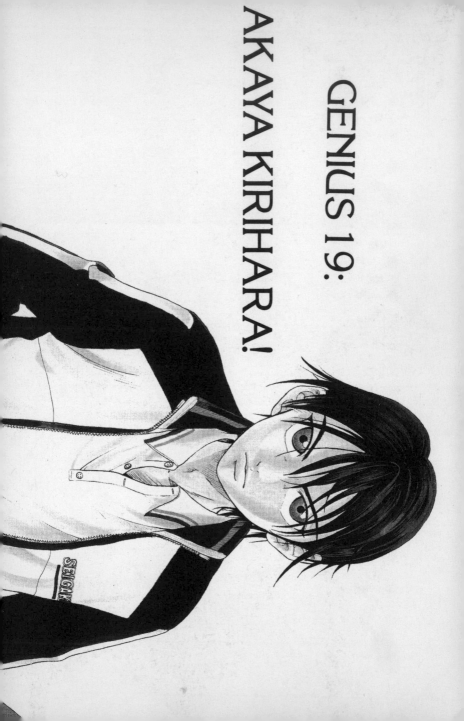

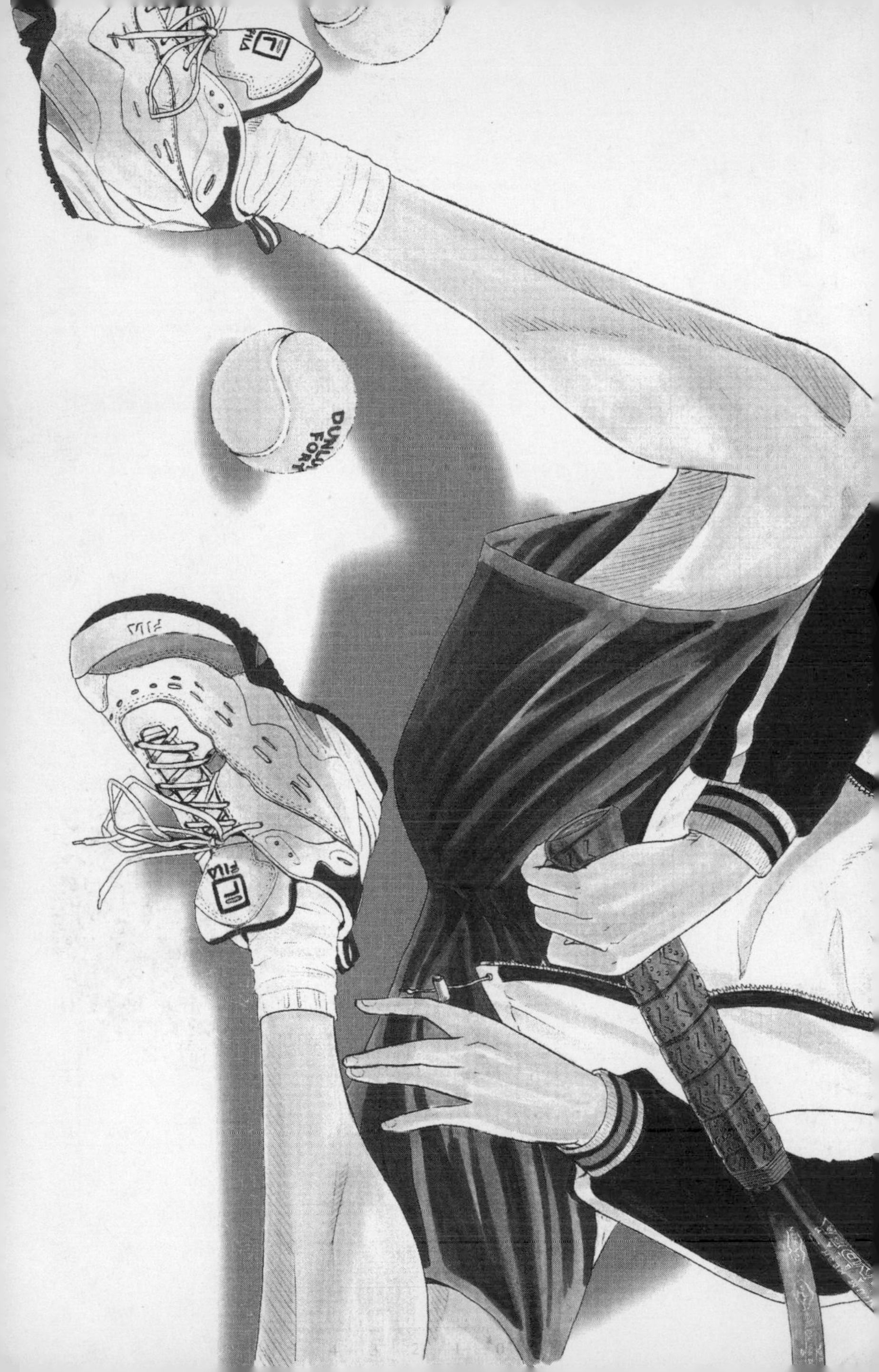
FILA

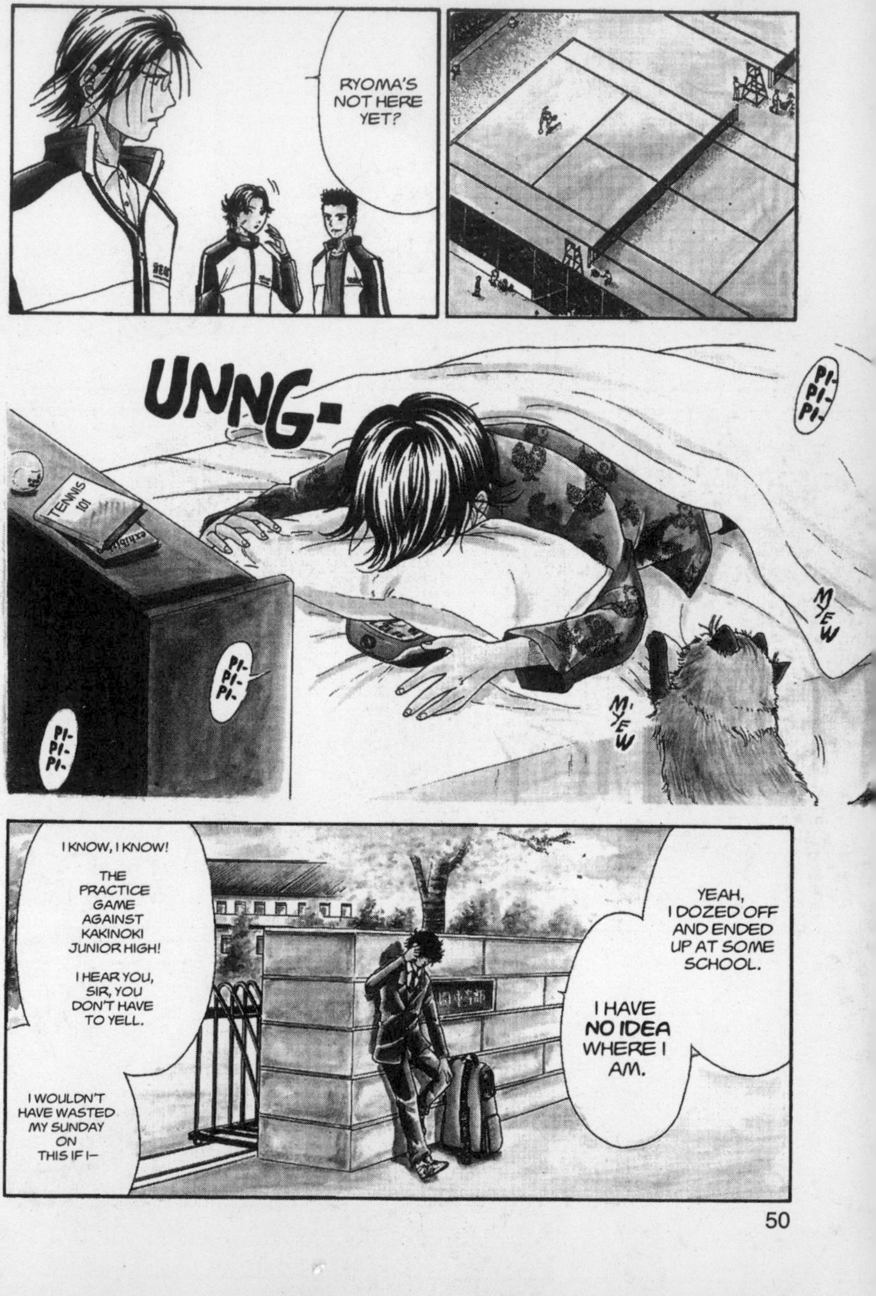
RYOMA'S NOT HERE YET?
PI-PI-PI-
MYEW
MYEW
UNNG-
PI-PI-PI-
PI-PI-PI-
TENNIS 101
YEAH, I DOZED OFF AND ENDED UP AT SOME SCHOOL.
I HAVE NO IDEA WHERE I AM.
I KNOW, I KNOW!
THE PRACTICE GAME AGAINST KAKINOKI JUNIOR HIGH!
I HEAR YOU, SIR, YOU DON'T HAVE TO YELL.
I WOULDN'T HAVE WASTED MY SUNDAY ON THIS IF I–

...HEY.

I SEE A SIGN.

SEISHUN ACADEMY

SEISHUN ACADEMY, EH...?

I KNOW WHERE I AM! HELLO...?

HELLO?!

HE HUNG UP...

CHUMP.

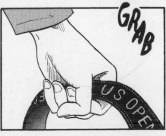

GRAB

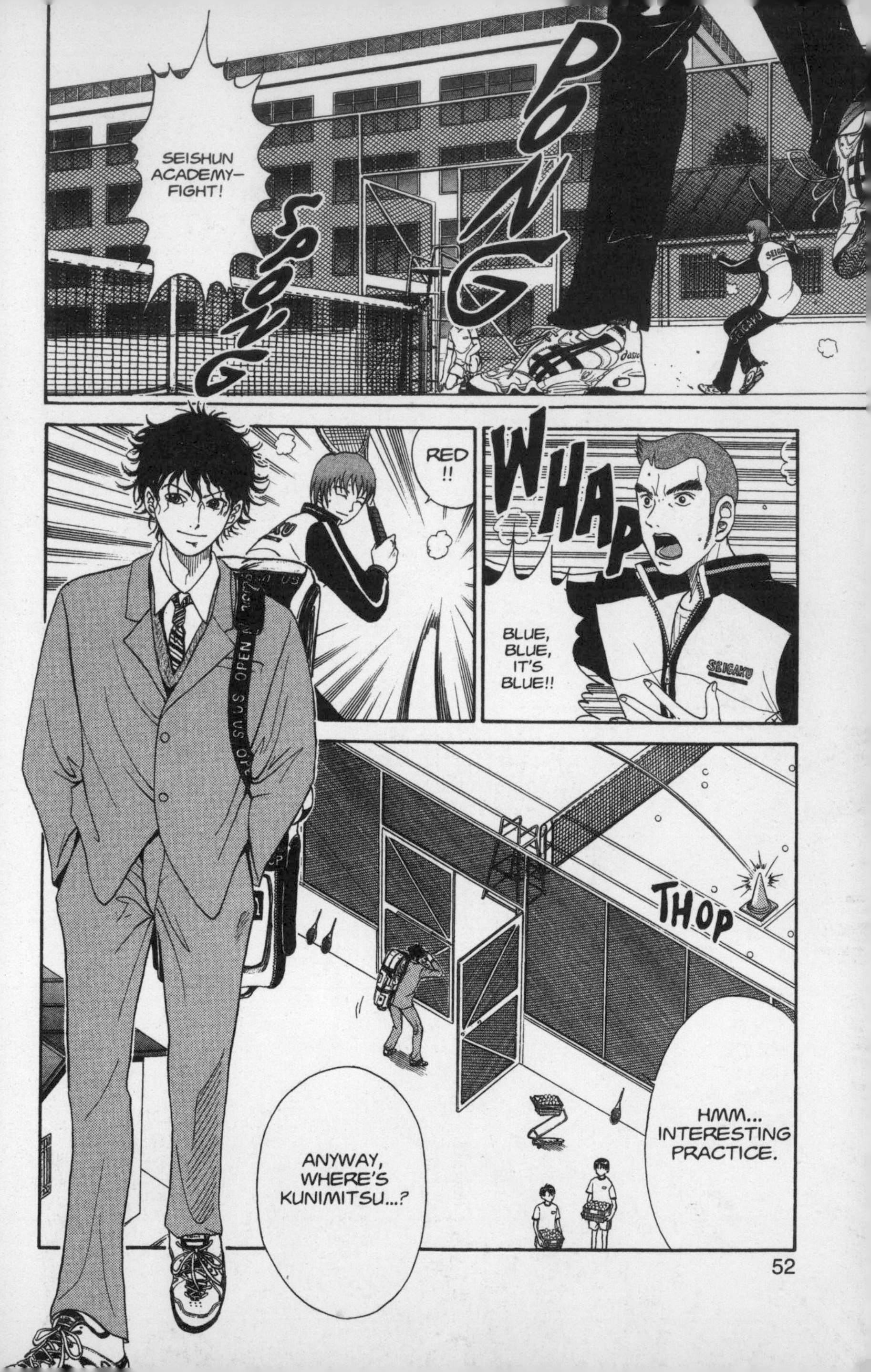
PONG
SEISHUN ACADEMY— FIGHT!
SPONG
WHAP
BLUE, BLUE, IT'S BLUE!!
RED !!
THOP
HMM... INTERESTING PRACTICE.
ANYWAY, WHERE'S KUNIMITSU...?

READ THIS WAY

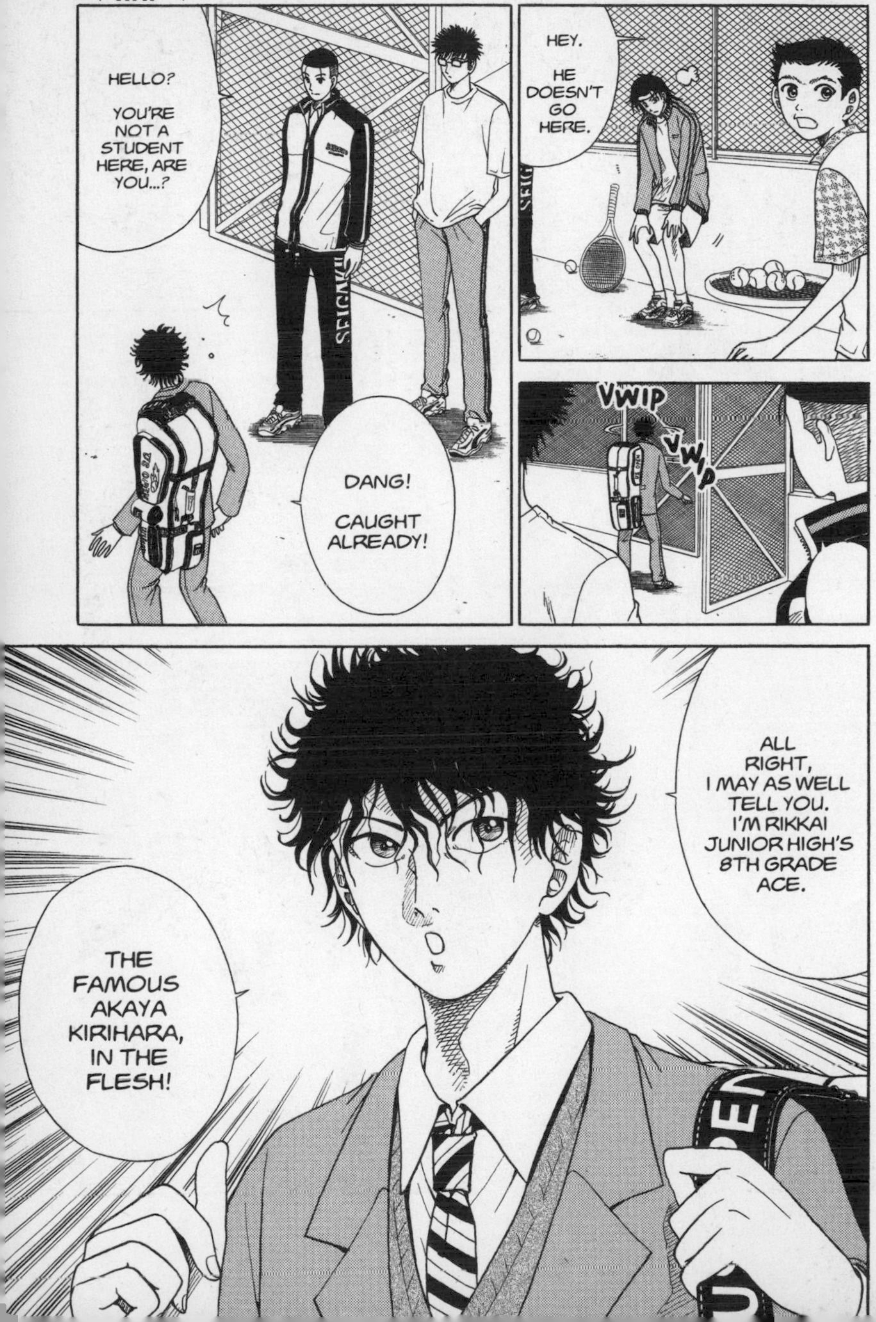
HEY. HE DOESN'T GO HERE.
VWIP
VWIP
HELLO? YOU'RE NOT A STUDENT HERE, ARE YOU...?
DANG! CAUGHT ALREADY!
ALL RIGHT, I MAY AS WELL TELL YOU. I'M RIKKAI JUNIOR HIGH'S 8TH GRADE ACE.
THE FAMOUS AKAYA KIRIHARA, IN THE FLESH!

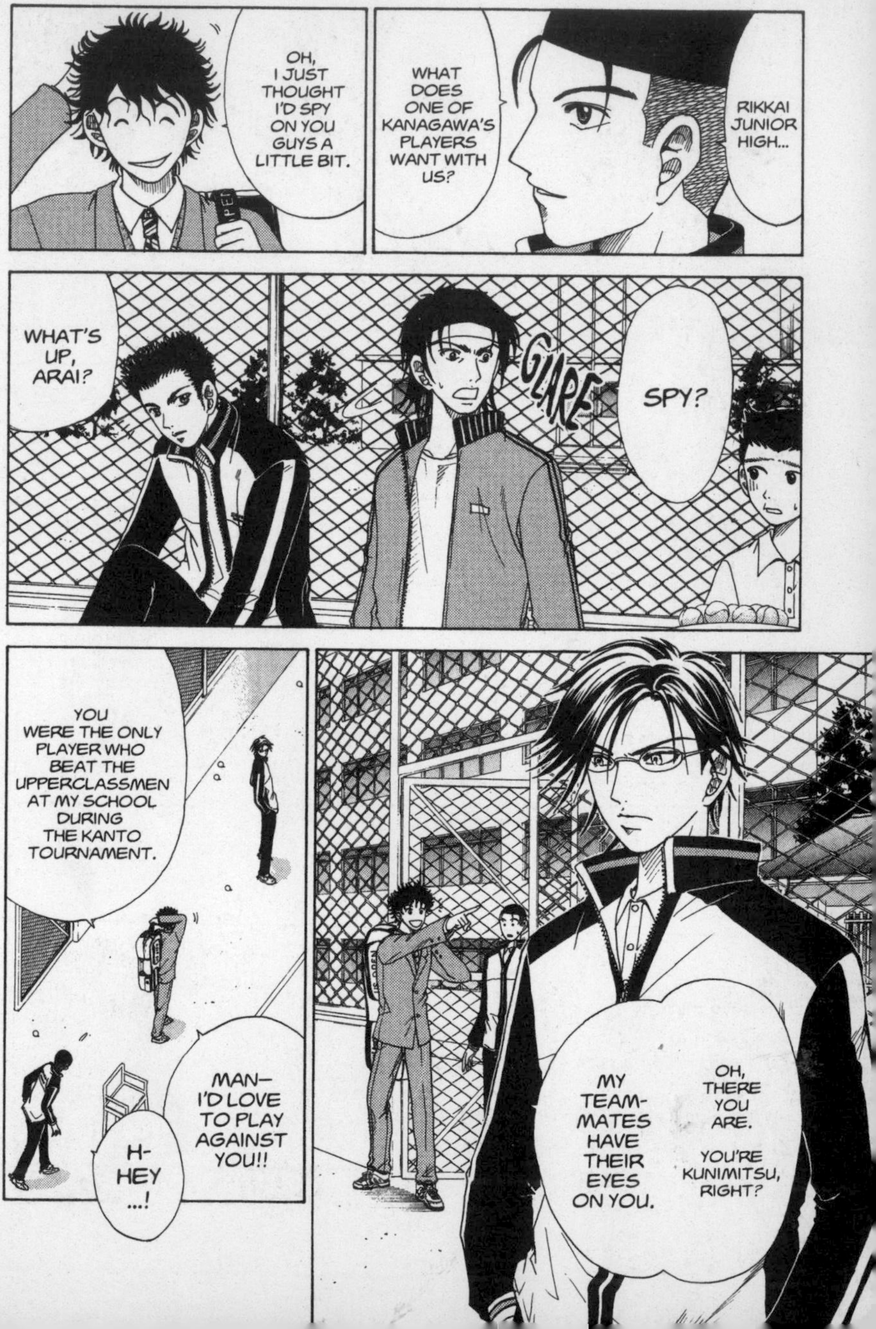
RIKKAI JUNIOR HIGH...
WHAT DOES ONE OF KANAGAWA'S PLAYERS WANT WITH US?
OH, I JUST THOUGHT I'D SPY ON YOU GUYS A LITTLE BIT.
SPY?
GLARE
WHAT'S UP, ARAI?
OH, THERE YOU ARE. YOU'RE KUNIMITSU, RIGHT?
MY TEAM-MATES HAVE THEIR EYES ON YOU.
YOU WERE THE ONLY PLAYER WHO BEAT THE UPPERCLASSMEN AT MY SCHOOL DURING THE KANTO TOURNAMENT.
MAN— I'D LOVE TO PLAY AGAINST YOU!!
H-HEY ...!

READ THIS WAY

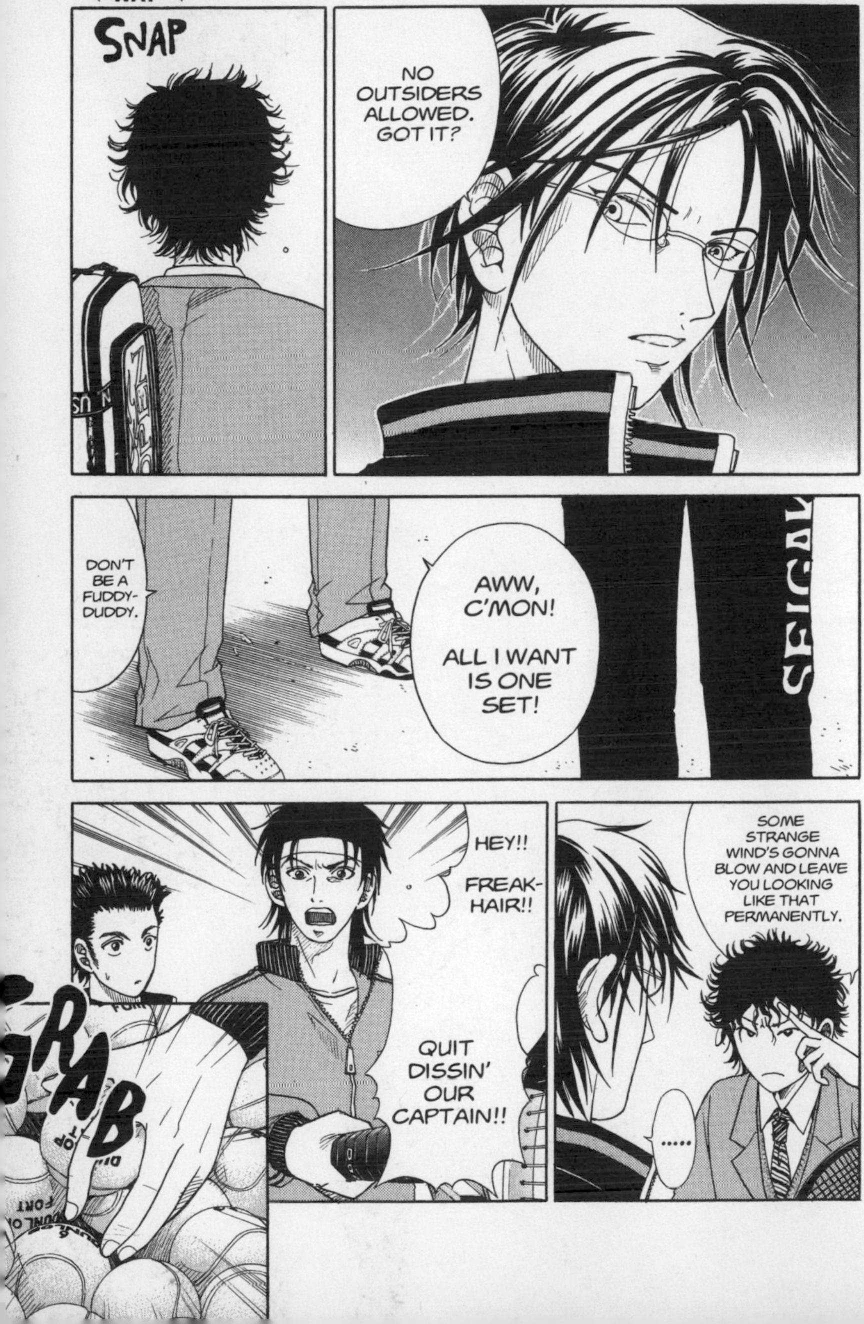
NO OUTSIDERS ALLOWED. GOT IT?
SNAP
AWW, C'MON!
ALL I WANT IS ONE SET!
DON'T BE A FUDDY-DUDDY.
SOME STRANGE WIND'S GONNA BLOW AND LEAVE YOU LOOKING LIKE THAT PERMANENTLY.
......
HEY!!
FREAK-HAIR!!
QUIT DISSIN' OUR CAPTAIN!!
GRAB

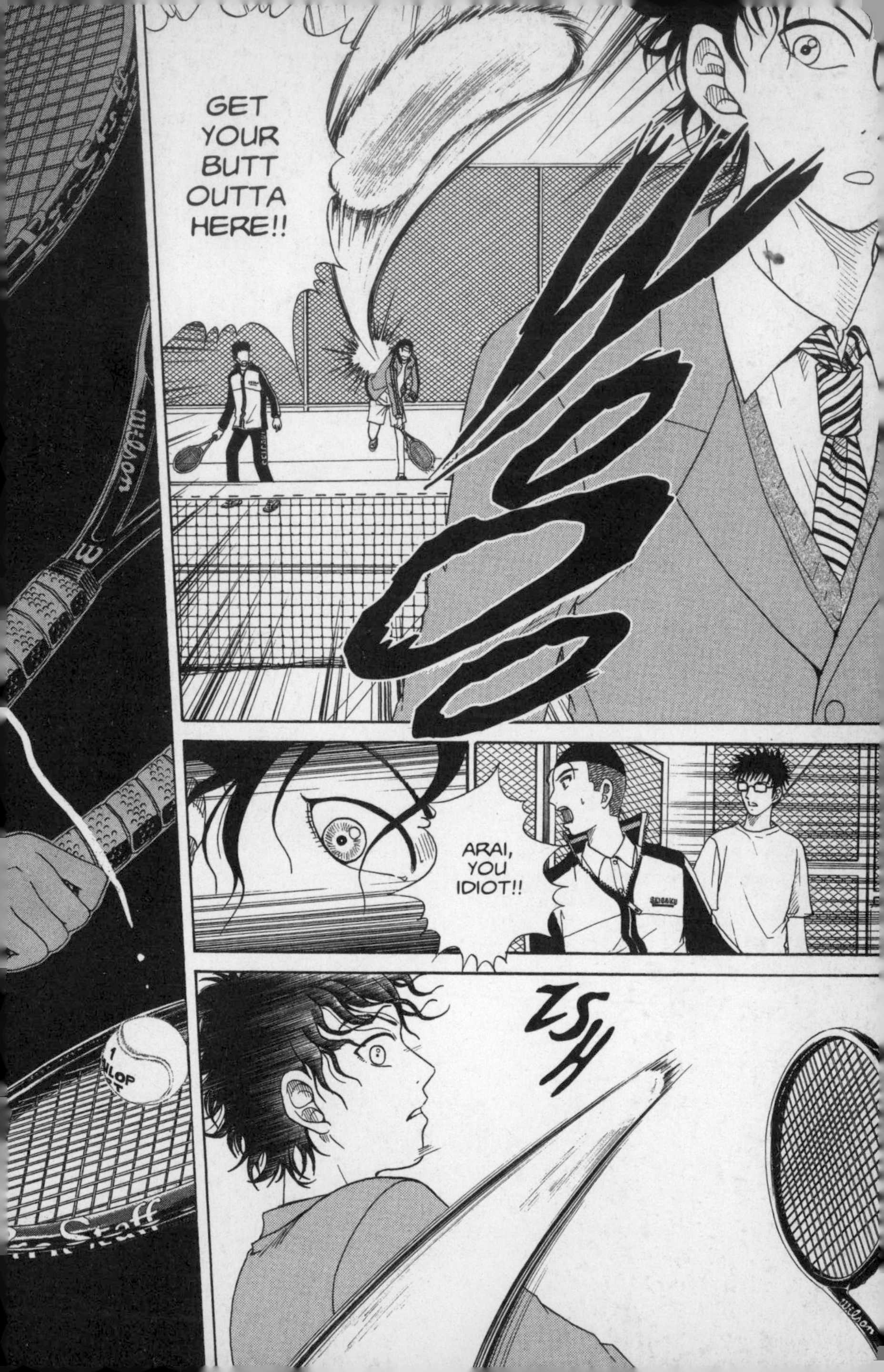
GET YOUR BUTT OUTTA HERE!!
ARAI, YOU IDIOT!!

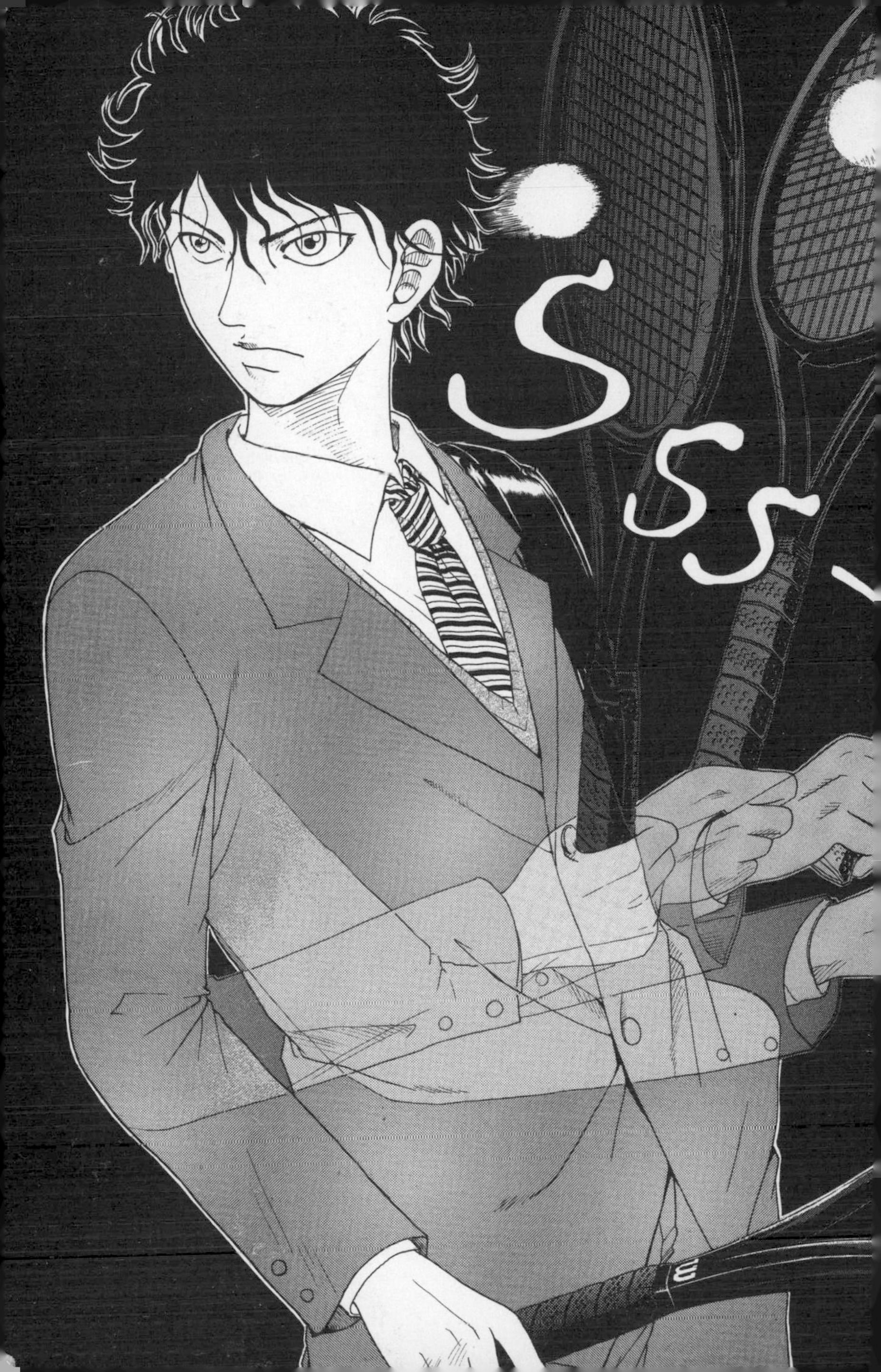

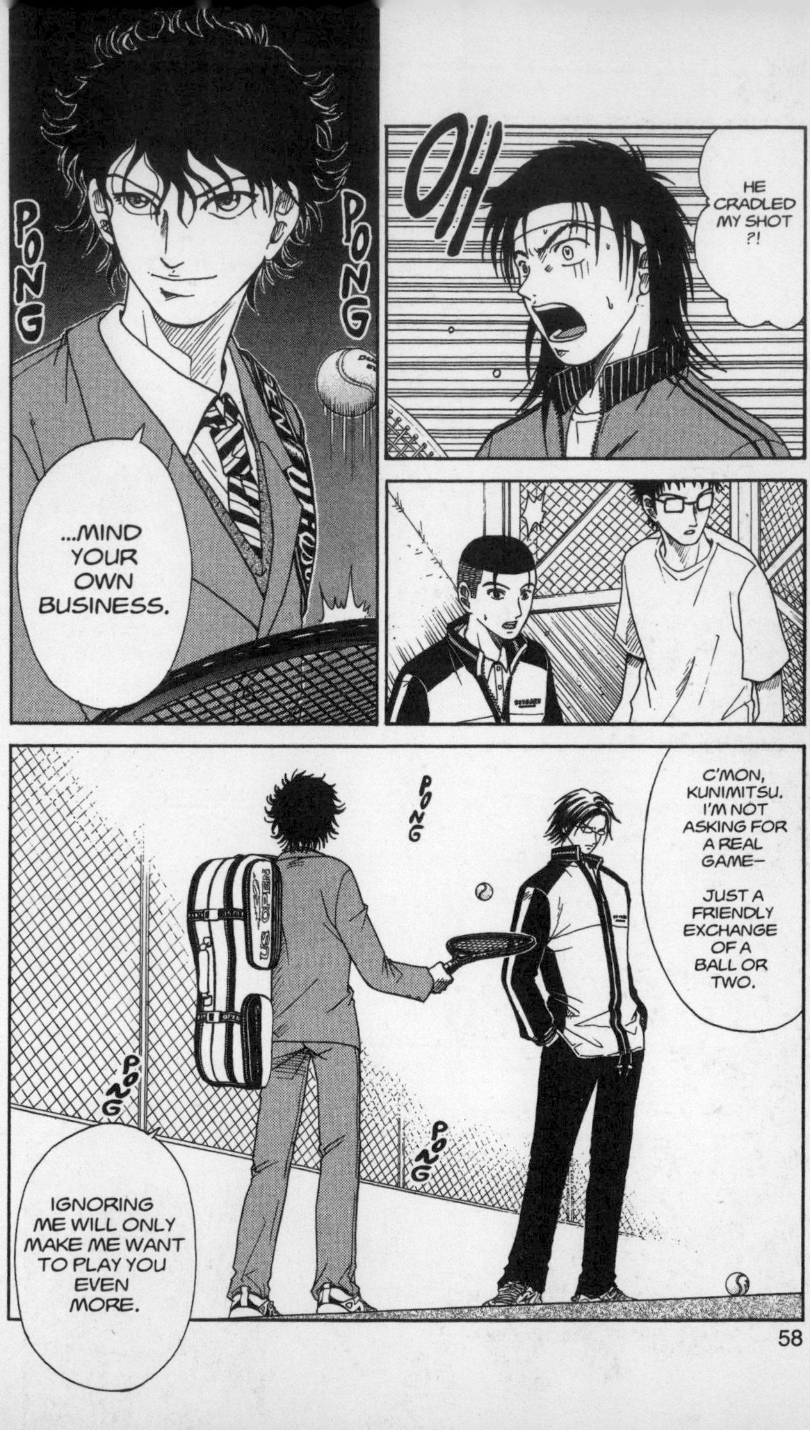
OH
HE CRADLED MY SHOT ?!
PONG
PONG
...MIND YOUR OWN BUSINESS.
C'MON, KUNIMITSU. I'M NOT ASKING FOR A REAL GAME–
JUST A FRIENDLY EXCHANGE OF A BALL OR TWO.
PONG
PONG
PONG
IGNORING ME WILL ONLY MAKE ME WANT TO PLAY YOU EVEN MORE.

READ THIS WAY

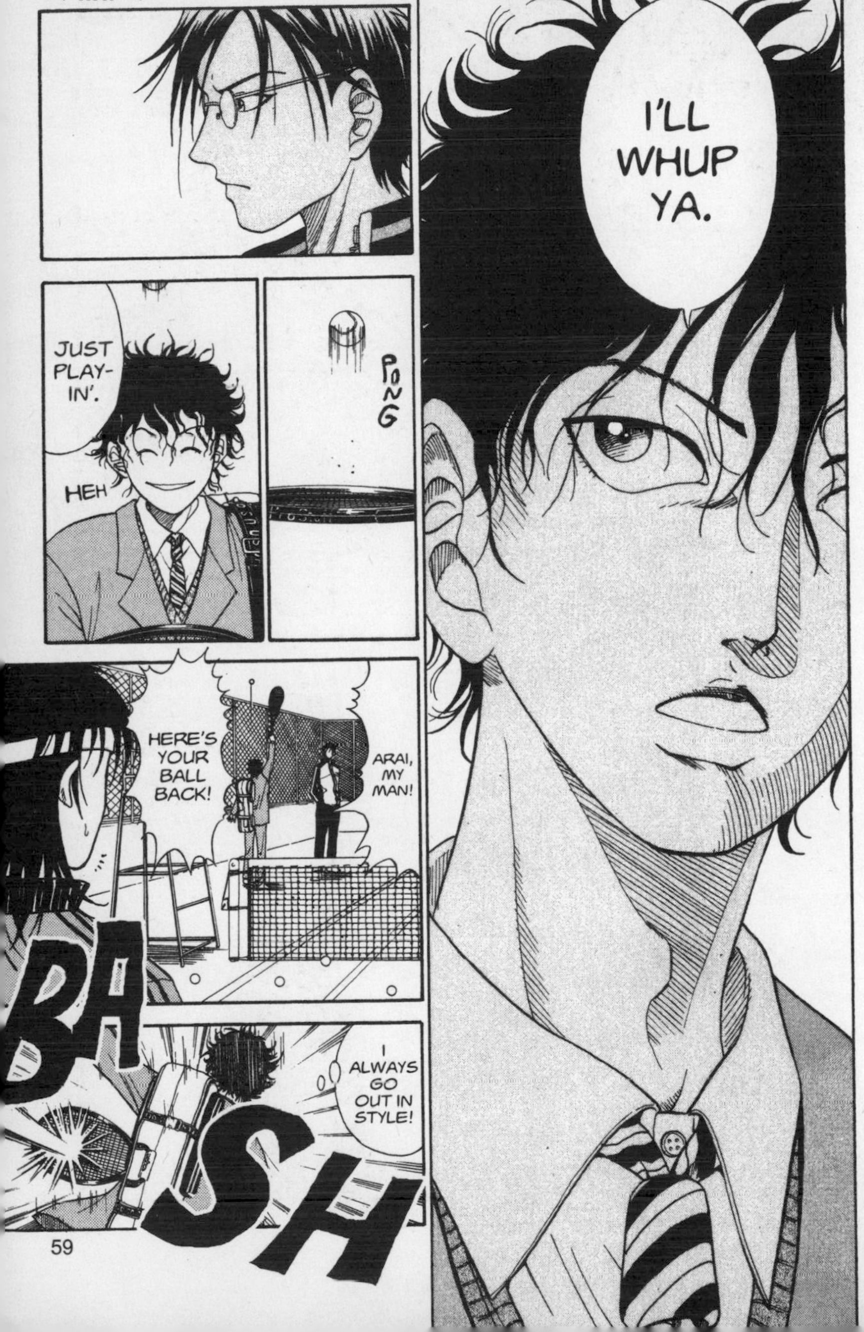

I'LL WHUP YA.
PONG
JUST PLAY-IN'.
HEH
ARAI, MY MAN!
HERE'S YOUR BALL BACK!
I ALWAYS GO OUT IN STYLE!
BASH

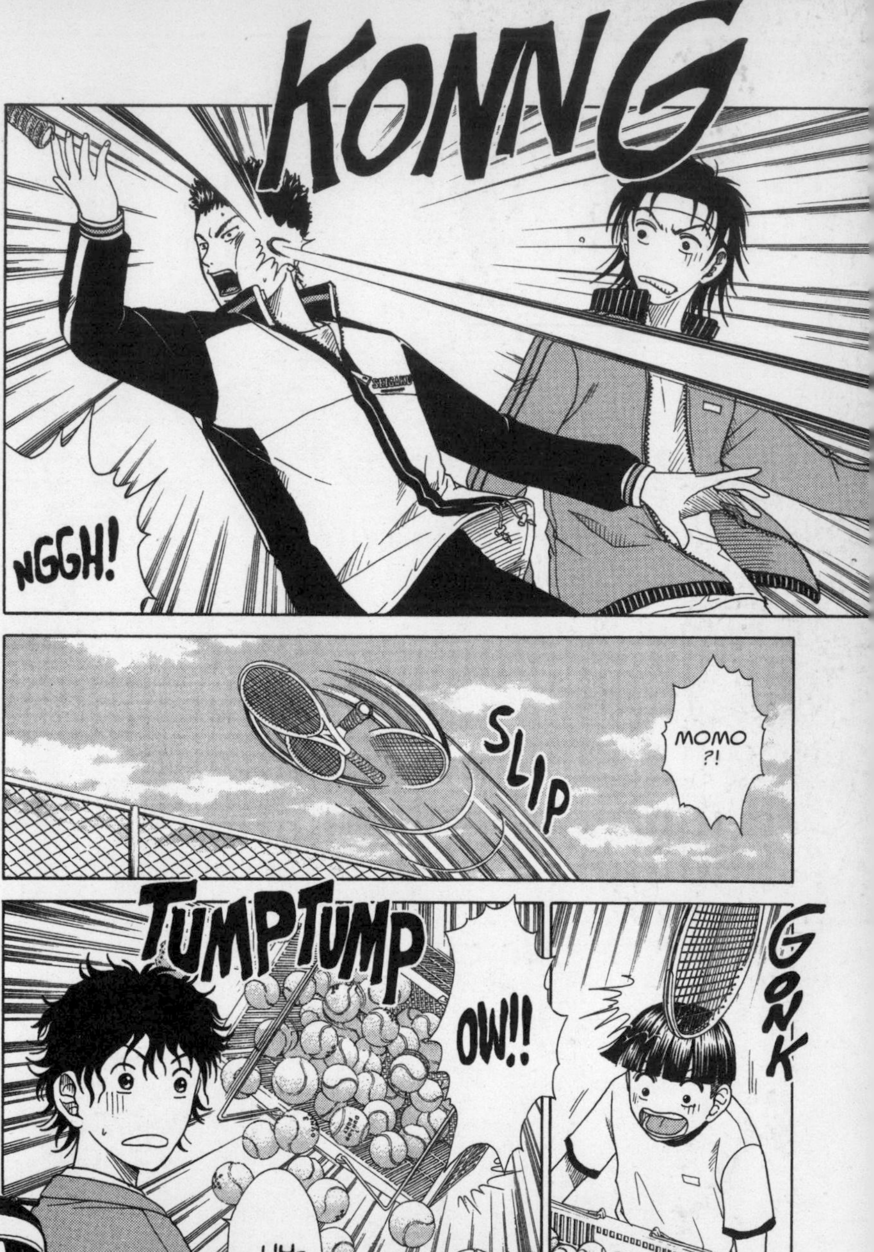
KONNG
NGGH!
MOMO ?!
SLIP
GONK
OW!!
TUMP TUMP
...UH- OH....

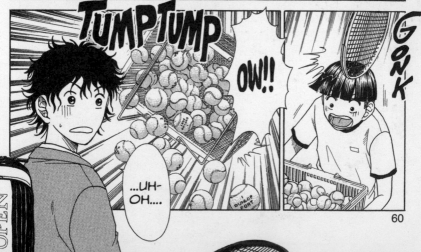

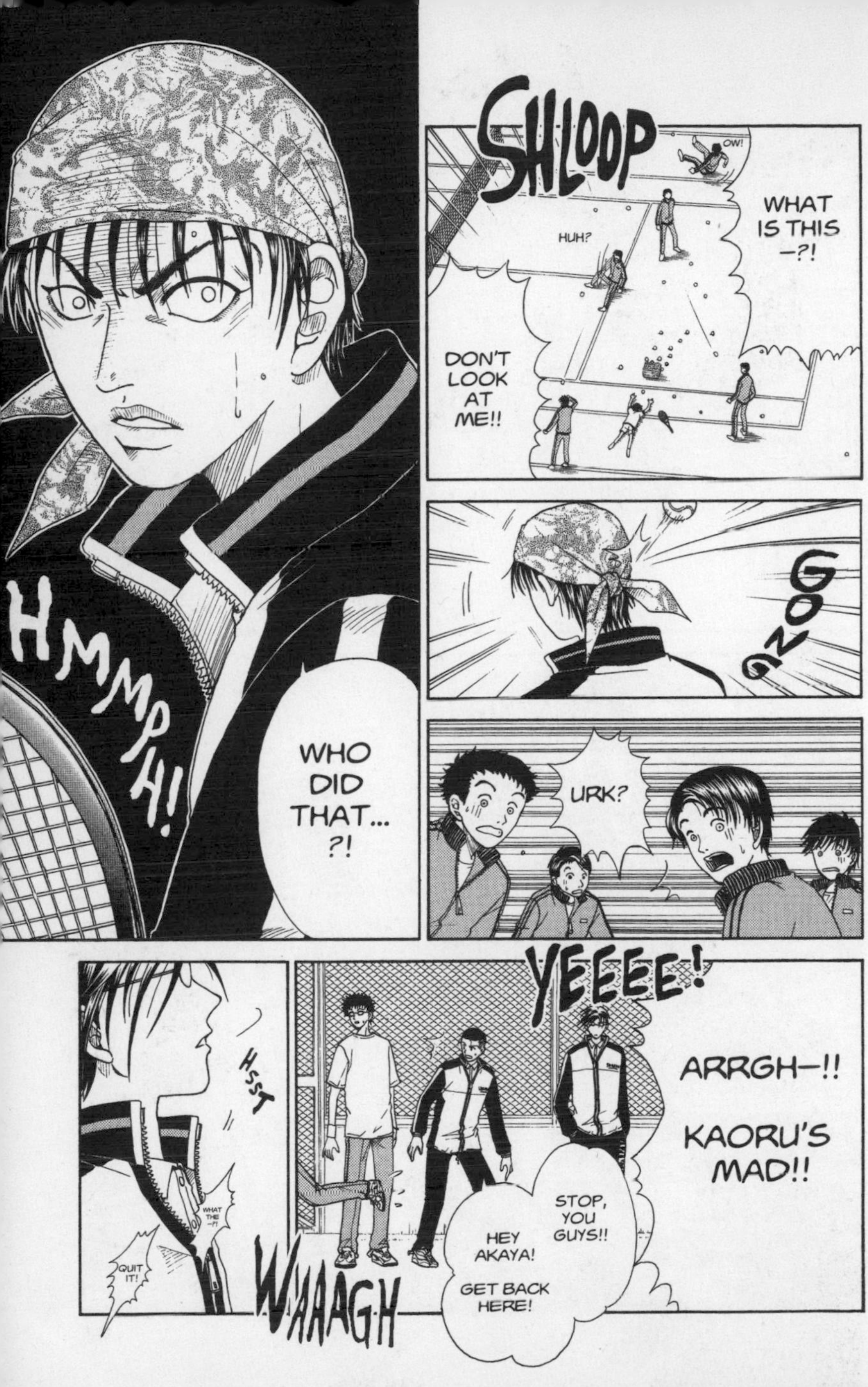
SHLOOP
OW!
WHAT IS THIS —?!
HUH?
DON'T LOOK AT ME!!
GONG
URK?
HMMPH!
WHO DID THAT...?!
YEEEE!
ARRGH—!!
KAORU'S MAD!!
STOP, YOU GUYS!!
HEY AKAYA!
GET BACK HERE!
WAAAGH
HSST
WHAT THE—?!
QUIT IT!

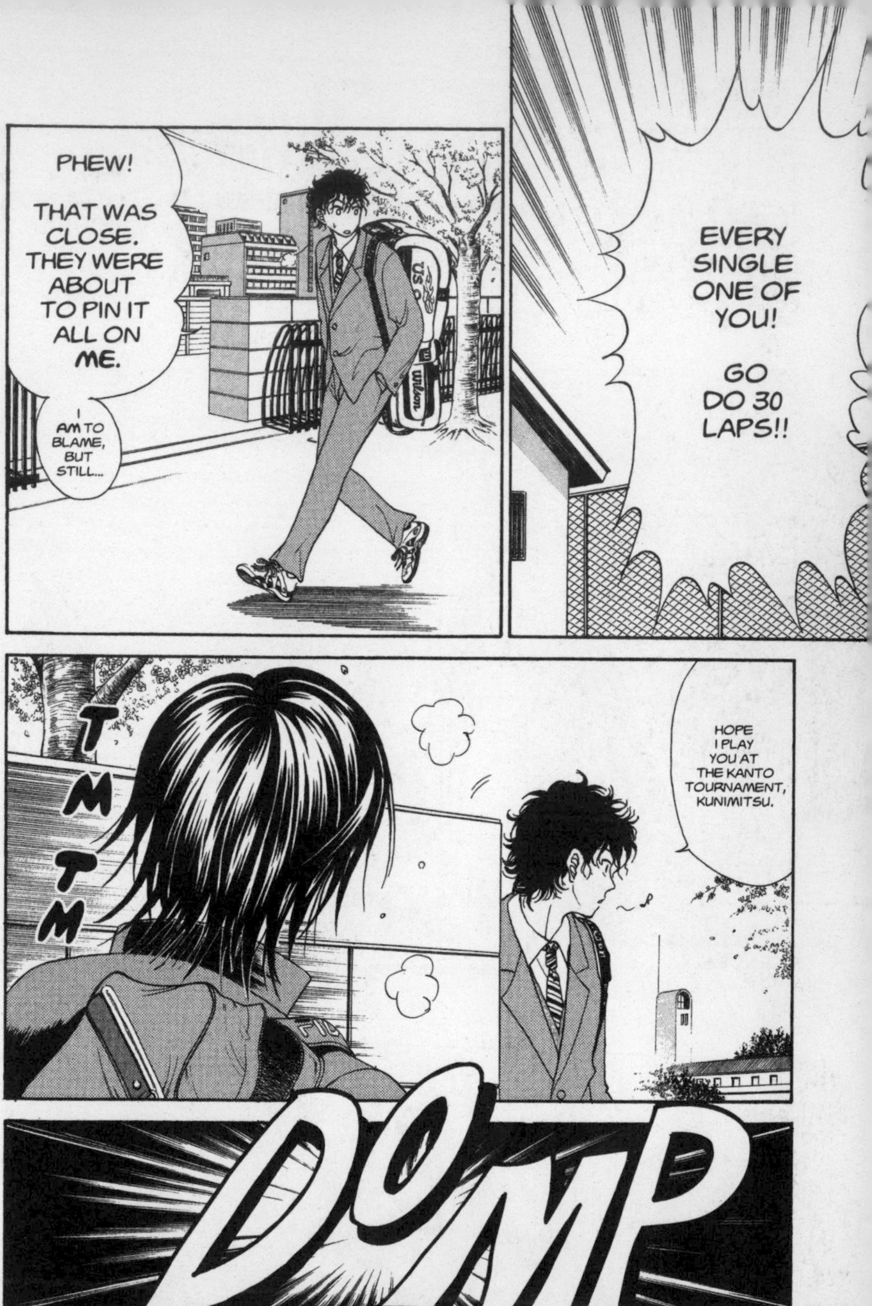
EVERY SINGLE ONE OF YOU!
GO DO 30 LAPS!!
PHEW!
THAT WAS CLOSE. THEY WERE ABOUT TO PIN IT ALL ON ME.
I AM TO BLAME, BUT STILL...
HOPE I PLAY YOU AT THE KANTO TOURNAMENT, KUNIMITSU.
TMTM
DOMP

READ THIS WAY

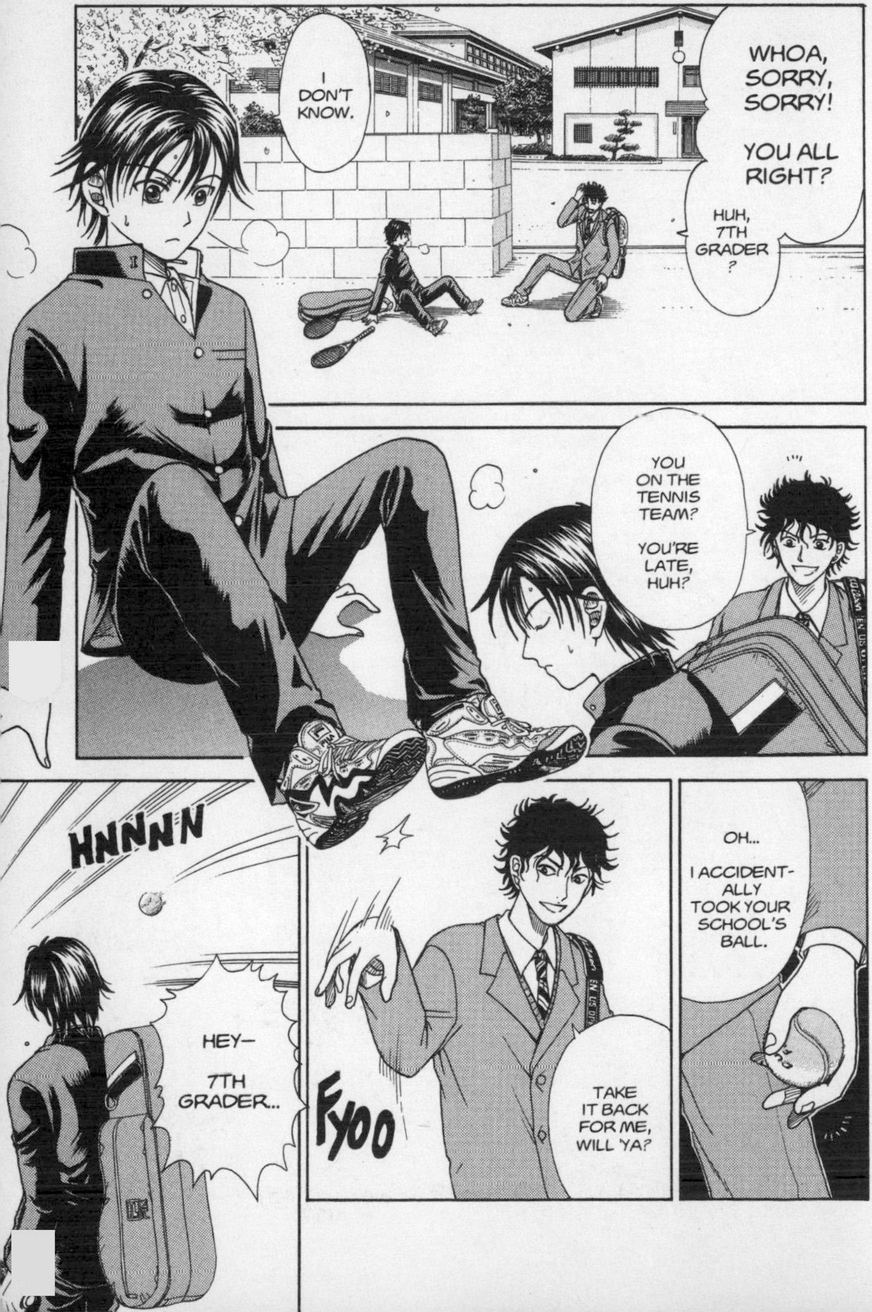
WHOA, SORRY, SORRY!
YOU ALL RIGHT?
HUH, 7TH GRADER?
I DON'T KNOW.
YOU ON THE TENNIS TEAM?
YOU'RE LATE, HUH?
OH...
I ACCIDENTALLY TOOK YOUR SCHOOL'S BALL.
TAKE IT BACK FOR ME, WILL 'YA?
FYOO
HNNNN
HEY—
7TH GRADER...

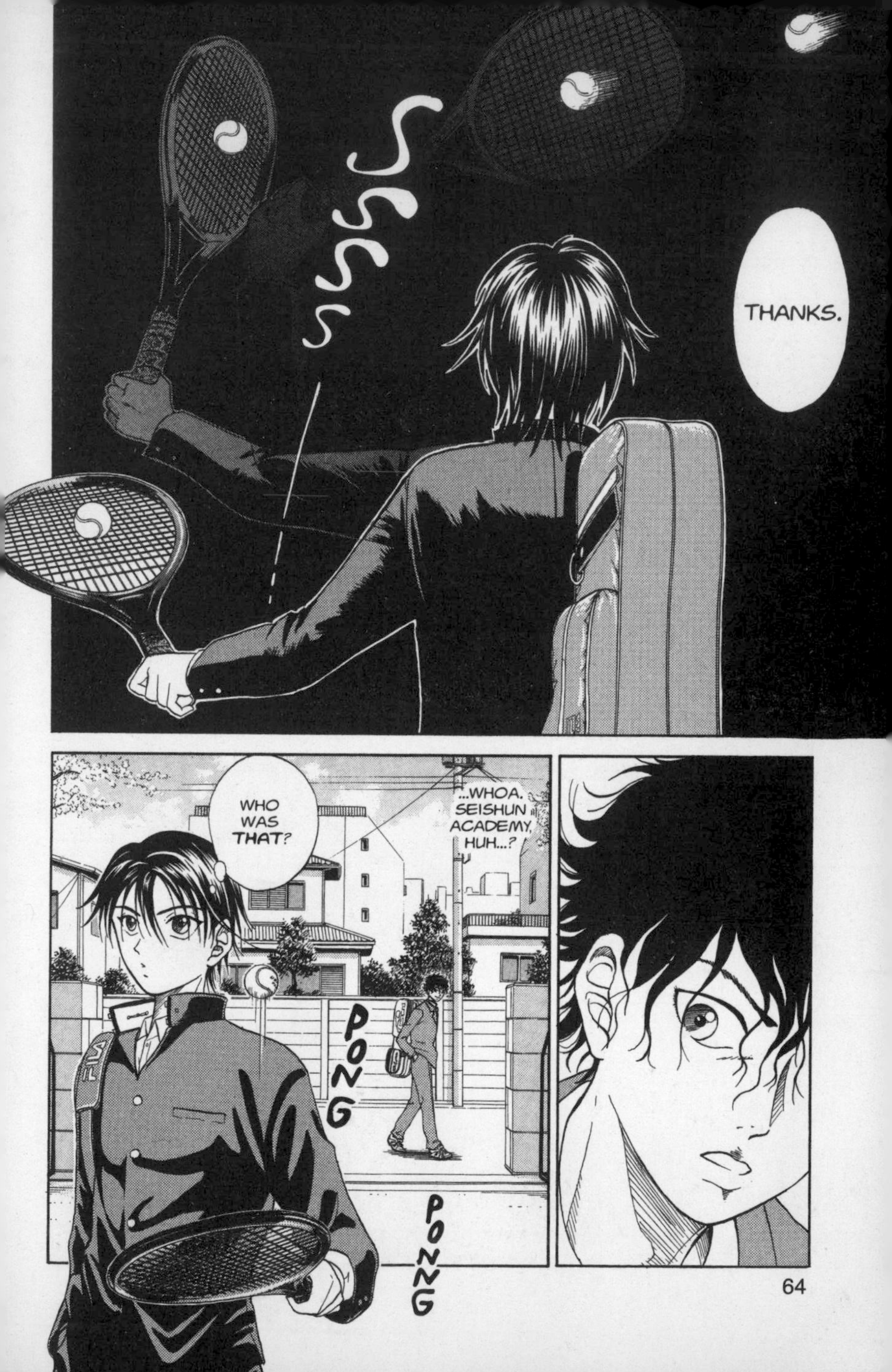
SSSS
THANKS.
...WHOA. SEISHUN ACADEMY, HUH...?
WHO WAS THAT?
PONG
PONNG

READ THIS WAY

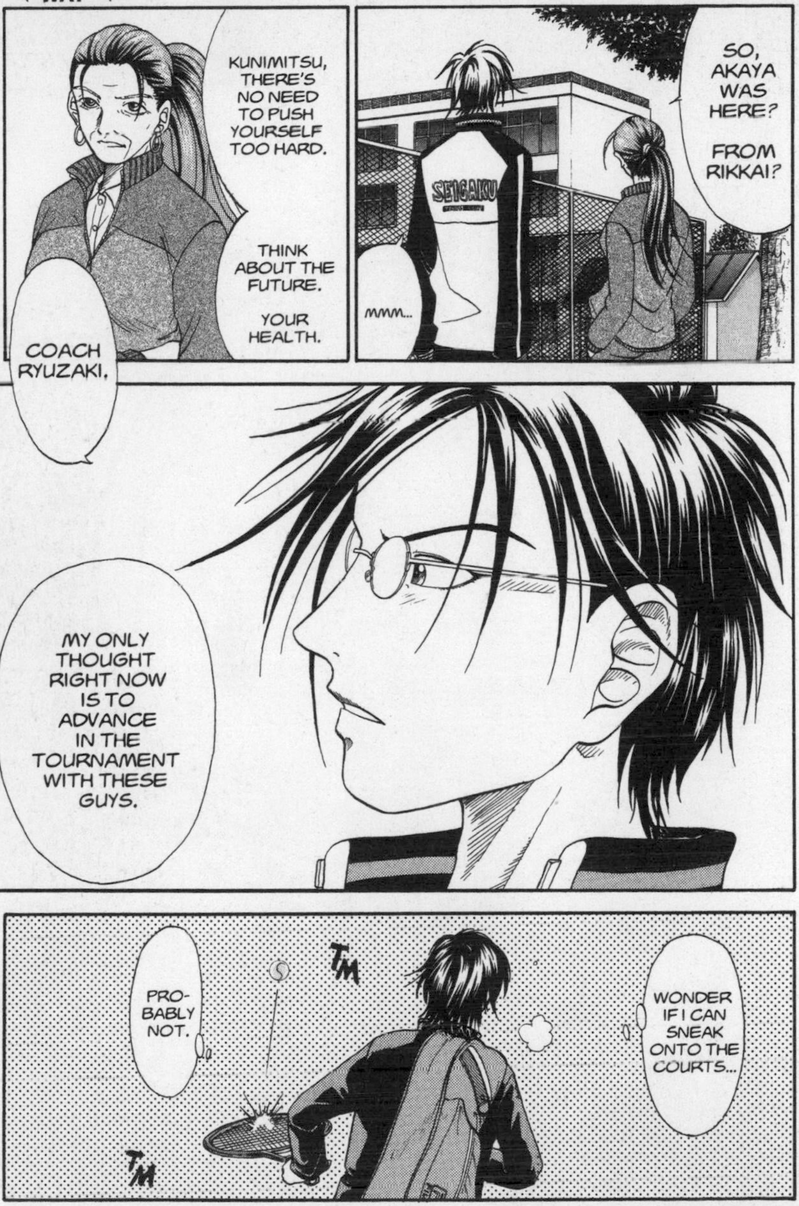
SO, AKAYA WAS HERE?
FROM RIKKAI?
MMM...
KUNIMITSU, THERE'S NO NEED TO PUSH YOURSELF TOO HARD.
THINK ABOUT THE FUTURE.
YOUR HEALTH.
COACH RYUZAKI,
MY ONLY THOUGHT RIGHT NOW IS TO ADVANCE IN THE TOURNAMENT WITH THESE GUYS.
WONDER IF I CAN SNEAK ONTO THE COURTS...
PRO-BABLY NOT.
TM
TM

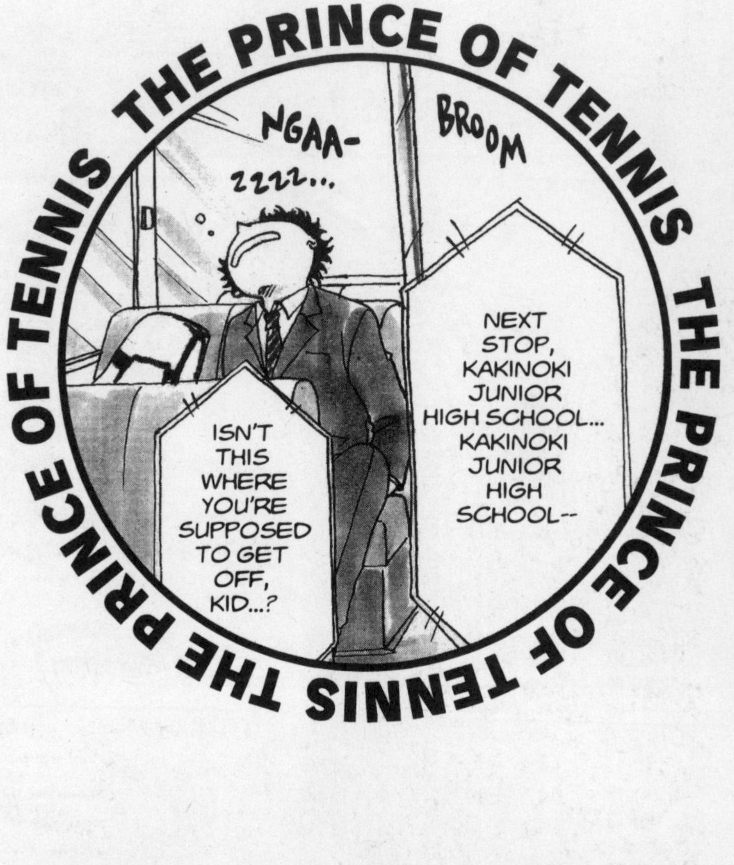
THE PRINCE OF TENNIS THE PRINCE OF TENNIS THE PRINCE OF TENNIS
BROOM
NGAA-
ZZZZ...
NEXT STOP, KAKINOKI JUNIOR HIGH SCHOOL... KAKINOKI JUNIOR HIGH SCHOOL--
ISN'T THIS WHERE YOU'RE SUPPOSED TO GET OFF, KID...?

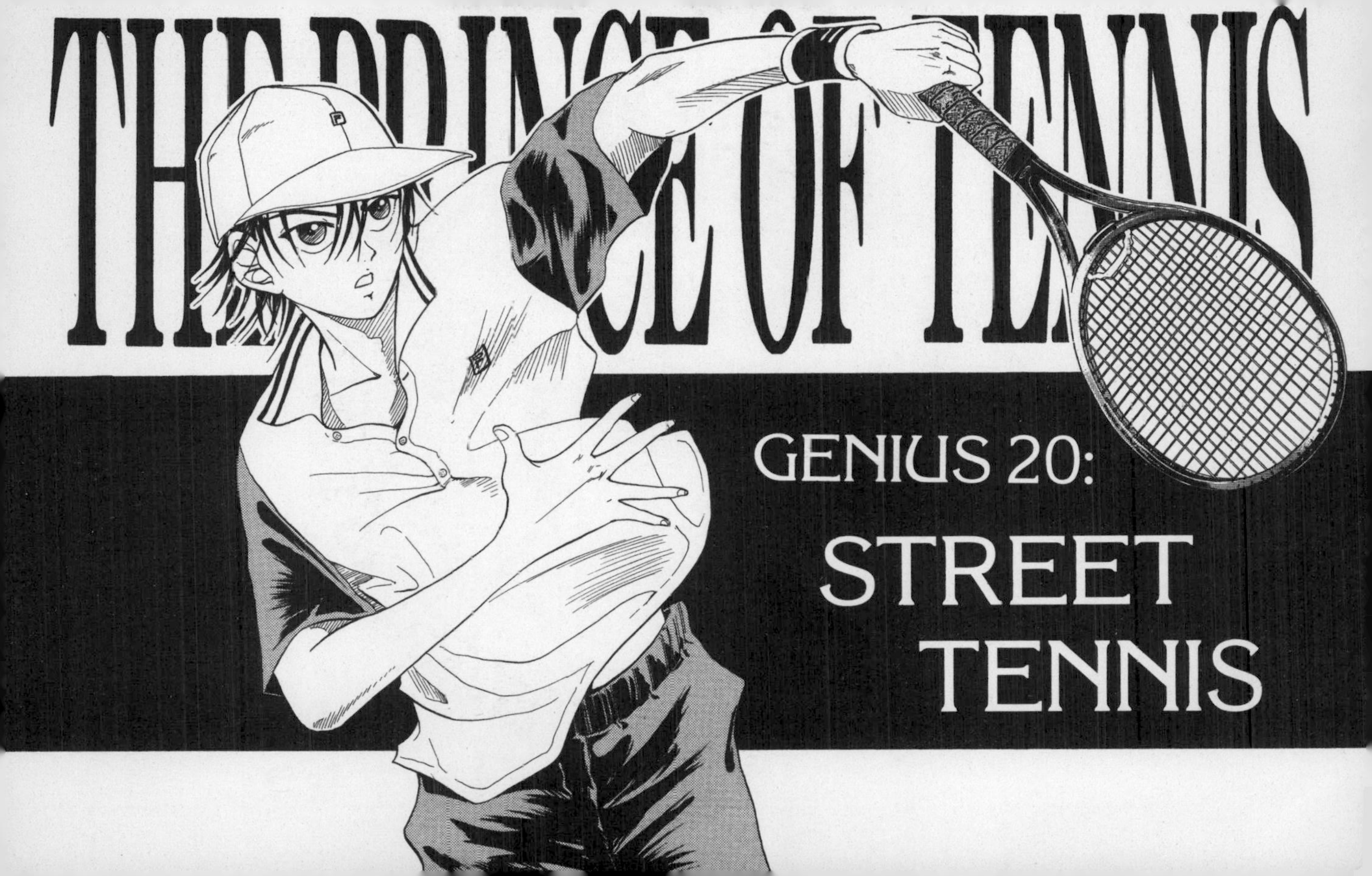
THE PRINCE OF TENNIS
GENIUS 20:
STREET
TENNIS

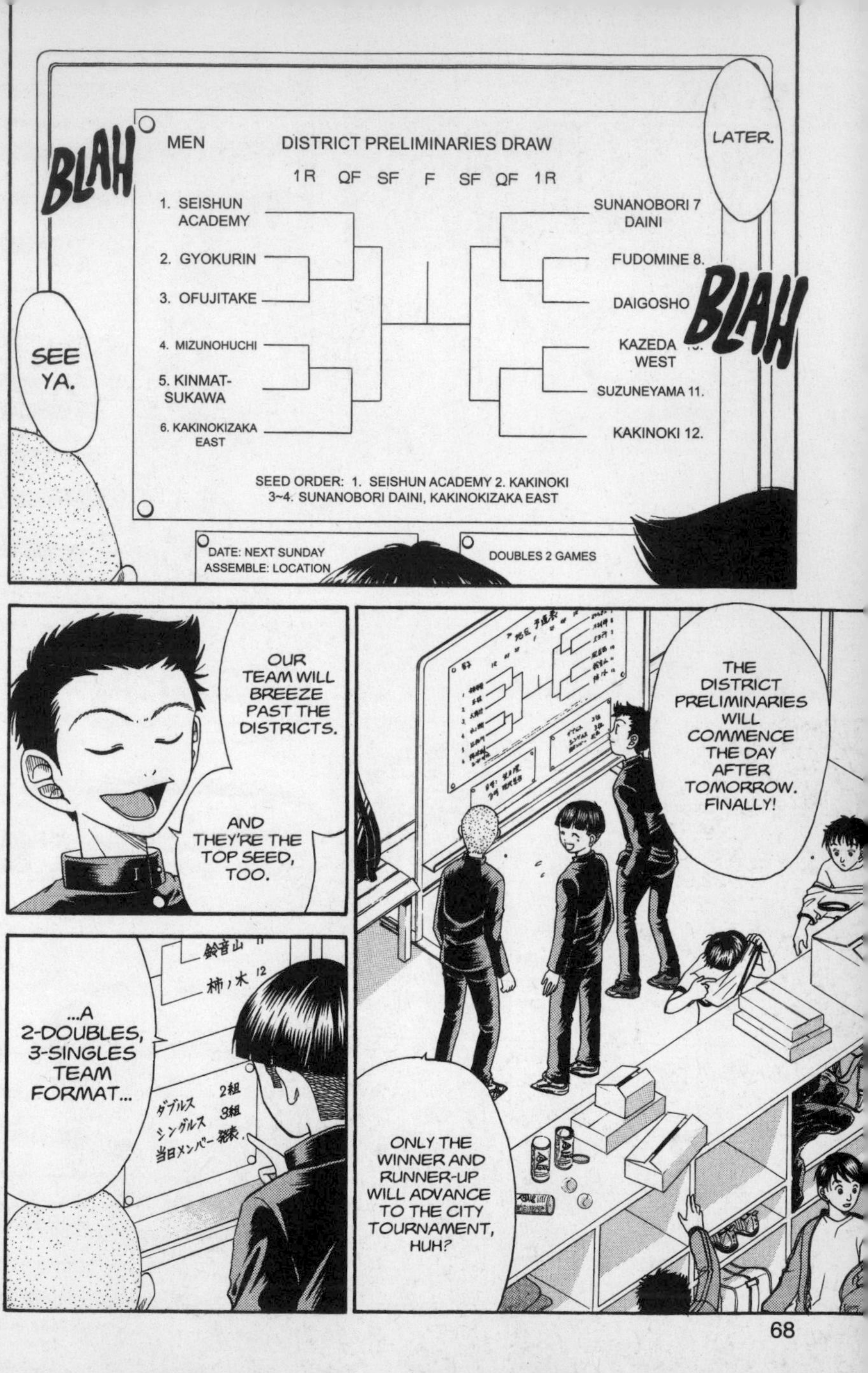
LATER.
BLAH
SEE YA.
BLAH
MEN
DISTRICT PRELIMINARIES DRAW
1R QF SF F SF QF 1R
1. SEISHUN ACADEMY
2. GYOKURIN
3. OFUJITAKE
4. MIZUNOHUCHI
5. KINMAT-SUKAWA
6. KAKINOKIZAKA EAST
SUNANOBORI 7 DAINI
FUDOMINE 8.
DAIGOSHO
KAZEDA WEST
SUZUNEYAMA 11.
KAKINOKI 12.
SEED ORDER: 1. SEISHUN ACADEMY 2. KAKINOKI
3~4. SUNANOBORI DAINI, KAKINOKIZAKA EAST
DATE: NEXT SUNDAY
ASSEMBLE: LOCATION
DOUBLES 2 GAMES
THE DISTRICT PRELIMINARIES WILL COMMENCE THE DAY AFTER TOMORROW. FINALLY!
ONLY THE WINNER AND RUNNER-UP WILL ADVANCE TO THE CITY TOURNAMENT, HUH?
OUR TEAM WILL BREEZE PAST THE DISTRICTS.
AND THEY'RE THE TOP SEED, TOO.
鈴音山 11
柿ノ木 12
...A 2-DOUBLES, 3-SINGLES TEAM FORMAT...
ダブルス 2組
シングルス 3組
当日メンバー発表

READ THIS WAY

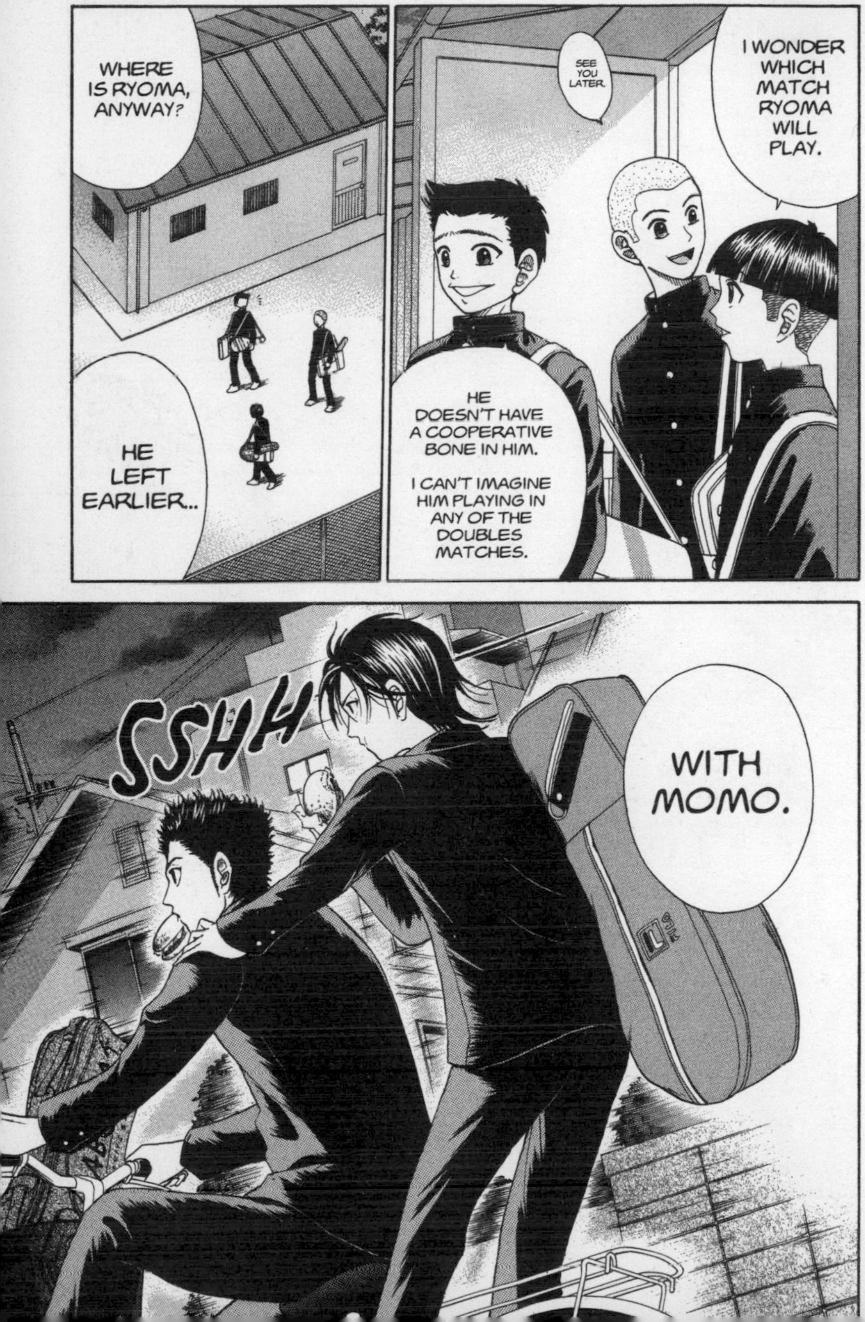
I WONDER WHICH MATCH RYOMA WILL PLAY.
SEE YOU LATER.
HE DOESN'T HAVE A COOPERATIVE BONE IN HIM.
I CAN'T IMAGINE HIM PLAYING IN ANY OF THE DOUBLES MATCHES.
WHERE IS RYOMA, ANYWAY?
HE LEFT EARLIER...
SSHH
WITH MOMO.

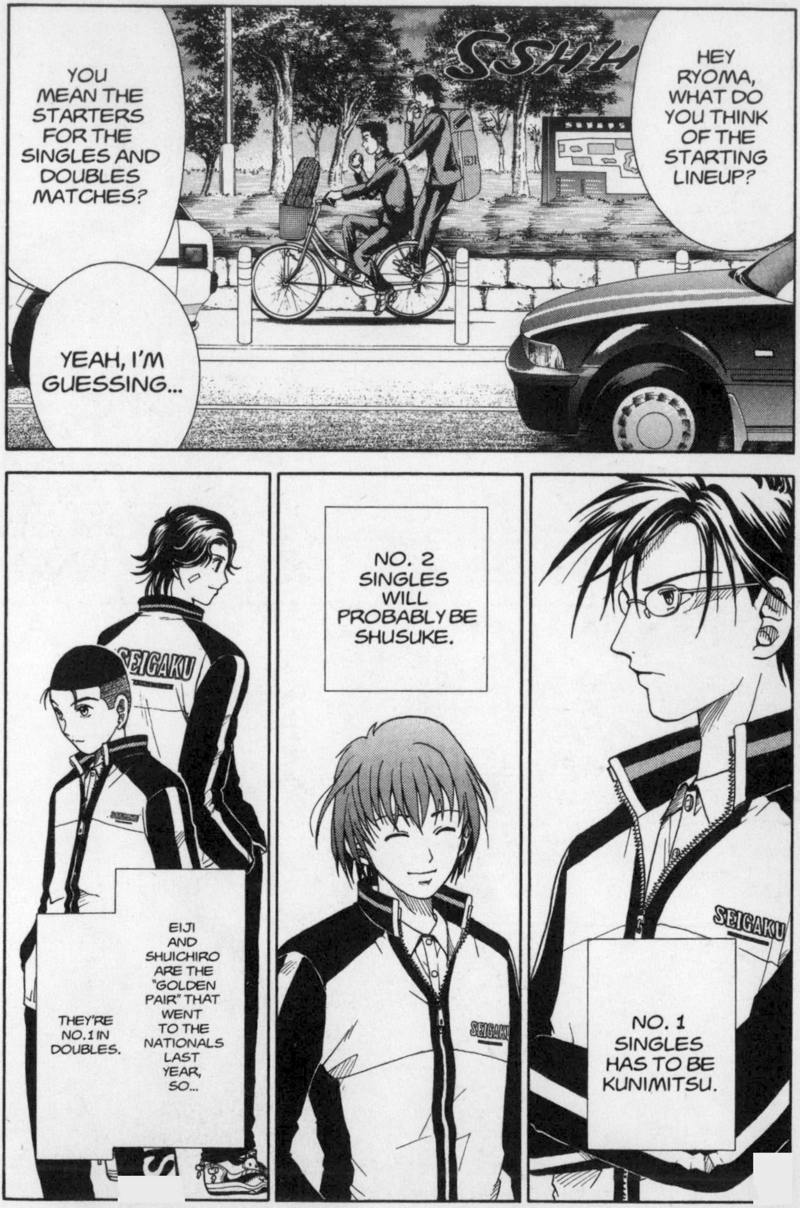
HEY RYOMA, WHAT DO YOU THINK OF THE STARTING LINEUP?
SSHH
YOU MEAN THE STARTERS FOR THE SINGLES AND DOUBLES MATCHES?
YEAH, I'M GUESSING...
SEIGAKU
NO. 1 SINGLES HAS TO BE KUNIMITSU.
NO. 2 SINGLES WILL PROBABLY BE SHUSUKE.
SEIGAKU
SEIGAKU
EIJI AND SHUICHIRO ARE THE "GOLDEN PAIR" THAT WENT TO THE NATIONALS LAST YEAR, SO...
THEY'RE NO.1 IN DOUBLES.

READ THIS WAY

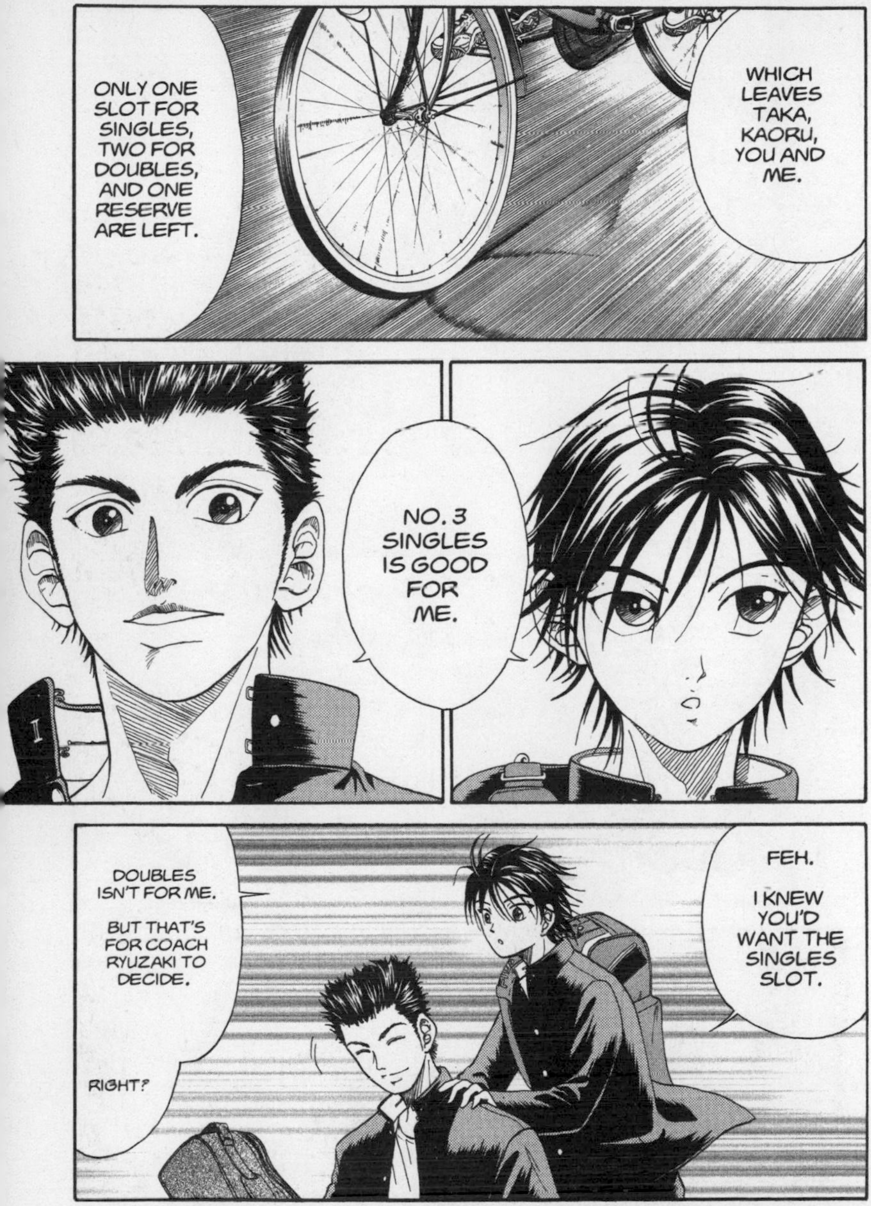
ONLY ONE SLOT FOR SINGLES, TWO FOR DOUBLES, AND ONE RESERVE ARE LEFT.
WHICH LEAVES TAKA, KAORU, YOU AND ME.
NO. 3 SINGLES IS GOOD FOR ME.
FEH.
I KNEW YOU'D WANT THE SINGLES SLOT.
DOUBLES ISN'T FOR ME.
BUT THAT'S FOR COACH RYUZAKI TO DECIDE.
RIGHT?

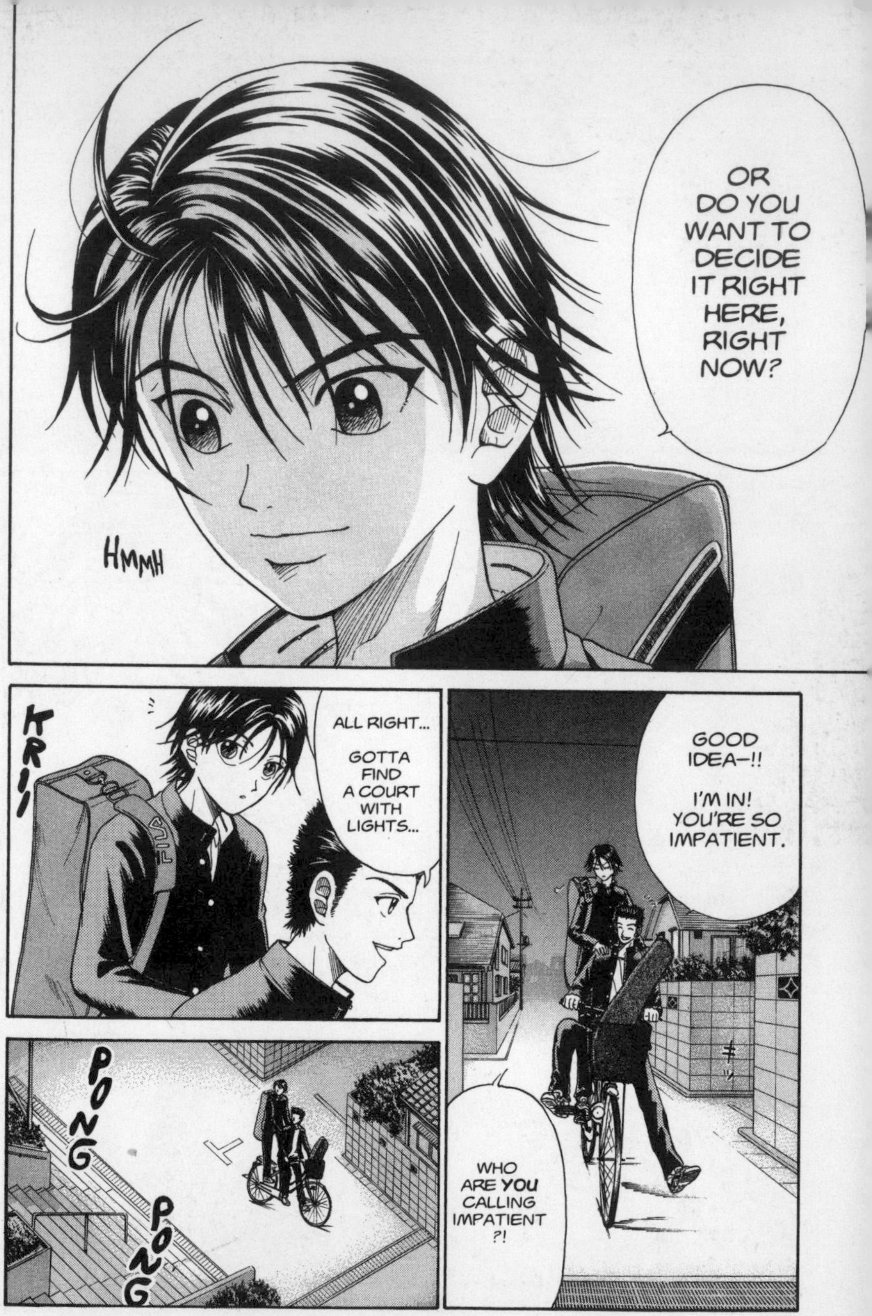
OR DO YOU WANT TO DECIDE IT RIGHT HERE, RIGHT NOW?
HMMH
GOOD IDEA–!!
I'M IN! YOU'RE SO IMPATIENT.
WHO ARE YOU CALLING IMPATIENT?!
KRII
ALL RIGHT...
GOTTA FIND A COURT WITH LIGHTS...
PONG
PONG

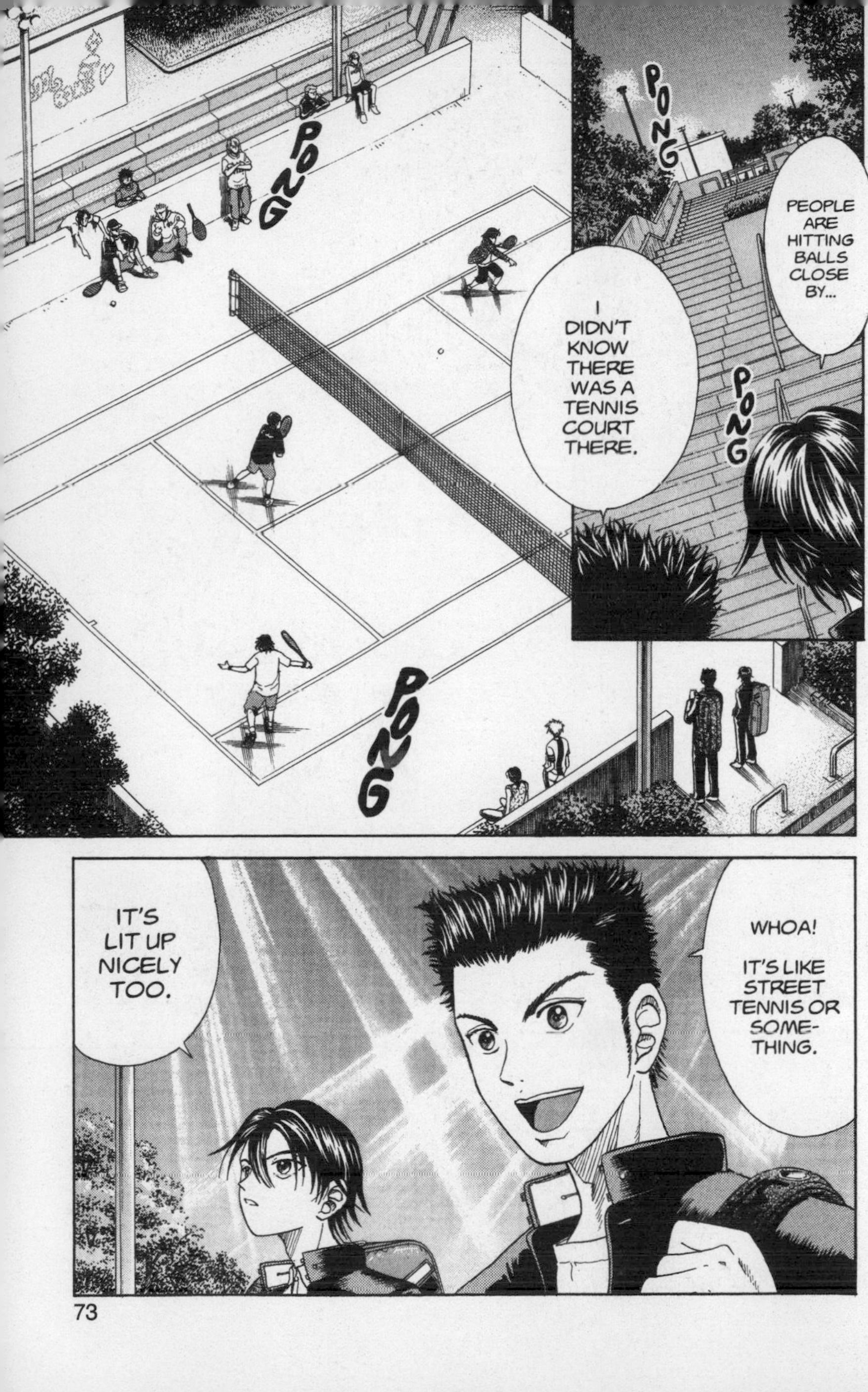

PONG
PONG
PEOPLE ARE HITTING BALLS CLOSE BY...
I DIDN'T KNOW THERE WAS A TENNIS COURT THERE.
PONG
PONG
WHOA!
IT'S LIKE STREET TENNIS OR SOME-THING.
IT'S LIT UP NICELY TOO.

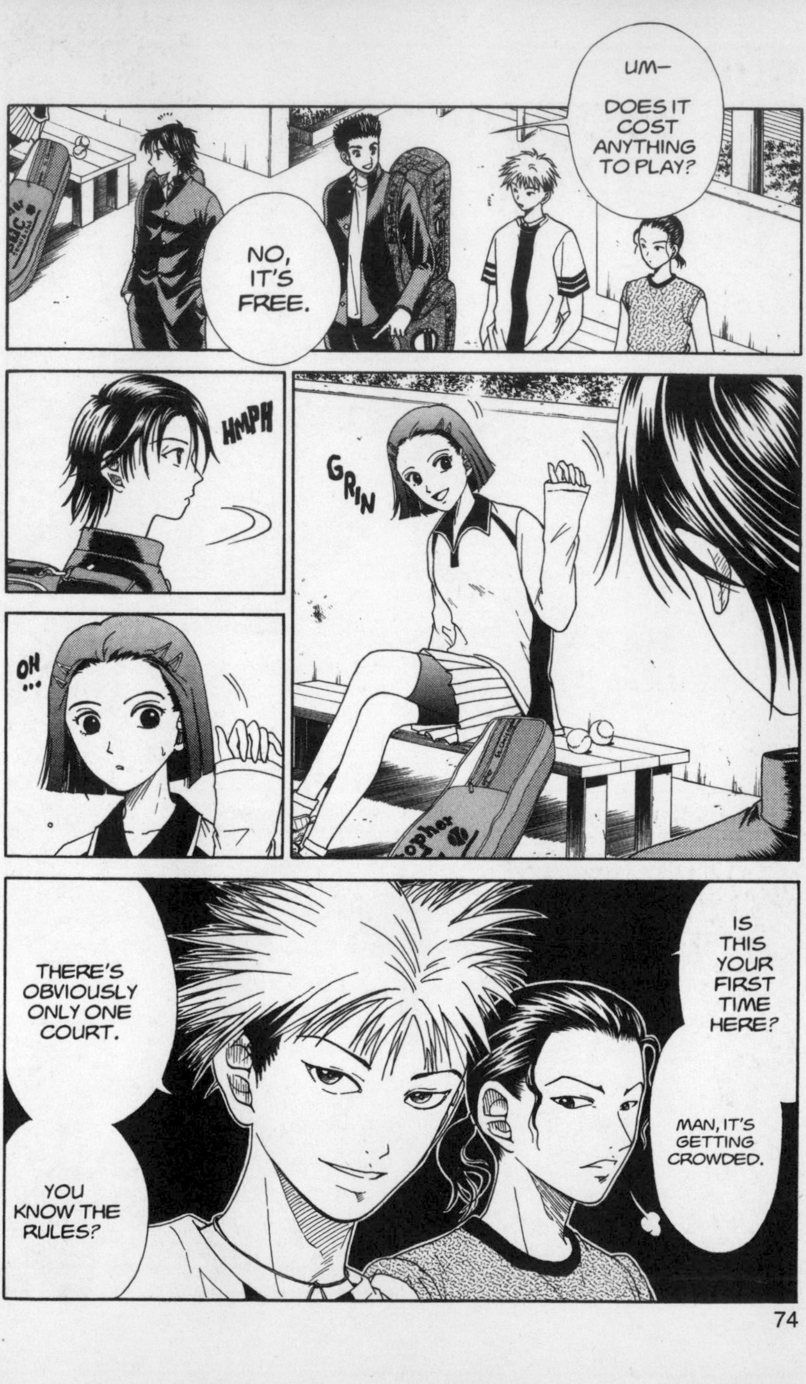
UM—
DOES IT COST ANYTHING TO PLAY?
NO, IT'S FREE.
GRIN
HMPH
OH...
IS THIS YOUR FIRST TIME HERE?
MAN, IT'S GETTING CROWDED.
THERE'S OBVIOUSLY ONLY ONE COURT.
YOU KNOW THE RULES?

READ THIS WAY

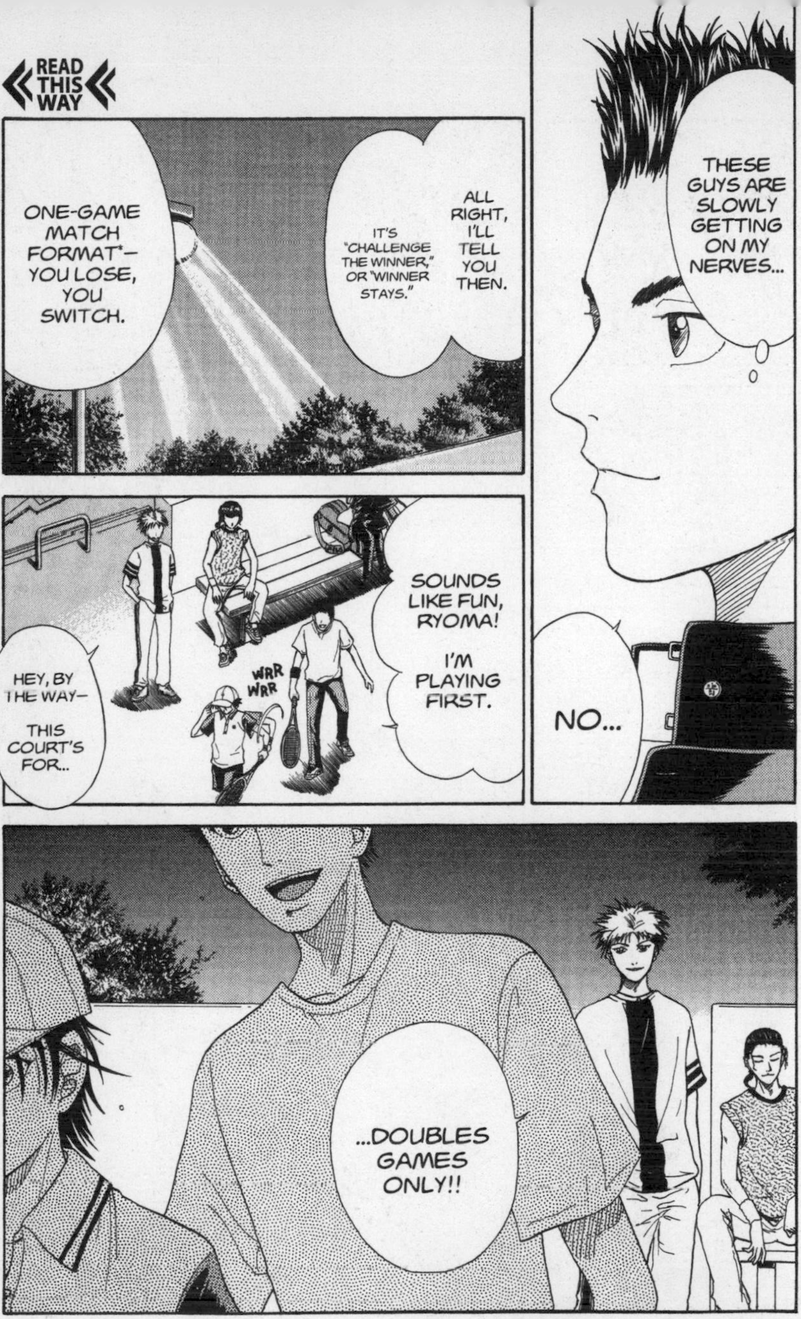
THESE GUYS ARE SLOWLY GETTING ON MY NERVES...
NO...
ALL RIGHT, I'LL TELL YOU THEN.
IT'S "CHALLENGE THE WINNER," OR "WINNER STAYS."
ONE-GAME MATCH FORMAT*—YOU LOSE, YOU SWITCH.
SOUNDS LIKE FUN, RYOMA!
I'M PLAYING FIRST.
WRR WRR
HEY, BY THE WAY—
THIS COURT'S FOR..
...DOUBLES GAMES ONLY!!

*ONE GAME = FOUR POINTS

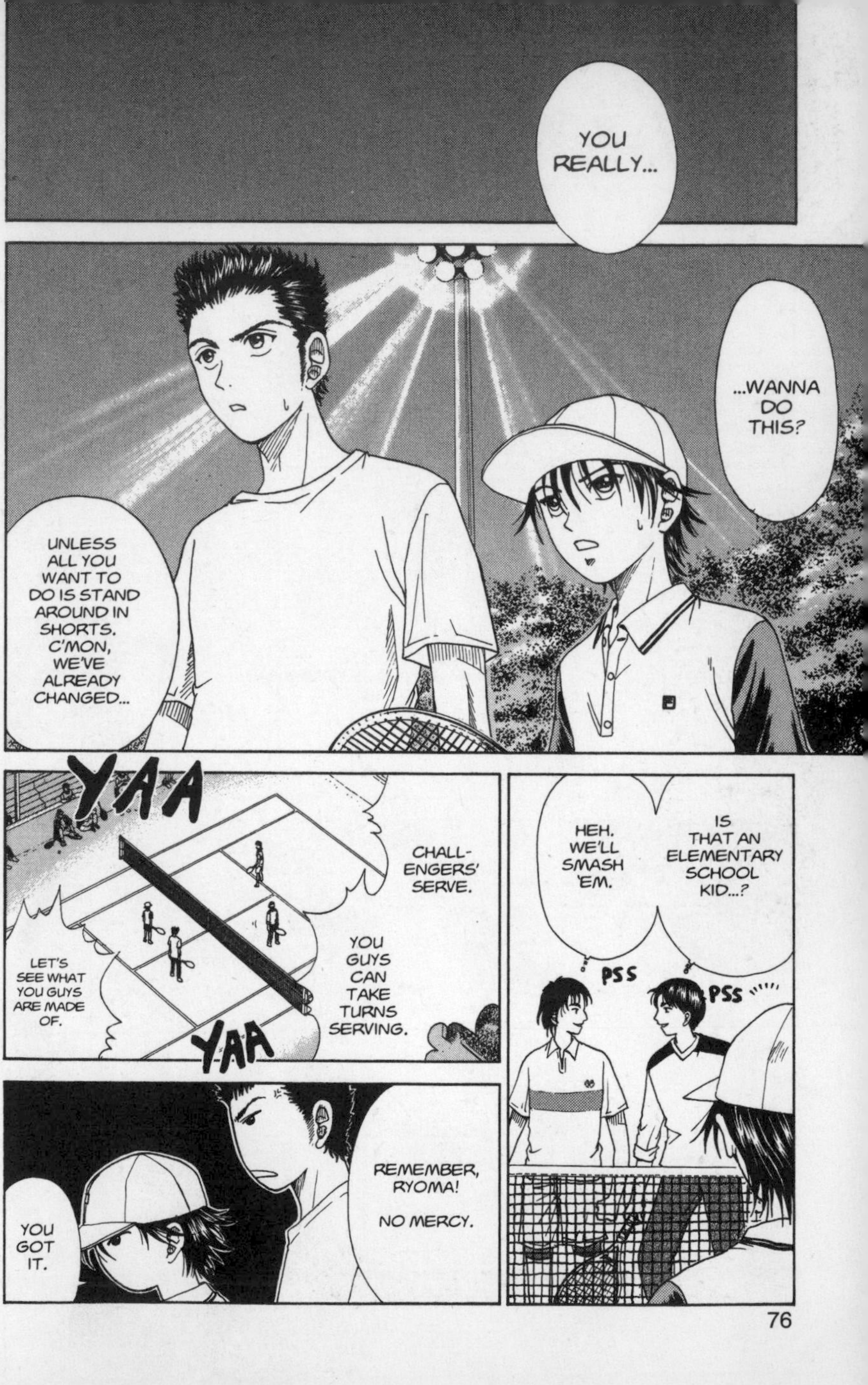
YOU REALLY...
...WANNA DO THIS?
UNLESS ALL YOU WANT TO DO IS STAND AROUND IN SHORTS. C'MON, WE'VE ALREADY CHANGED...
IS THAT AN ELEMENTARY SCHOOL KID...?
HEH. WE'LL SMASH 'EM.
PSS
PSS
YAA
CHALL-ENGERS' SERVE.
YOU GUYS CAN TAKE TURNS SERVING.
LET'S SEE WHAT YOU GUYS ARE MADE OF.
YAA
REMEMBER, RYOMA!
NO MERCY.
YOU GOT IT.

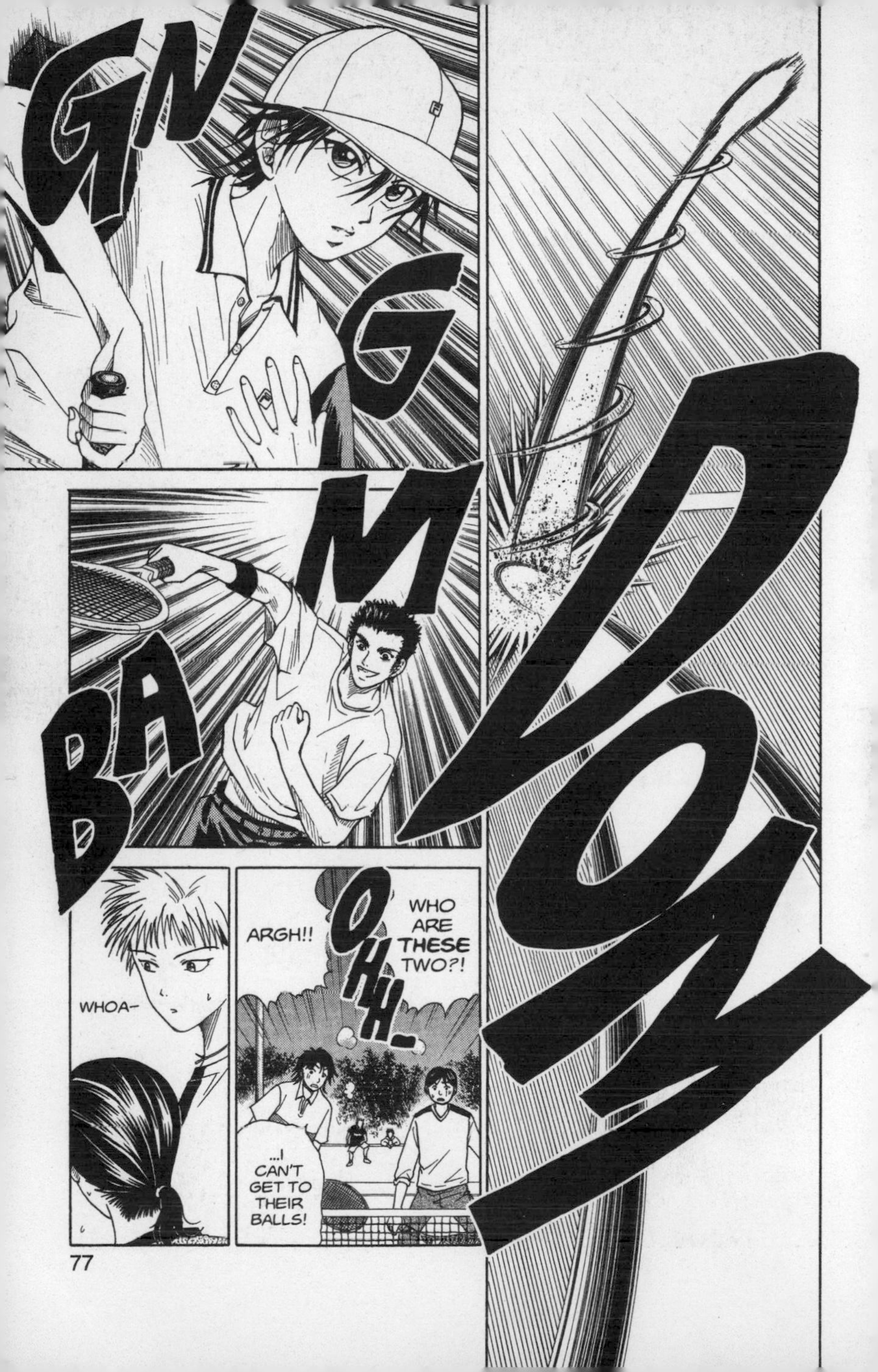
BAM
WHO ARE THESE TWO?!
ARGH!!
OHHH–
...I CAN'T GET TO THEIR BALLS!
WHOA–

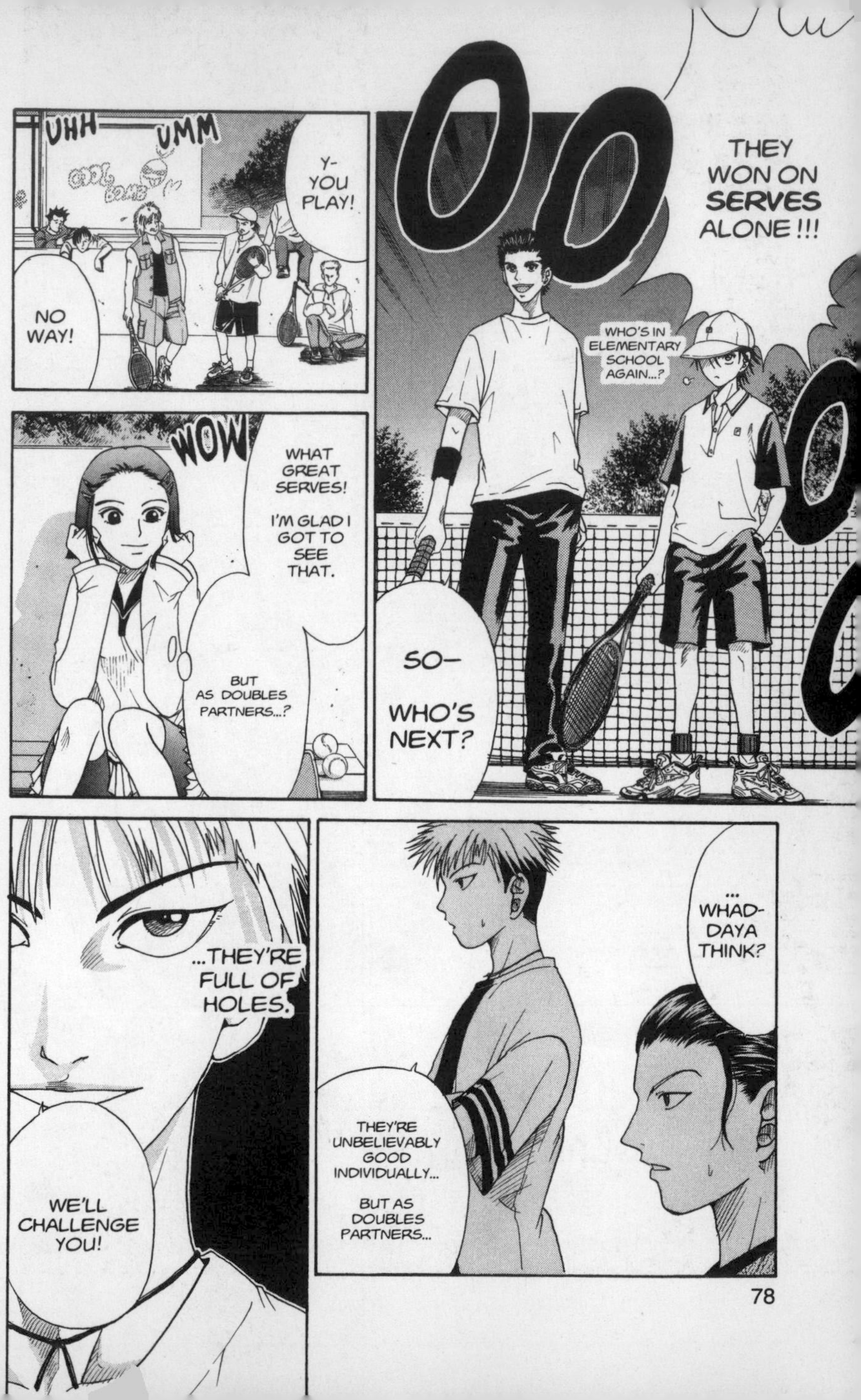

OOO
THEY WON ON SERVES ALONE!!!
WHO'S IN ELEMENTARY SCHOOL AGAIN...?
SO—
WHO'S NEXT?
UHH
UMM
Y- YOU PLAY!
NO WAY!
WOW
WHAT GREAT SERVES!
I'M GLAD I GOT TO SEE THAT.
BUT AS DOUBLES PARTNERS...?
... WHAD- DAYA THINK?
THEY'RE UNBELIEVABLY GOOD INDIVIDUALLY...
BUT AS DOUBLES PARTNERS...
...THEY'RE FULL OF HOLES.
WE'LL CHALLENGE YOU!

READ THIS WAY

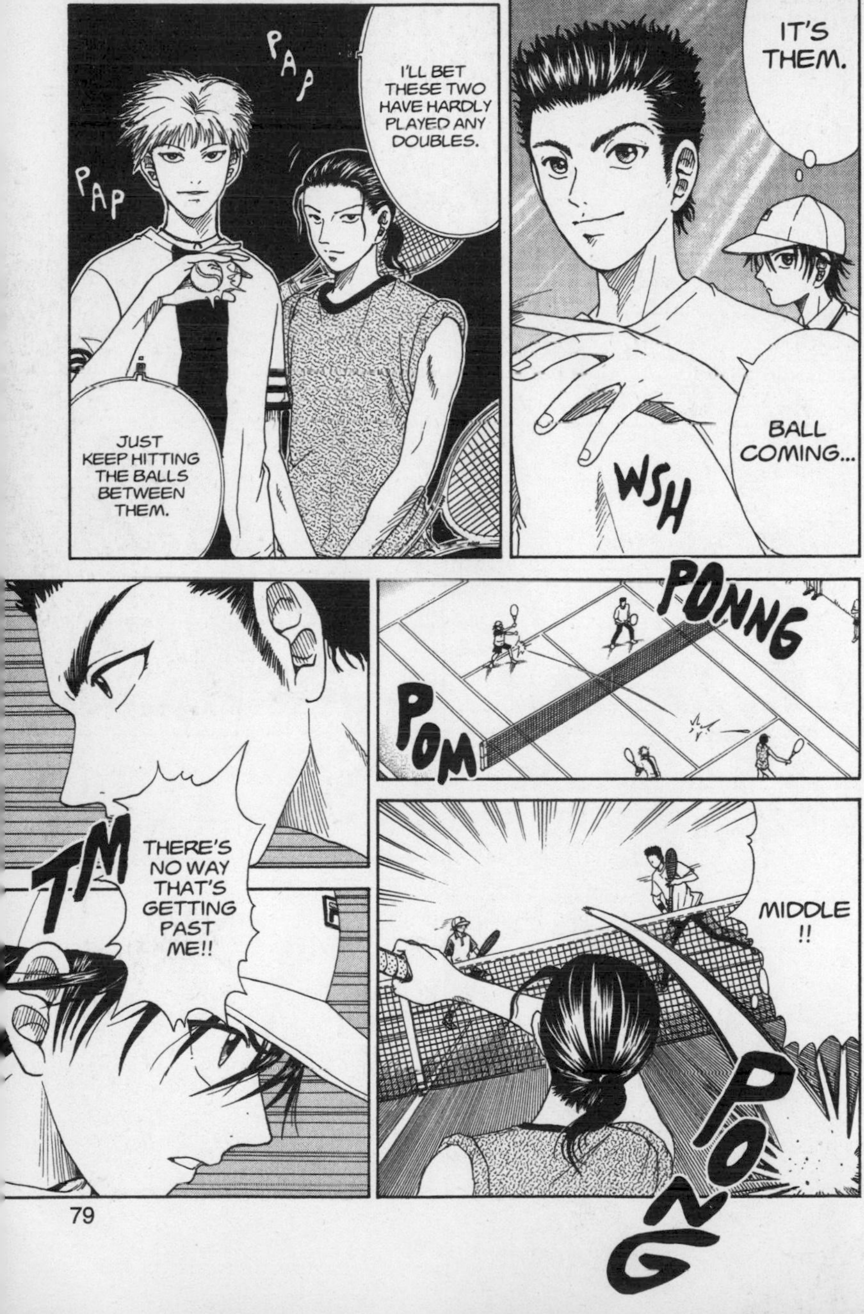
IT'S THEM.
BALL COMING...
WSH
I'LL BET THESE TWO HAVE HARDLY PLAYED ANY DOUBLES.
PAP PAP
PAP
JUST KEEP HITTING THE BALLS BETWEEN THEM.
PONNG
POM
MIDDLE !!
PONG
TM
THERE'S NO WAY THAT'S GETTING PAST ME!!

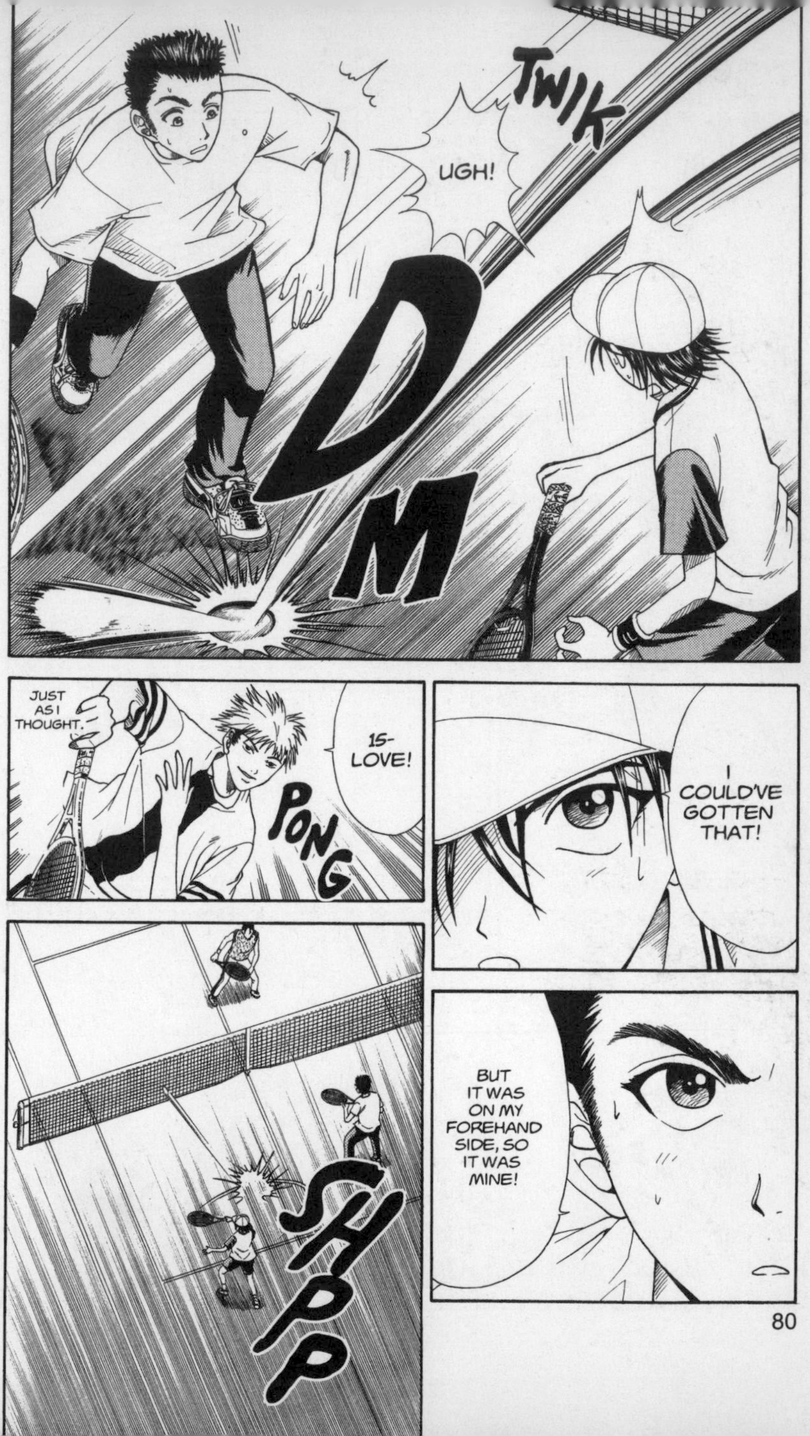
TWIK
UGH!
DM
I COULD'VE GOTTEN THAT!
15-LOVE!
PONG
JUST AS I THOUGHT.
BUT IT WAS ON MY FOREHAND SIDE, SO IT WAS MINE!
SHPP

READ THIS WAY

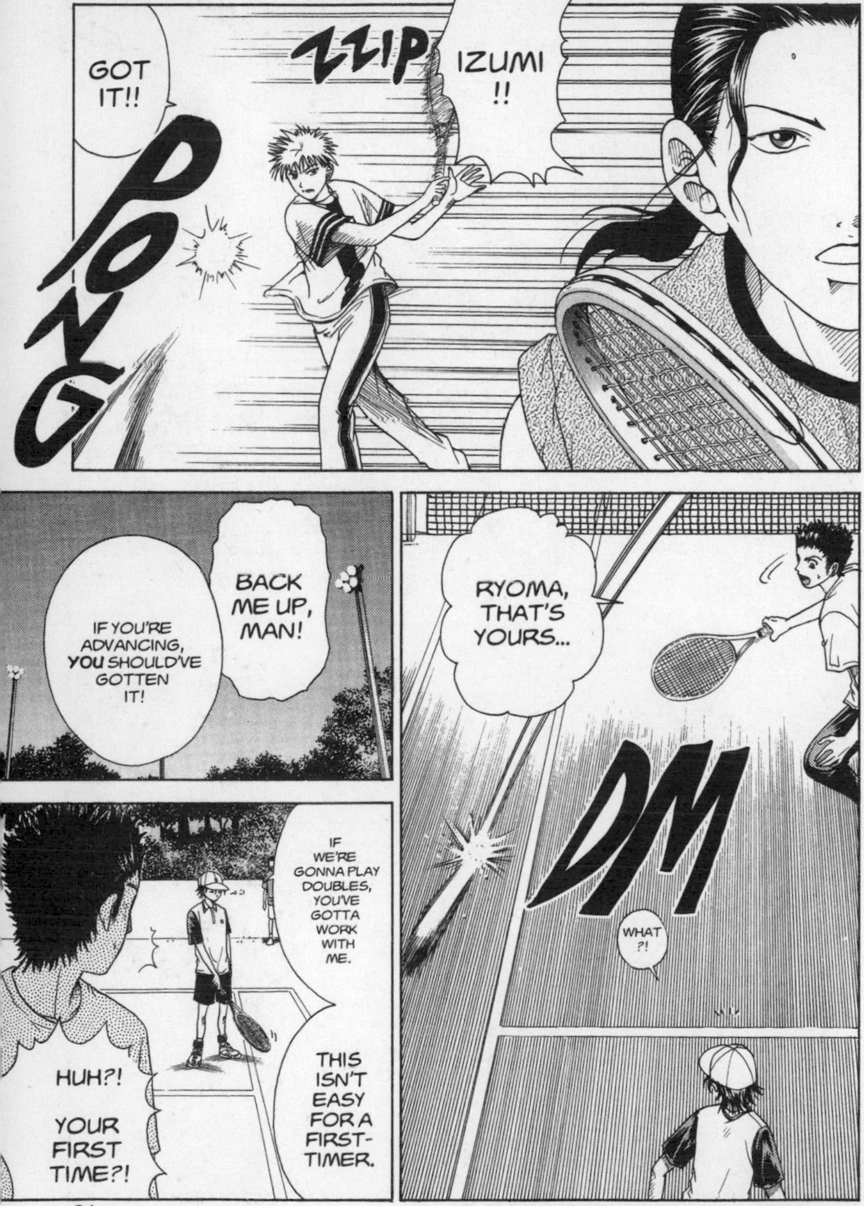
IZUMI !!
ZZIP
GOT IT!!
PONG
RYOMA, THAT'S YOURS...
DM
WHAT ?!
BACK ME UP, MAN!
IF YOU'RE ADVANCING, YOU SHOULD'VE GOTTEN IT!
IF WE'RE GONNA PLAY DOUBLES, YOU'VE GOTTA WORK WITH ME.
THIS ISN'T EASY FOR A FIRST-TIMER.
HUH?!
YOUR FIRST TIME?!

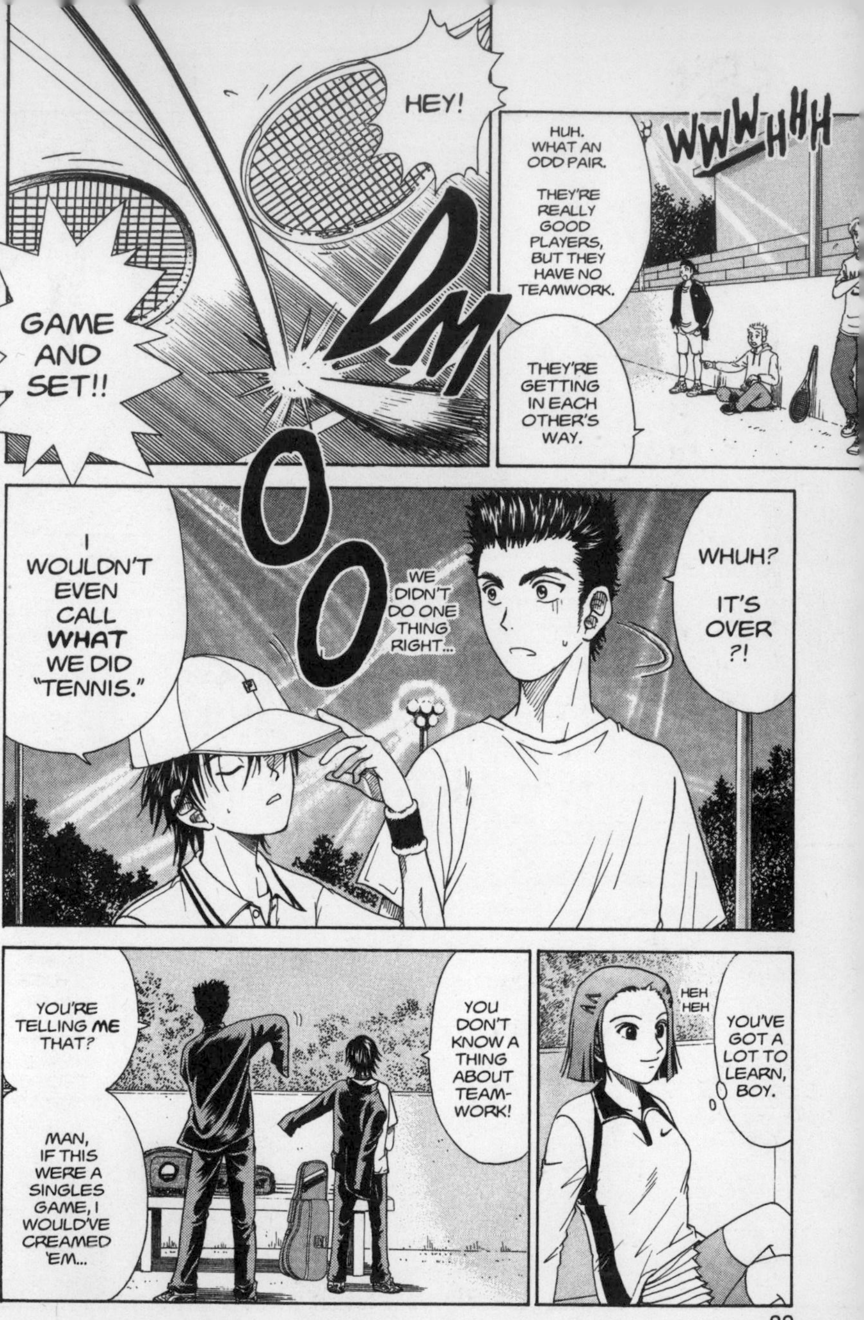

HUH. WHAT AN ODD PAIR.
THEY'RE REALLY GOOD PLAYERS, BUT THEY HAVE NO TEAMWORK.
THEY'RE GETTING IN EACH OTHER'S WAY.
WWWHHH
HEY!
DMOO
GAME AND SET!!
WHUH?
IT'S OVER ?!
WE DIDN'T DO ONE THING RIGHT...
I WOULDN'T EVEN CALL **WHAT** WE DID "TENNIS."
HEH HEH
YOU'VE GOT A LOT TO LEARN, BOY.
YOU DON'T KNOW A THING ABOUT TEAM-WORK!
YOU'RE TELLING **ME** THAT?
MAN, IF THIS WERE A SINGLES GAME, I WOULD'VE CREAMED 'EM...

READ THIS WAY

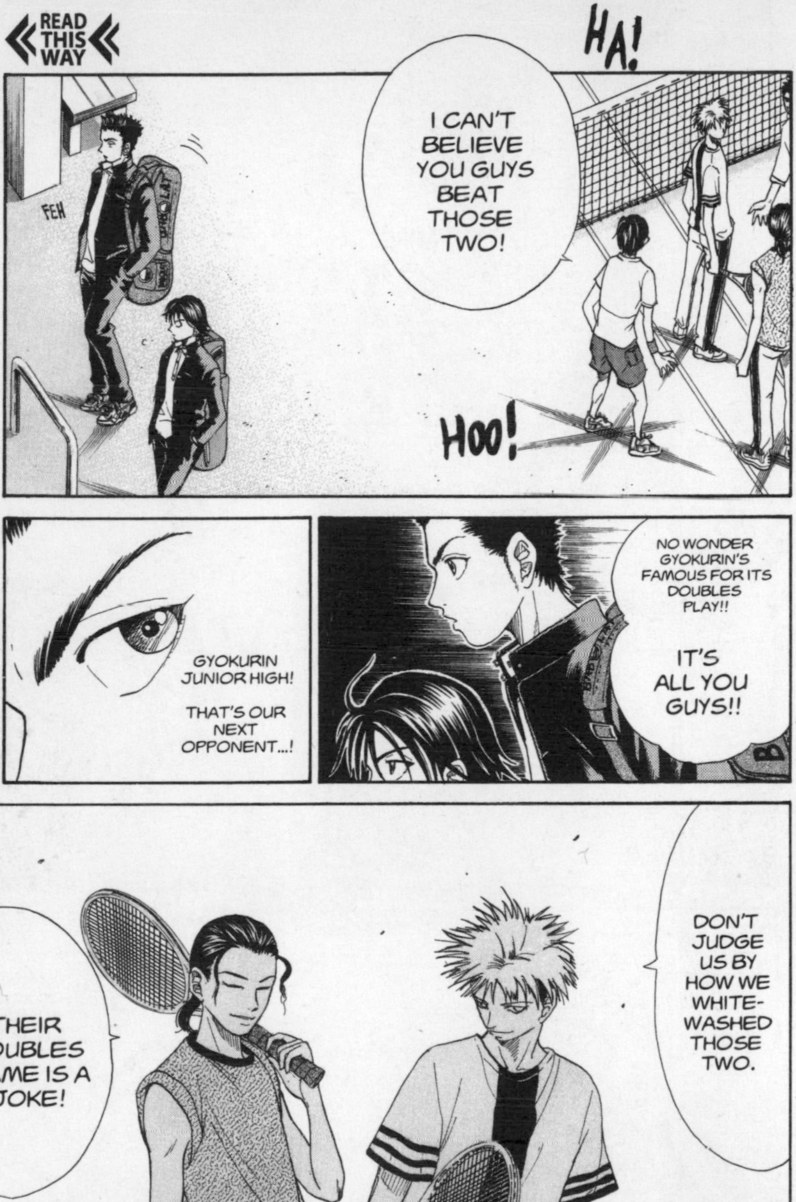
HA!
I CAN'T BELIEVE YOU GUYS BEAT THOSE TWO!
HOO!
FEH
NO WONDER GYOKURIN'S FAMOUS FOR ITS DOUBLES PLAY!!
IT'S ALL YOU GUYS!!
GYOKURIN JUNIOR HIGH!
THAT'S OUR NEXT OPPONENT...!
DON'T JUDGE US BY HOW WE WHITE-WASHED THOSE TWO.
THEIR DOUBLES GAME IS A JOKE!

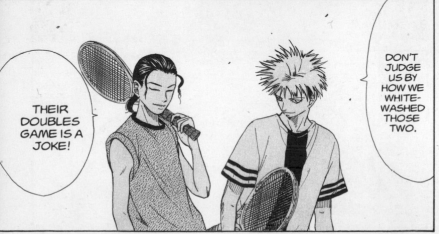

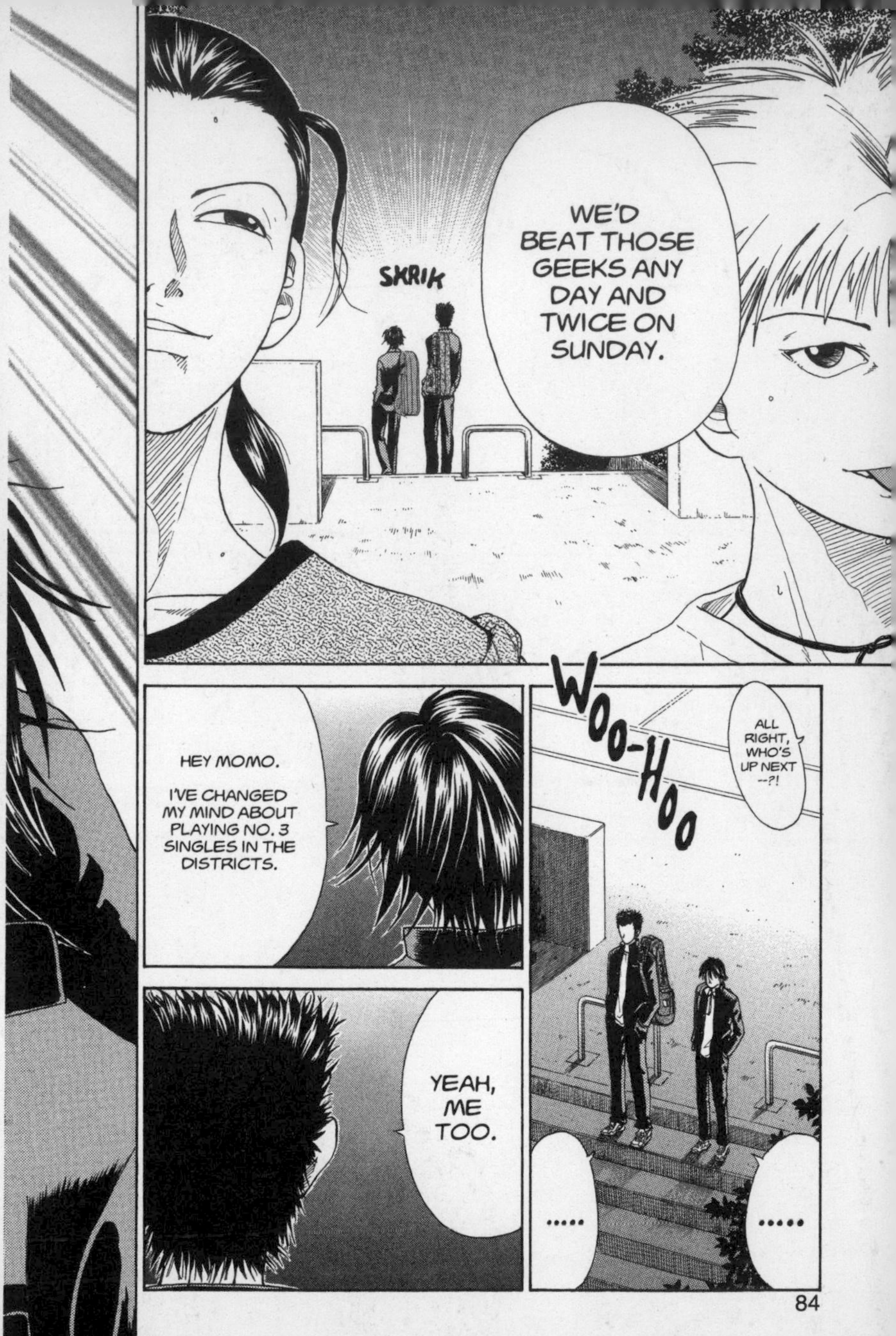
WE'D BEAT THOSE GEEKS ANY DAY AND TWICE ON SUNDAY.
SKRIK
WOO-HOO
ALL RIGHT, WHO'S UP NEXT --?!
......
......
HEY MOMO.
I'VE CHANGED MY MIND ABOUT PLAYING NO. 3 SINGLES IN THE DISTRICTS.
YEAH, ME TOO.

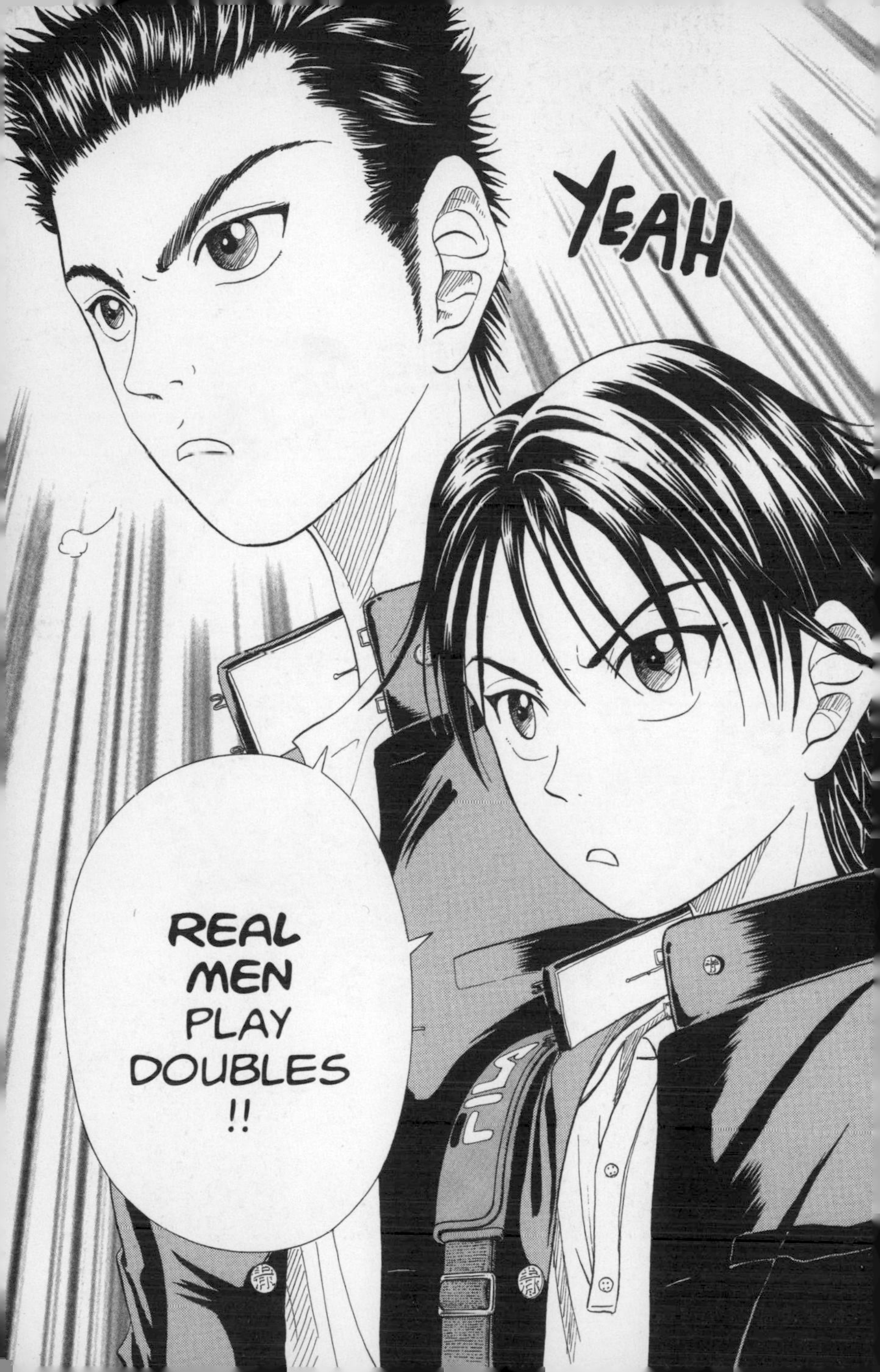
YEAH
REAL MEN PLAY DOUBLES !!

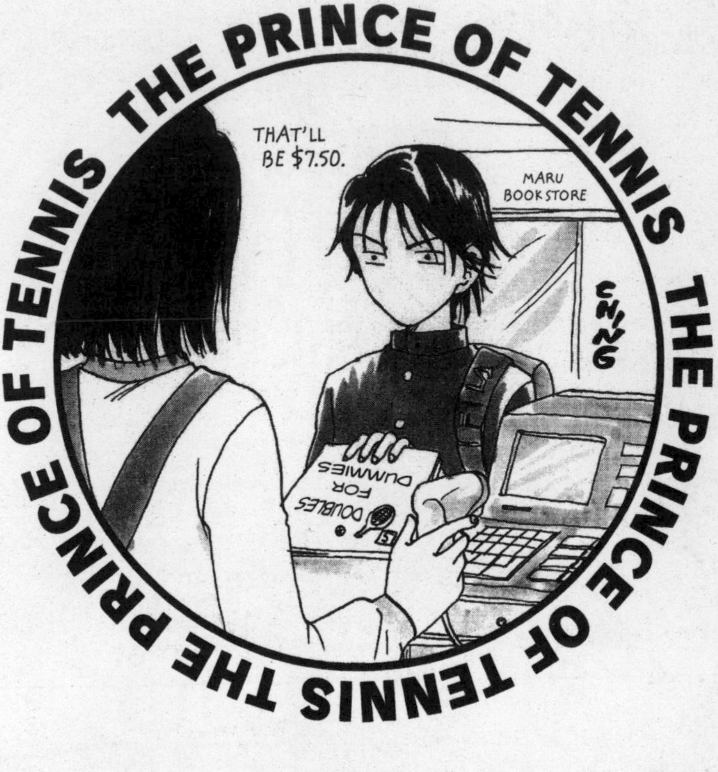
THE PRINCE OF TENNIS THE PRINCE OF TENNIS THE PRINCE OF TENNIS
THAT'LL BE $7.50.
MARU BOOKSTORE
CHING
DOUBLES FOR DUMMIES

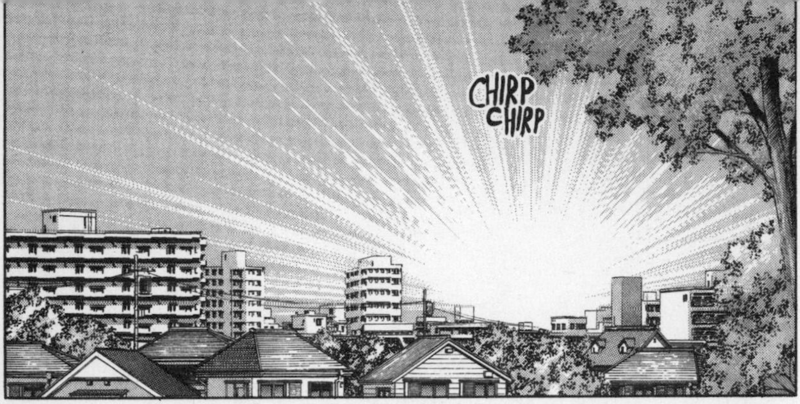
CHIRP CHIRP

GENIUS 21: THE DISTRICT PRELIMINARIES BEGIN

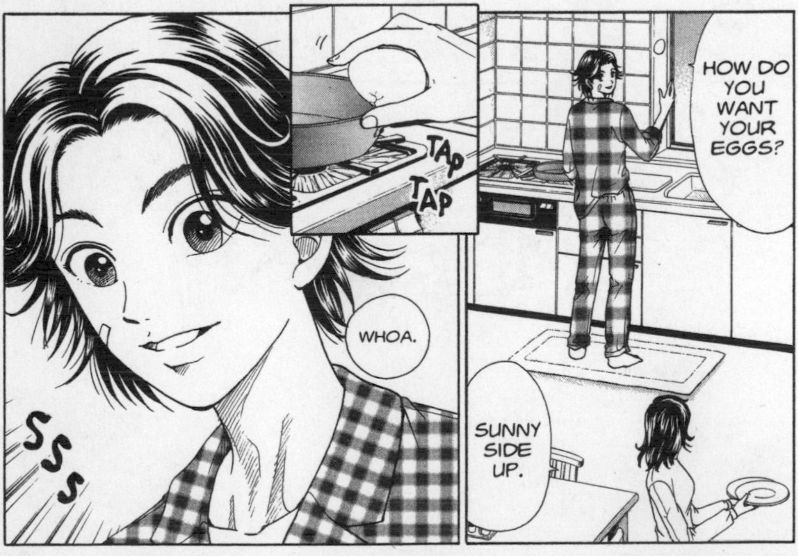
HOW DO YOU WANT YOUR EGGS?
SUNNY SIDE UP.
TAP TAP
WHOA.
SSS

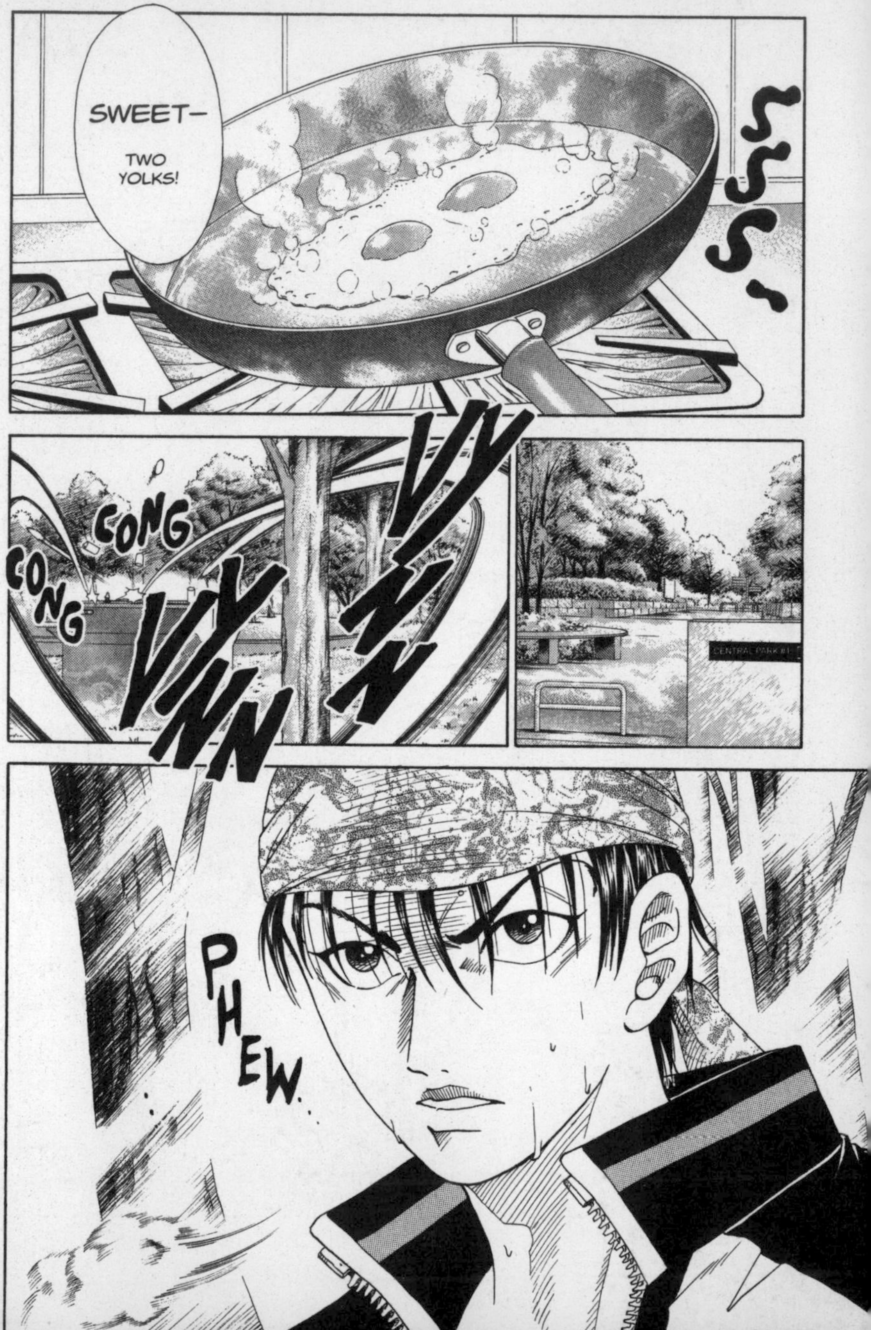
SWEET-
TWO YOLKS!
SSSS
VYYNN
VYYNN
CONG
CONG
PHEW.

READ THIS WAY

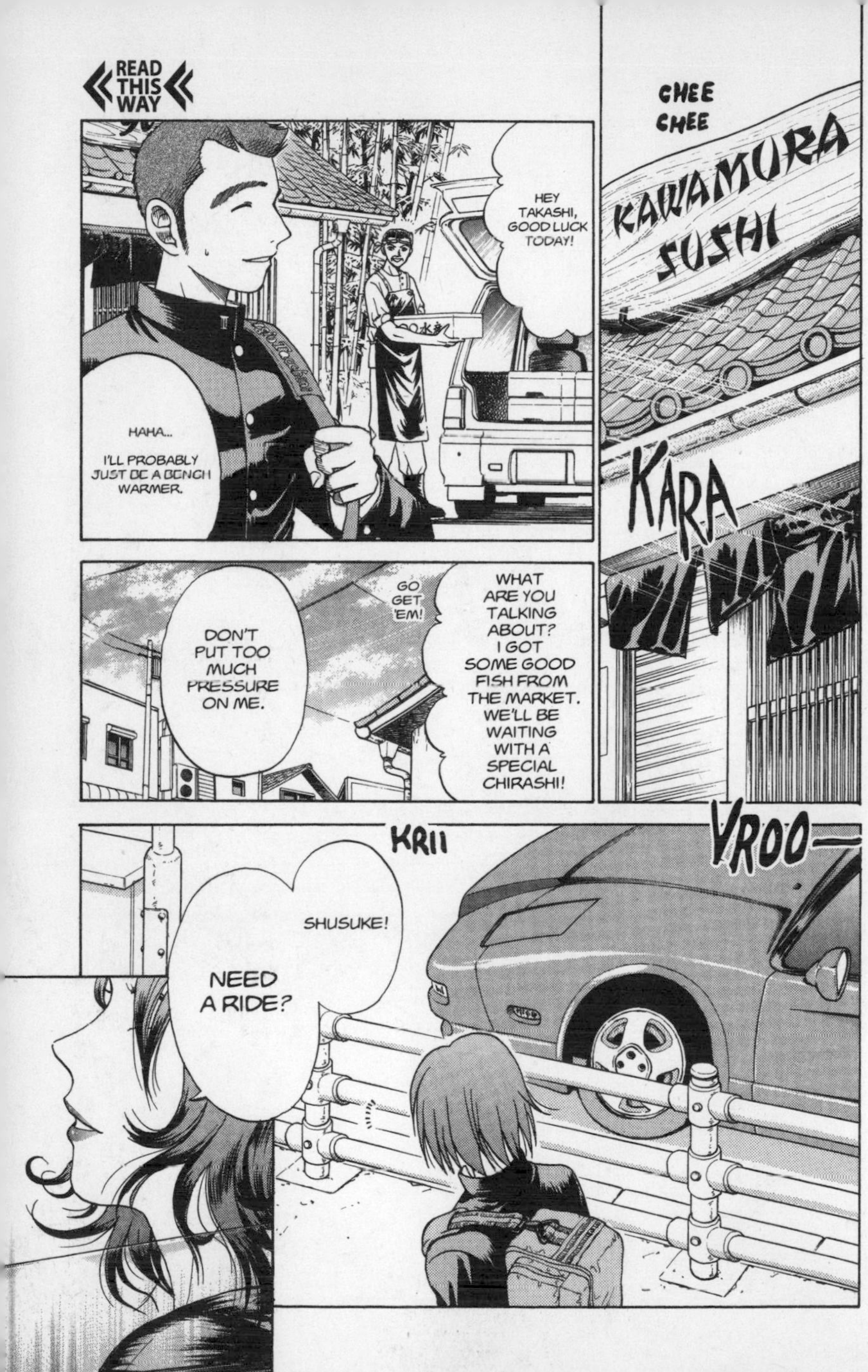
CHEE CHEE
KAWAMURA SUSHI
KARA
HEY TAKASHI, GOOD LUCK TODAY!
HAHA... I'LL PROBABLY JUST BE A BENCH WARMER.
WHAT ARE YOU TALKING ABOUT? I GOT SOME GOOD FISH FROM THE MARKET. WE'LL BE WAITING WITH A SPECIAL CHIRASHI!
GO GET 'EM!
DON'T PUT TOO MUCH PRESSURE ON ME.
VROO—
KRII
SHUSUKE!
NEED A RIDE?

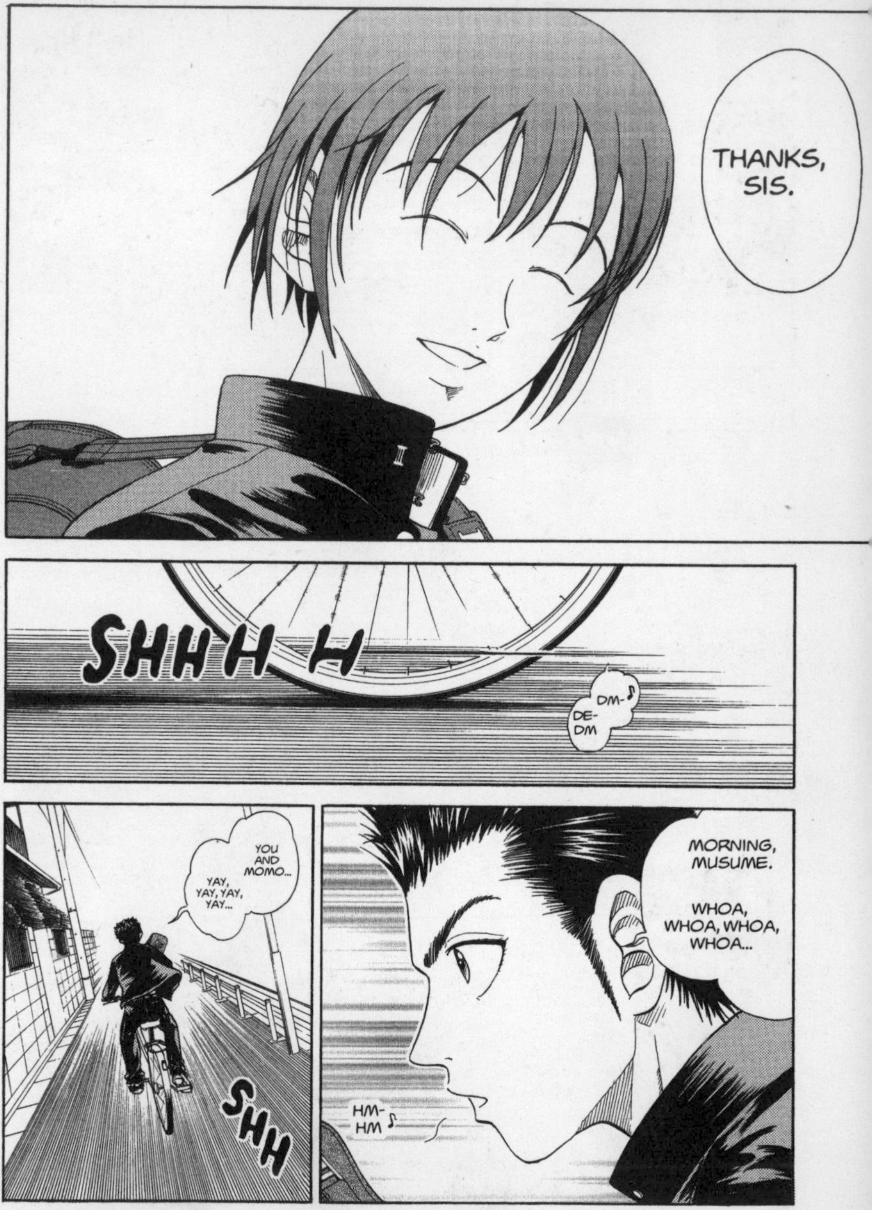
THANKS, SIS.
SHHHH H
DM-♪ DE-DM
MORNING, MUSUME.
WHOA, WHOA, WHOA, WHOA...
HM-HM ♪
YOU AND MOMO...
YAY, YAY, YAY, YAY...
SHH

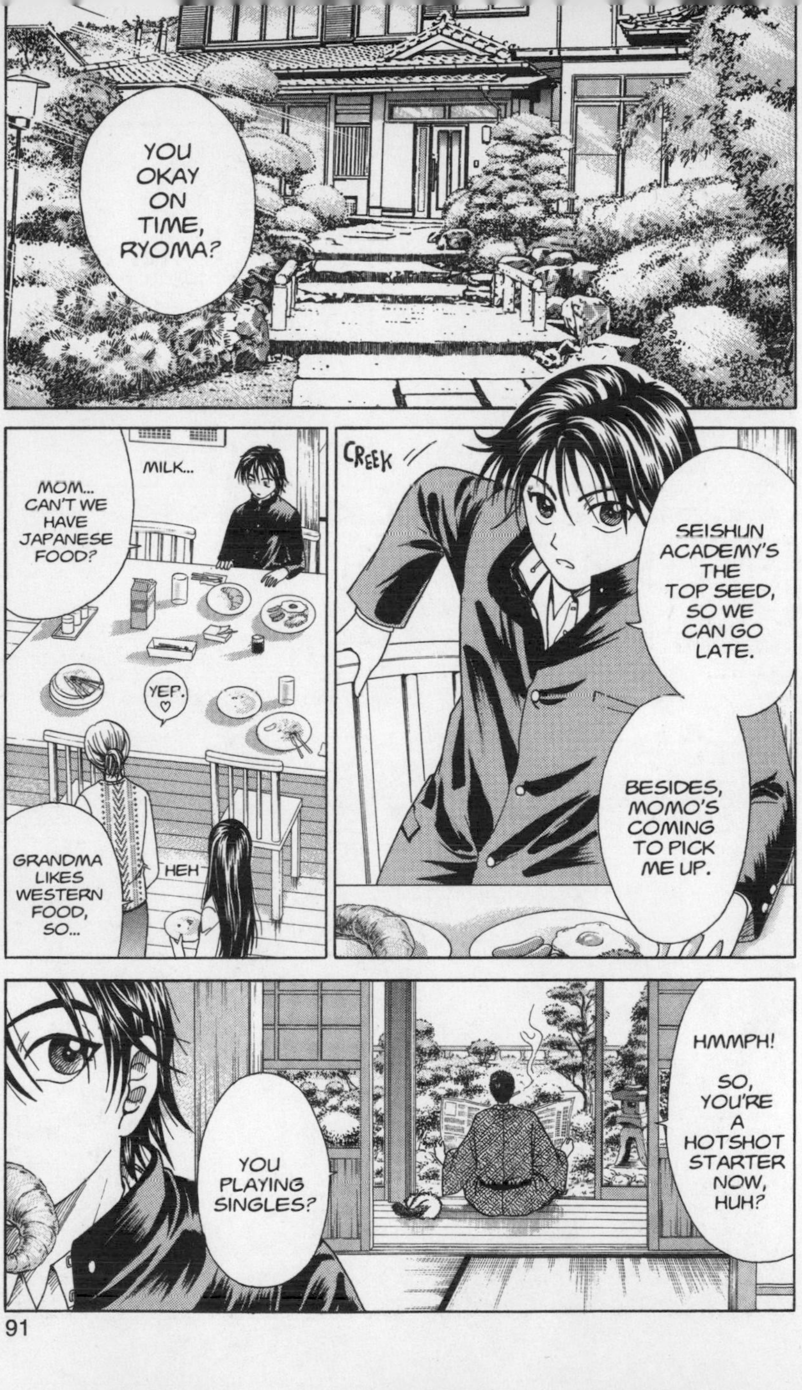
YOU OKAY ON TIME, RYOMA?
CREEK
SEISHUN ACADEMY'S THE TOP SEED, SO WE CAN GO LATE.
BESIDES, MOMO'S COMING TO PICK ME UP.
MILK...
MOM... CAN'T WE HAVE JAPANESE FOOD?
YEP. ♡
HEH
GRANDMA LIKES WESTERN FOOD, SO...
HMMPH!
SO, YOU'RE A HOTSHOT STARTER NOW, HUH?
YOU PLAYING SINGLES?

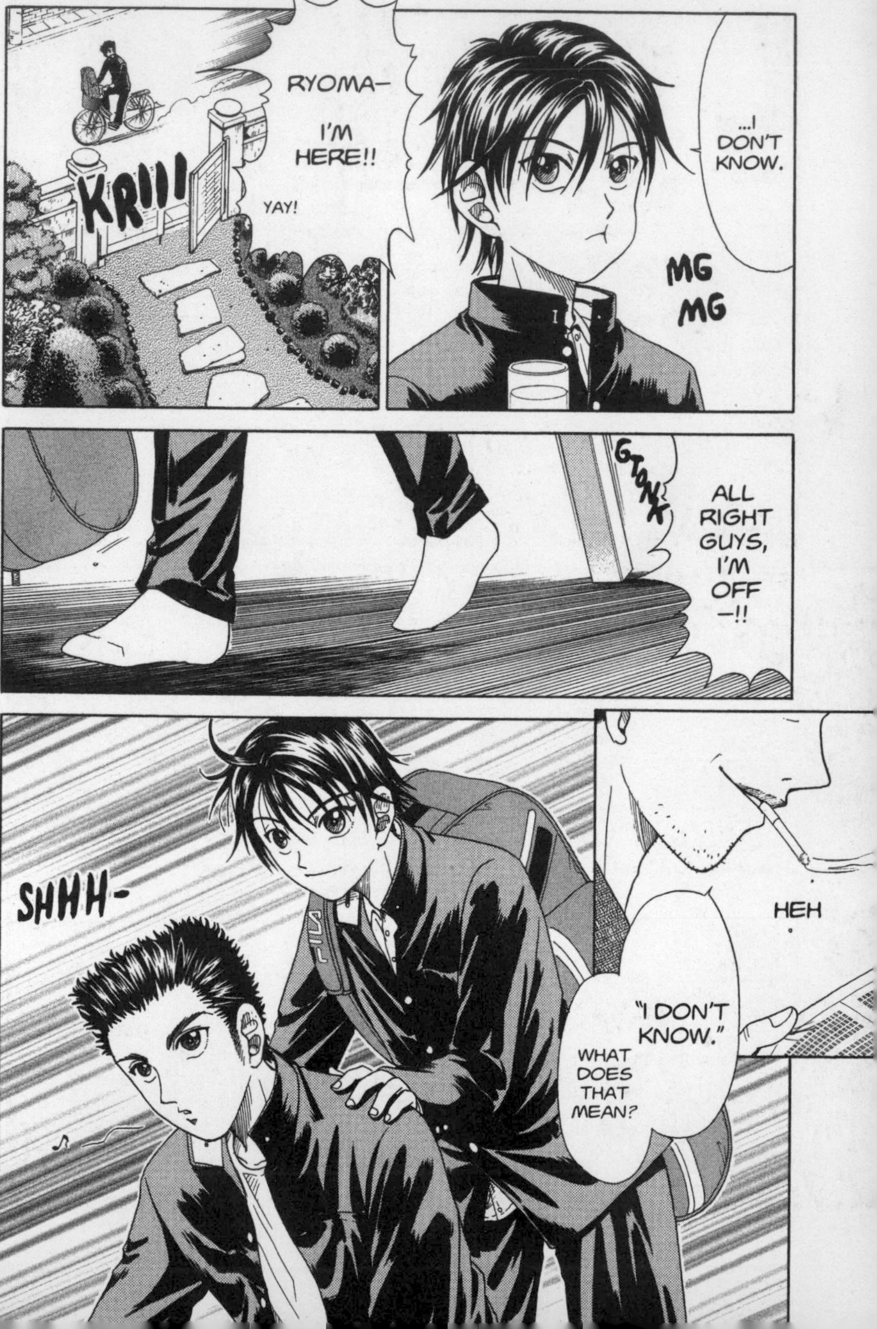

...I DON'T KNOW.
MG MG
RYOMA— I'M HERE!!
YAY!
KRIII
GTONK
ALL RIGHT GUYS, I'M OFF—!!
HEH
"I DON'T KNOW." WHAT DOES THAT MEAN?
SHHH-

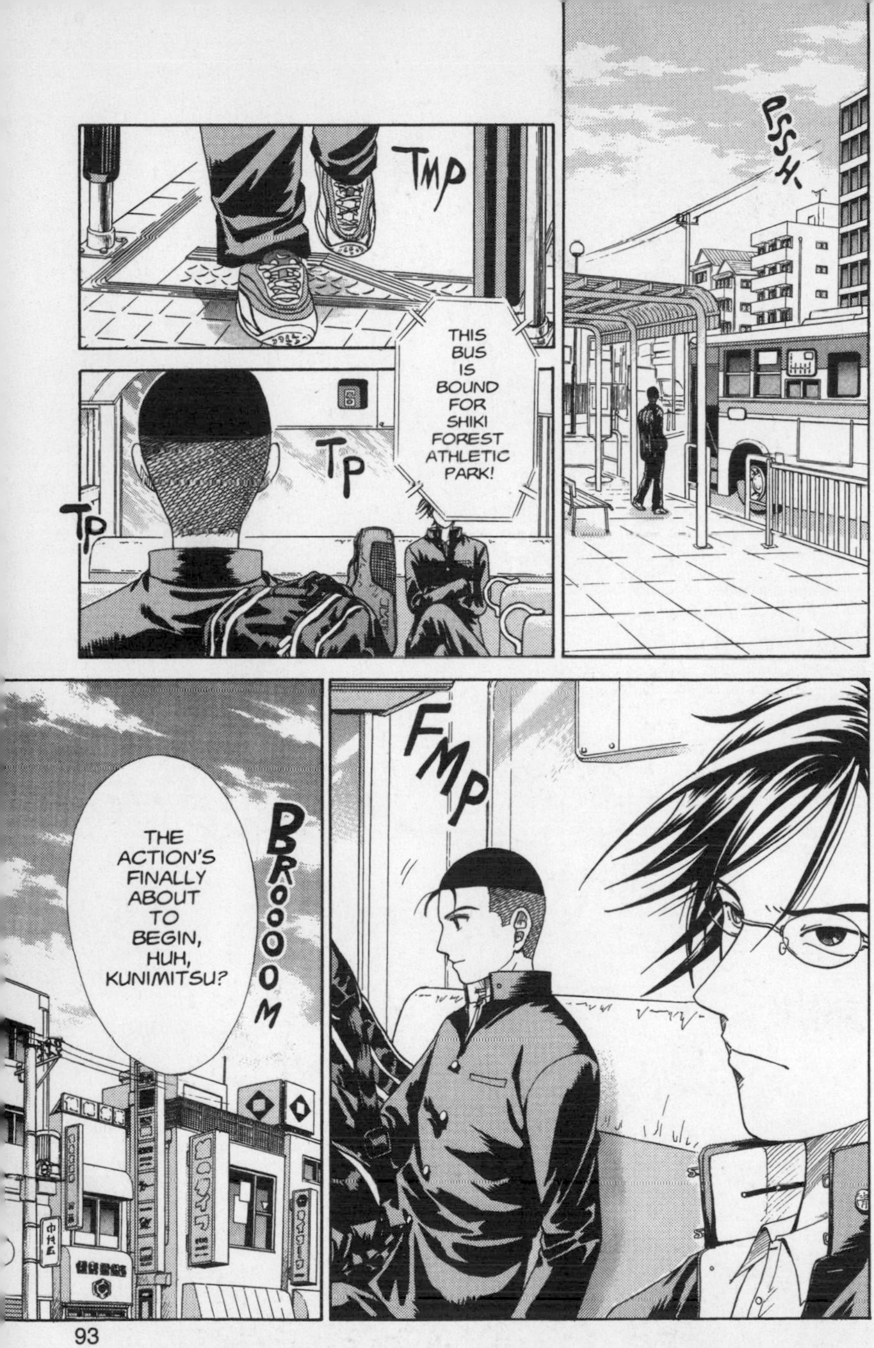
PSSH
TMP
THIS BUS IS BOUND FOR SHIKI FOREST ATHLETIC PARK!
TP
TP
FMP
BROOOOOM
THE ACTION'S FINALLY ABOUT TO BEGIN, HUH, KUNIMITSU?

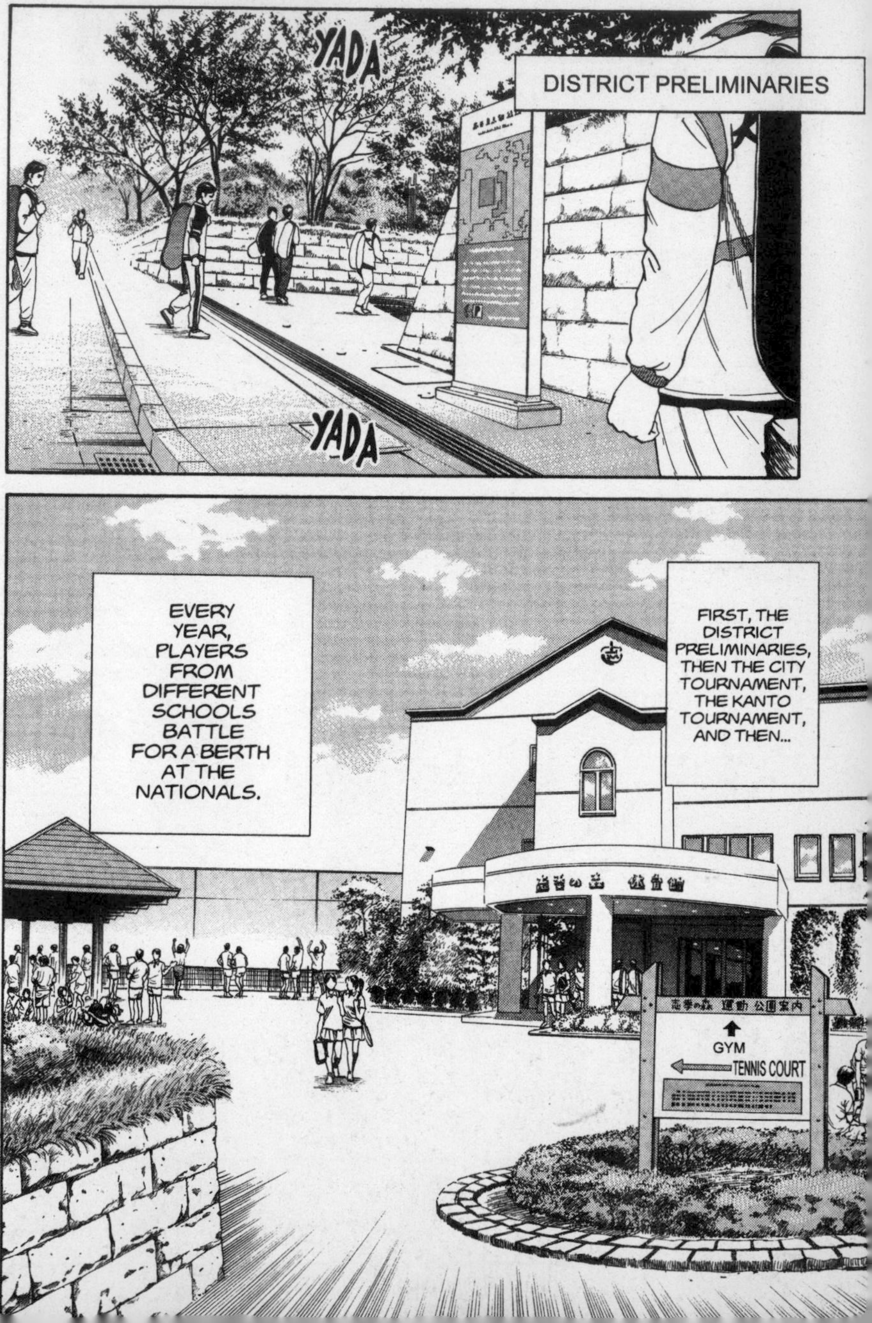
DISTRICT PRELIMINARIES
YADA
YADA
FIRST, THE DISTRICT PRELIMINARIES, THEN THE CITY TOURNAMENT, THE KANTO TOURNAMENT, AND THEN...
EVERY YEAR, PLAYERS FROM DIFFERENT SCHOOLS BATTLE FOR A BERTH AT THE NATIONALS.
GYM
TENNIS COURT

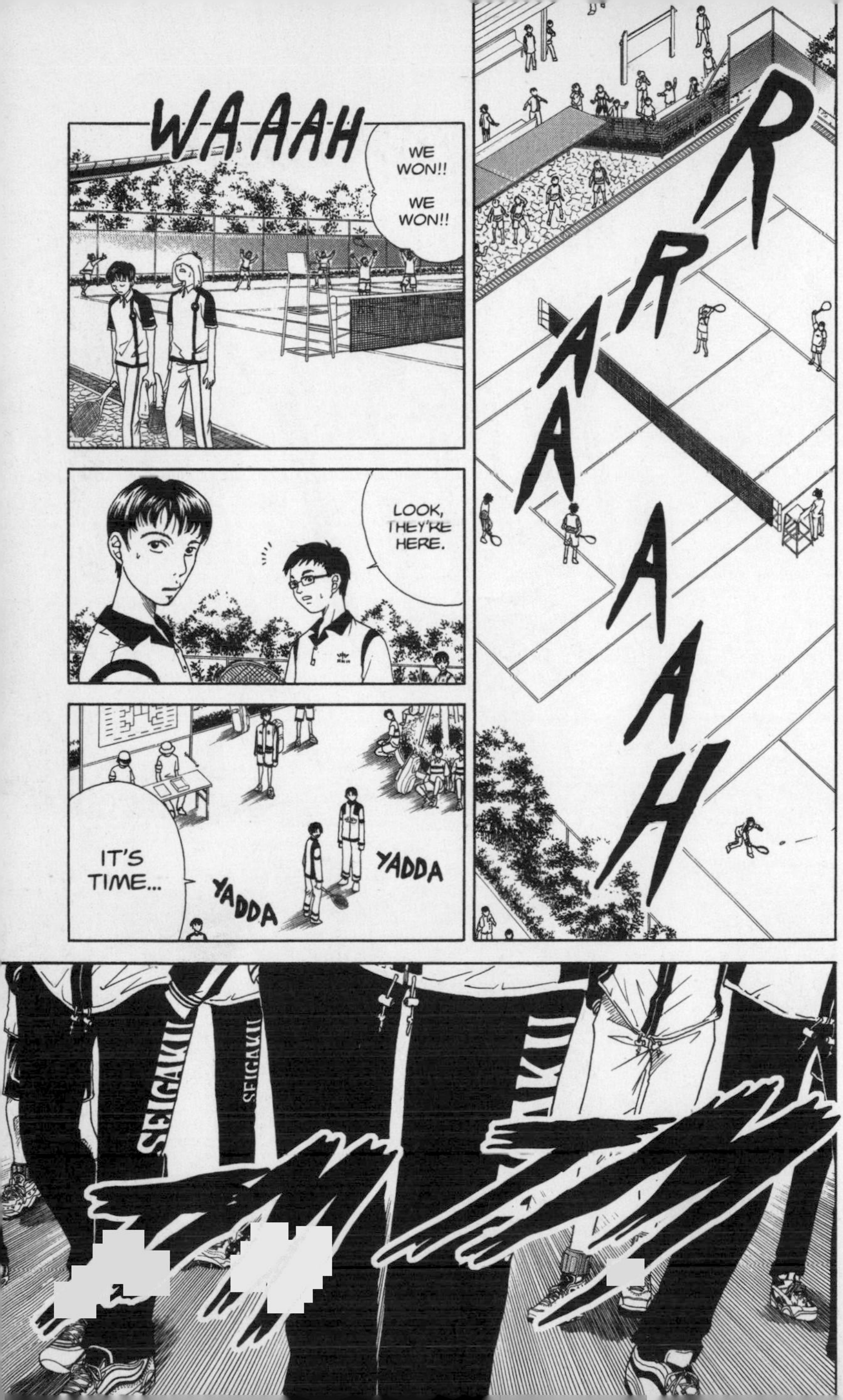
RRAAAAH
WAAAH
WE WON!!
WE WON!!
LOOK, THEY'RE HERE.
IT'S TIME...
YADDA
YADDA
SEIGAKU
SEIGAKU
SEIGAKU

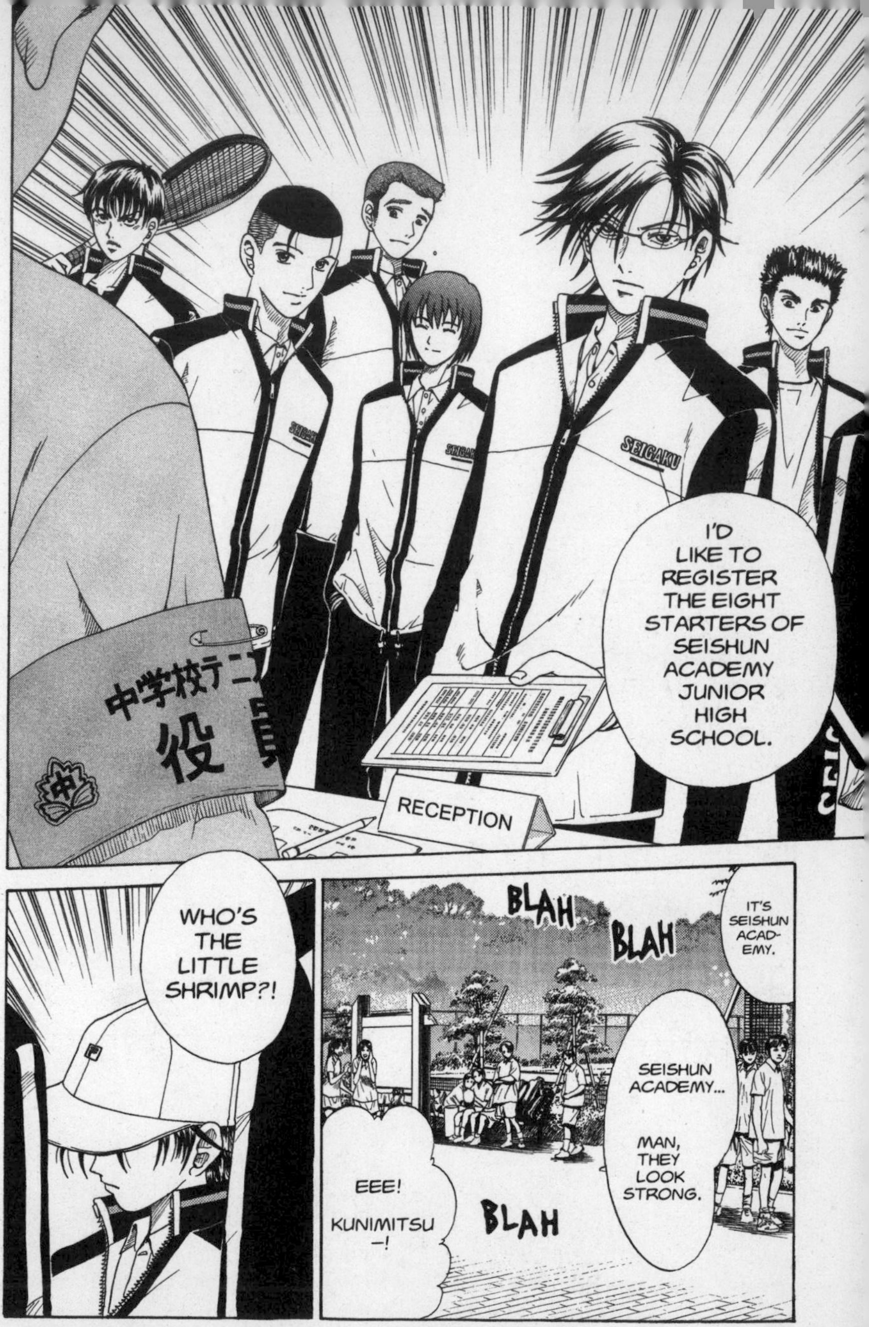
I'D LIKE TO REGISTER THE EIGHT STARTERS OF SEISHUN ACADEMY JUNIOR HIGH SCHOOL.
RECEPTION
SEIGAKU
中学校テニ
役
IT'S SEISHUN ACAD-EMY.
BLAH
BLAH
SEISHUN ACADEMY...
MAN, THEY LOOK STRONG.
BLAH
EEE!
KUNIMITSU—!
WHO'S THE LITTLE SHRIMP?!

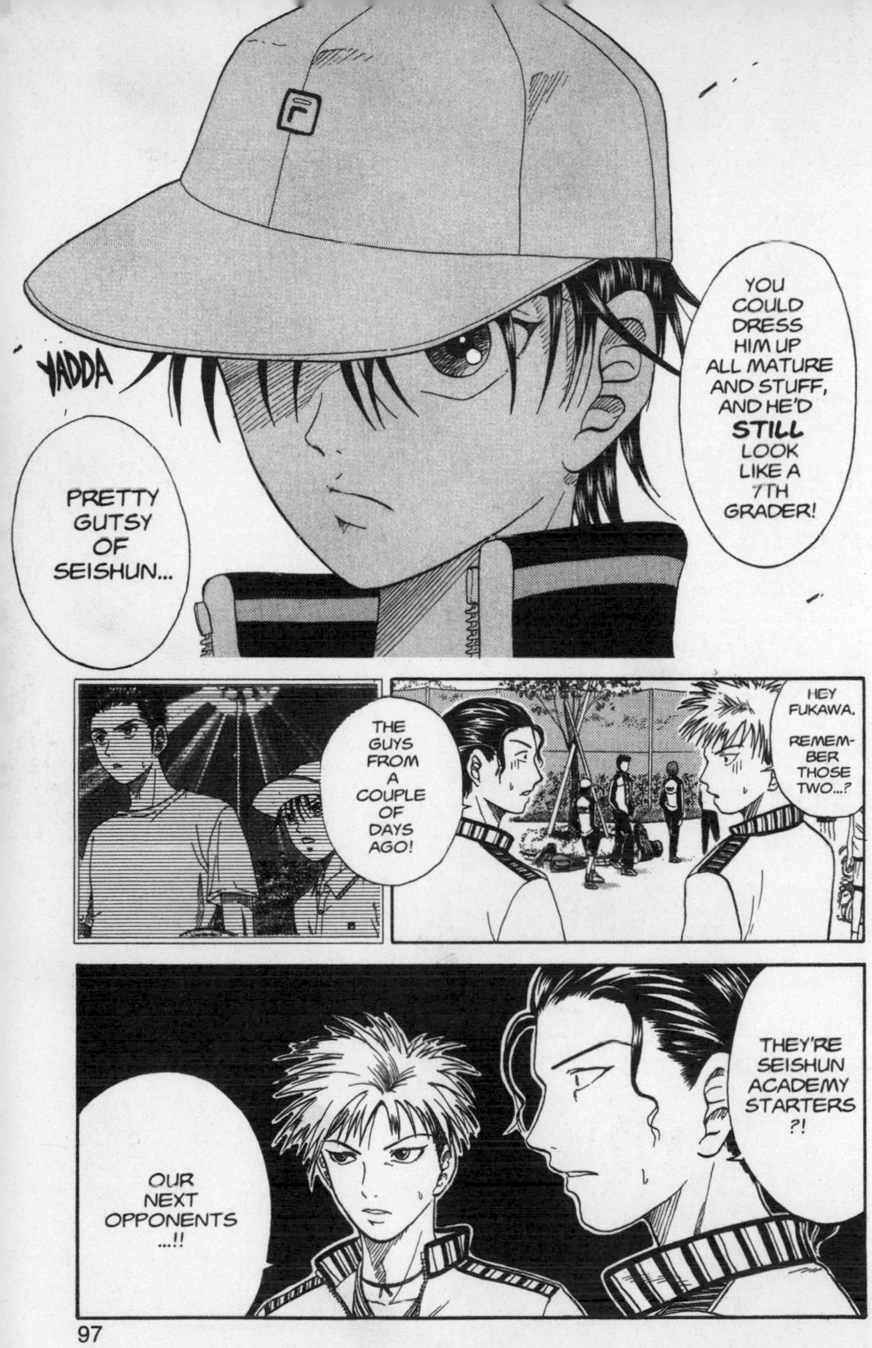
YOU COULD DRESS HIM UP ALL MATURE AND STUFF, AND HE'D **STILL** LOOK LIKE A 7TH GRADER!
YADDA
PRETTY GUTSY OF SEISHUN...
HEY FUKAWA.
REMEMBER THOSE TWO...?
THE GUYS FROM A COUPLE OF DAYS AGO!
THEY'RE SEISHUN ACADEMY STARTERS ?!
OUR NEXT OPPONENTS ...!!

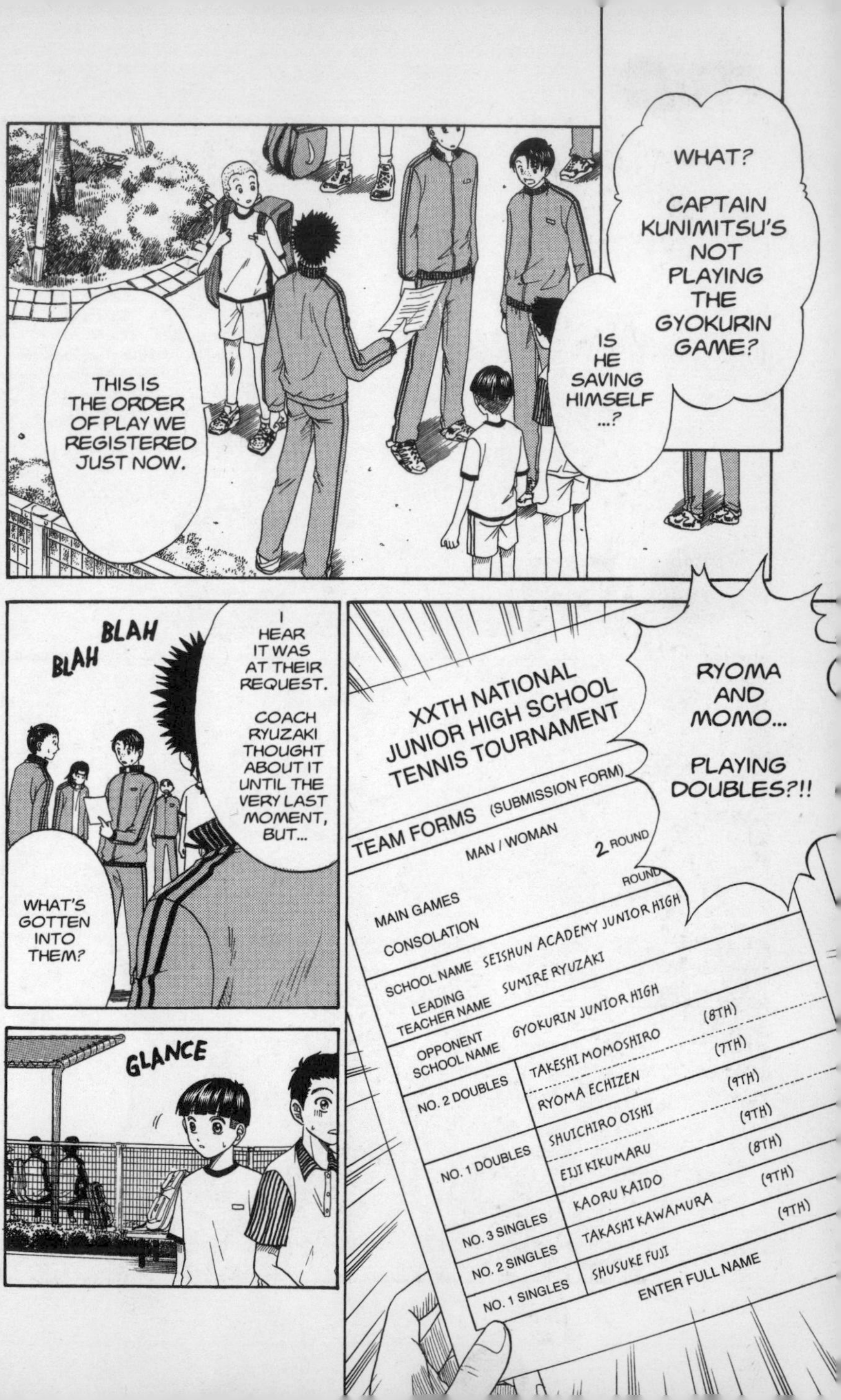
WHAT?
CAPTAIN KUNIMITSU'S NOT PLAYING THE GYOKURIN GAME?
IS HE SAVING HIMSELF ...?
THIS IS THE ORDER OF PLAY WE REGISTERED JUST NOW.
RYOMA AND MOMO...
PLAYING DOUBLES?!!
XXTH NATIONAL JUNIOR HIGH SCHOOL TENNIS TOURNAMENT
TEAM FORMS (SUBMISSION FORM)
MAN / WOMAN
MAIN GAMES 2 ROUND
CONSOLATION ROUND
SCHOOL NAME SEISHUN ACADEMY JUNIOR HIGH
LEADING TEACHER NAME SUMIRE RYUZAKI
OPPONENT SCHOOL NAME GYOKURIN JUNIOR HIGH
NO. 2 DOUBLES TAKESHI MOMOSHIRO (8TH)
RYOMA ECHIZEN (7TH)
NO. 1 DOUBLES SHUICHIRO OISHI (9TH)
EIJI KIKUMARU (9TH)
NO. 3 SINGLES KAORU KAIDO (8TH)
NO. 2 SINGLES TAKASHI KAWAMURA (9TH)
NO. 1 SINGLES SHUSUKE FUJI (9TH)
ENTER FULL NAME
BLAH BLAH
I HEAR IT WAS AT THEIR REQUEST.
COACH RYUZAKI THOUGHT ABOUT IT UNTIL THE VERY LAST MOMENT, BUT...
WHAT'S GOTTEN INTO THEM?
GLANCE

READ THIS WAY

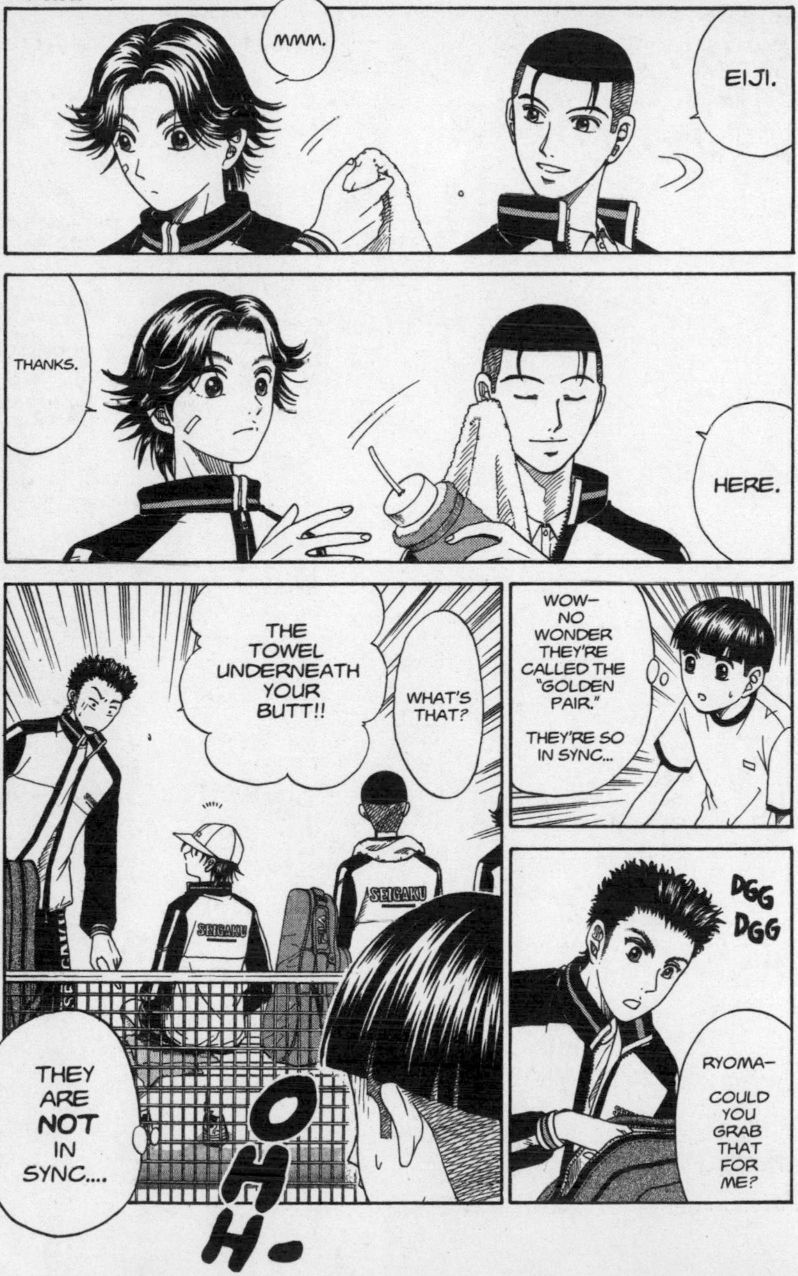
EIJI.
MMM.
HERE.
THANKS.
WOW— NO WONDER THEY'RE CALLED THE "GOLDEN PAIR." THEY'RE SO IN SYNC...
DGG DGG
RYOMA— COULD YOU GRAB THAT FOR ME?
WHAT'S THAT?
THE TOWEL UNDERNEATH YOUR BUTT!!
OHH-
THEY ARE NOT IN SYNC....

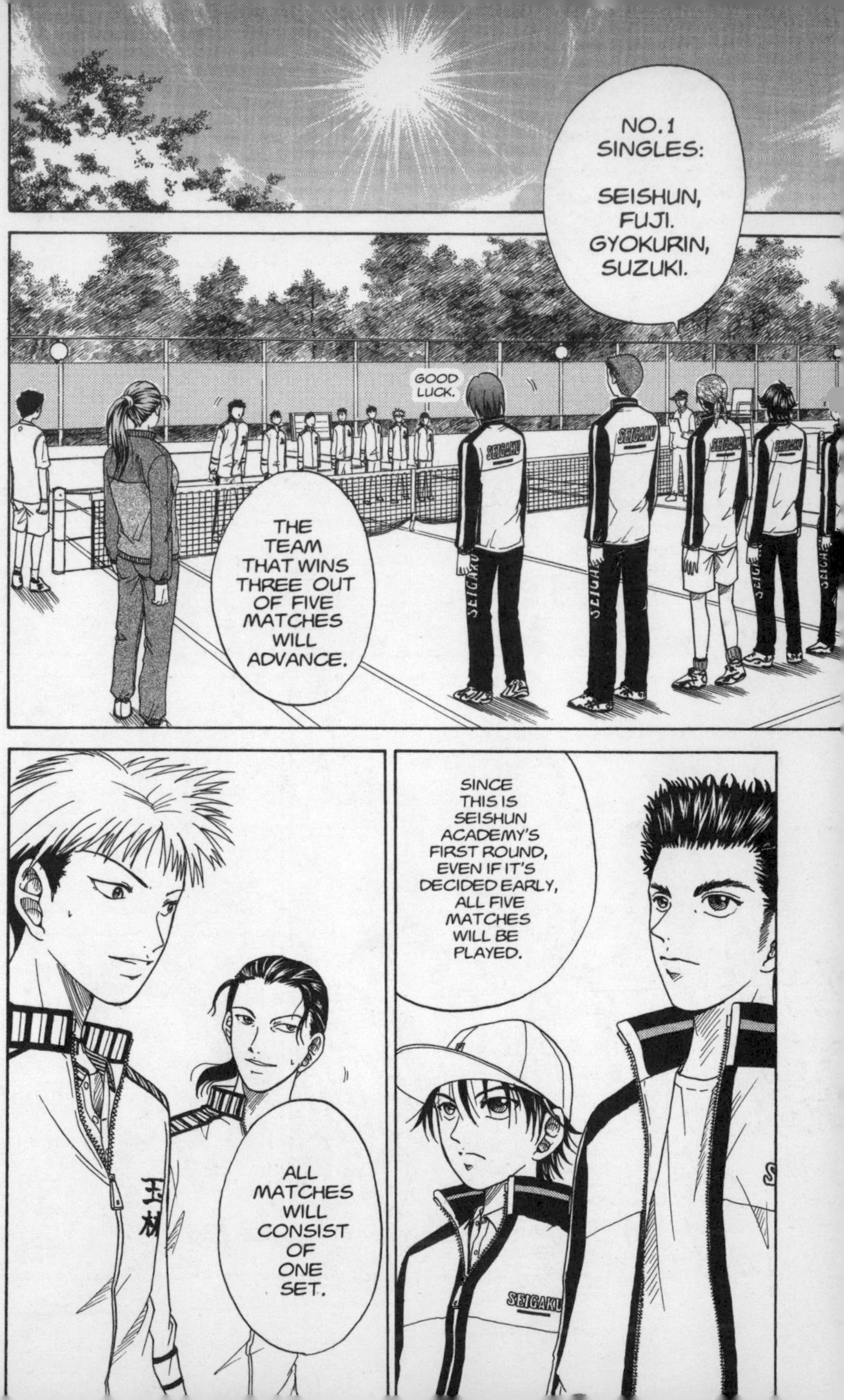
NO.1 SINGLES: SEISHUN, FUJI. GYOKURIN, SUZUKI.
GOOD LUCK.
THE TEAM THAT WINS THREE OUT OF FIVE MATCHES WILL ADVANCE.
SINCE THIS IS SEISHUN ACADEMY'S FIRST ROUND, EVEN IF IT'S DECIDED EARLY, ALL FIVE MATCHES WILL BE PLAYED.
ALL MATCHES WILL CONSIST OF ONE SET.

READ THIS WAY

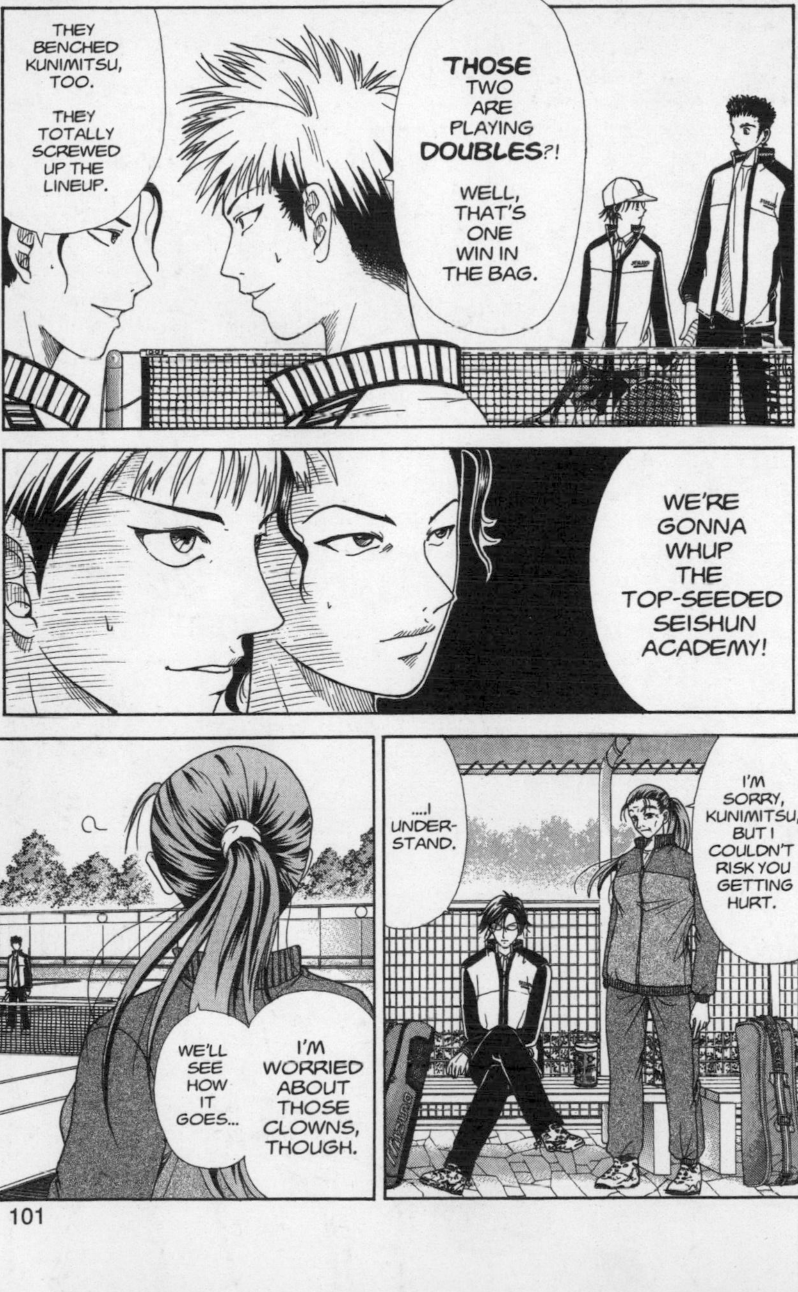
THOSE TWO ARE PLAYING DOUBLES?!
WELL, THAT'S ONE WIN IN THE BAG.
THEY BENCHED KUNIMITSU, TOO.
THEY TOTALLY SCREWED UP THE LINEUP.
WE'RE GONNA WHUP THE TOP-SEEDED SEISHUN ACADEMY!
I'M SORRY, KUNIMITSU, BUT I COULDN'T RISK YOU GETTING HURT.
....I UNDERSTAND.
I'M WORRIED ABOUT THOSE CLOWNS, THOUGH.
WE'LL SEE HOW IT GOES...

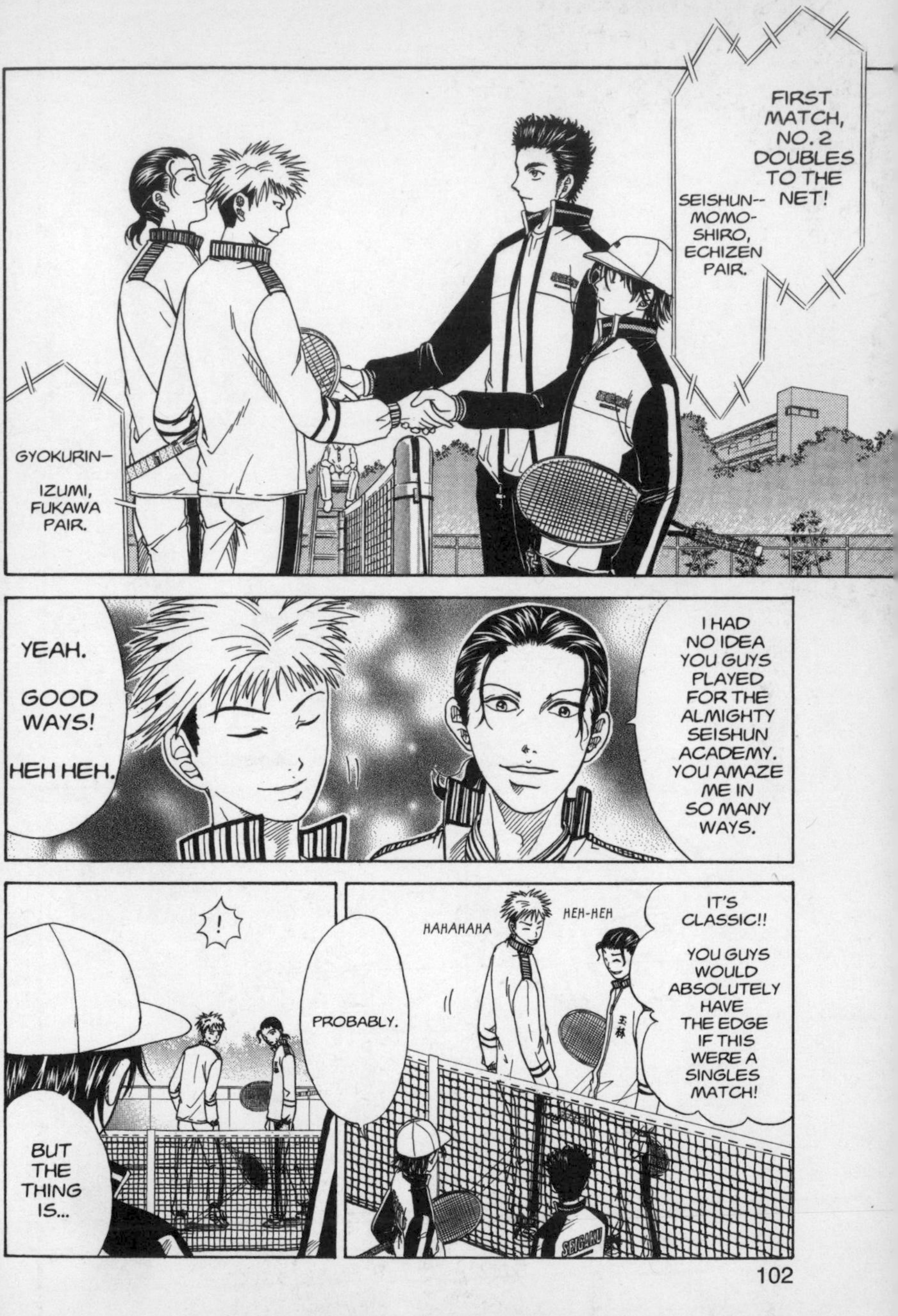
FIRST MATCH, NO. 2 DOUBLES TO THE NET!
SEISHUN-- MOMO-SHIRO, ECHIZEN PAIR.
GYOKURIN— IZUMI, FUKAWA PAIR.
I HAD NO IDEA YOU GUYS PLAYED FOR THE ALMIGHTY SEISHUN ACADEMY. YOU AMAZE ME IN SO MANY WAYS.
YEAH. GOOD WAYS! HEH HEH.
IT'S CLASSIC!! YOU GUYS WOULD ABSOLUTELY HAVE THE EDGE IF THIS WERE A SINGLES MATCH!
HEH-HEH
HAHAHAHA
PROBABLY.
!
BUT THE THING IS...

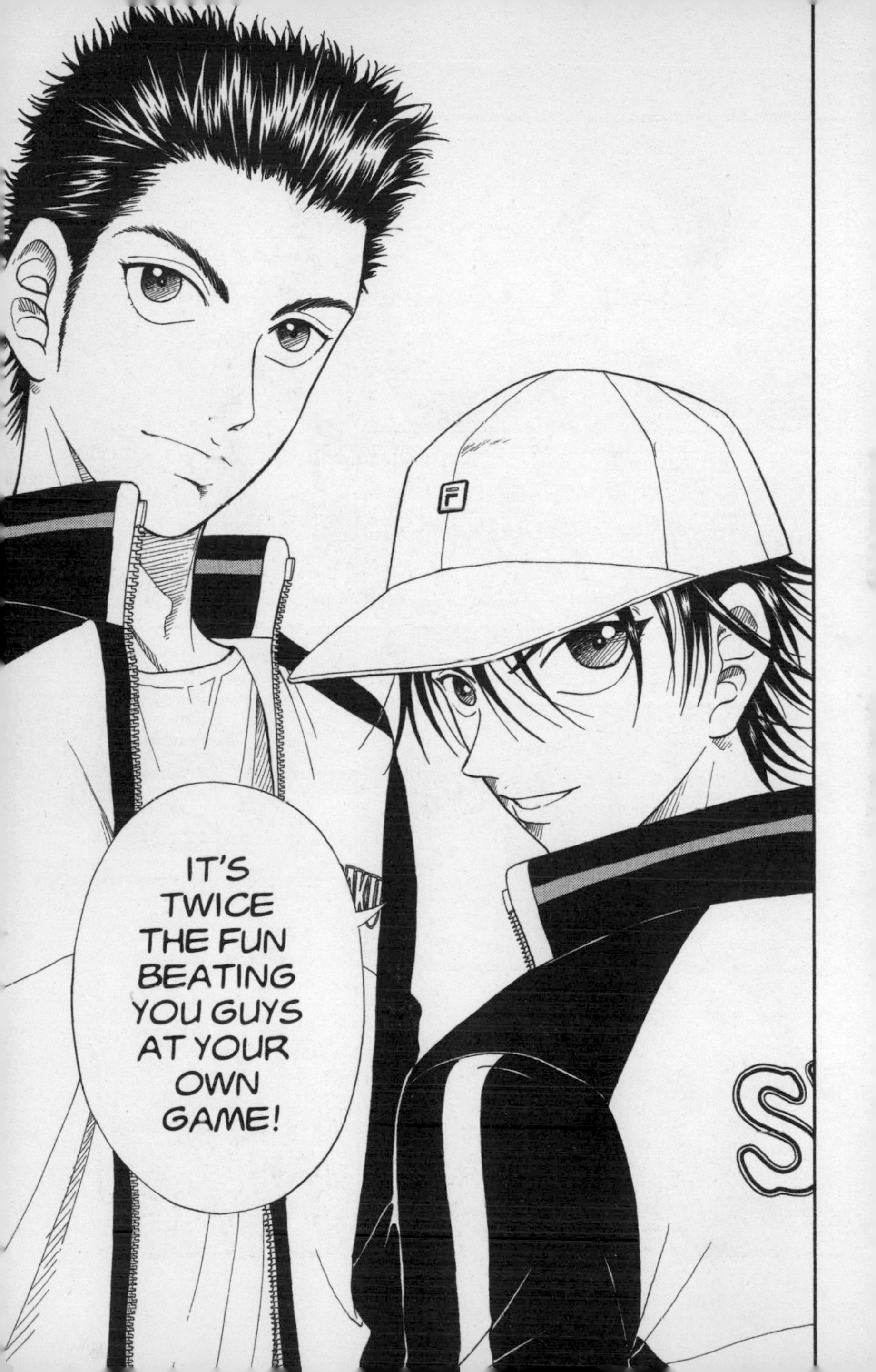
IT'S TWICE THE FUN BEATING YOU GUYS AT YOUR OWN GAME!

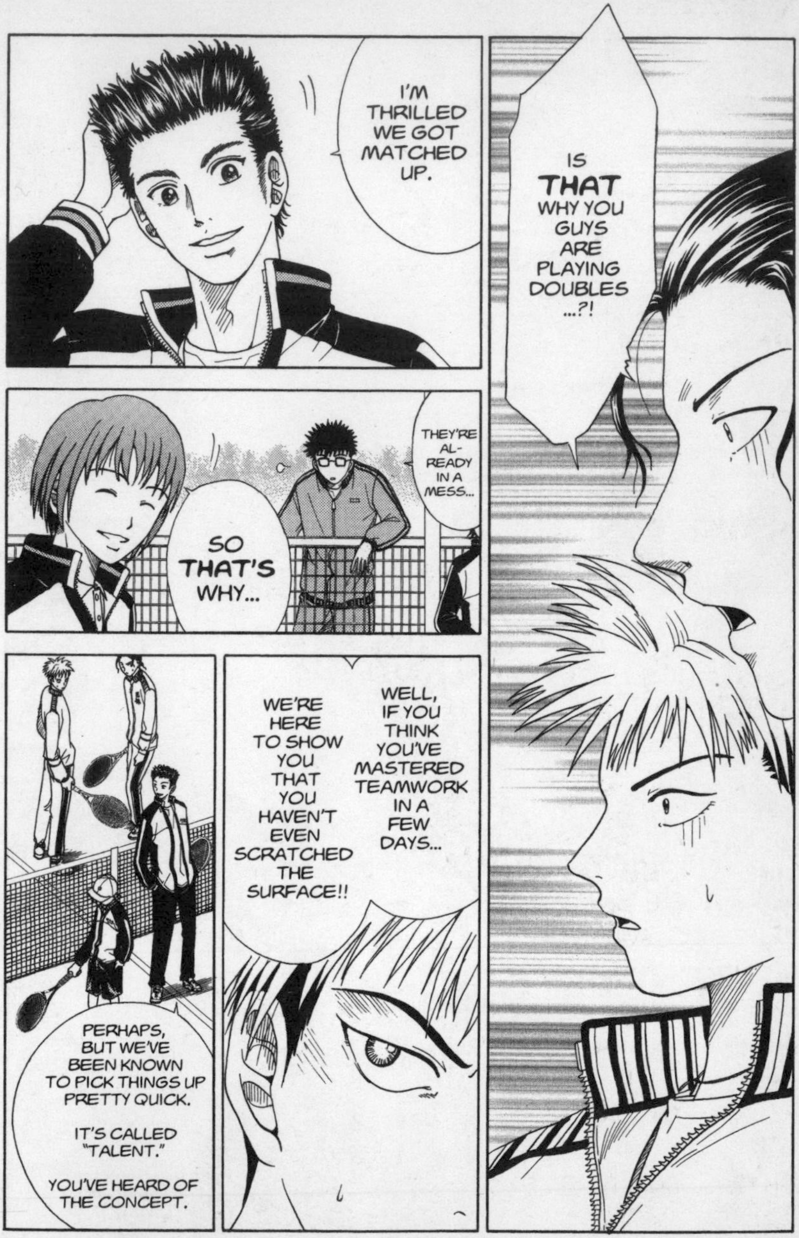
IS THAT WHY YOU GUYS ARE PLAYING DOUBLES ...?!
I'M THRILLED WE GOT MATCHED UP.
THEY'RE AL-READY IN A MESS...
SO THAT'S WHY...
WELL, IF YOU THINK YOU'VE MASTERED TEAMWORK IN A FEW DAYS...
WE'RE HERE TO SHOW YOU THAT YOU HAVEN'T EVEN SCRATCHED THE SURFACE!!
PERHAPS, BUT WE'VE BEEN KNOWN TO PICK THINGS UP PRETTY QUICK.
IT'S CALLED "TALENT."
YOU'VE HEARD OF THE CONCEPT.

READ THIS WAY

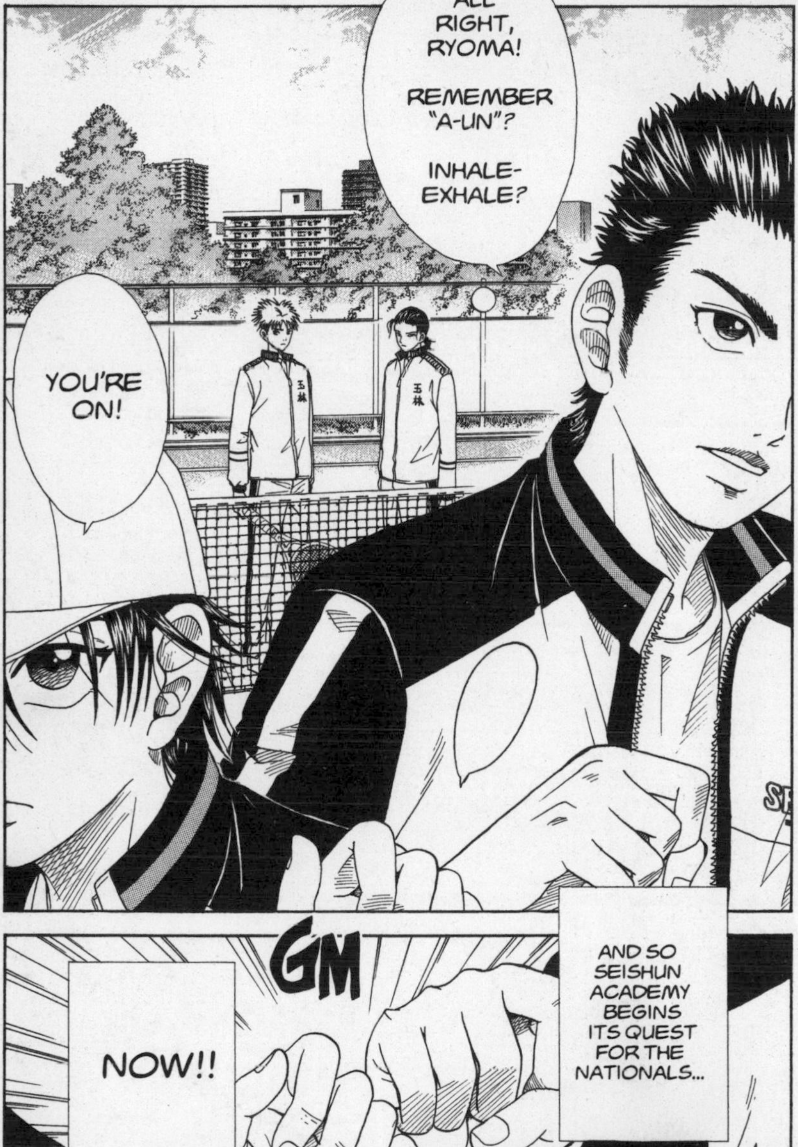
ALL RIGHT, RYOMA!
REMEMBER "A-UN"?
INHALE-EXHALE?
YOU'RE ON!
AND SO SEISHUN ACADEMY BEGINS ITS QUEST FOR THE NATIONALS...
GM
NOW!!

Date · · No. 28

RYOMA ECHIZEN/LEFT-HANDED

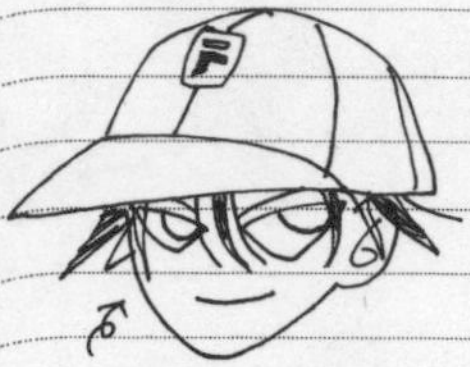
SQUINTS, ARROGANT

SEISHUN ACADEMY JUNIOR HIGH, 7TH GRADE, CLASS 2

HEIGHT: 151 CM/BLOOD TYPE: O/BORN: 12/24

FAVORITE BRAND CAP: FILA

GEAR: FILA

SHOES: FILA (MARK PHILIPPOUSSIS MID)

RACKET: BRIDGESTONE (DYNABEAM GRANDEA)

BEST SHOT: TWIST SERVE

FAVORITE FOOD: GRILLED FISH, STEAM POT, SHRIMP RICE CRACKERS (PLUM, KIMCHI FLAVOR)

HOBBIES/PASTIMES: BATHING WITH HOT SPRING POWDER FROM ALL OVER THE COUNTRY

TAKESHI MOMOSHIRO/RIGHT-HANDED

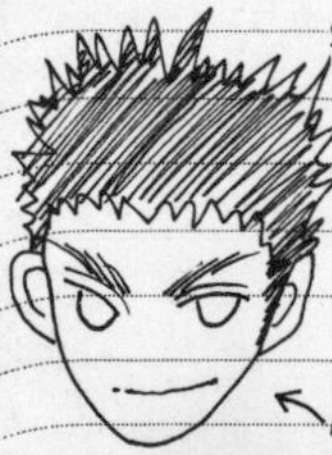
SPIKY HAIR
MISCHIEVOUS

SEISHUN ACADEMY JUNIOR HIGH, 8TH GRADE, CLASS 8

HEIGHT: 170 CM/BLOOD TYPE: O/BORN: 7/23

FAVORITE BRAND SHOES: PUMA (ASPIRATION PT0631 0020)

RACKET: MIZUNO (PROLIGHT P10 TI HYPER)

BEST SHOT: DUNK SMASH

FAVORITE FOOD: SHRIMP CUTLET BURGER, VERY BERRY COCO PARFAIT

HOBBIES/PASTIMES: LISTENING TO MUSIC, SENSORY GAMES

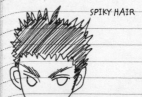

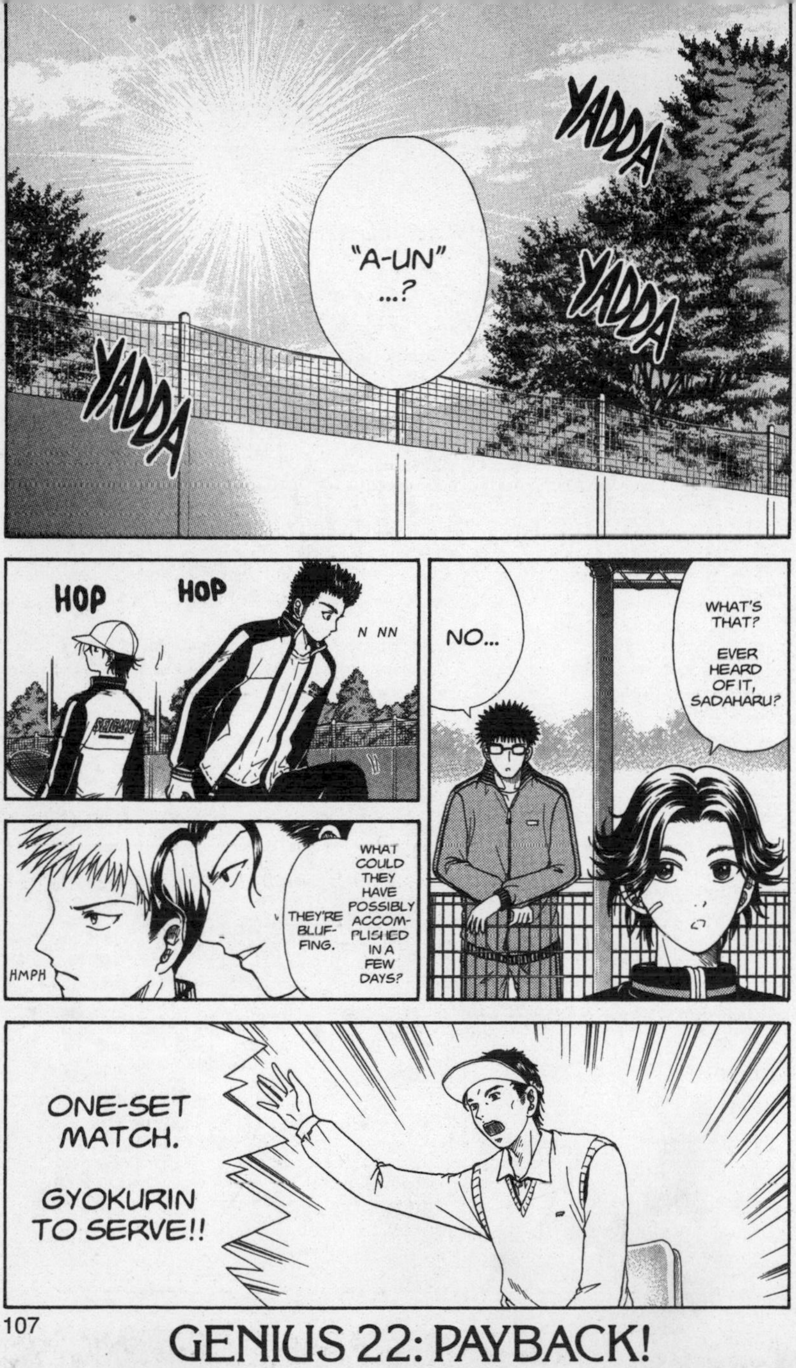
YADDA
YADDA
"A-UN" ...?
YADDA
WHAT'S THAT?
EVER HEARD OF IT, SADAHARU?
NO...
N NN
HOP
HOP
WHAT COULD THEY HAVE POSSIBLY ACCOMPLISHED IN A FEW DAYS?
THEY'RE BLUFFING.
HMPH
ONE-SET MATCH.
GYOKURIN TO SERVE!!

GENIUS 22: PAYBACK!

GENIUS 22: PAYBACK!

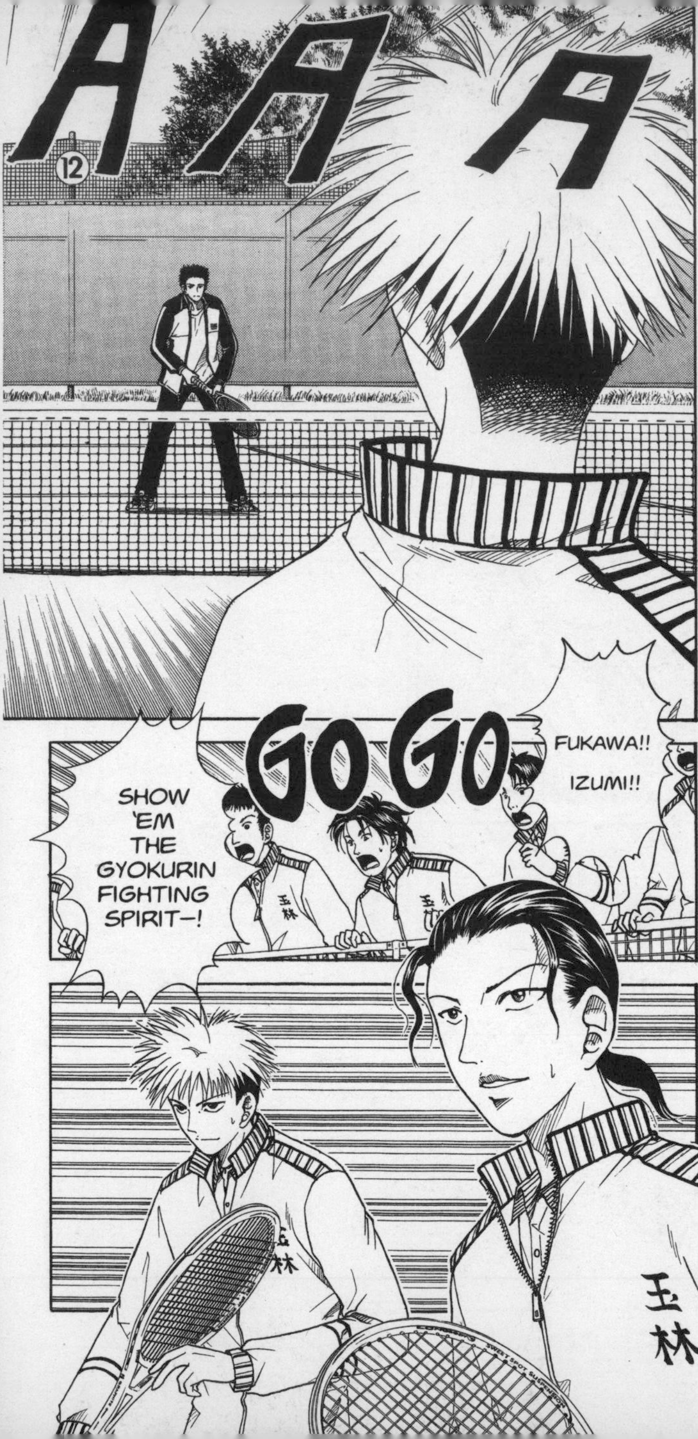
AAA
FUKAWA!!
IZUMI!!
GO GO
SHOW 'EM THE GYOKURIN FIGHTING SPIRIT—!

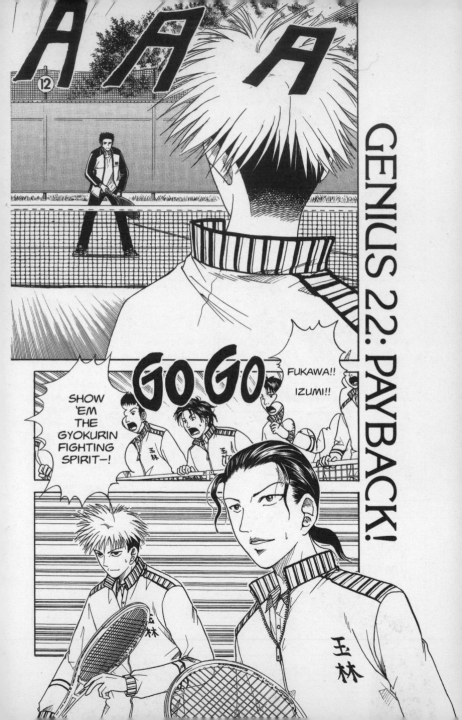

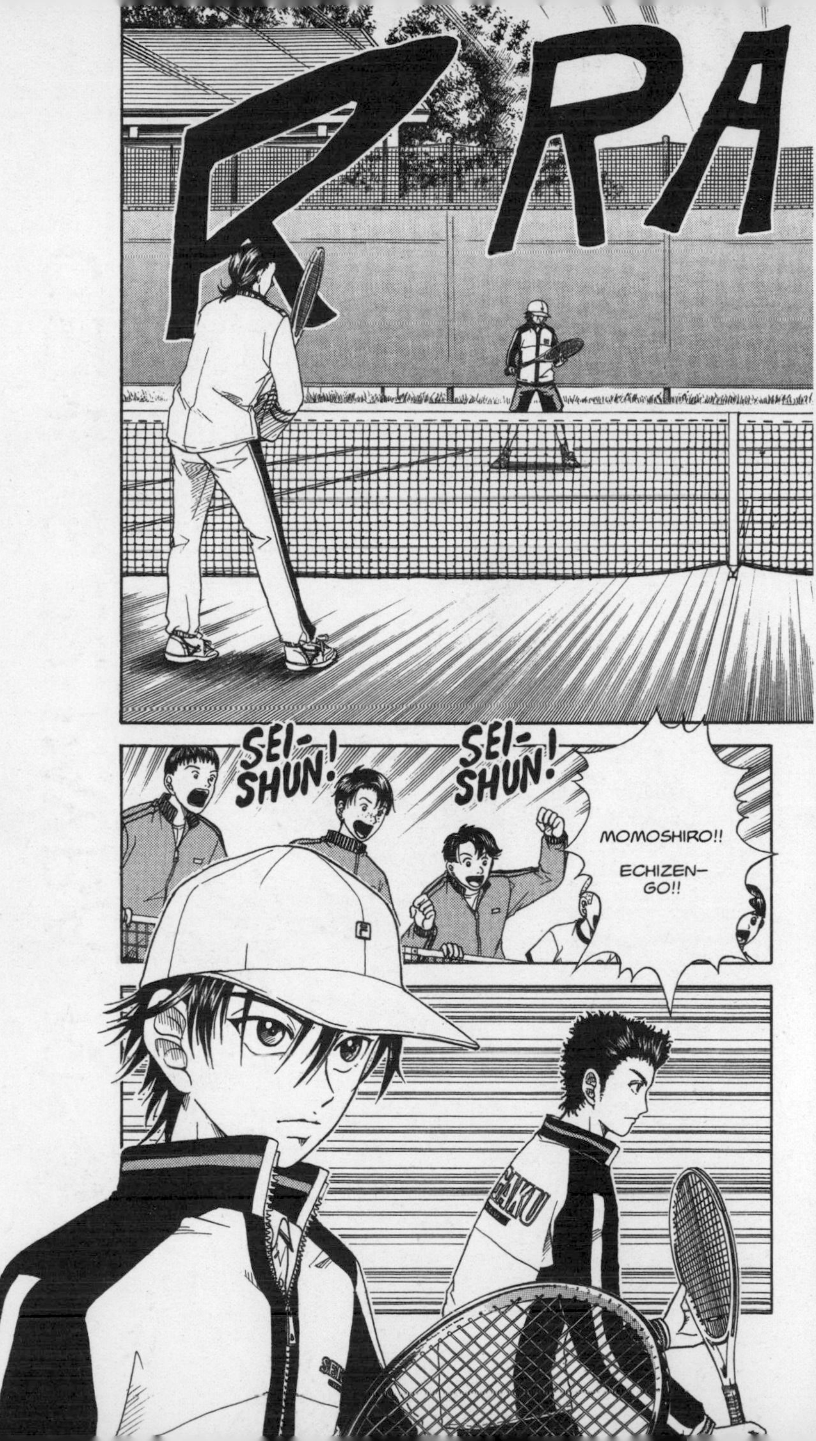
RRA
MOMOSHIRO!!
ECHIZEN-GO!!
SEI-SHUN!
SEI-SHUN!

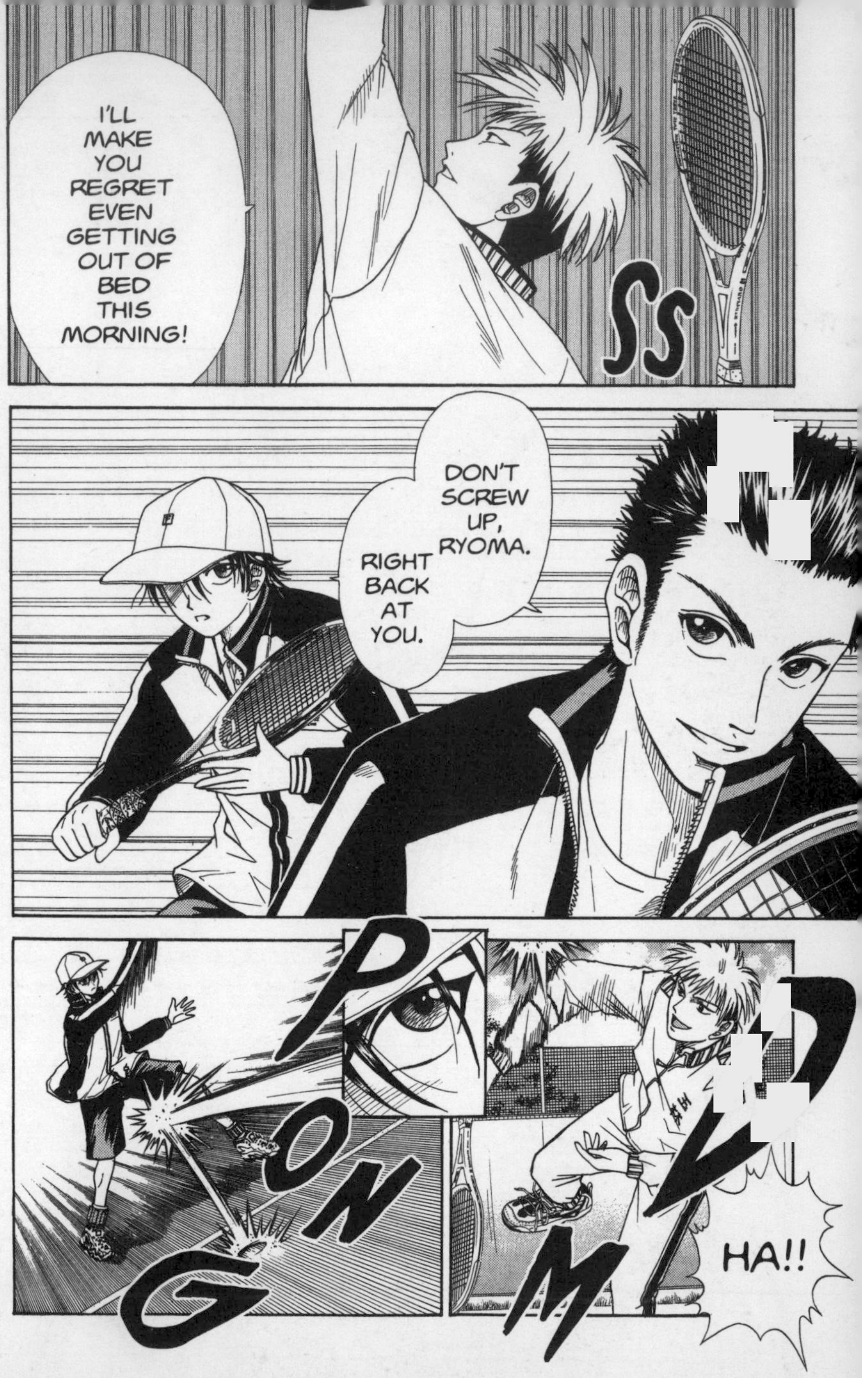
I'LL MAKE YOU REGRET EVEN GETTING OUT OF BED THIS MORNING!
DON'T SCREW UP, RYOMA.
RIGHT BACK AT YOU.
HA!!
PONG

READ THIS WAY

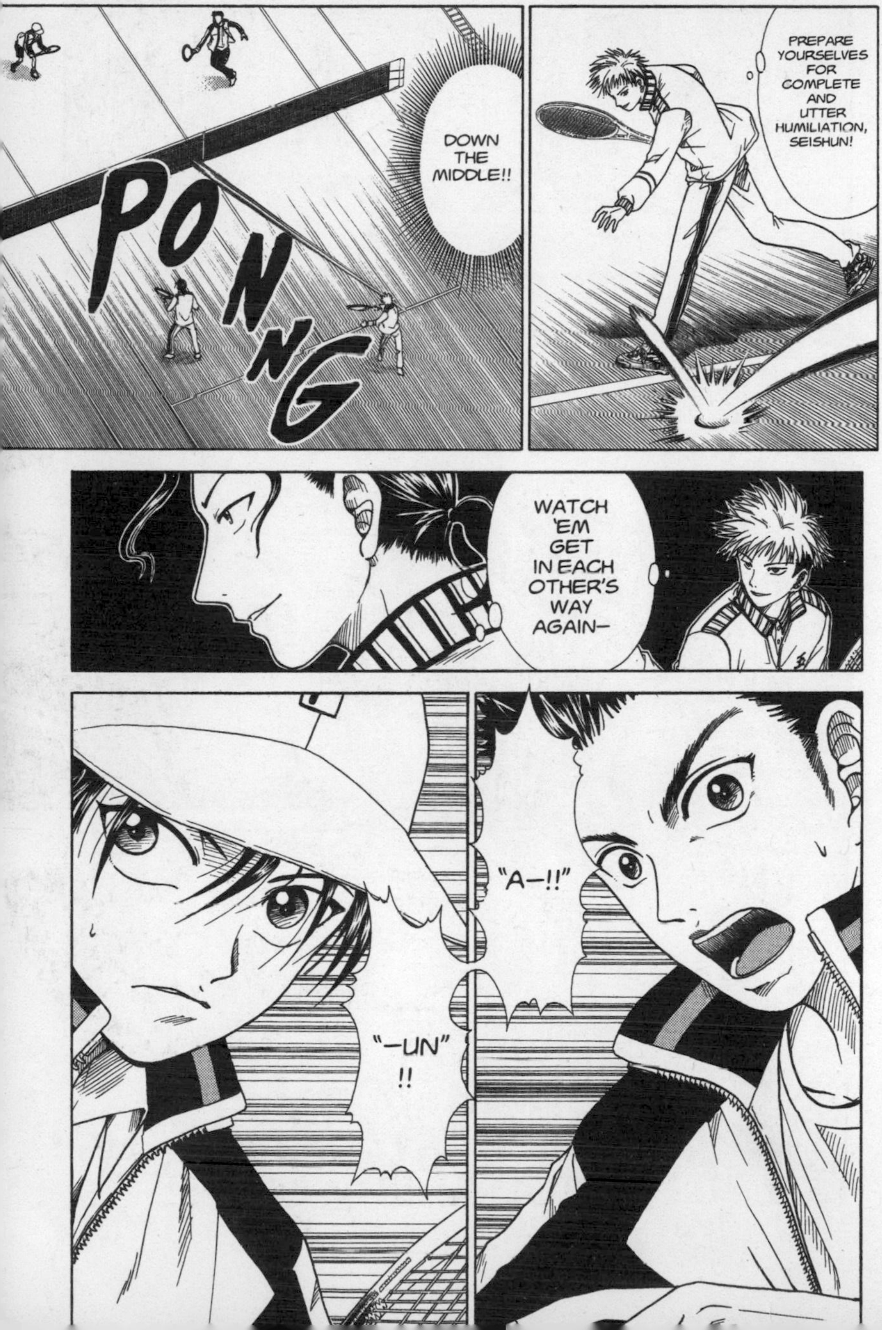
PREPARE YOURSELVES FOR COMPLETE AND UTTER HUMILIATION, SEISHUN!
DOWN THE MIDDLE!!
PONNG
WATCH 'EM GET IN EACH OTHER'S WAY AGAIN—
"A—!!"
"—UN" !!

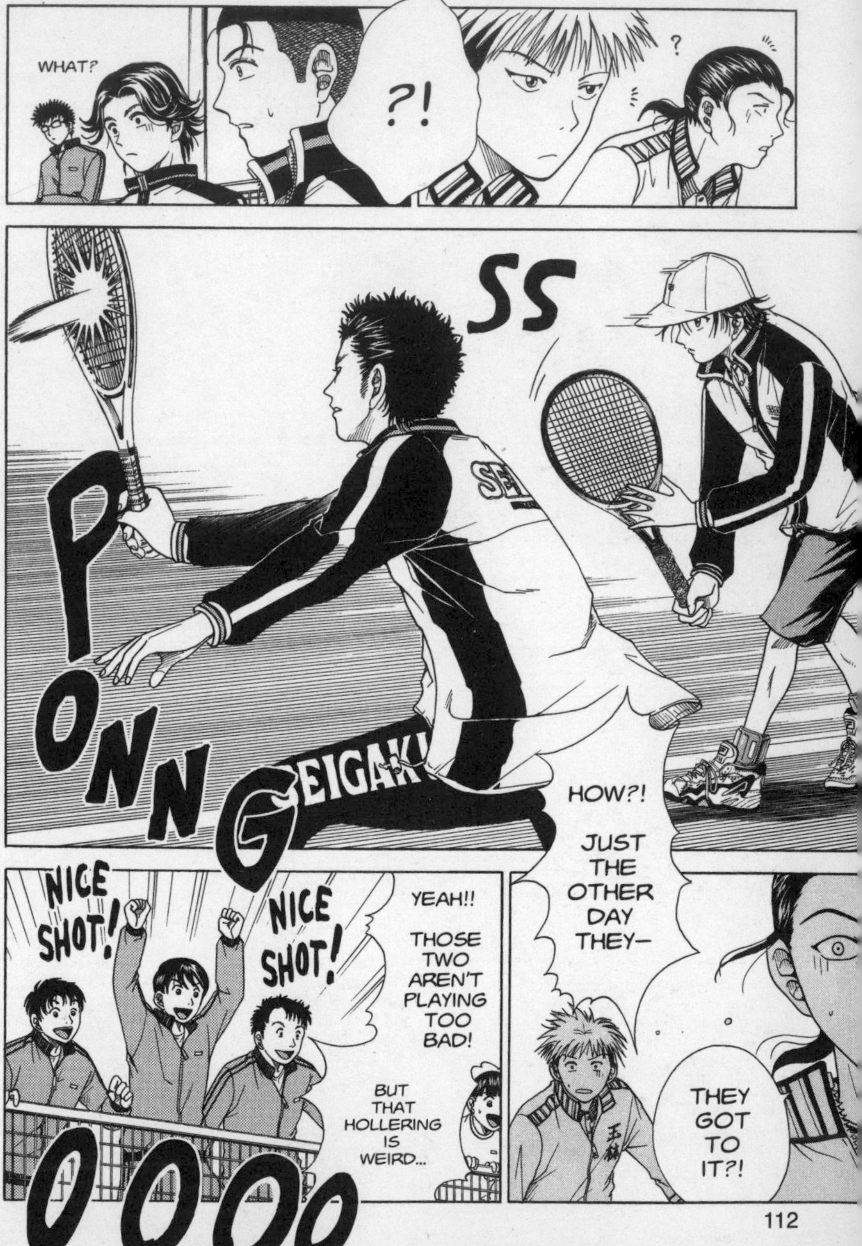
?
?!
WHAT?
SS
PONNG
HOW?!
JUST THE OTHER DAY THEY—
THEY GOT TO IT?!
NICE SHOT!
NICE SHOT!
YEAH!!
THOSE TWO AREN'T PLAYING TOO BAD!
BUT THAT HOLLERING IS WEIRD...
OOOOO

READ THIS WAY

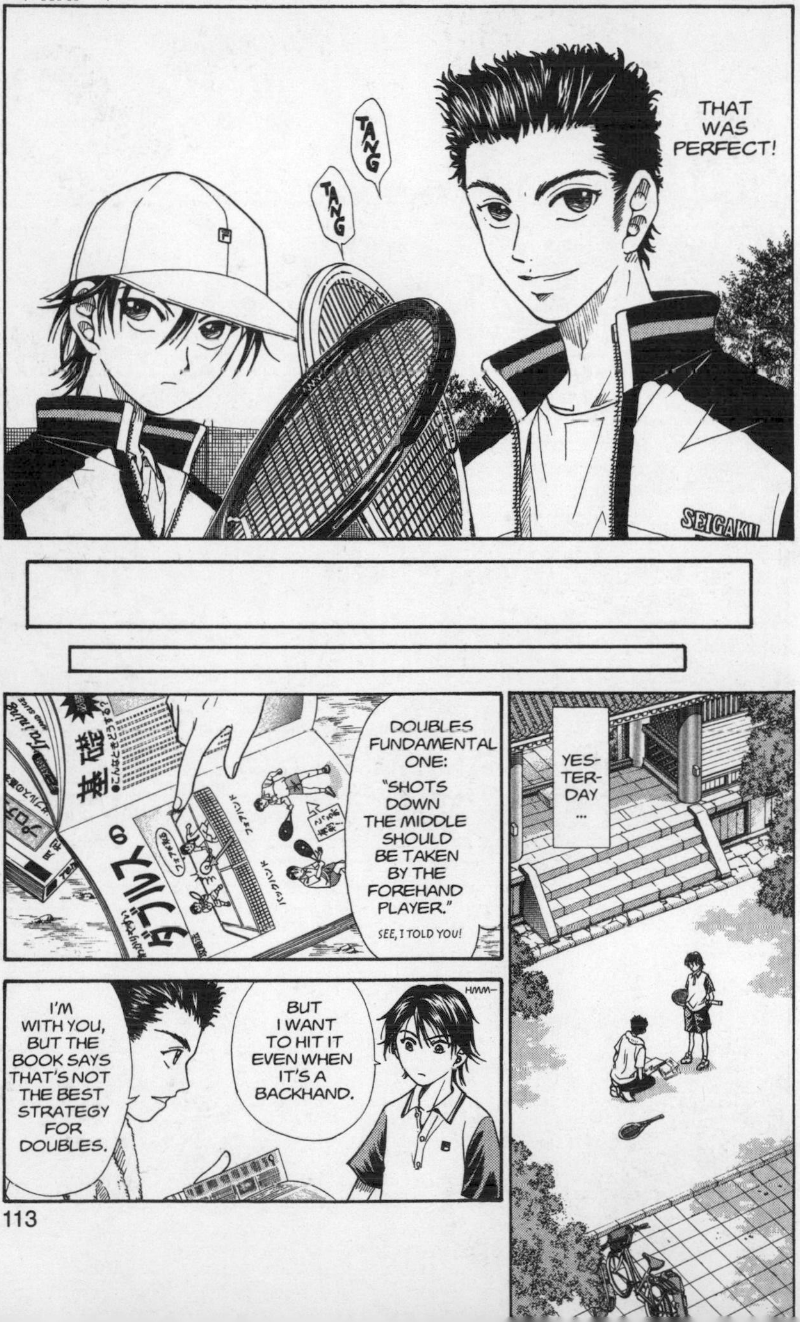
THAT WAS PERFECT!
TANG
TANG
YESTERDAY...
DOUBLES FUNDAMENTAL ONE: "SHOTS DOWN THE MIDDLE SHOULD BE TAKEN BY THE FOREHAND PLAYER."
SEE, I TOLD YOU!
HMM—
BUT I WANT TO HIT IT EVEN WHEN IT'S A BACKHAND.
I'M WITH YOU, BUT THE BOOK SAYS THAT'S NOT THE BEST STRATEGY FOR DOUBLES.
SEIGAKU

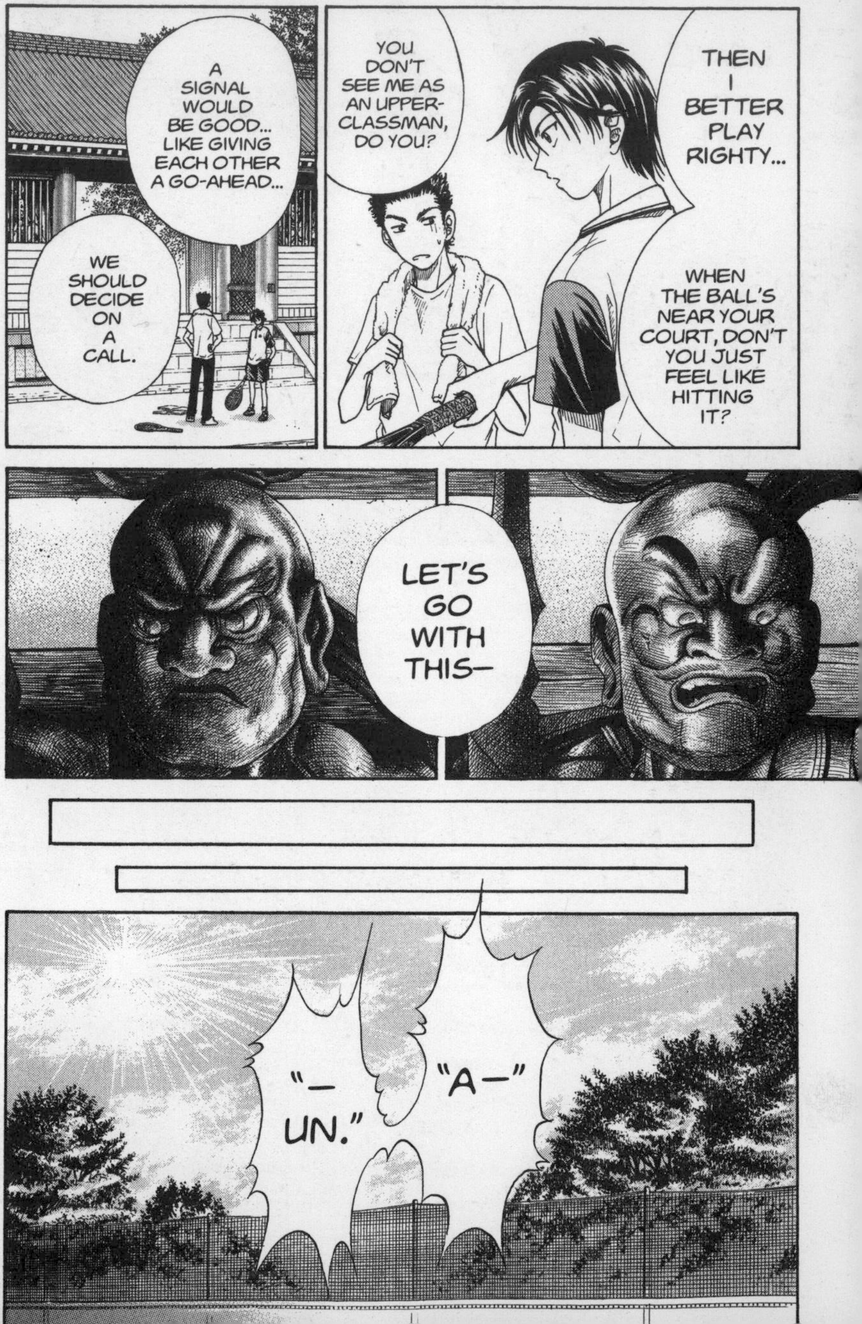
THEN I BETTER PLAY RIGHTY...
YOU DON'T SEE ME AS AN UPPER-CLASSMAN, DO YOU?
WHEN THE BALL'S NEAR YOUR COURT, DON'T YOU JUST FEEL LIKE HITTING IT?
A SIGNAL WOULD BE GOOD... LIKE GIVING EACH OTHER A GO-AHEAD...
WE SHOULD DECIDE ON A CALL.
LET'S GO WITH THIS—
"A—"
"— UN."

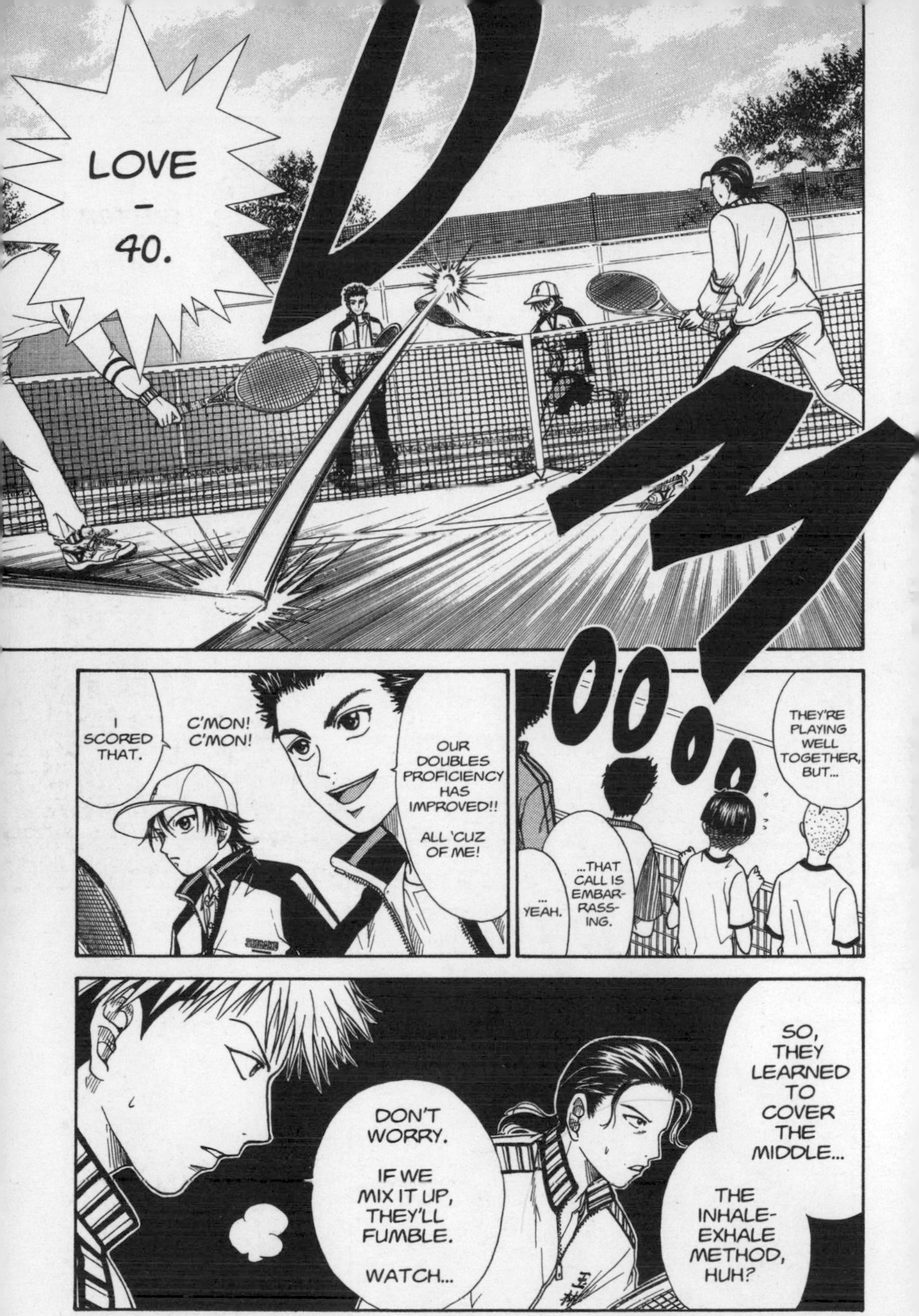
LOVE - 40.
THEY'RE PLAYING WELL TOGETHER, BUT...
...THAT CALL IS EMBARRASSING.
...YEAH.
OUR DOUBLES PROFICIENCY HAS IMPROVED!!
ALL 'CUZ OF ME!
C'MON! C'MON!
I SCORED THAT.
SO, THEY LEARNED TO COVER THE MIDDLE...
THE INHALE-EXHALE METHOD, HUH?
DON'T WORRY.
IF WE MIX IT UP, THEY'LL FUMBLE.
WATCH...

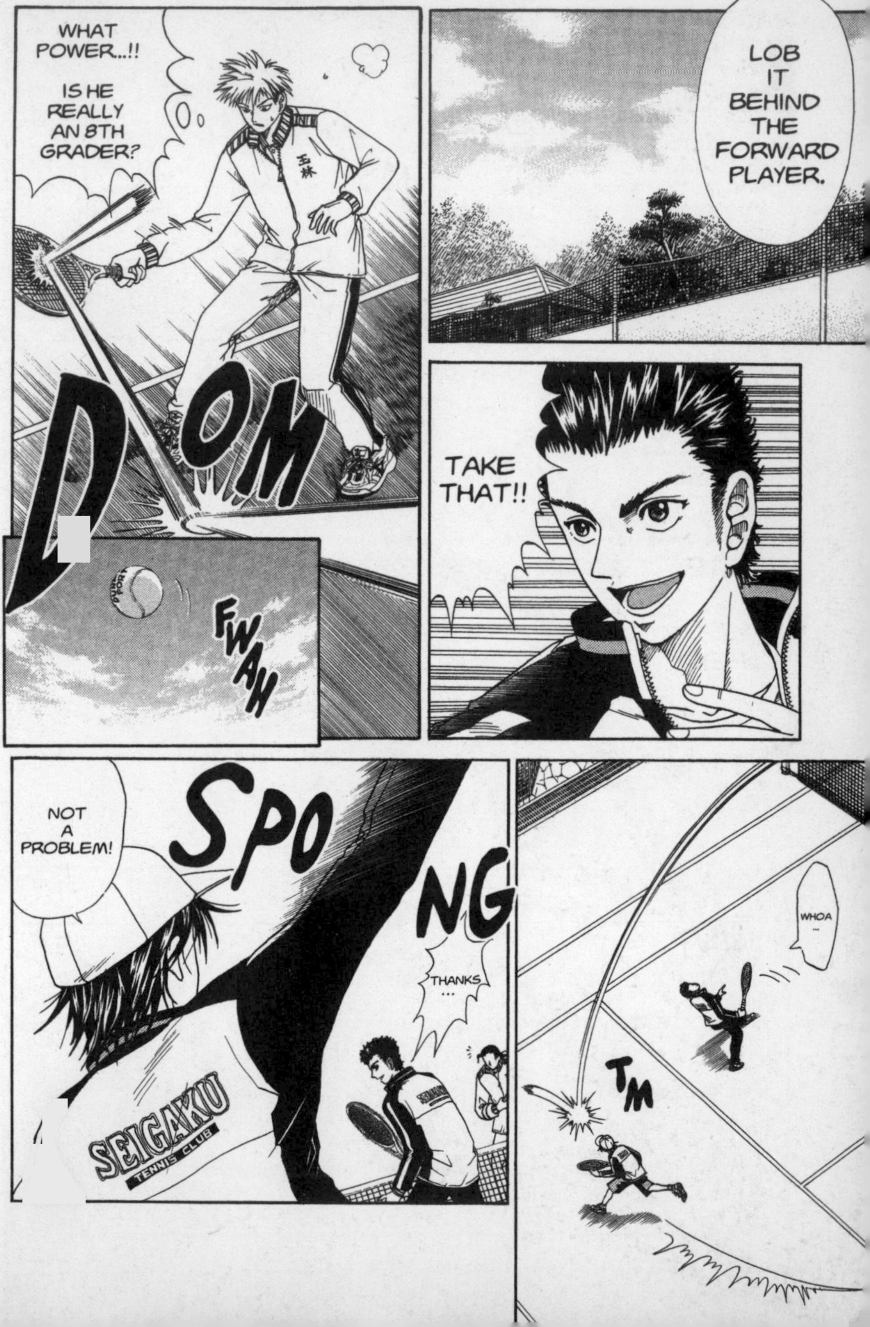
LOB IT BEHIND THE FORWARD PLAYER.
WHAT POWER...!!
IS HE REALLY AN 8TH GRADER?
DOM
TAKE THAT!!
FWAH
WHOA ...
TM
NOT A PROBLEM!
SPONG
THANKS ...
SEIGAKU
TENNIS CLUB

READ THIS WAY

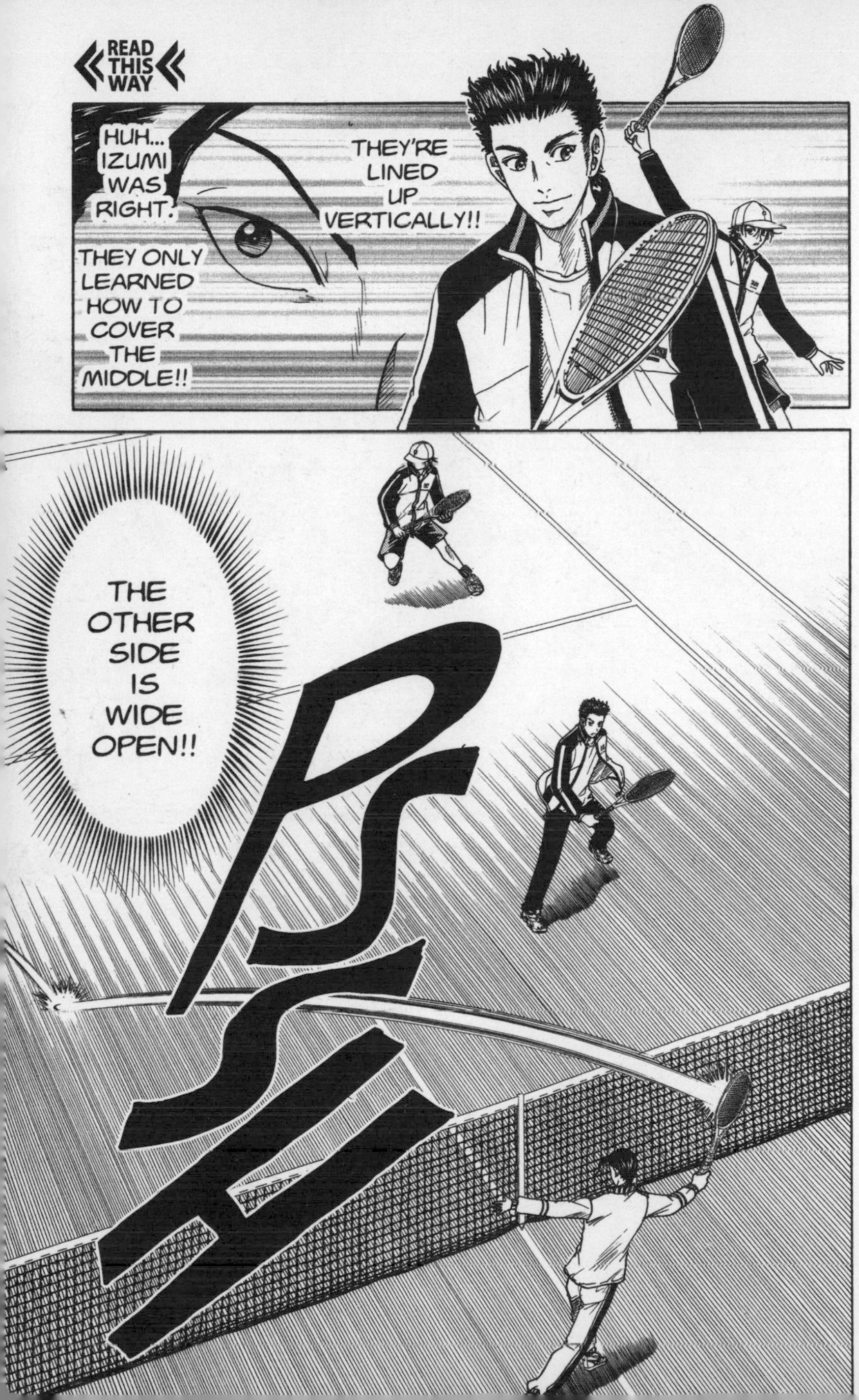
THEY'RE LINED UP VERTICALLY!!
HUH... IZUMI WAS RIGHT.
THEY ONLY LEARNED HOW TO COVER THE MIDDLE!!
THE OTHER SIDE IS WIDE OPEN!!
PSSH

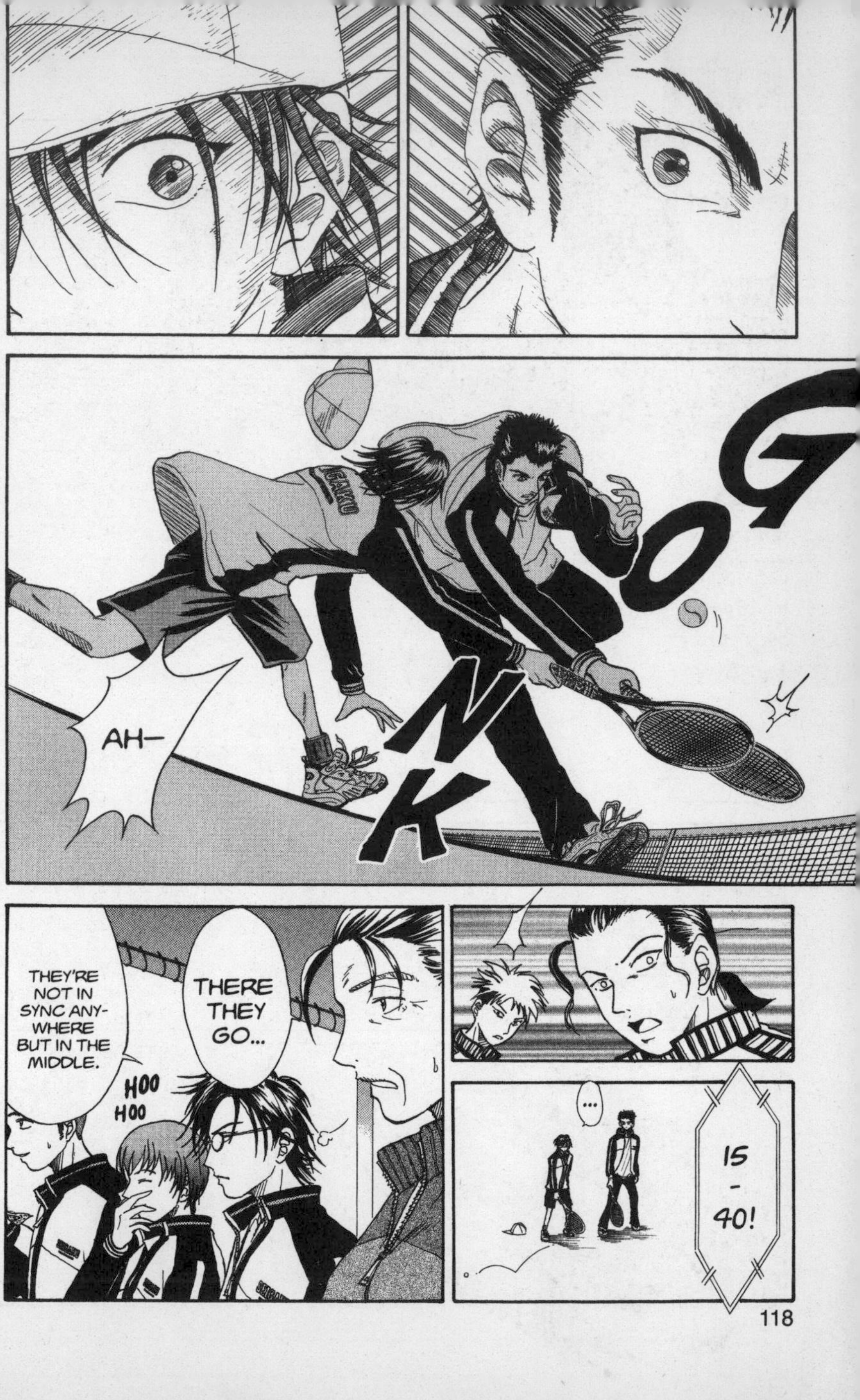
GONK
AH—
...
15 - 40!
THERE THEY GO...
THEY'RE NOT IN SYNC ANYWHERE BUT IN THE MIDDLE.
HOO HOO

READ THIS WAY

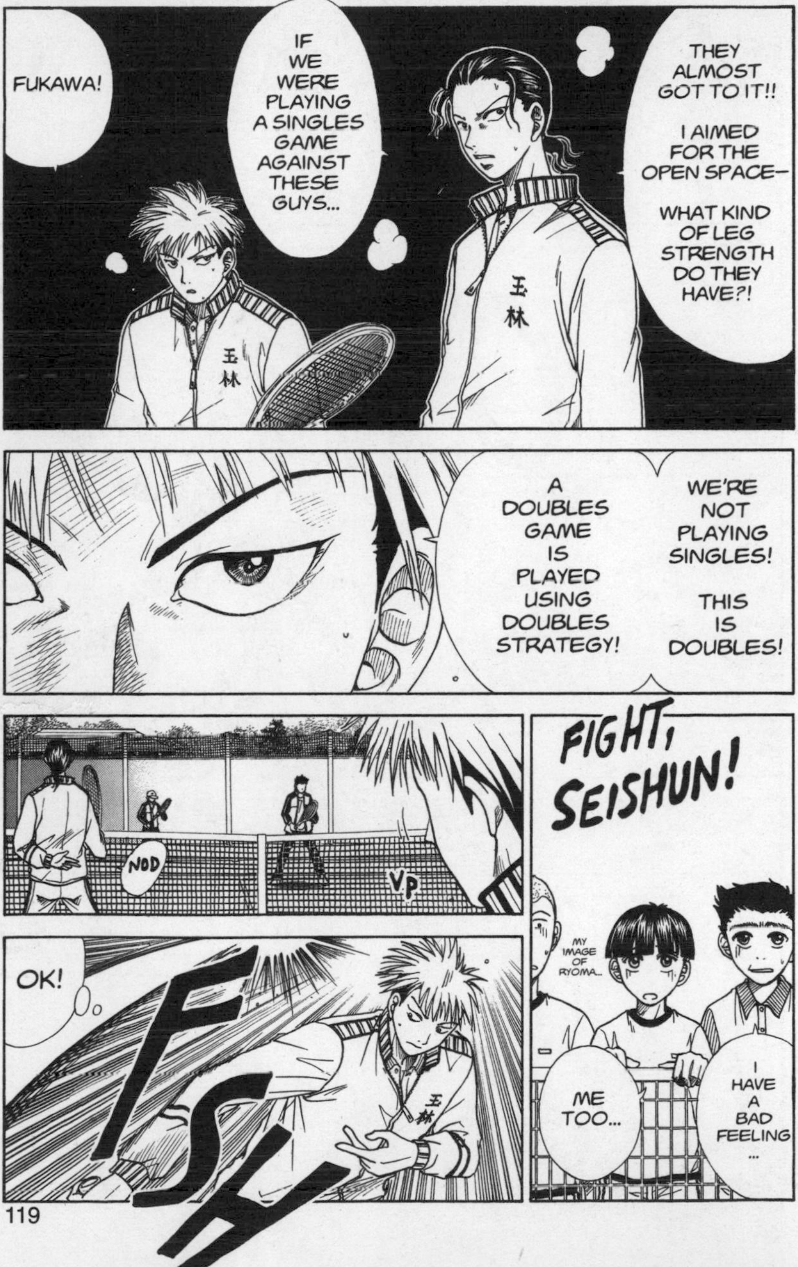

THEY ALMOST GOT TO IT!! I AIMED FOR THE OPEN SPACE— WHAT KIND OF LEG STRENGTH DO THEY HAVE?!
IF WE WERE PLAYING A SINGLES GAME AGAINST THESE GUYS...
FUKAWA!
WE'RE NOT PLAYING SINGLES! THIS IS DOUBLES!
A DOUBLES GAME IS PLAYED USING DOUBLES STRATEGY!
FIGHT, SEISHUN!
MY IMAGE OF RYOMA...
I HAVE A BAD FEELING ...
ME TOO...
VP
NOD
OK!
FSH

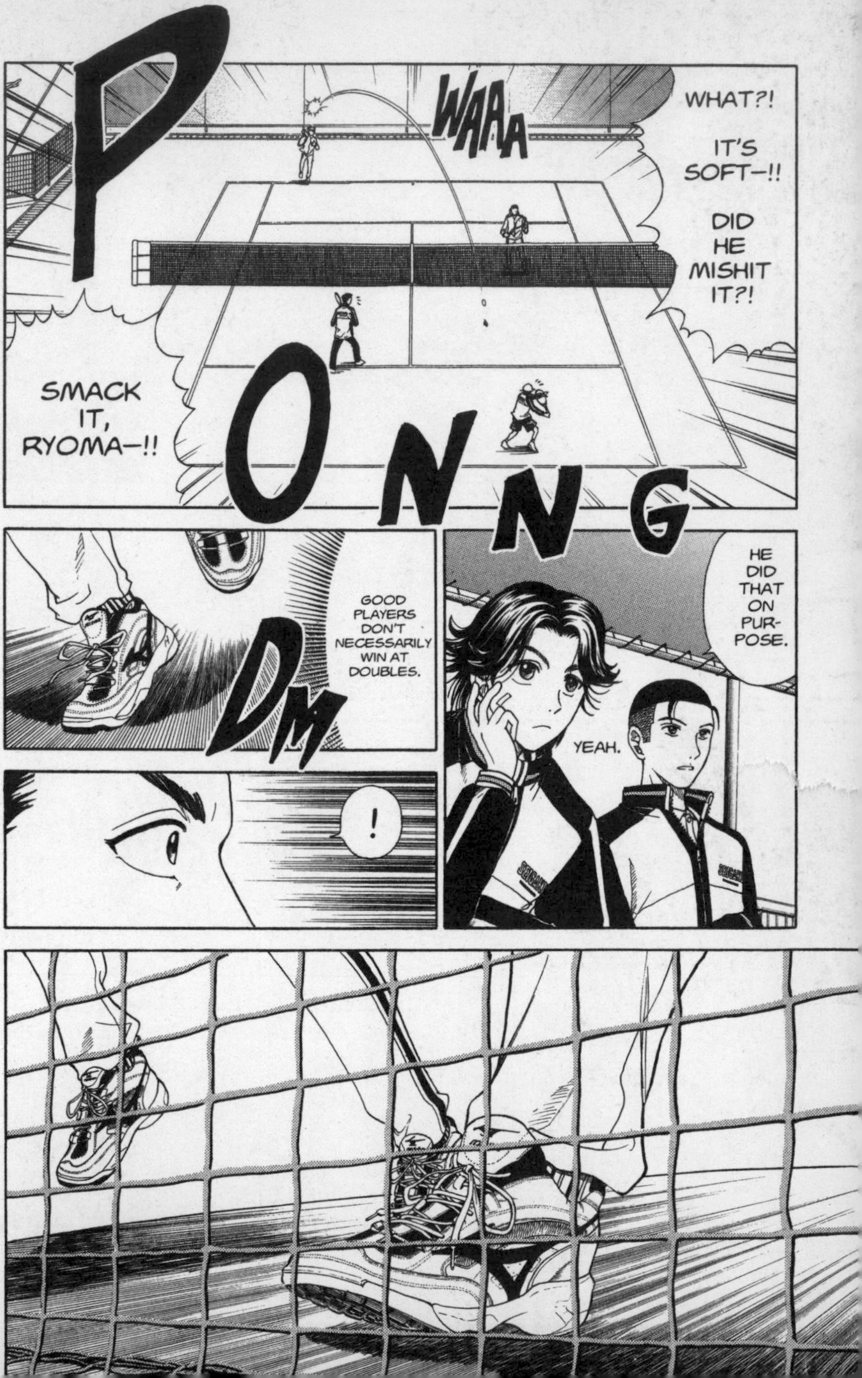
WHAT?!
IT'S SOFT—!!
DID HE MISHIT IT?!
WAAA
PONNG
SMACK IT, RYOMA—!!
HE DID THAT ON PURPOSE.
YEAH.
GOOD PLAYERS DON'T NECESSARILY WIN AT DOUBLES.
DM
!

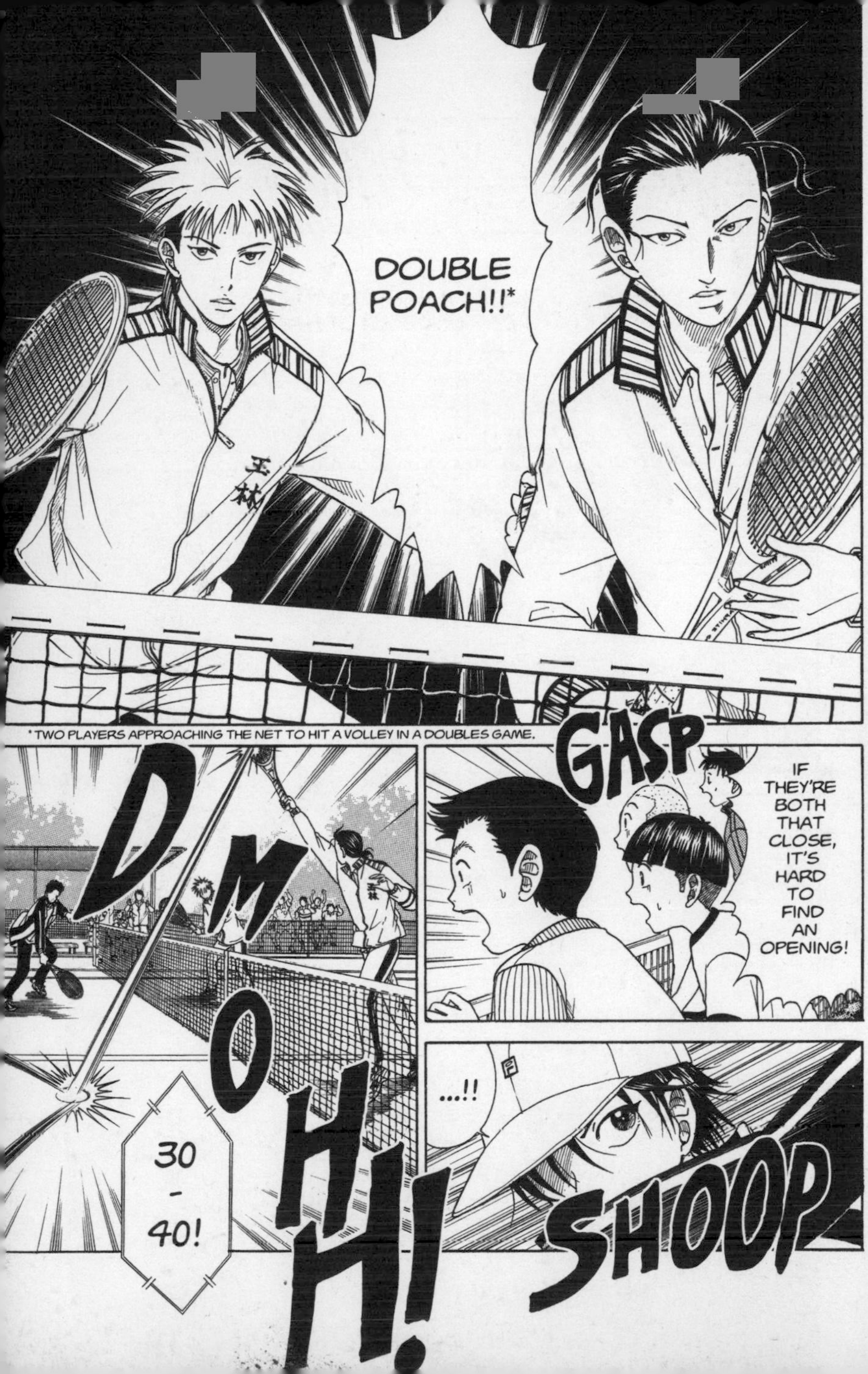
DOUBLE POACH!!*
GASP
IF THEY'RE BOTH THAT CLOSE, IT'S HARD TO FIND AN OPENING!
...!!
SHOOP
DMOHH!
30 - 40!

*TWO PLAYERS APPROACHING THE NET TO HIT A VOLLEY IN A DOUBLES GAME.

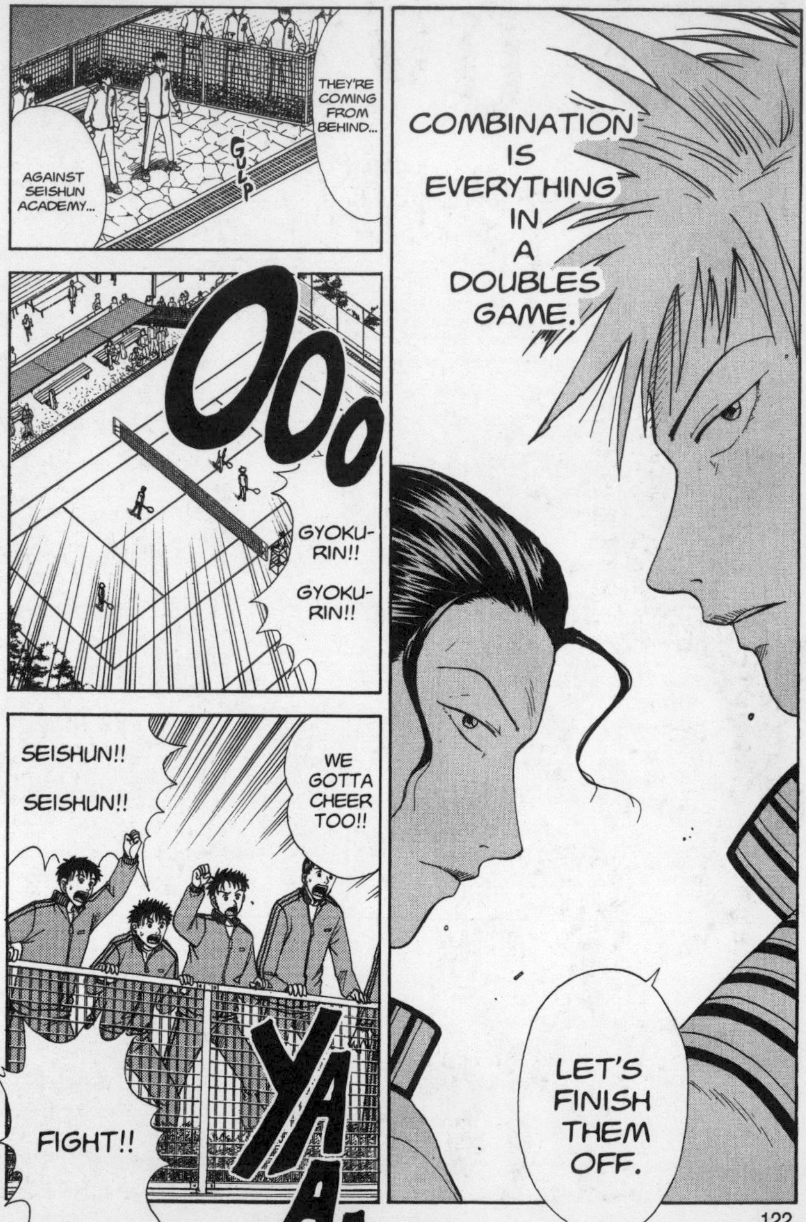
COMBINATION IS EVERYTHING IN A DOUBLES GAME.
LET'S FINISH THEM OFF.
THEY'RE COMING FROM BEHIND...
GULP
AGAINST SEISHUN ACADEMY...
OOO
GYOKU-RIN!!
GYOKU-RIN!!
WE GOTTA CHEER TOO!!
SEISHUN!!
SEISHUN!!
YAAA
FIGHT!!

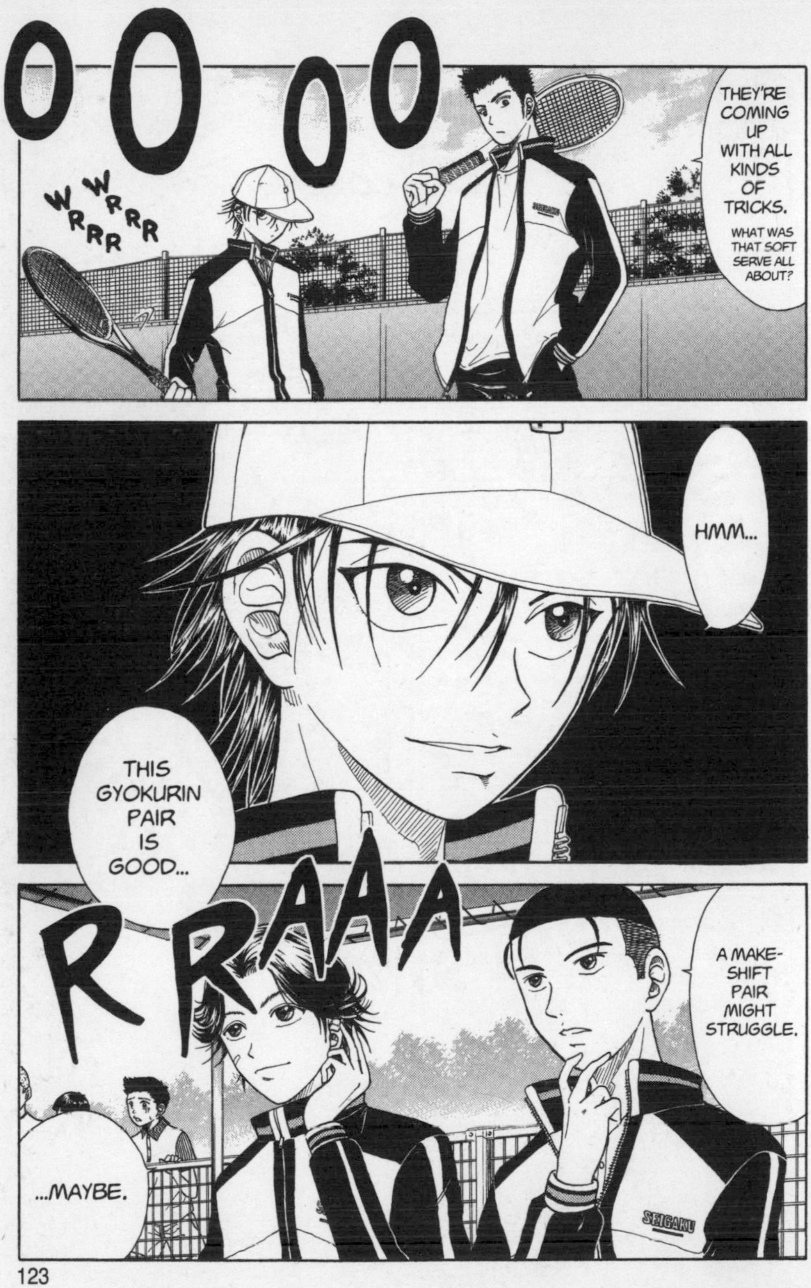
THEY'RE COMING UP WITH ALL KINDS OF TRICKS.
WHAT WAS THAT SOFT SERVE ALL ABOUT?
OOOO
WWRRRRRR
HMM...
THIS GYOKURIN PAIR IS GOOD...
A MAKE-SHIFT PAIR MIGHT STRUGGLE.
RRAAA
...MAYBE.

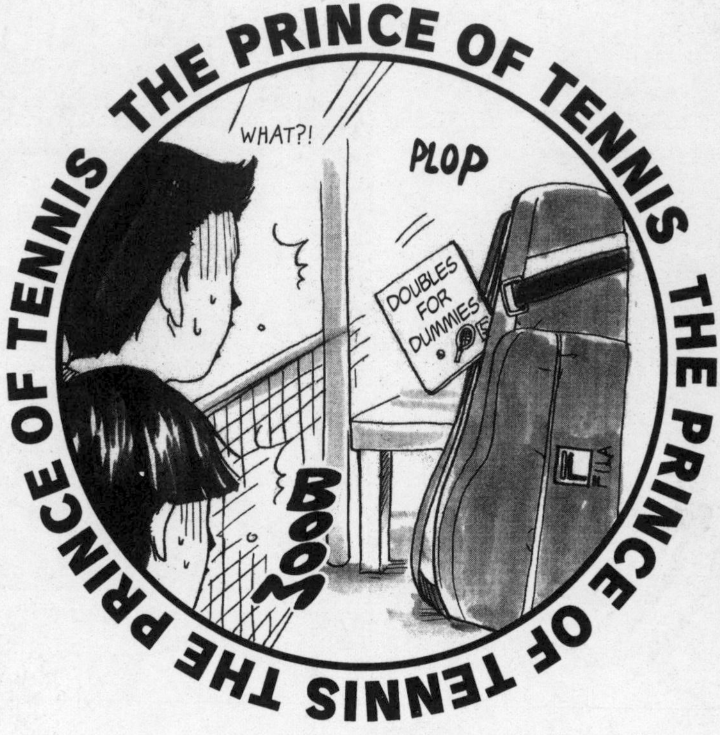
THE PRINCE OF TENNIS THE PRINCE OF TENNIS THE PRINCE OF TENNIS
PLOP
DOUBLES FOR DUMMIES
FILA
WHAT?!
BOOOM

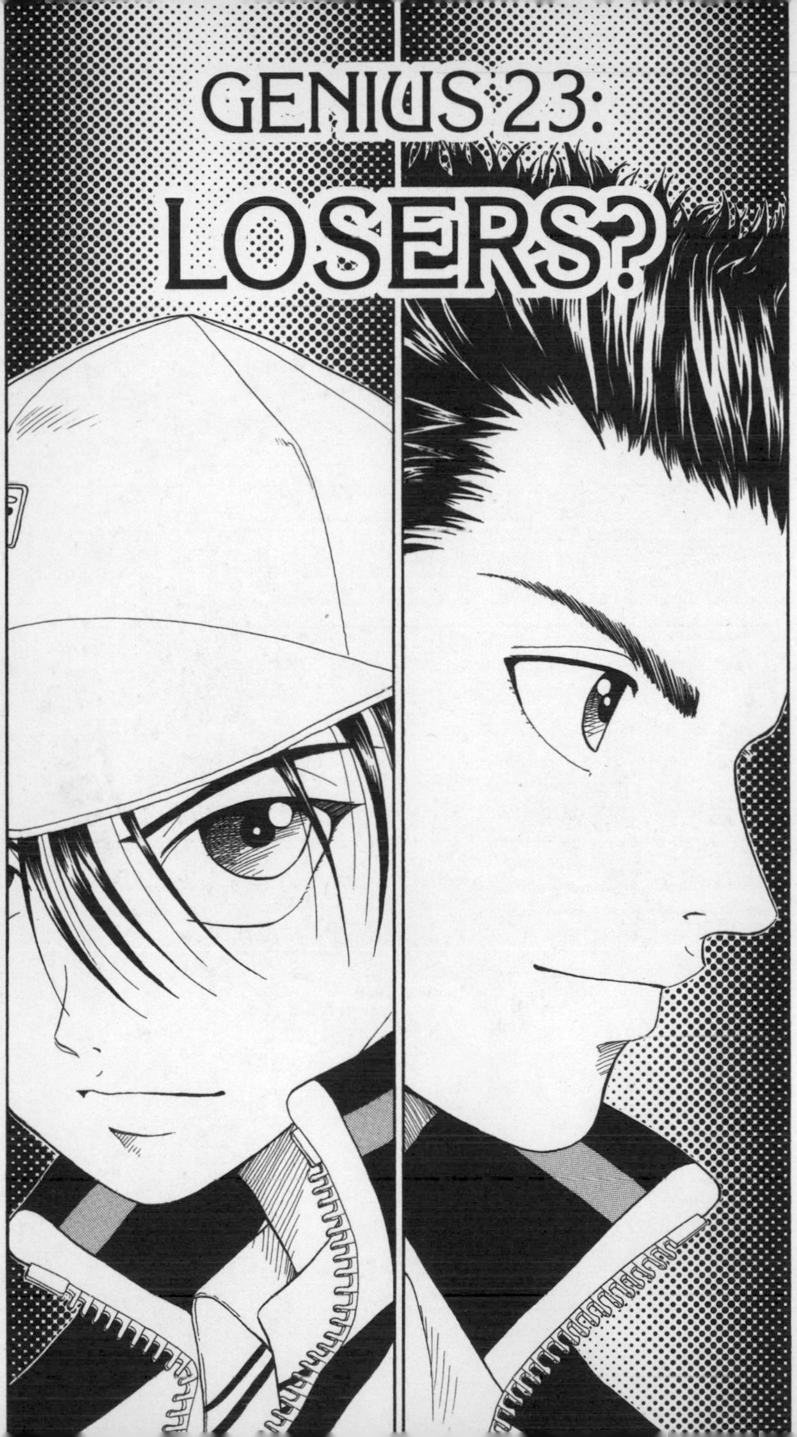
GENIUS 23:
LOSERS?

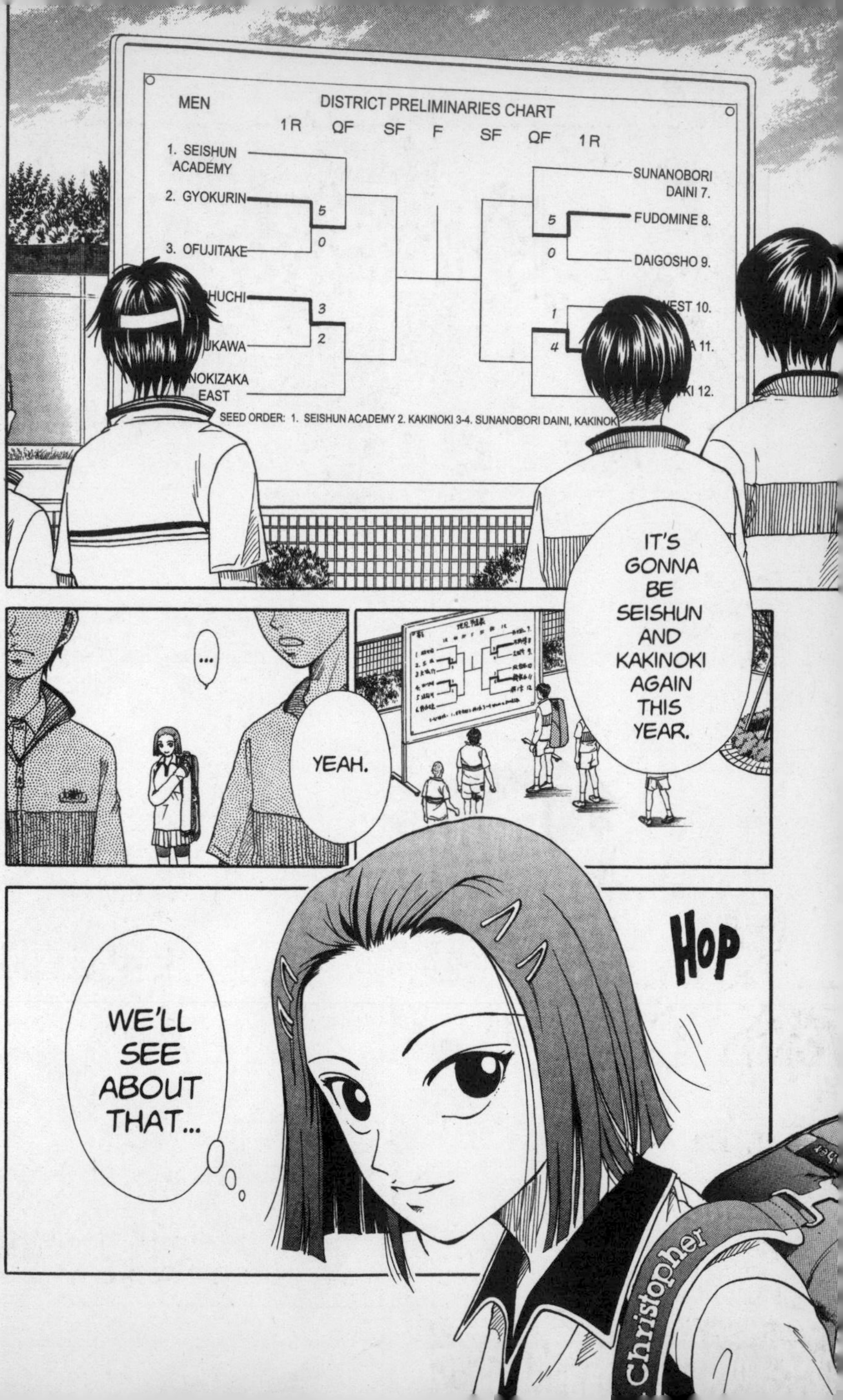
MEN
DISTRICT PRELIMINARIES CHART
1R QF SF F SF QF 1R
1. SEISHUN ACADEMY
2. GYOKURIN
3. OFUJITAKE
SUNANOBORI DAINI 7.
FUDOMINE 8.
DAIGOSHO 9.
5 0 3 2 5 0 1 4
SEED ORDER: 1. SEISHUN ACADEMY 2. KAKINOKI 3-4. SUNANOBORI DAINI, KAKINOK
IT'S GONNA BE SEISHUN AND KAKINOKI AGAIN THIS YEAR.
...
YEAH.
HOP
WE'LL SEE ABOUT THAT...
Christopher

READ THIS WAY

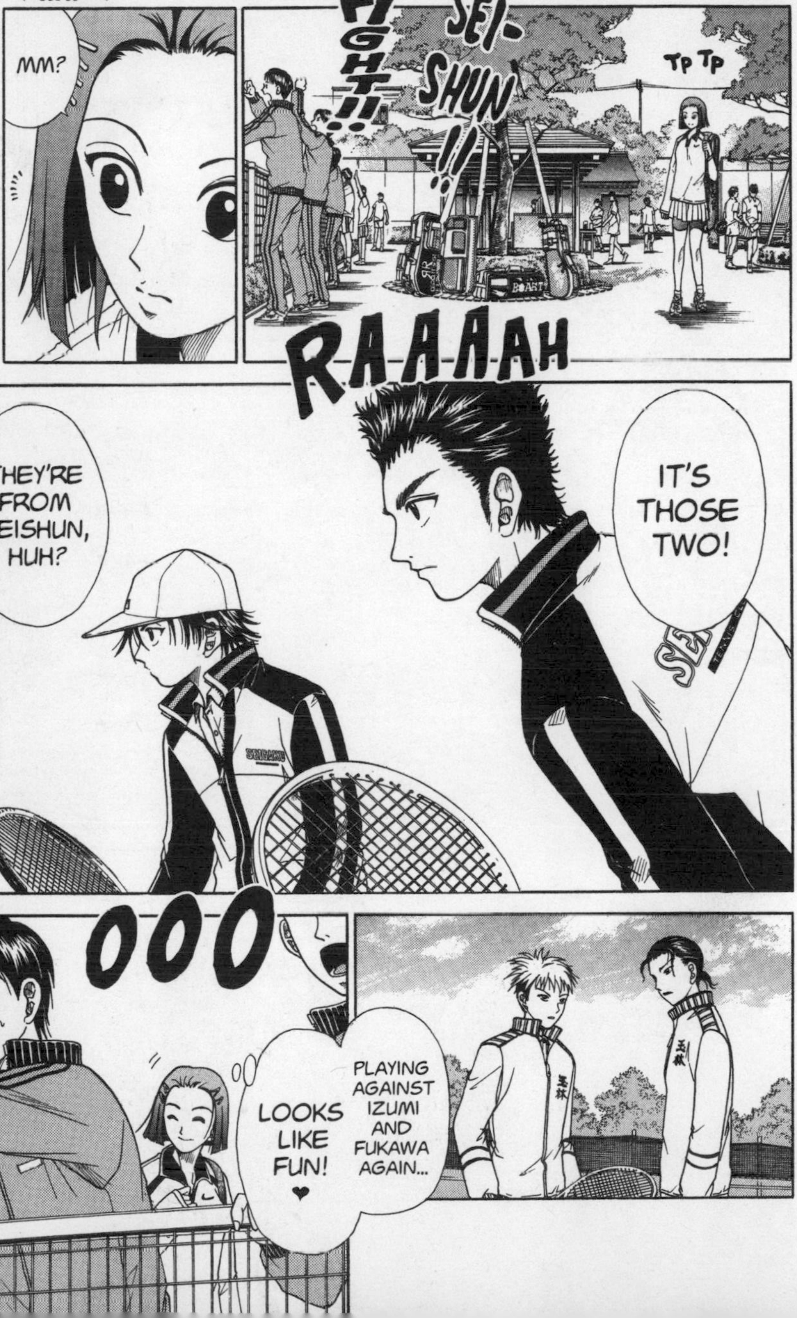
SEI-SHUN!!
FIGHT!!!
Tp Tp
MM?
RAAAAH
IT'S THOSE TWO!
THEY'RE FROM SEISHUN, HUH?
OOO
PLAYING AGAINST IZUMI AND FUKAWA AGAIN...
LOOKS LIKE FUN! ♥

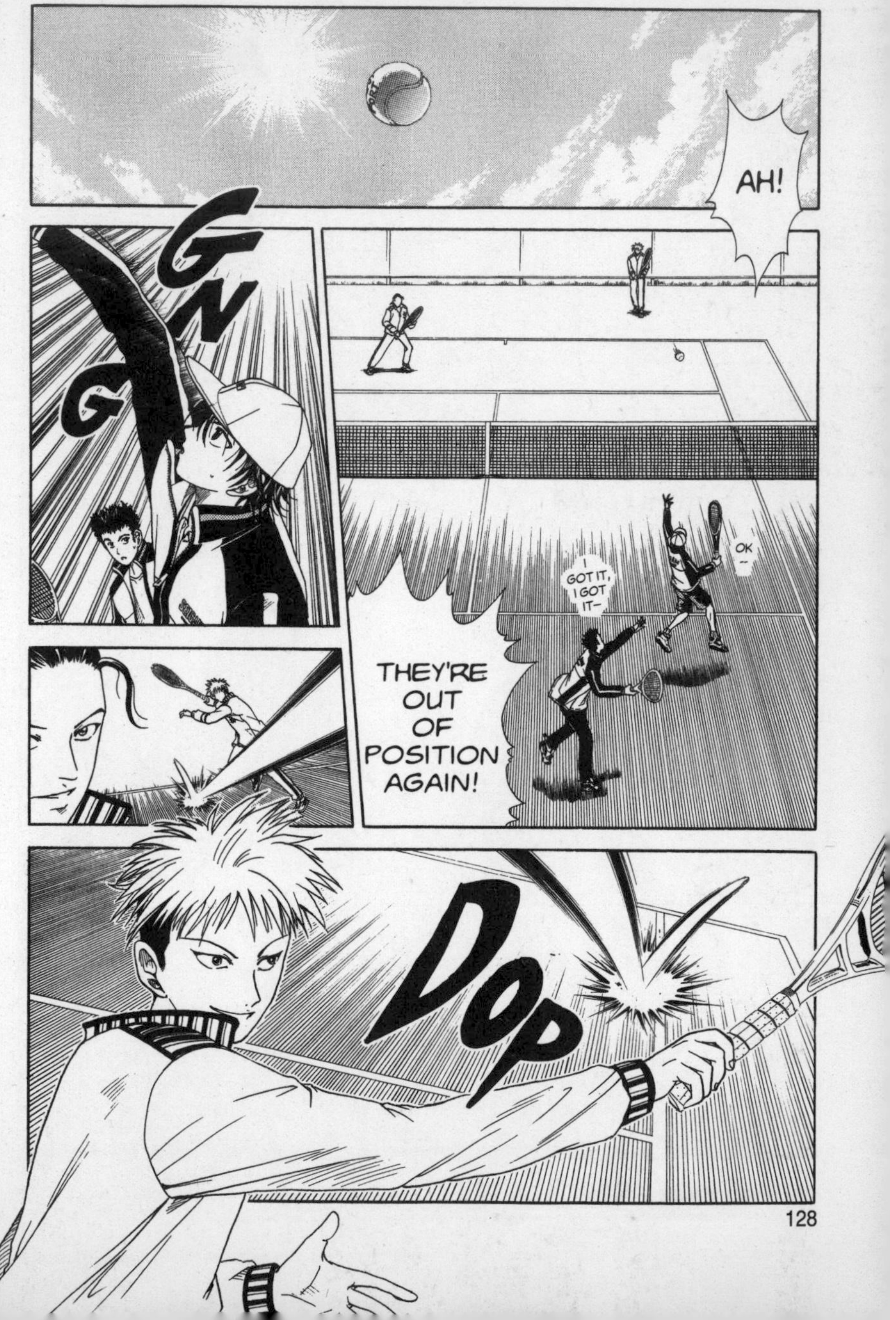
AH!
OK ~
I GOT IT, I GOT IT–
THEY'RE OUT OF POSITION AGAIN!
GNG
DOP

READ THIS WAY

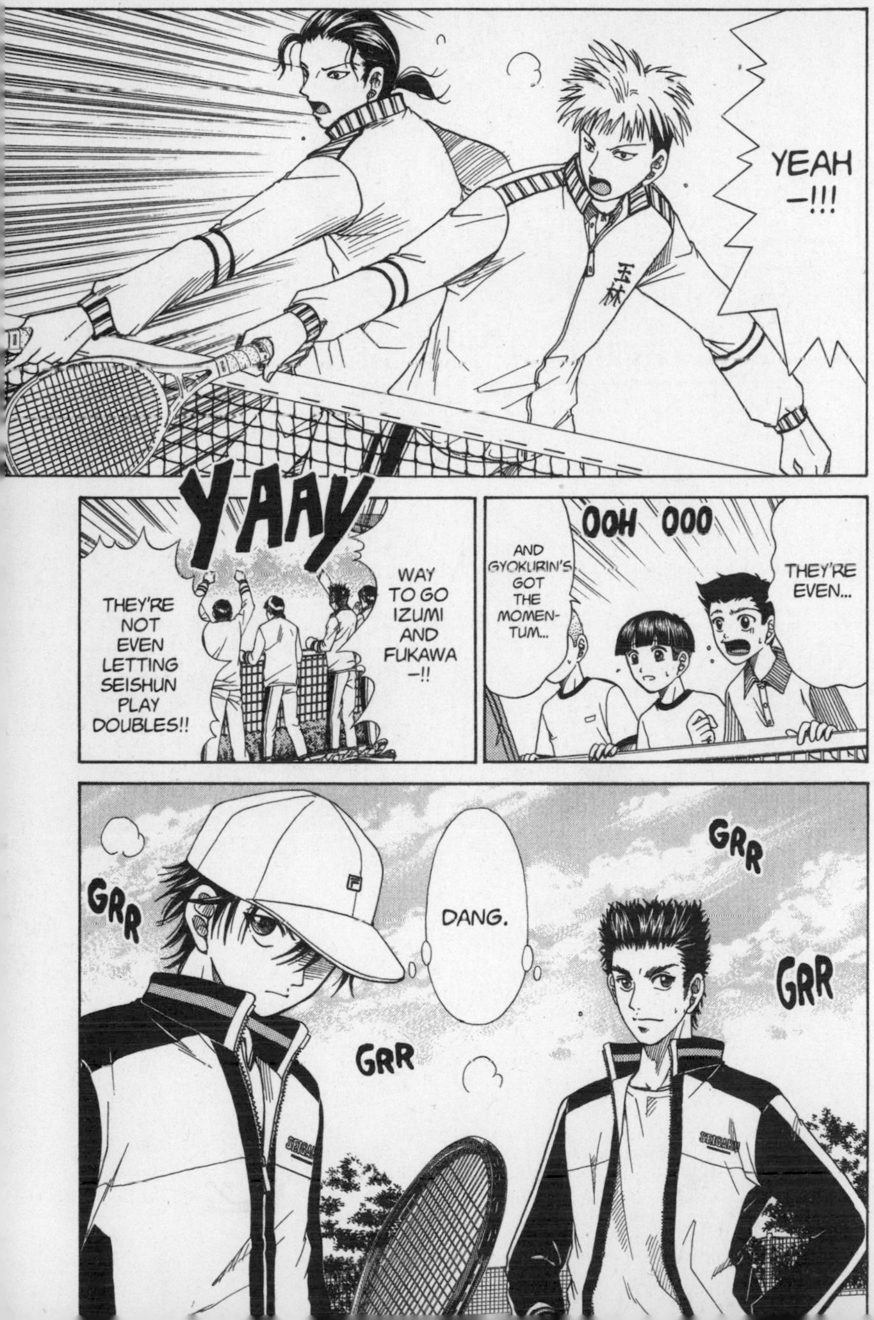
YEAH—!!!
OOH OOO
THEY'RE EVEN...
AND GYOKURIN'S GOT THE MOMENTUM...
YAAY
WAY TO GO IZUMI AND FUKAWA—!!
THEY'RE NOT EVEN LETTING SEISHUN PLAY DOUBLES!!
GRR
GRR
DANG.
GRR
GRR

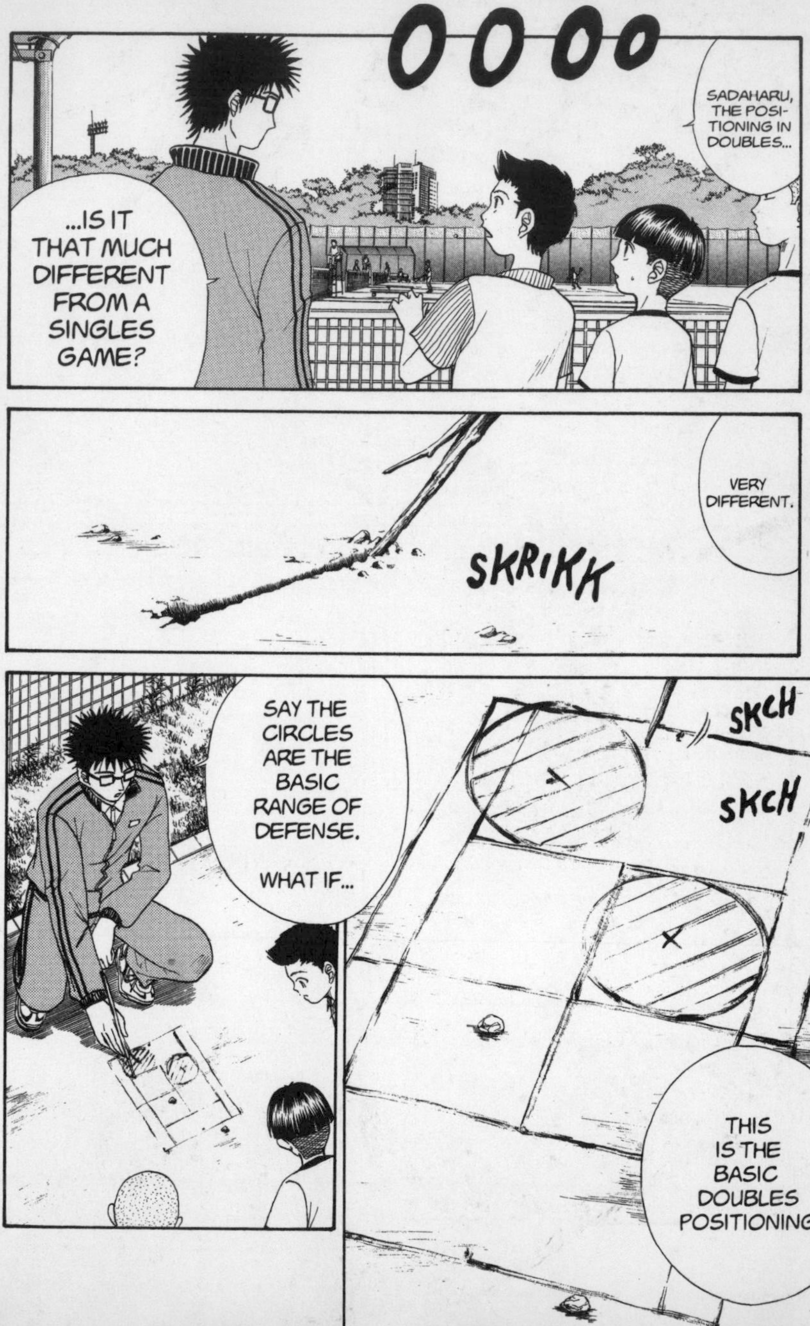
OOOO
SADAHARU, THE POSITIONING IN DOUBLES...
...IS IT THAT MUCH DIFFERENT FROM A SINGLES GAME?
VERY DIFFERENT.
SKRIKK
SKCH
SKCH
THIS IS THE BASIC DOUBLES POSITIONING.
SAY THE CIRCLES ARE THE BASIC RANGE OF DEFENSE.
WHAT IF...

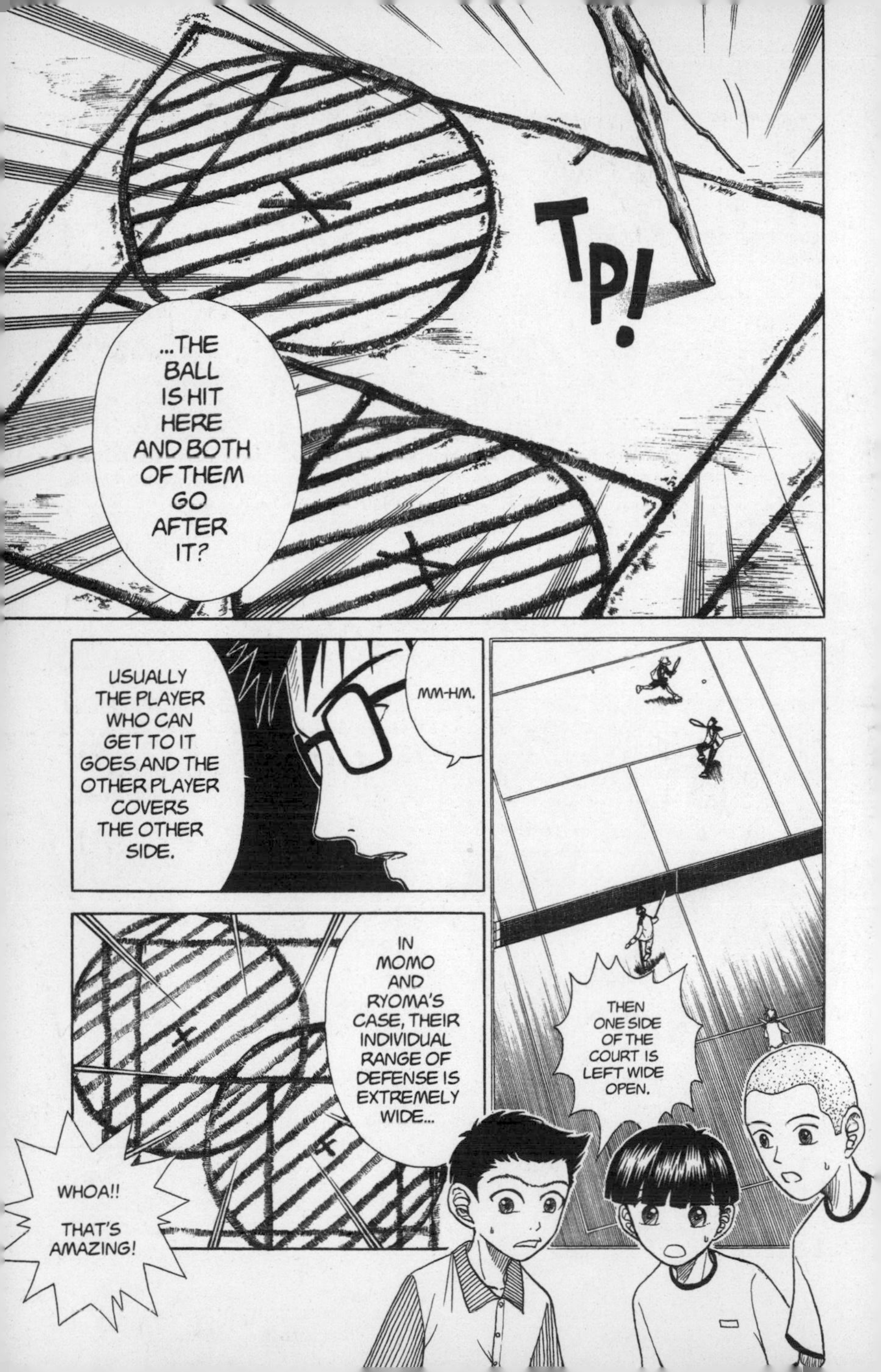
TP!
...THE BALL IS HIT HERE AND BOTH OF THEM GO AFTER IT?
THEN ONE SIDE OF THE COURT IS LEFT WIDE OPEN.
MM-HM.
USUALLY THE PLAYER WHO CAN GET TO IT GOES AND THE OTHER PLAYER COVERS THE OTHER SIDE.
IN MOMO AND RYOMA'S CASE, THEIR INDIVIDUAL RANGE OF DEFENSE IS EXTREMELY WIDE...
WHOA!! THAT'S AMAZING!

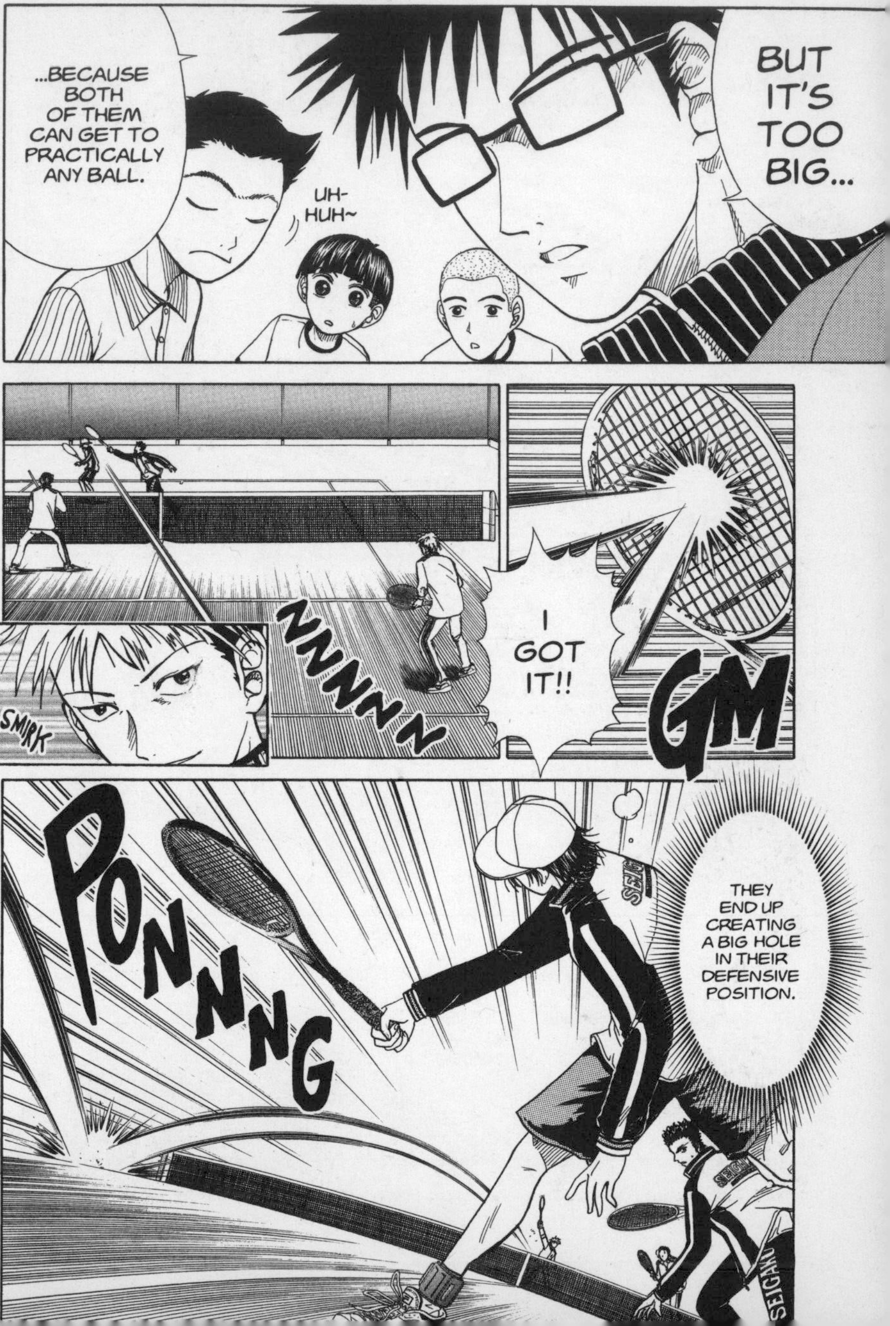
...BECAUSE BOTH OF THEM CAN GET TO PRACTICALLY ANY BALL.
UH-HUH~
BUT IT'S TOO BIG...
NNNNNN
SMIRK
I GOT IT!!
GM
PONNNG
THEY END UP CREATING A BIG HOLE IN THEIR DEFENSIVE POSITION.

READ THIS WAY

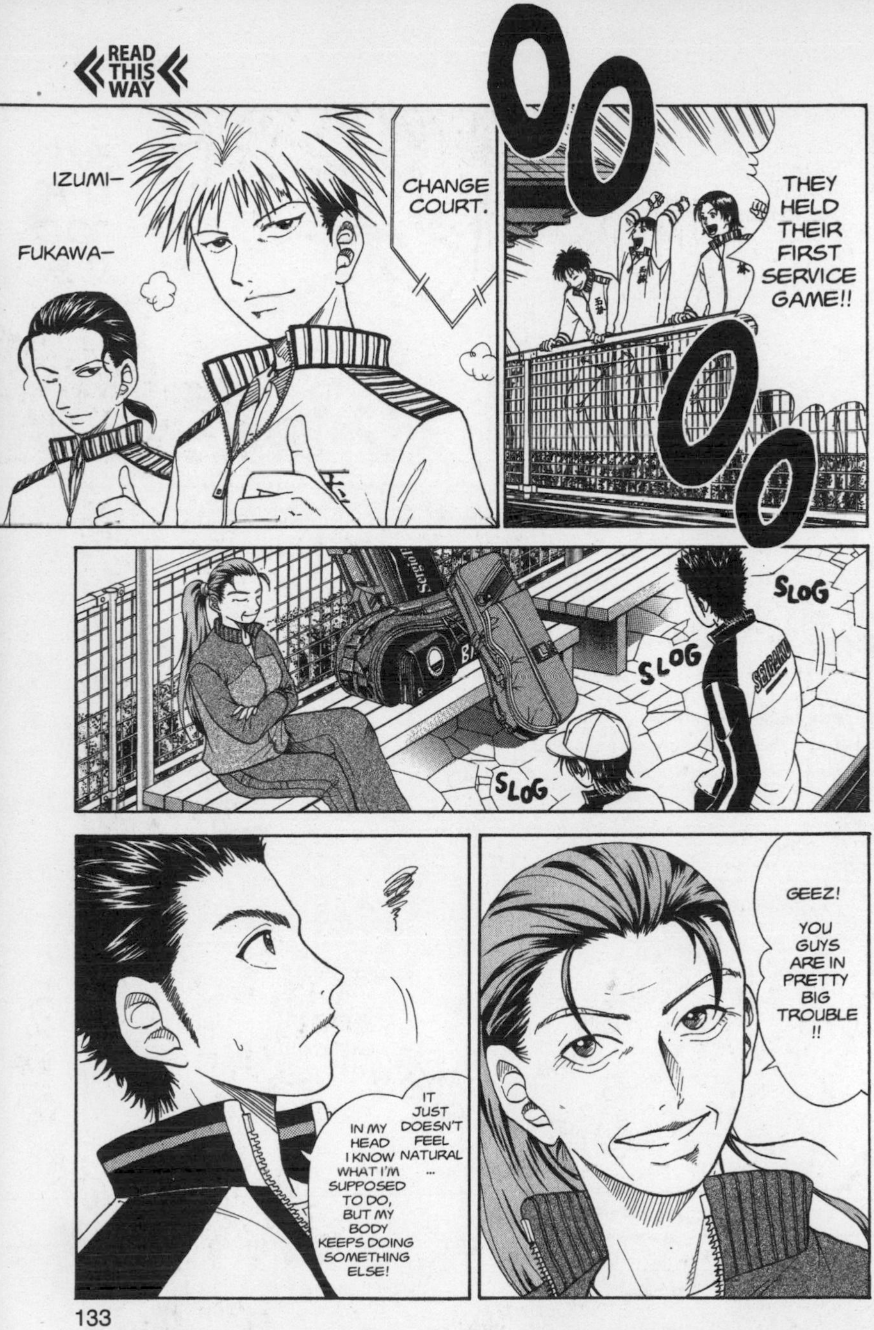

OOOO
THEY HELD THEIR FIRST SERVICE GAME!!
CHANGE COURT.
IZUMI–
FUKAWA–
SLOG
SLOG
SLOG
GEEZ!
YOU GUYS ARE IN PRETTY BIG TROUBLE!!
IT JUST DOESN'T FEEL NATURAL...
IN MY HEAD I KNOW WHAT I'M SUPPOSED TO DO, BUT MY BODY KEEPS DOING SOMETHING ELSE!

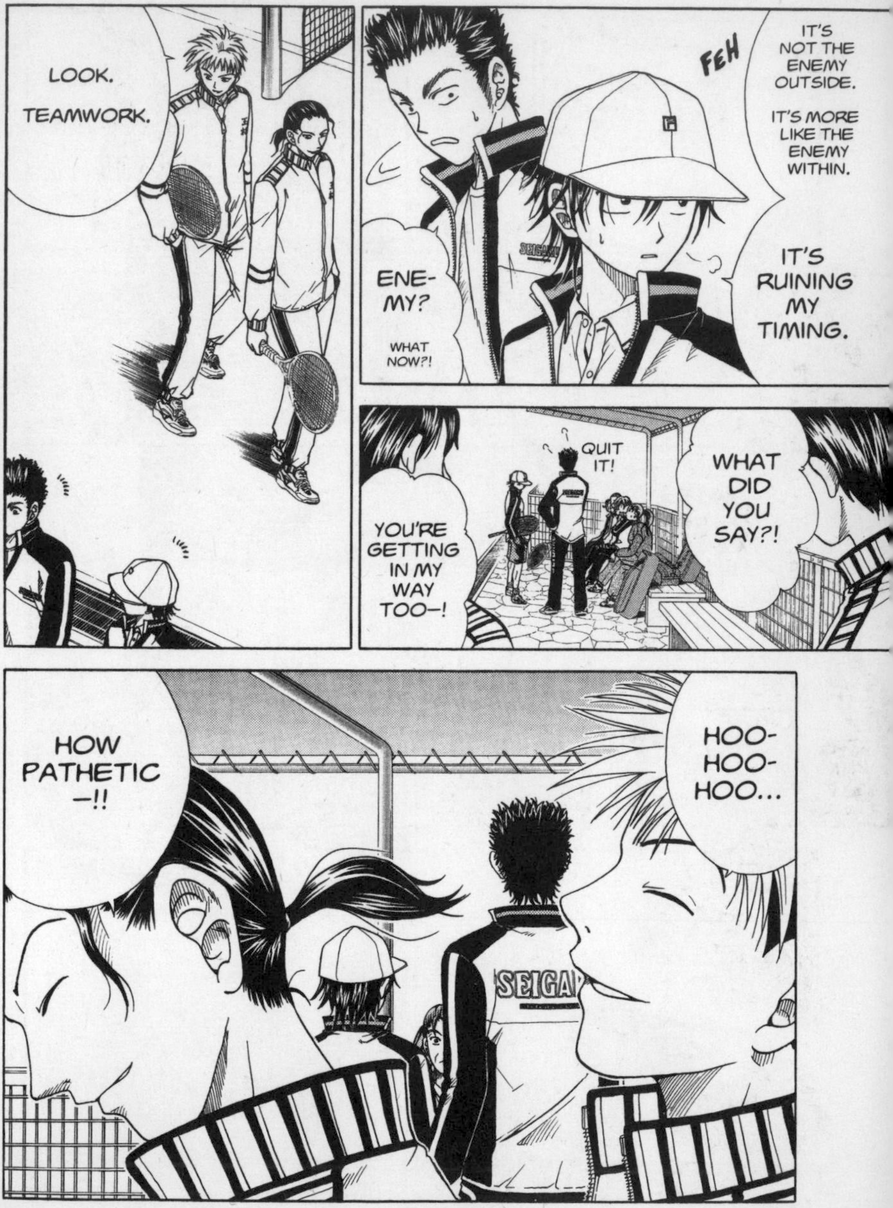
FEH
IT'S NOT THE ENEMY OUTSIDE.
IT'S MORE LIKE THE ENEMY WITHIN.
IT'S RUINING MY TIMING.
ENE-MY?
WHAT NOW?!
WHAT DID YOU SAY?!
QUIT IT!
YOU'RE GETTING IN MY WAY TOO—!
LOOK.
TEAMWORK.
HOO-HOO-HOO...
HOW PATHETIC—!!

READ THIS WAY

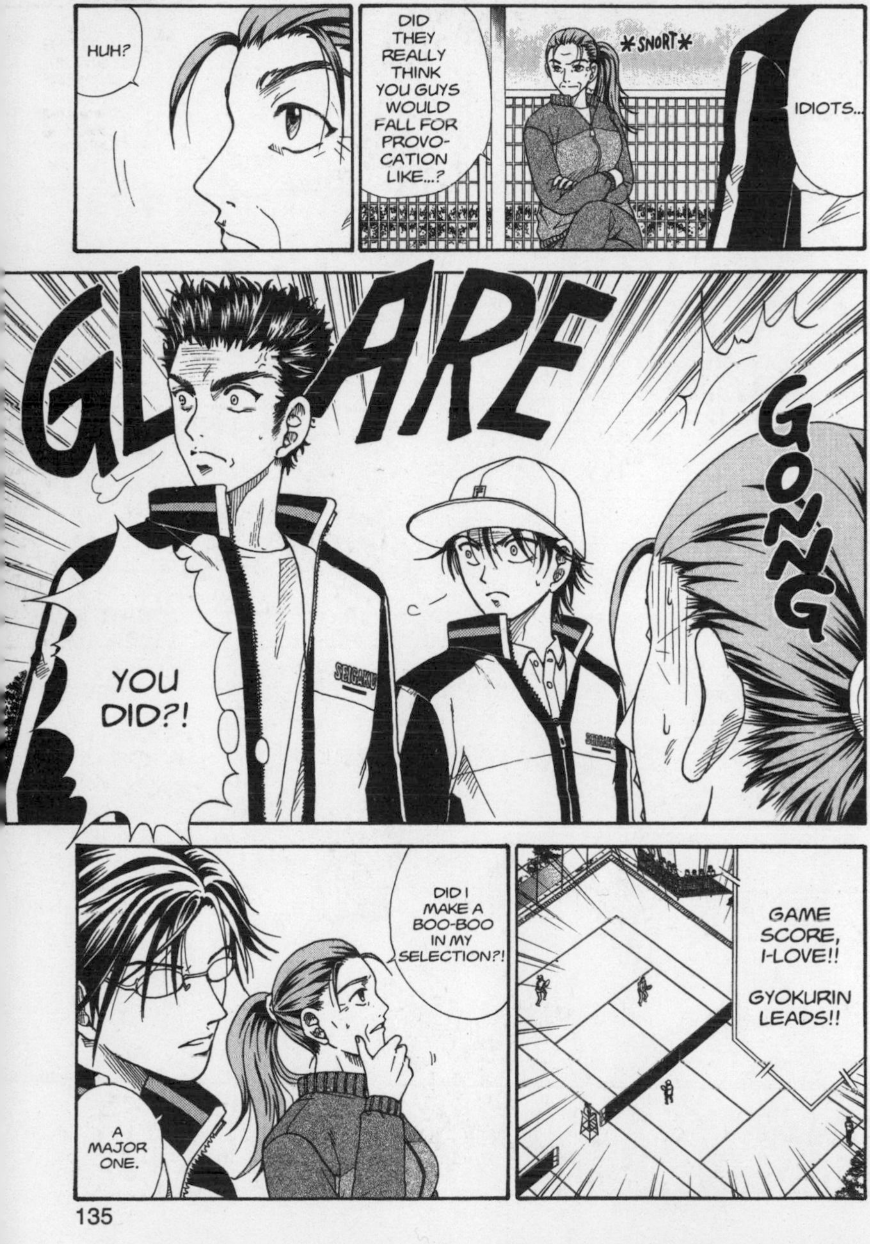

IDIOTS...
SNORT
DID THEY REALLY THINK YOU GUYS WOULD FALL FOR PROVOCATION LIKE...?
HUH?
GONG
GLARE
YOU DID?!
GAME SCORE, I-LOVE!!
GYOKURIN LEADS!!
DID I MAKE A BOO-BOO IN MY SELECTION?!
A MAJOR ONE.

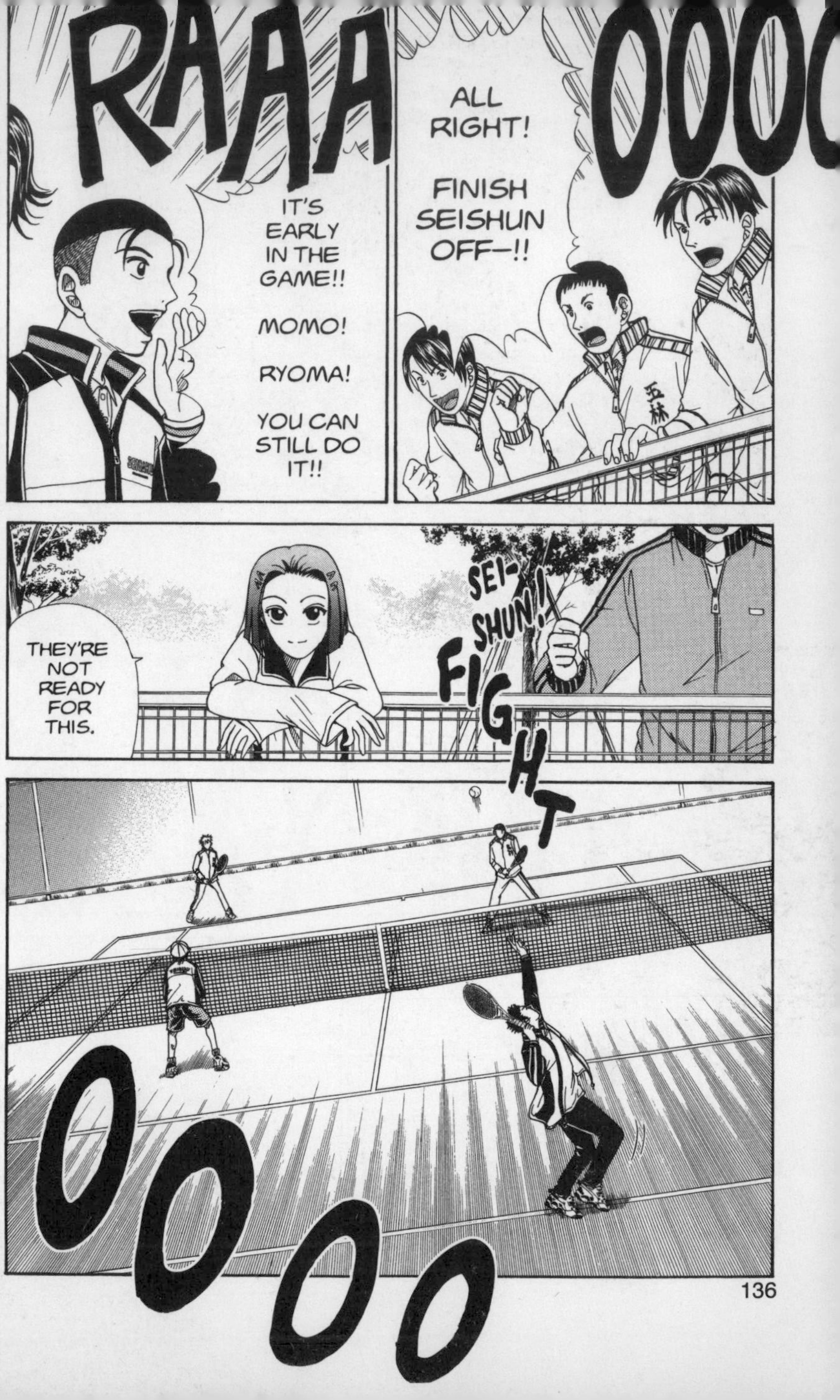
OOOO
ALL RIGHT!
FINISH SEISHUN OFF—!!
RAAA
IT'S EARLY IN THE GAME!!
MOMO!
RYOMA!
YOU CAN STILL DO IT!!
SEI-SHUN!!
FIGHT
THEY'RE NOT READY FOR THIS.
OOOO

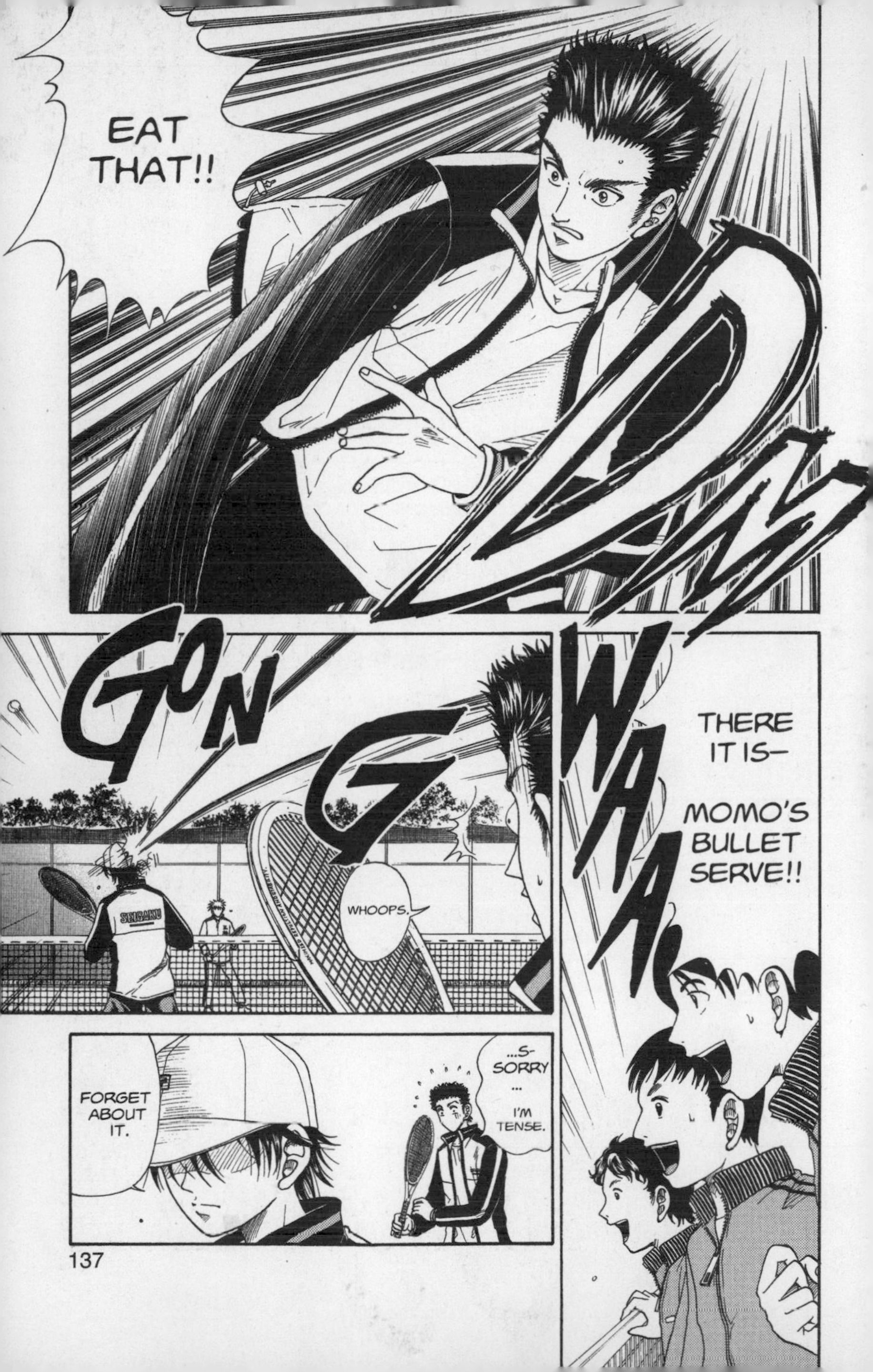
EAT THAT!!
THERE IT IS—
MOMO'S BULLET SERVE!!
GON
WHOOPS.
...S-SORRY ... I'M TENSE.
FORGET ABOUT IT.

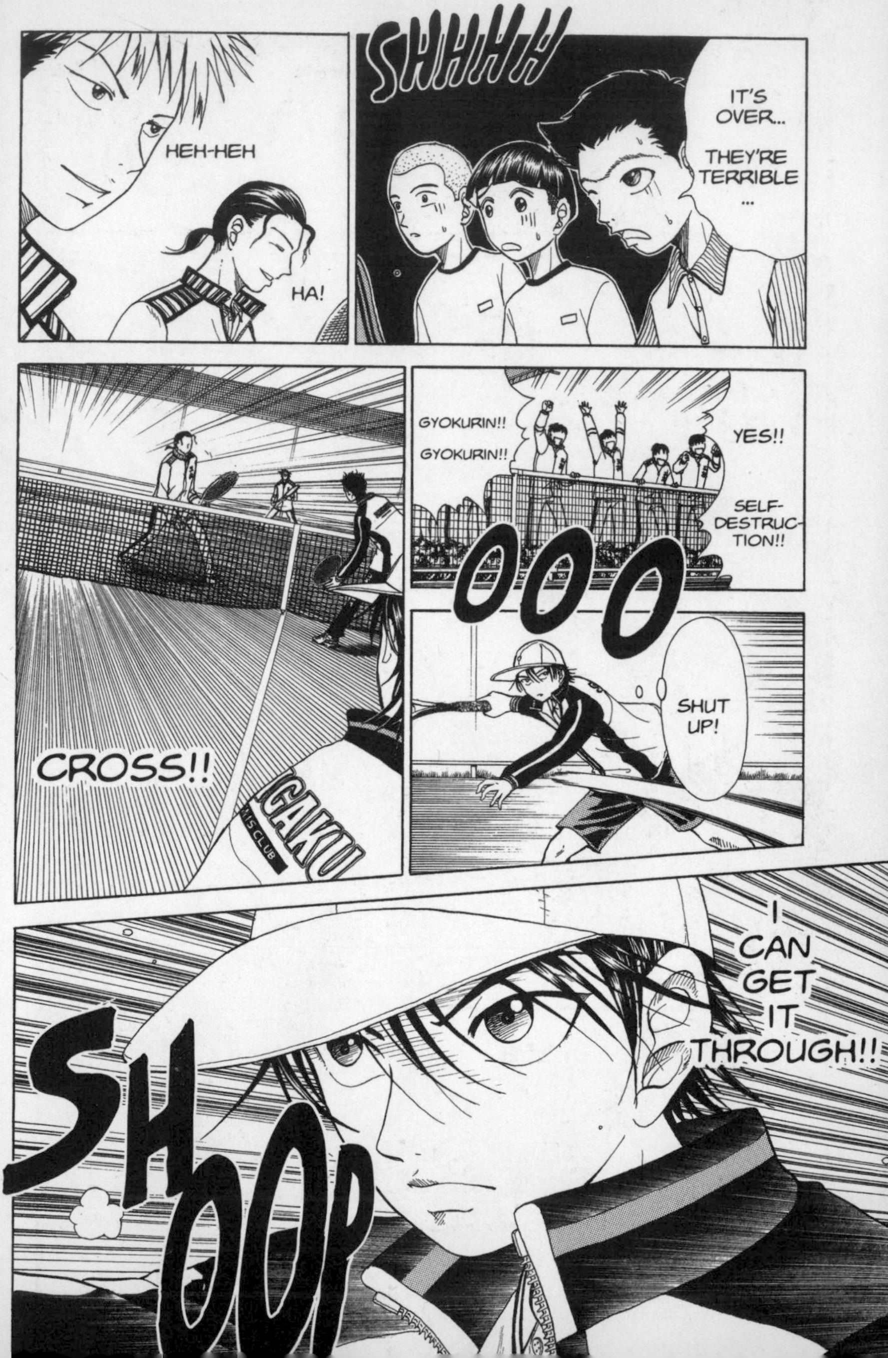
SHHHH
IT'S OVER...
THEY'RE TERRIBLE ...
HEH-HEH
HA!
YES!!
GYOKURIN!!
GYOKURIN!!
SELF-DESTRUCTION!!
OOO
SHUT UP!
CROSS!!
I CAN GET IT THROUGH!!
SHOOP

READ THIS WAY

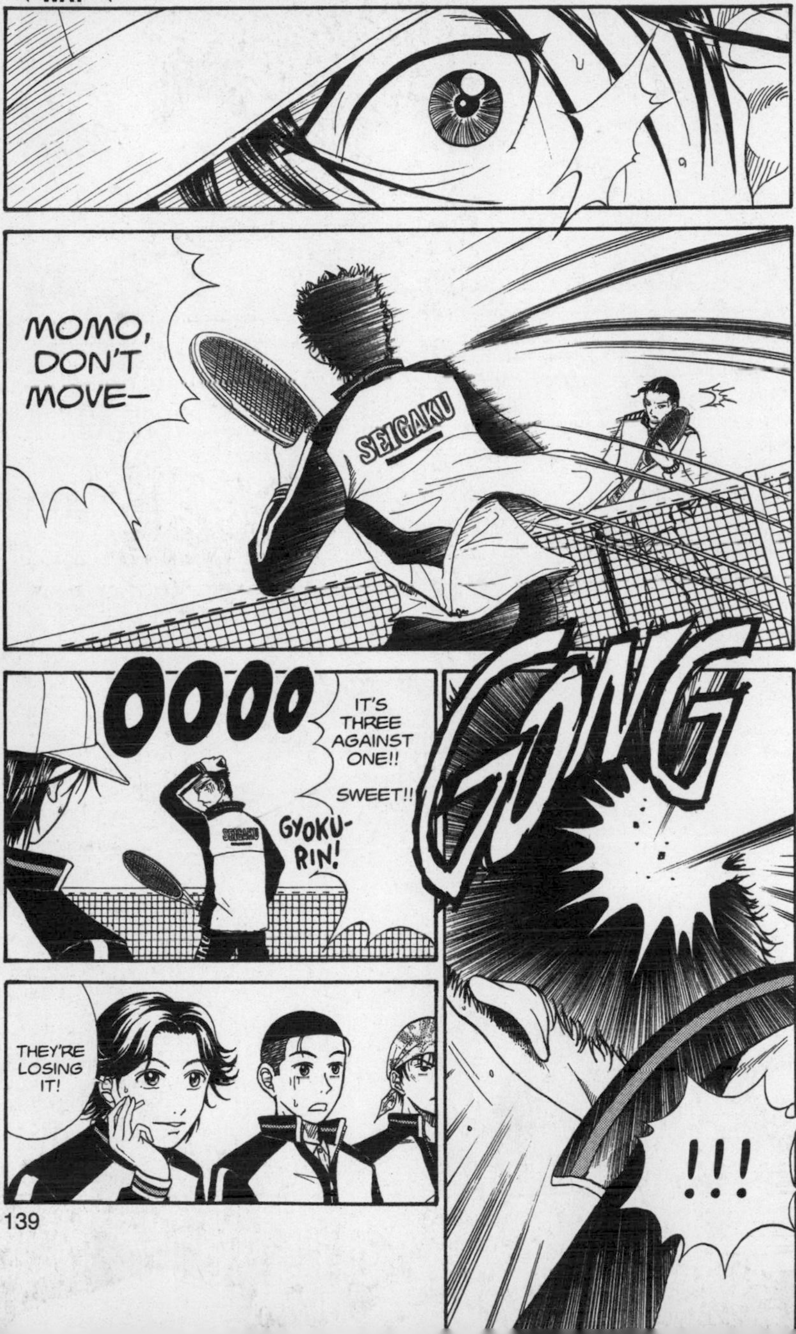

MOMO, DON'T MOVE–
GONG
!!!
IT'S THREE AGAINST ONE!!
SWEET!!
OOOO
GYOKU-RIN!
THEY'RE LOSING IT!

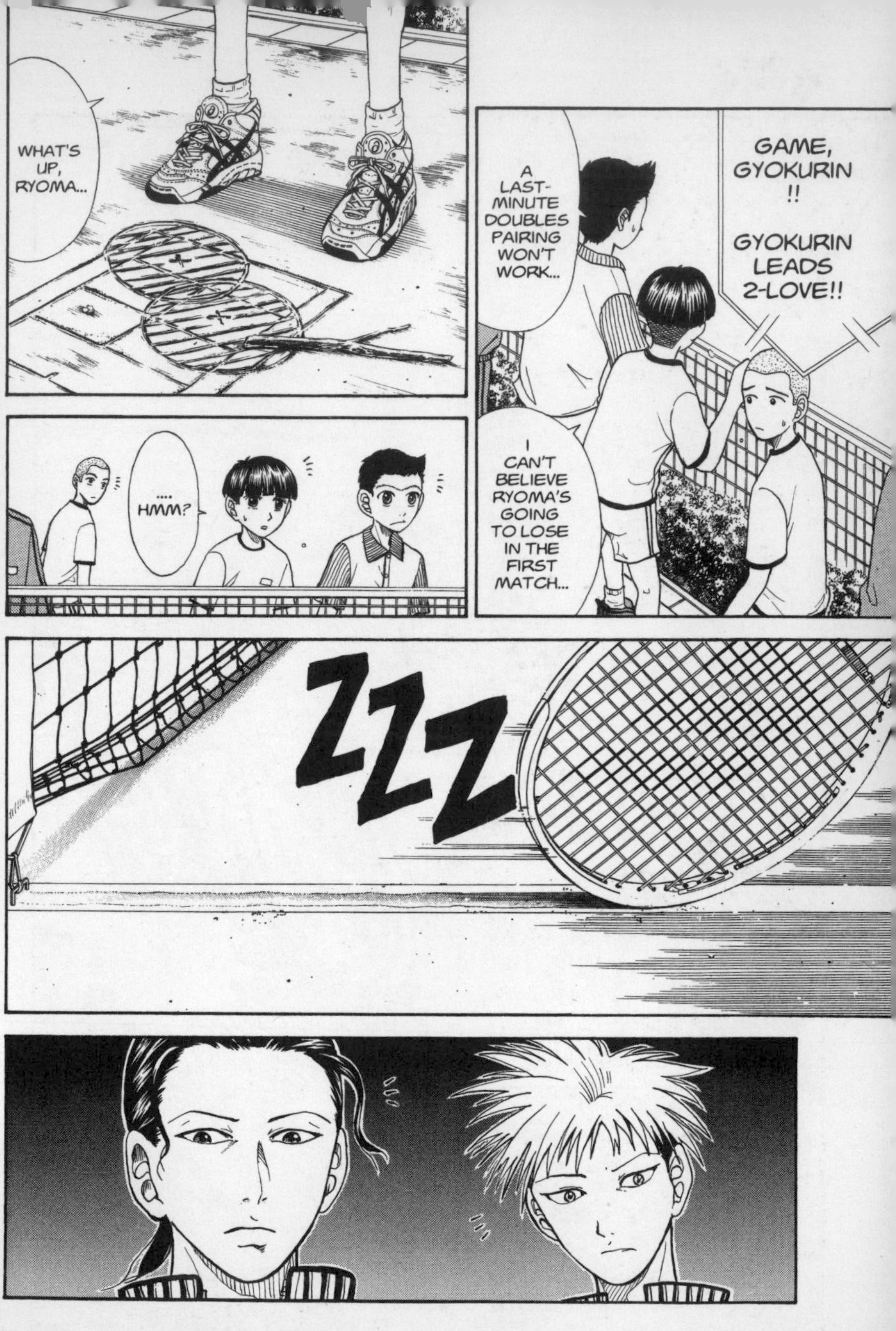
GAME, GYOKURIN !!
GYOKURIN LEADS 2-LOVE!!
A LAST-MINUTE DOUBLES PAIRING WON'T WORK...
I CAN'T BELIEVE RYOMA'S GOING TO LOSE IN THE FIRST MATCH...
WHAT'S UP, RYOMA...
.... HMM?
ZZZ

READ THIS WAY

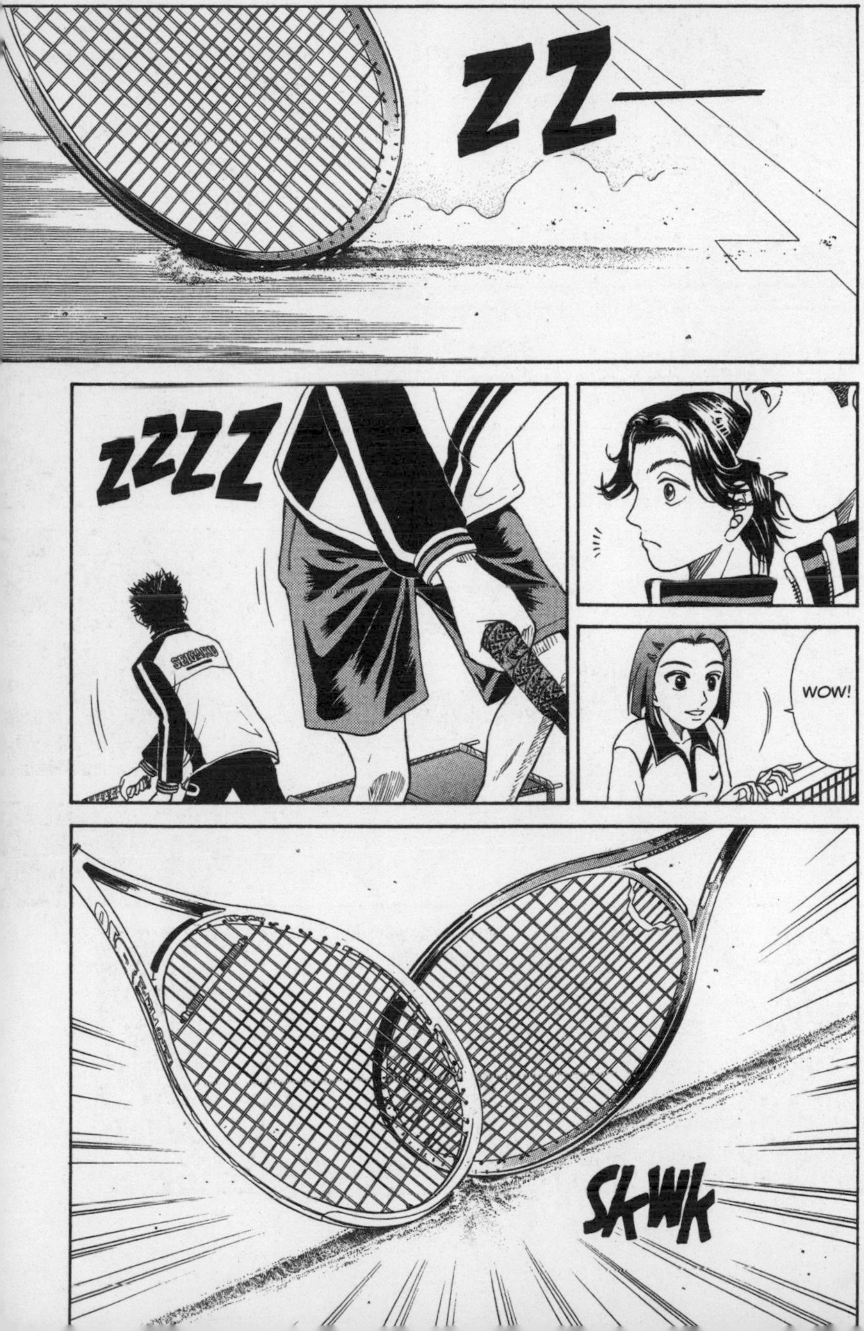
ZZ—
WOW!
ZZZZ
SK-WK

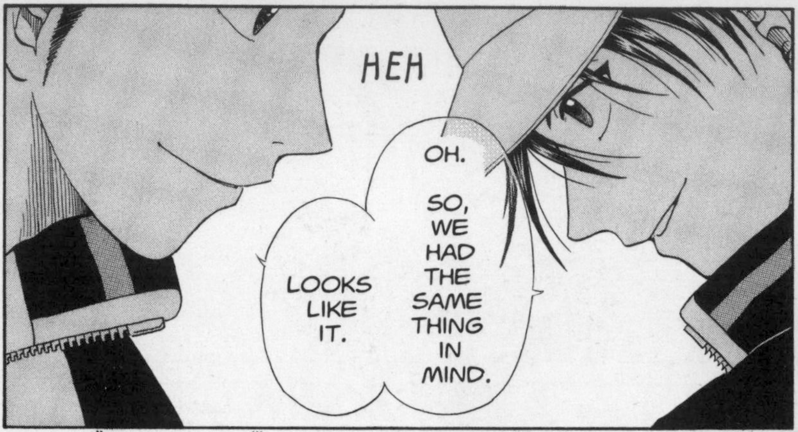
HEH
OH. SO, WE HAD THE SAME THING IN MIND.
LOOKS LIKE IT.
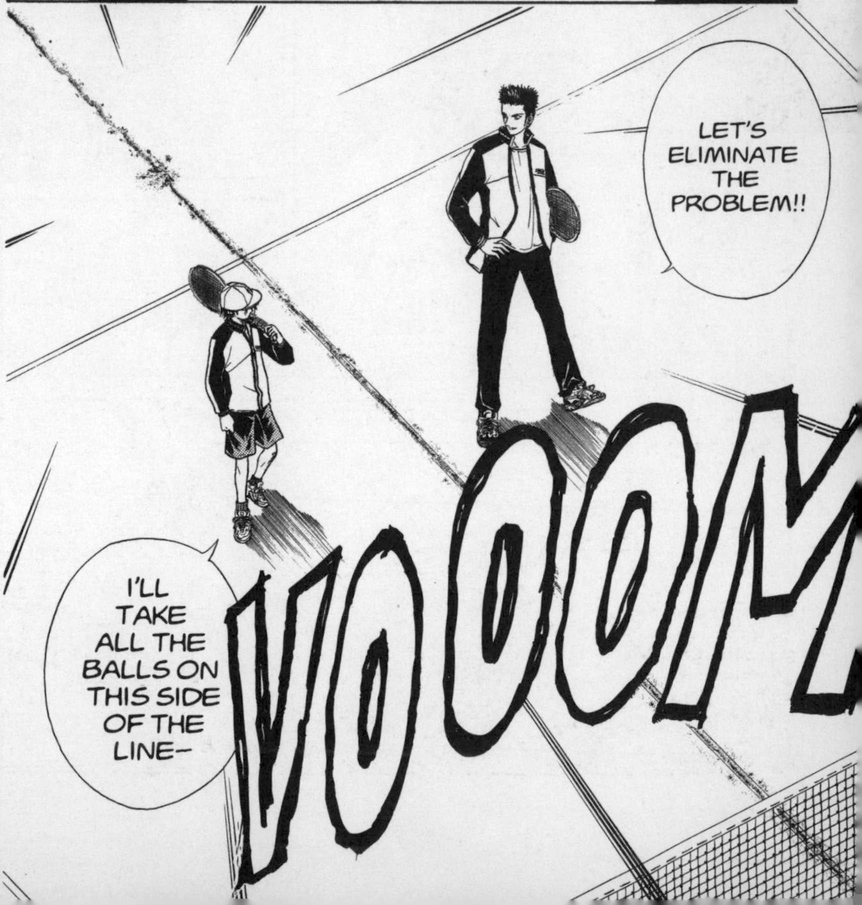
LET'S ELIMINATE THE PROBLEM!!
VOOOM
I'LL TAKE ALL THE BALLS ON THIS SIDE OF THE LINE—

READ THIS WAY

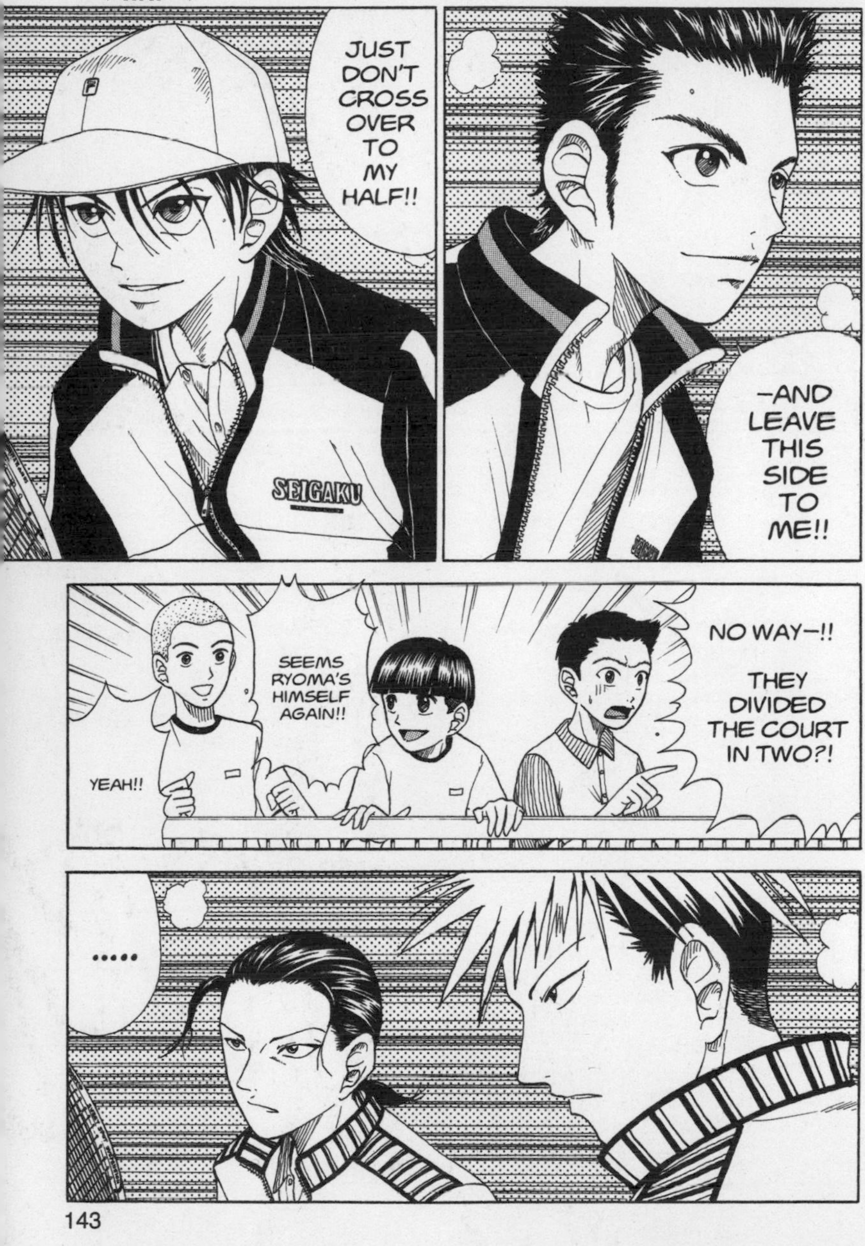

—AND LEAVE THIS SIDE TO ME!!
JUST DON'T CROSS OVER TO MY HALF!!
SEIGAKU
NO WAY—!!
THEY DIVIDED THE COURT IN TWO?!
SEEMS RYOMA'S HIMSELF AGAIN!!
YEAH!!
.....

テニスの王子

THE PRINCE OF TENNIS

I COULD'VE FILLED TWO OR THREE SCHOOLS, LET ALONE A CLASS. TWO DAYS AFTER *THE PRINCE OF TENNIS* VOL. 1 SAW PRINT I HAD BOXES FILLED WITH LETTERS! KINDA LIKE AN ELECTION!

I WAS TOUCHED BY YOUR FEELINGS FOR THE CHARACTERS! I WANT TO MAKE ALL OF YOU THEIR CLASSMATES!! BUT I COULD ONLY CHOOSE 36 BOYS AND GIRLS... I'D LIKE TO THANK AND APOLOGIZE TO THE REST OF YOU. I'M GUESSING THOSE WHO WEREN'T CHOSEN ARE FEELING DOWN– I'M REALLY, REALLY SORRY– YOU'RE SUCH LOYAL FANS. AS THE WRITER,

I WANT ALL OF YOU TO ATTEND SEISHUN ACADEMY!!

SO HERE'S 9TH GRADE CLASS 6'S STUDENT LIST!!

STUDENT NUMBER	(BOYS)		(GIRLS)
1.	TAKAYUKI AOYAMA	1.	IZUMI ASAHI
2.	KAZUYA IHARA	2.	YUMI KAWAI
3.	RYOHEI OGAWA	3.	AKIKO KAMIHARA
4.	YUTA KATO	4.	YOKO KITAGISHI
5.	TAKEHIRO KANAZAWA	5.	HIROMI KISU
6.	TAKENOBU KIKUCHI	6.	YOSHIKO KOBA
7.	EIJI KIKUMARU	7.	YUUKI SHIMOMURA
8.	NAOYA KUWAHARA	8.	ERIKO TAKEGUCHI
9.	MAKOTO KOBAYASHI	9.	MIYOKO NARAZAKI
10.	HIROTAKA SEGAWA	10.	MARI HIRAKI
11.	JUNKI TAKAHASHI	11.	MEGUMI HOSHINO
12.	JOSHUA TAKANO	12.	KIMI MATSURA
13.	KOJIRO HAYASHI	13.	SACHIE MINAMI
14.	SHUSUKE FUJI	14.	CHIAKI MIYOSHI
15.	EIJI FUJIWARA	15.	ASUKA MURAI
16.	KENTA FUJII	16.	AKIKO MORIMOTO
17.	KOSEI MAKIHARA	17.	KAORU YAMASHITA
18.	SOJUN MORI	18.	KANA YAMASHITA
19.	YUYA YAGURA		
20.	SHINTARO YOSHIDA		

TOTAL: 38 (TITLES OMITTED FROM NAMES)

THESE ARE THE WINNERS. THANK YOU ALL.

A LOT SAID, "I'M WAITING FOR XX'S TURN." IT WAS SO POPULAR I MIGHT DO IT AGAIN...

WILL IT BE RYOMA'S CLASS... OR...?! THANKS FOR SUPPORTING *THE PRINCE OF TENNIS* AND RYOMA!!

SEE YOU NEXT VOLUME!!
TAKESHI KONOMI

T.KONOMI
2000.4.25

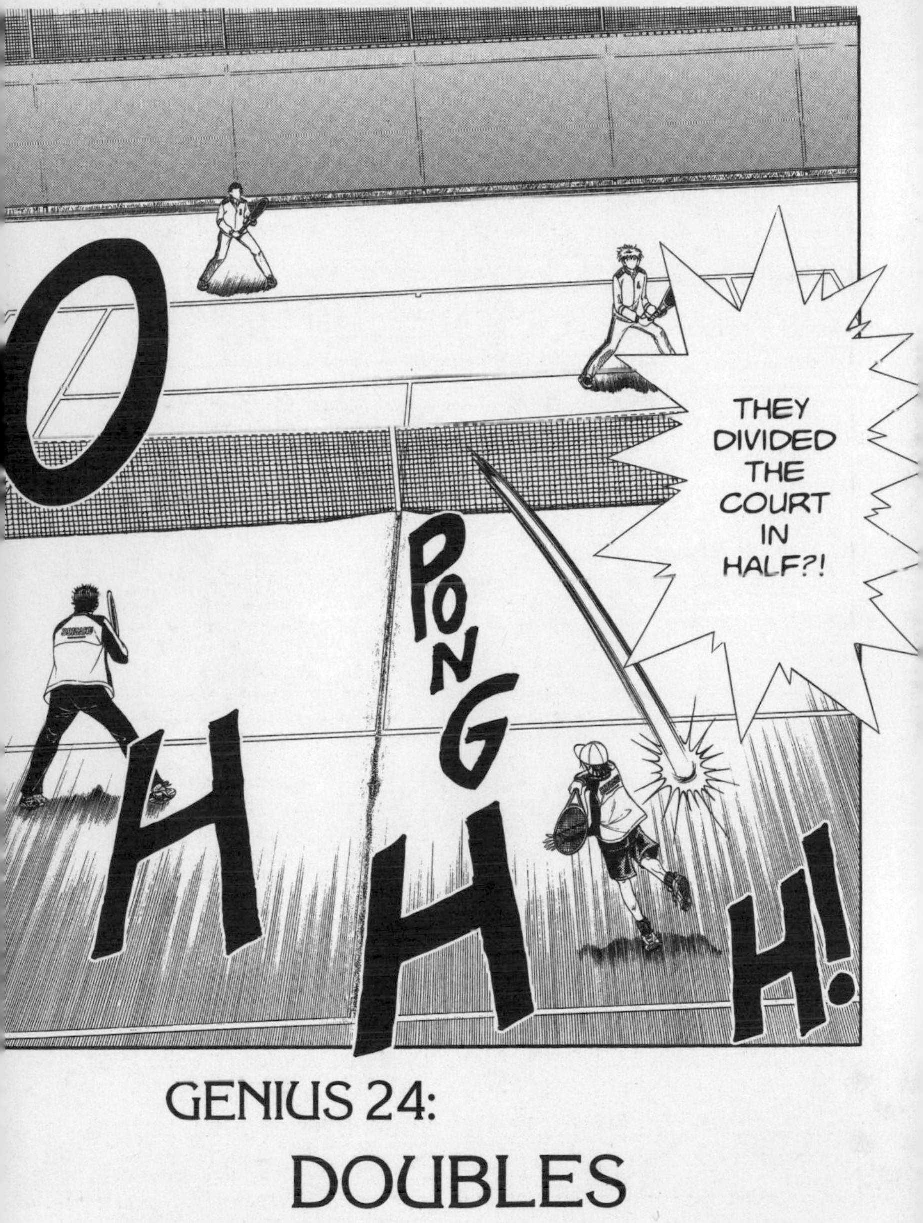
THEY DIVIDED THE COURT IN HALF?!
OHHHH!
PONG

GENIUS 24: DOUBLES

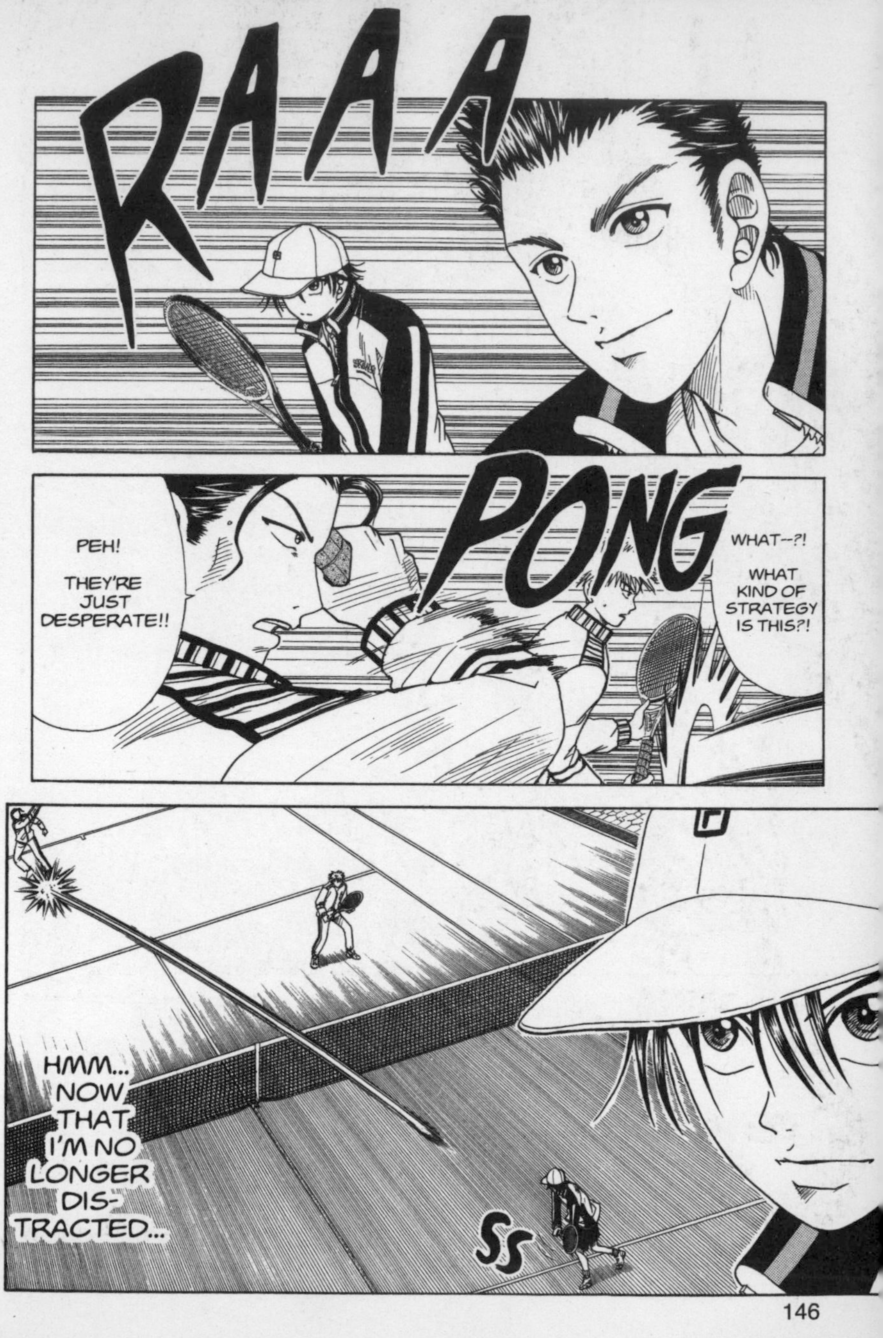
RAAA
WHAT--?!
WHAT KIND OF STRATEGY IS THIS?!
PONG
PEH!
THEY'RE JUST DESPERATE!!
HMM... NOW THAT I'M NO LONGER DIS-TRACTED...
SS

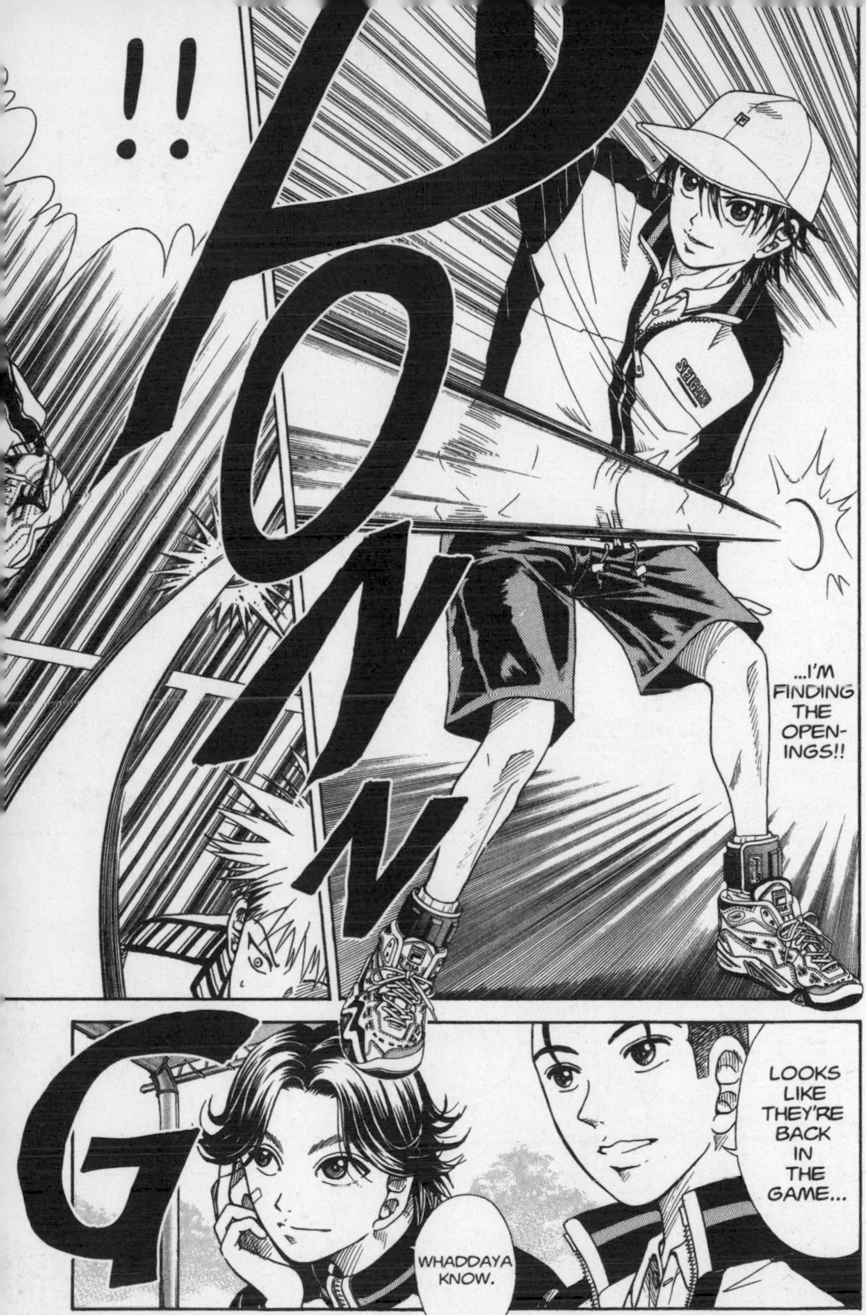
!!
...I'M FINDING THE OPENINGS!!
LOOKS LIKE THEY'RE BACK IN THE GAME...
WHADDAYA KNOW.

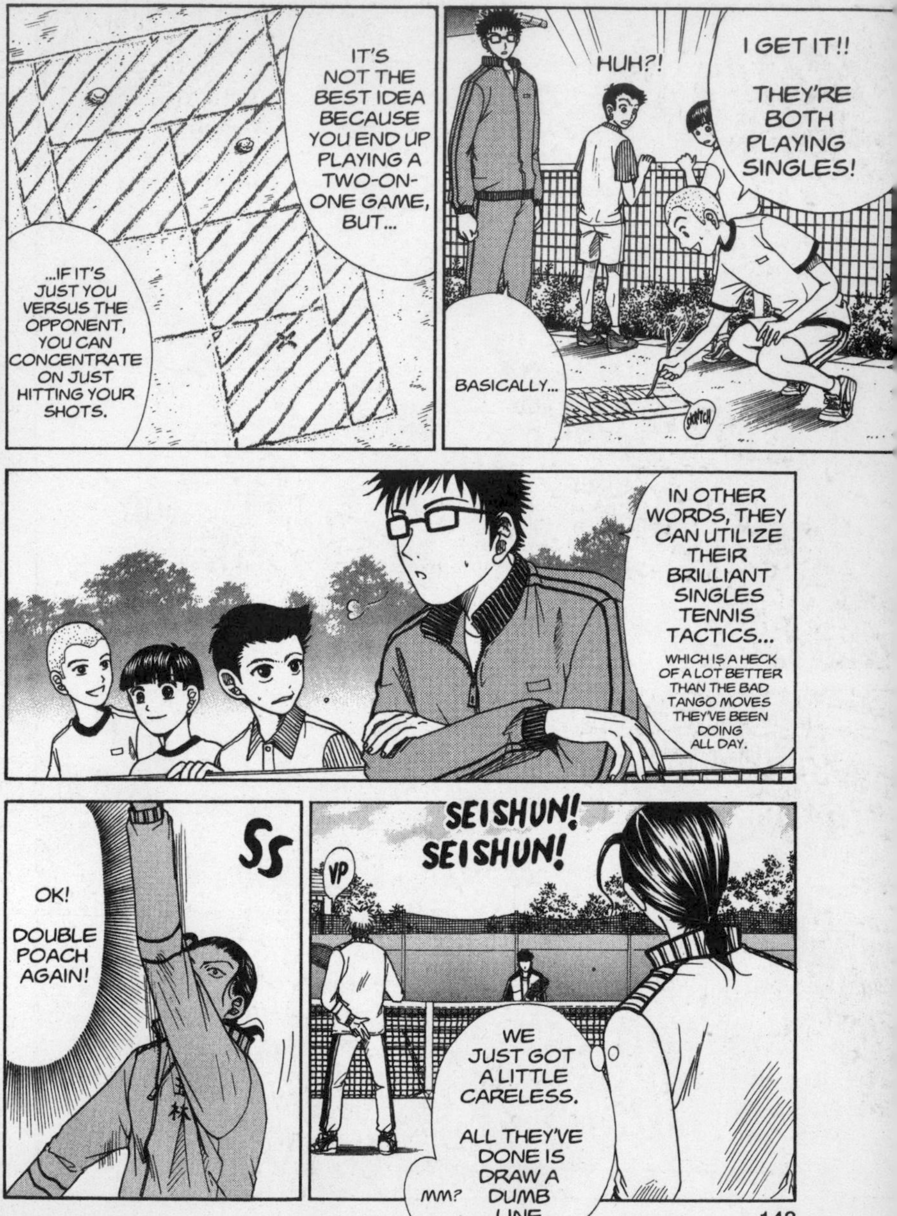
I GET IT!!
THEY'RE BOTH PLAYING SINGLES!
HUH?!
SKRITCH
BASICALLY...
IT'S NOT THE BEST IDEA BECAUSE YOU END UP PLAYING A TWO-ON-ONE GAME, BUT...
...IF IT'S JUST YOU VERSUS THE OPPONENT, YOU CAN CONCENTRATE ON JUST HITTING YOUR SHOTS.
IN OTHER WORDS, THEY CAN UTILIZE THEIR BRILLIANT SINGLES TENNIS TACTICS...
WHICH IS A HECK OF A LOT BETTER THAN THE BAD TANGO MOVES THEY'VE BEEN DOING ALL DAY.
SEISHUN! SEISHUN!
VP
WE JUST GOT A LITTLE CARELESS.
ALL THEY'VE DONE IS DRAW A DUMB LINE.
MM?
SS
OK!
DOUBLE POACH AGAIN!

READ THIS WAY

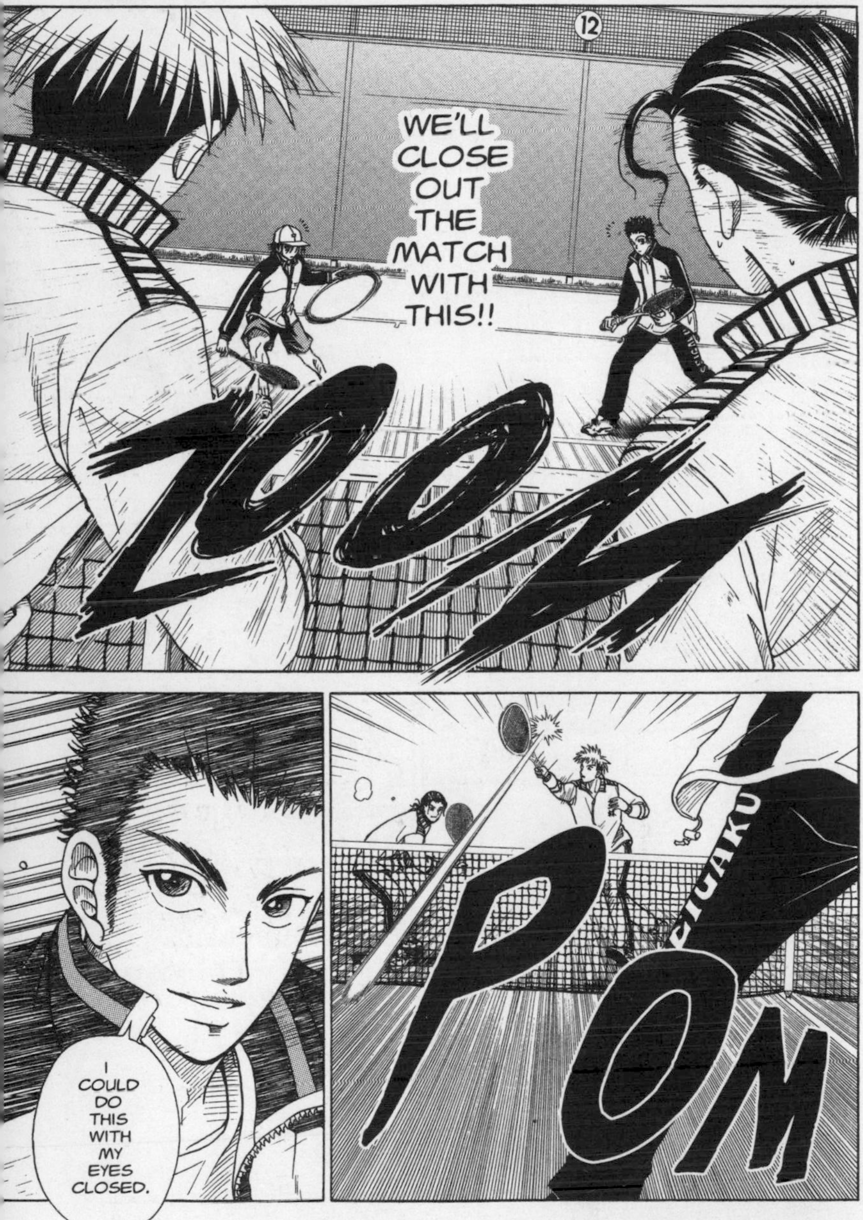
12
WE'LL CLOSE OUT THE MATCH WITH THIS!!
ZOOM
POM
I COULD DO THIS WITH MY EYES CLOSED.

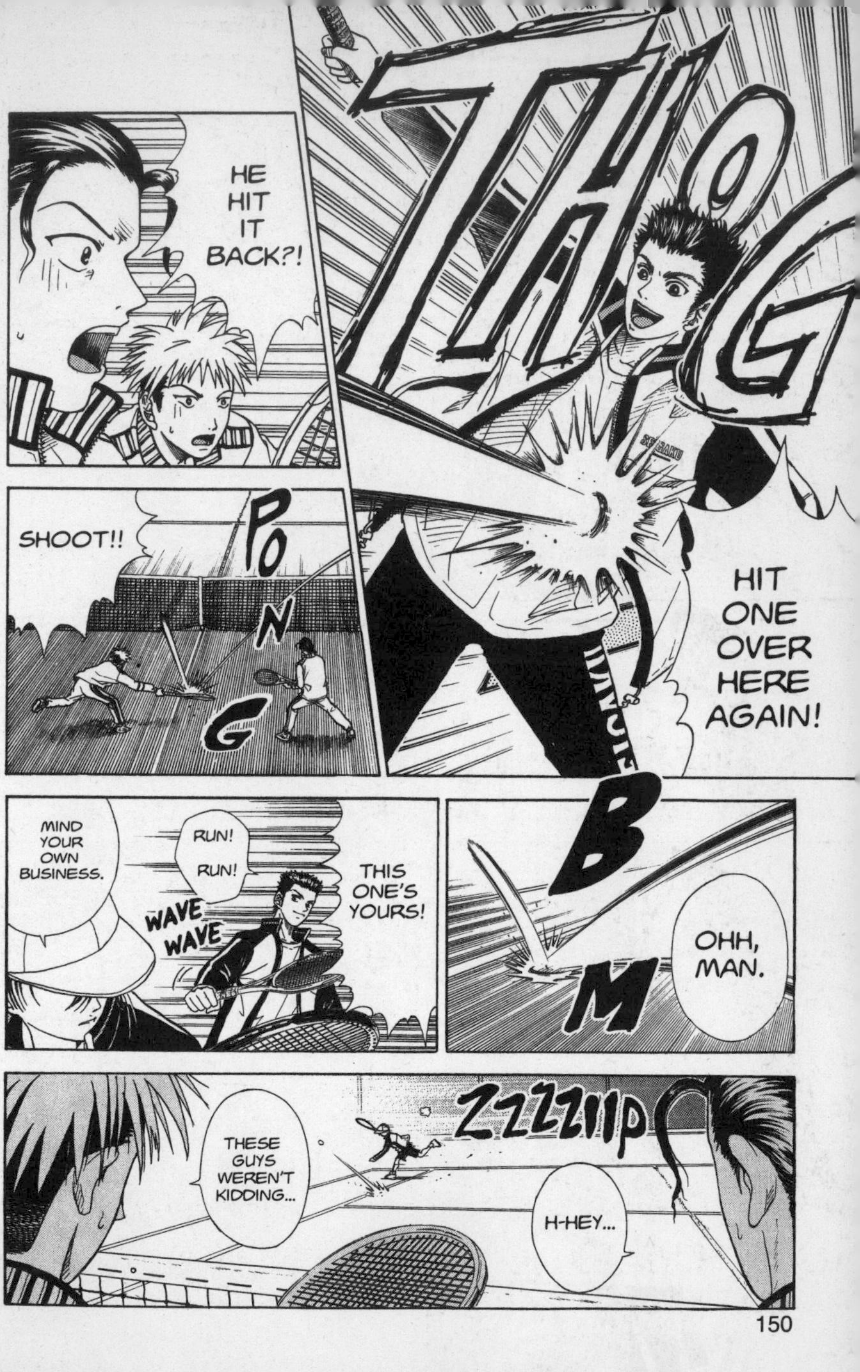
HIT ONE OVER HERE AGAIN!
HE HIT IT BACK?!
SHOOT!!
PONG
OHH, MAN.
THIS ONE'S YOURS!
RUN!
RUN!
WAVE WAVE
MIND YOUR OWN BUSINESS.
H-HEY...
ZZZZIIP
THESE GUYS WEREN'T KIDDING...

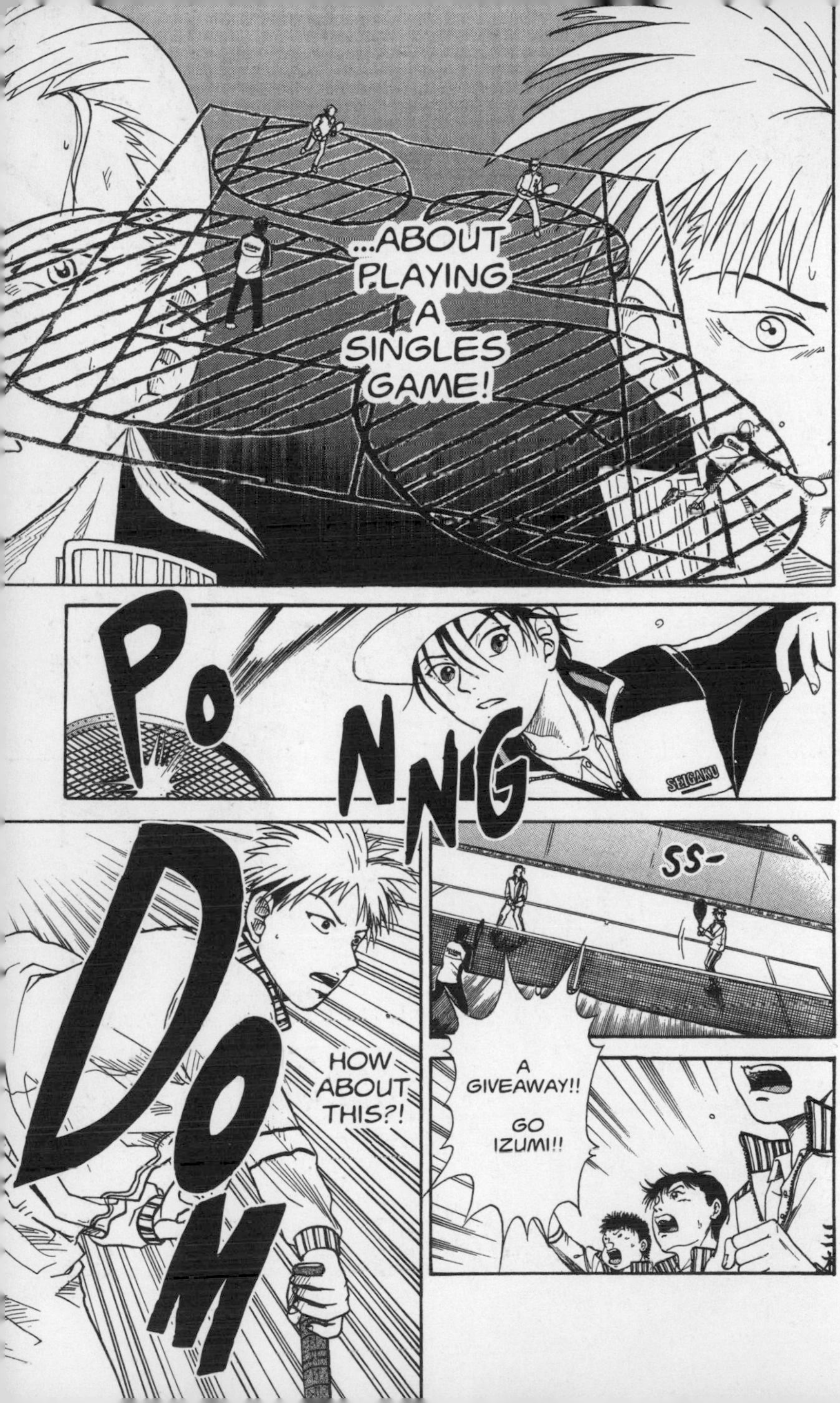
...ABOUT PLAYING A SINGLES GAME!
PONNG
SEIGAKU
SS-
A GIVEAWAY!!
GO IZUMI!!
DOM
HOW ABOUT THIS?!

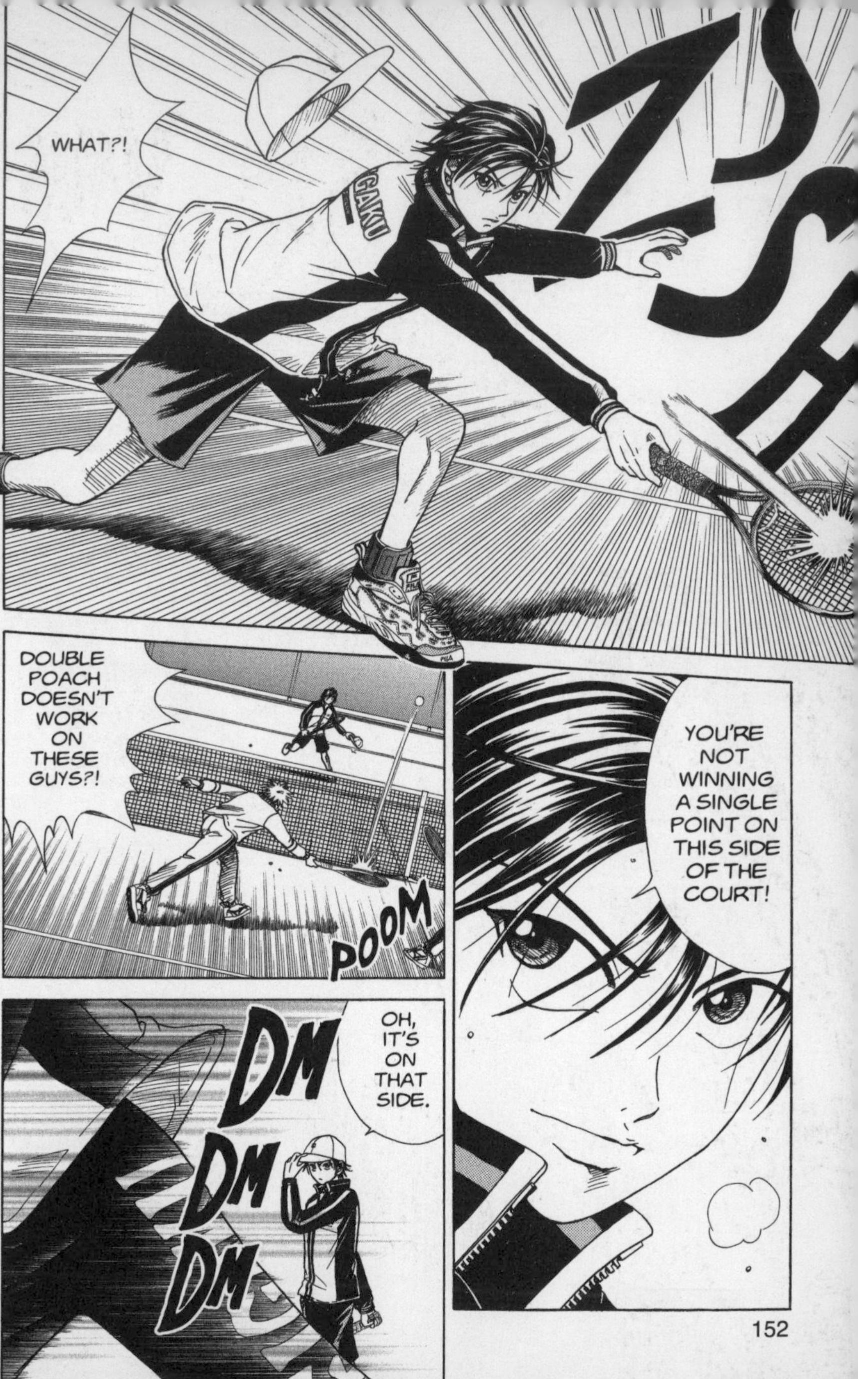
WHAT?!
YOU'RE NOT WINNING A SINGLE POINT ON THIS SIDE OF THE COURT!
DOUBLE POACH DOESN'T WORK ON THESE GUYS?!
POOM
OH, IT'S ON THAT SIDE.
DM DM DM

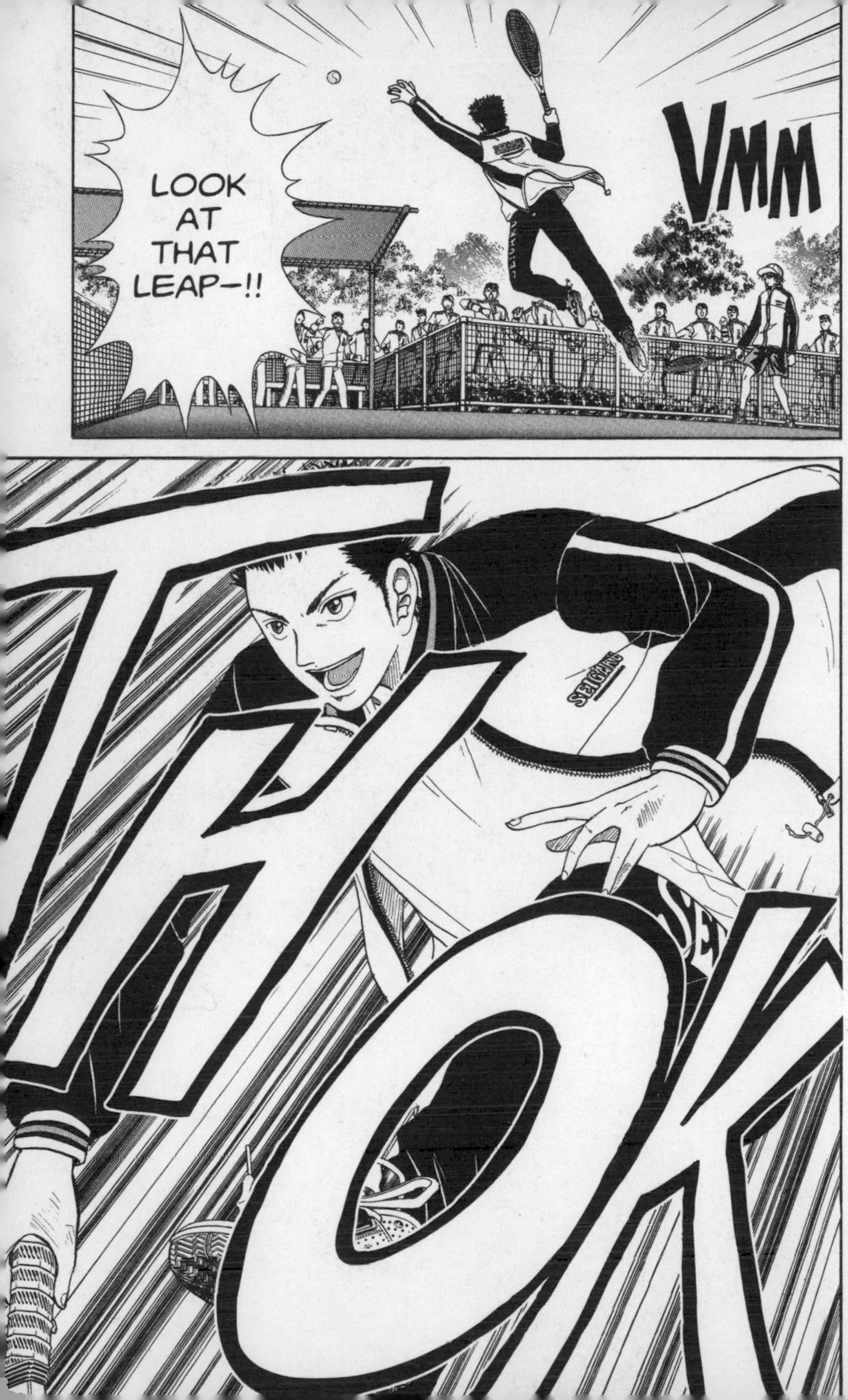
VMM
LOOK AT THAT LEAP—!!

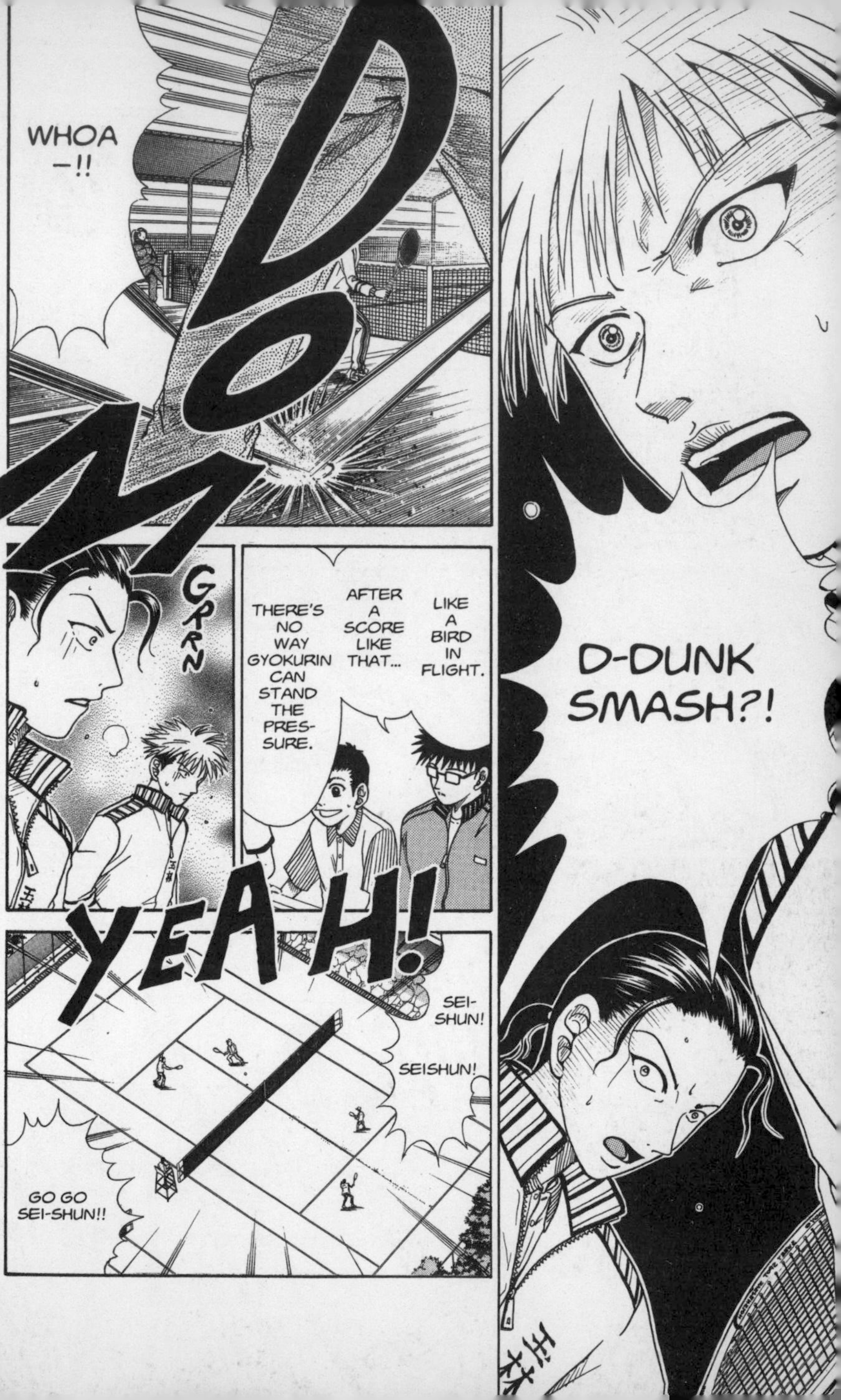
D-DUNK SMASH?!
DOM
WHOA —!!
LIKE A BIRD IN FLIGHT.
AFTER A SCORE LIKE THAT...
THERE'S NO WAY GYOKURIN CAN STAND THE PRES-SURE.
GRRN
YEAH!
SEI-SHUN!
SEISHUN!
GO GO SEI-SHUN!!

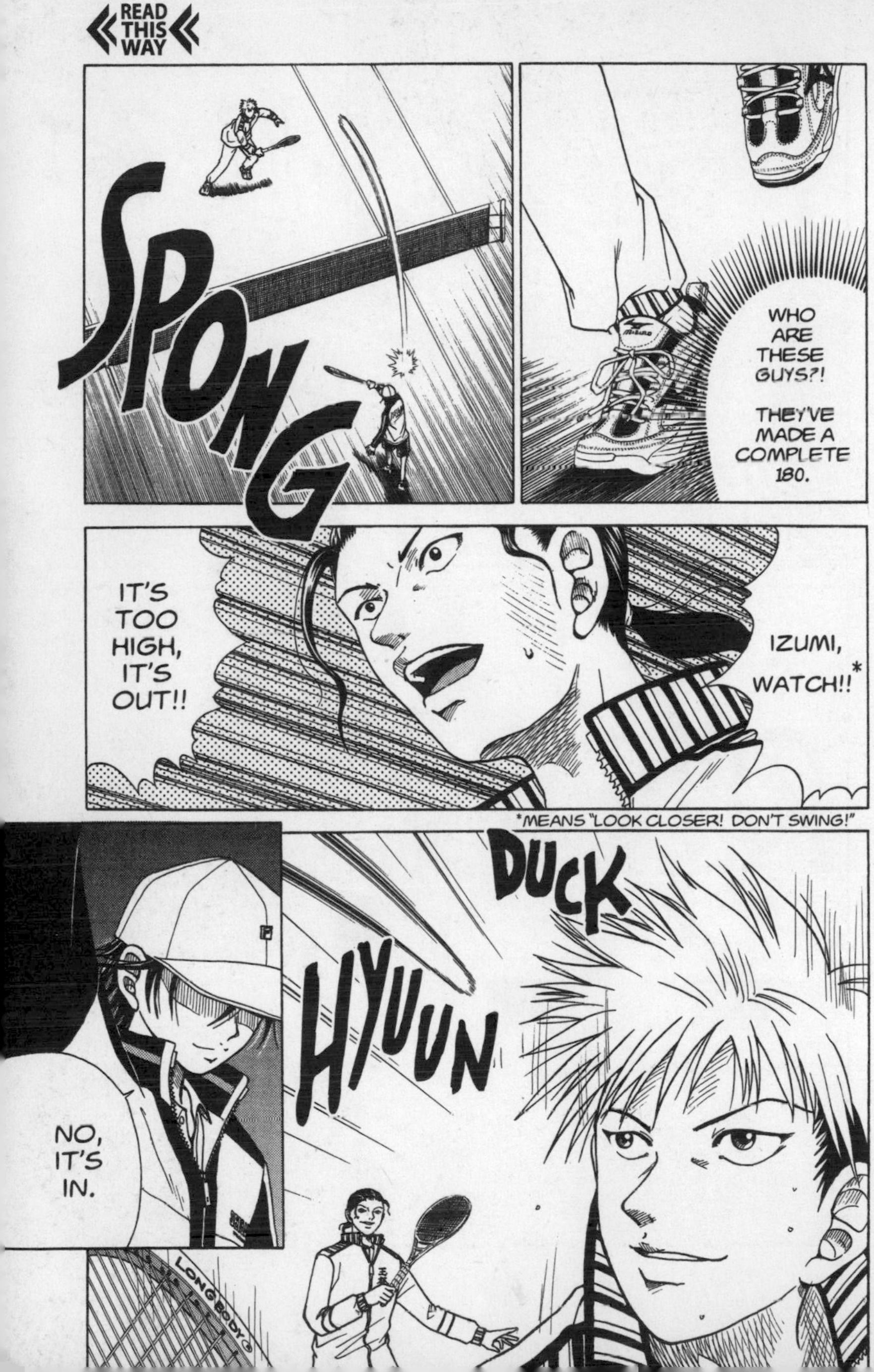
READ THIS WAY
WHO ARE THESE GUYS?!
THEY'VE MADE A COMPLETE 180.
SPONG
IZUMI, WATCH!!*
IT'S TOO HIGH, IT'S OUT!!
*MEANS "LOOK CLOSER! DON'T SWING!"
DUCK
HYUUN
NO, IT'S IN.

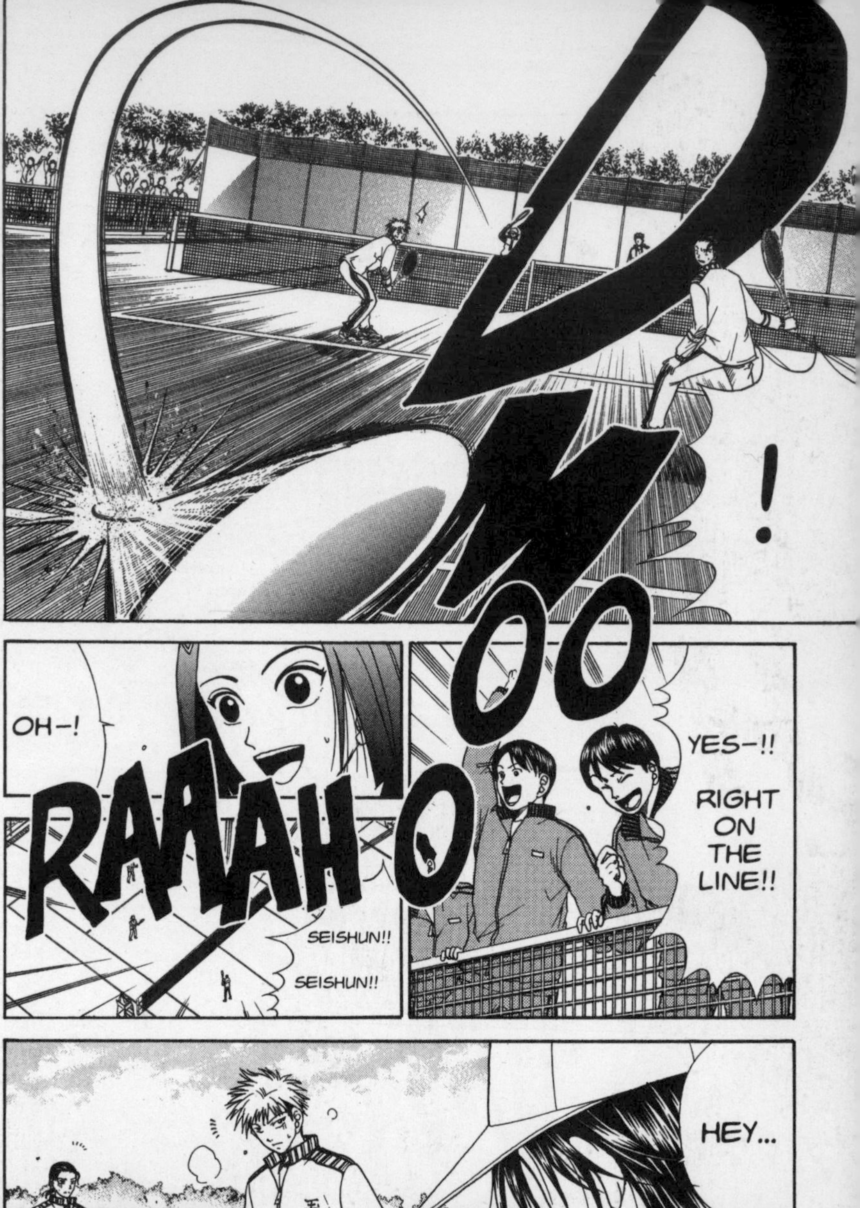
RAAAH
YES–!!
RIGHT ON THE LINE!!
OH–!
SEISHUN!!
SEISHUN!!
HEY...

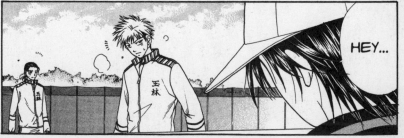

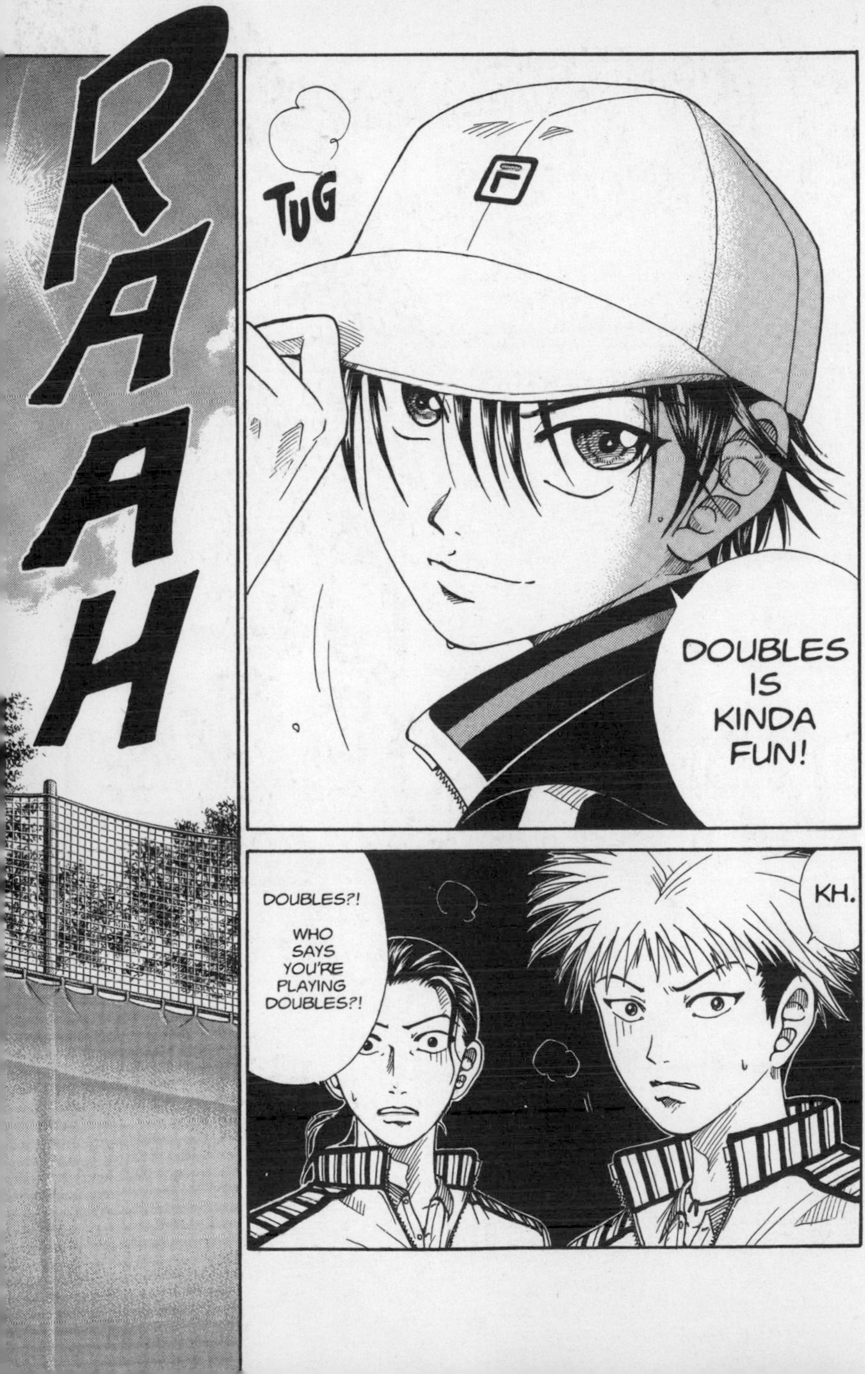
TUG
DOUBLES IS KINDA FUN!
KH.
DOUBLES?!
WHO SAYS YOU'RE PLAYING DOUBLES?!
RAAAH

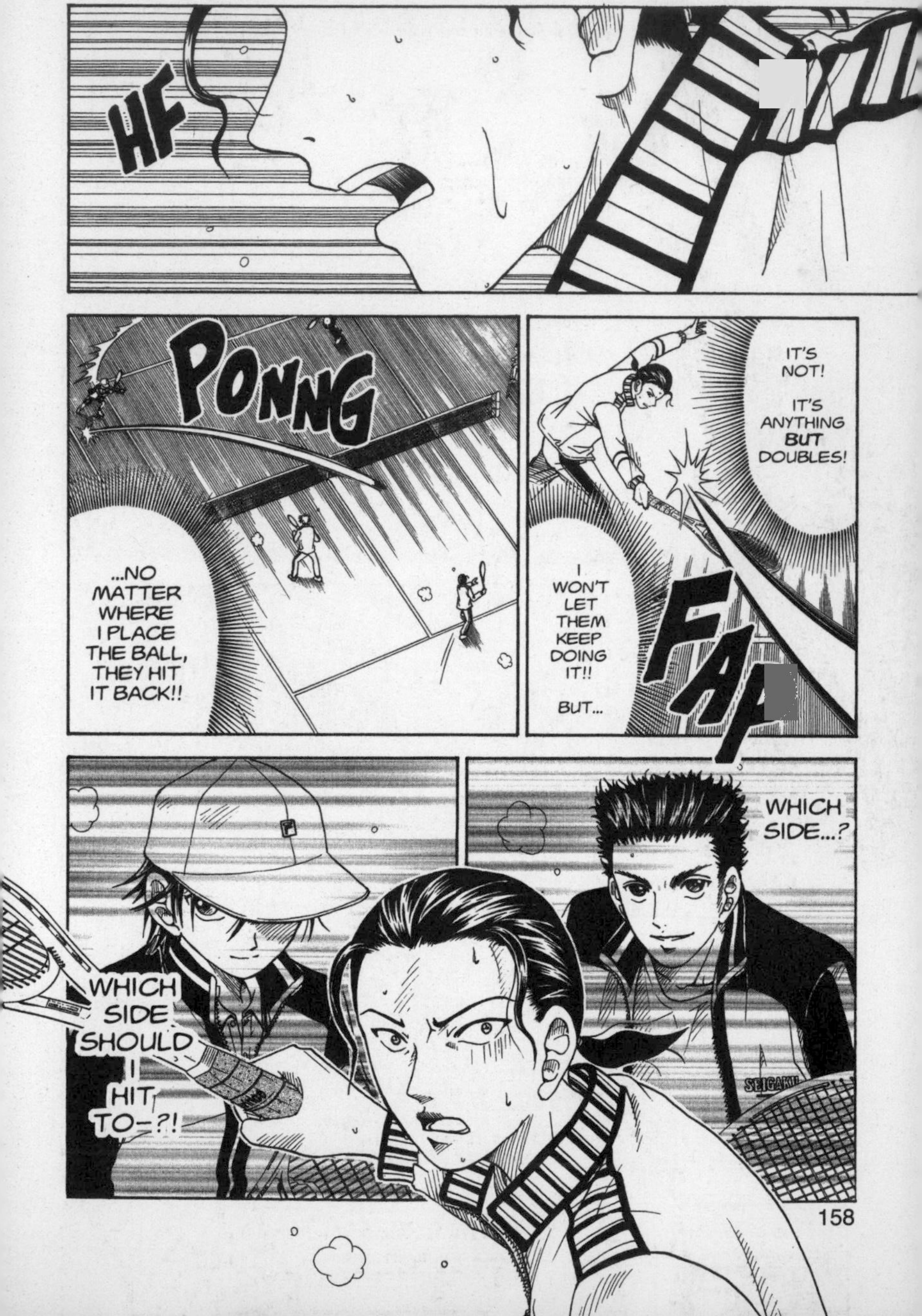
HF
IT'S NOT!
IT'S ANYTHING BUT DOUBLES!
I WON'T LET THEM KEEP DOING IT!!
BUT...
FAP
PONNG
...NO MATTER WHERE I PLACE THE BALL, THEY HIT IT BACK!!
WHICH SIDE...?
WHICH SIDE SHOULD I HIT TO–?!

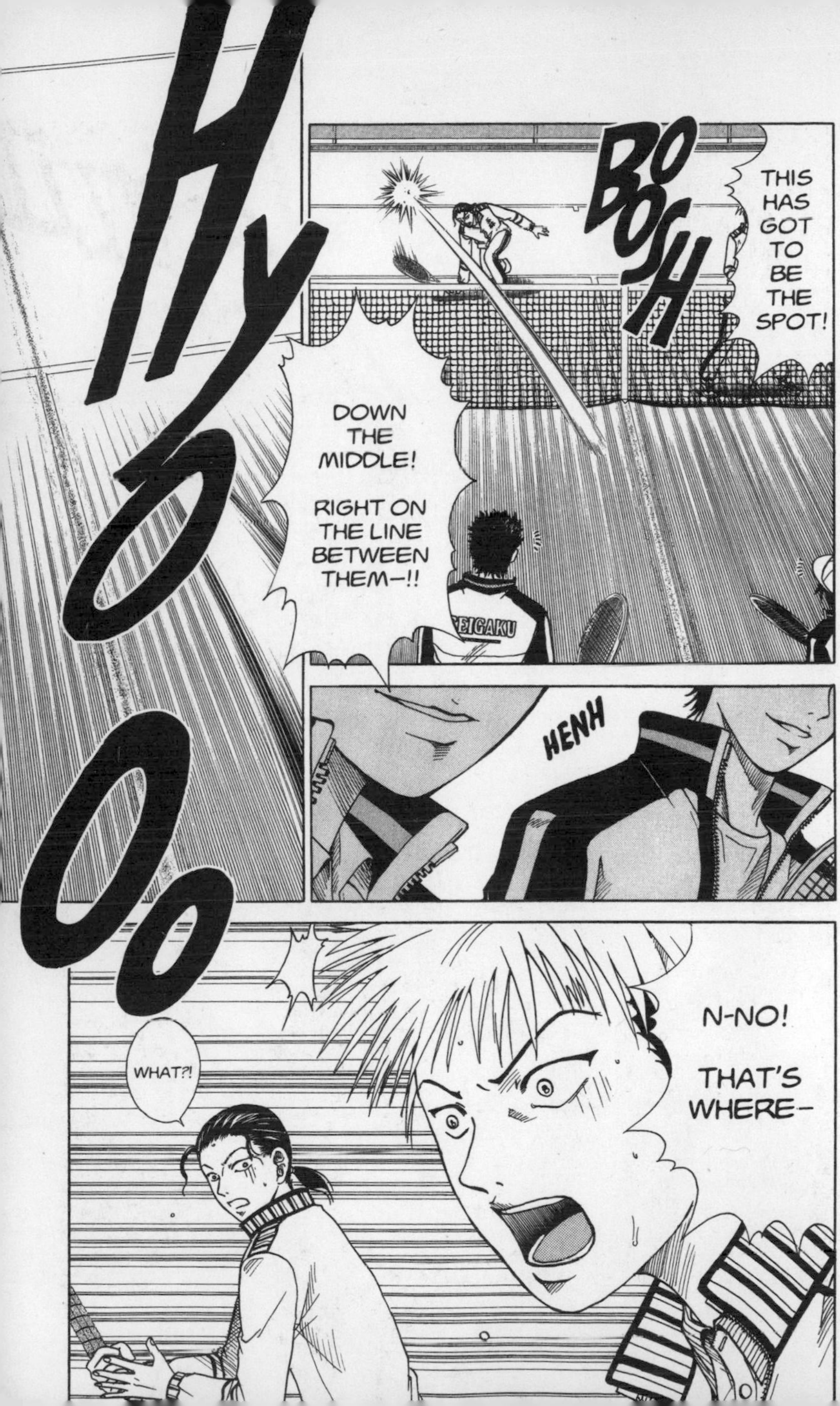
BOOSH
THIS HAS GOT TO BE THE SPOT!
DOWN THE MIDDLE!
RIGHT ON THE LINE BETWEEN THEM—!!
SEIGAKU
HENH
HYOOOO
N-NO!
THAT'S WHERE—
WHAT?!

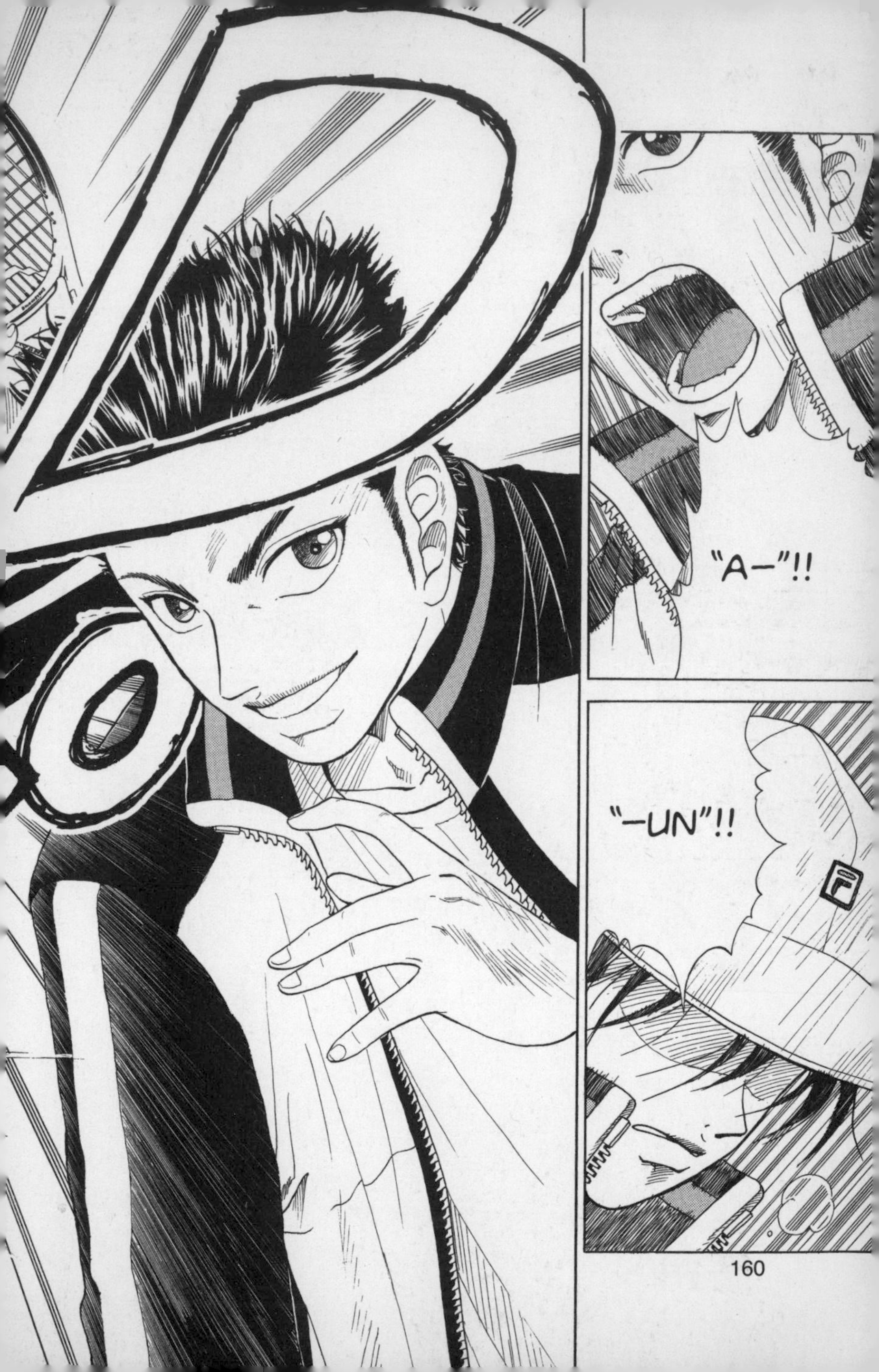
"A—"!!
"—UN"!!

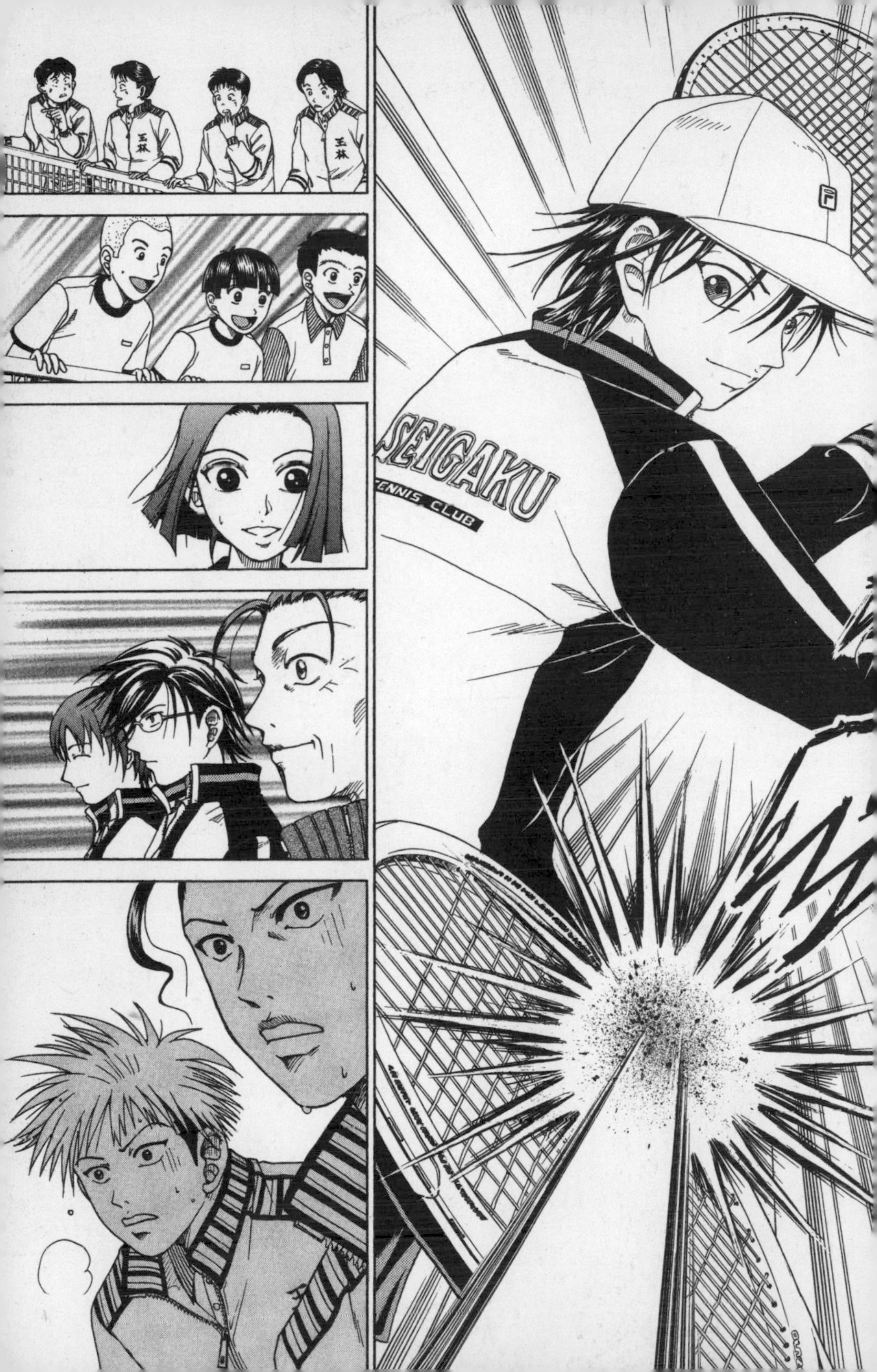
SEIGAKU
TENNIS CLUB

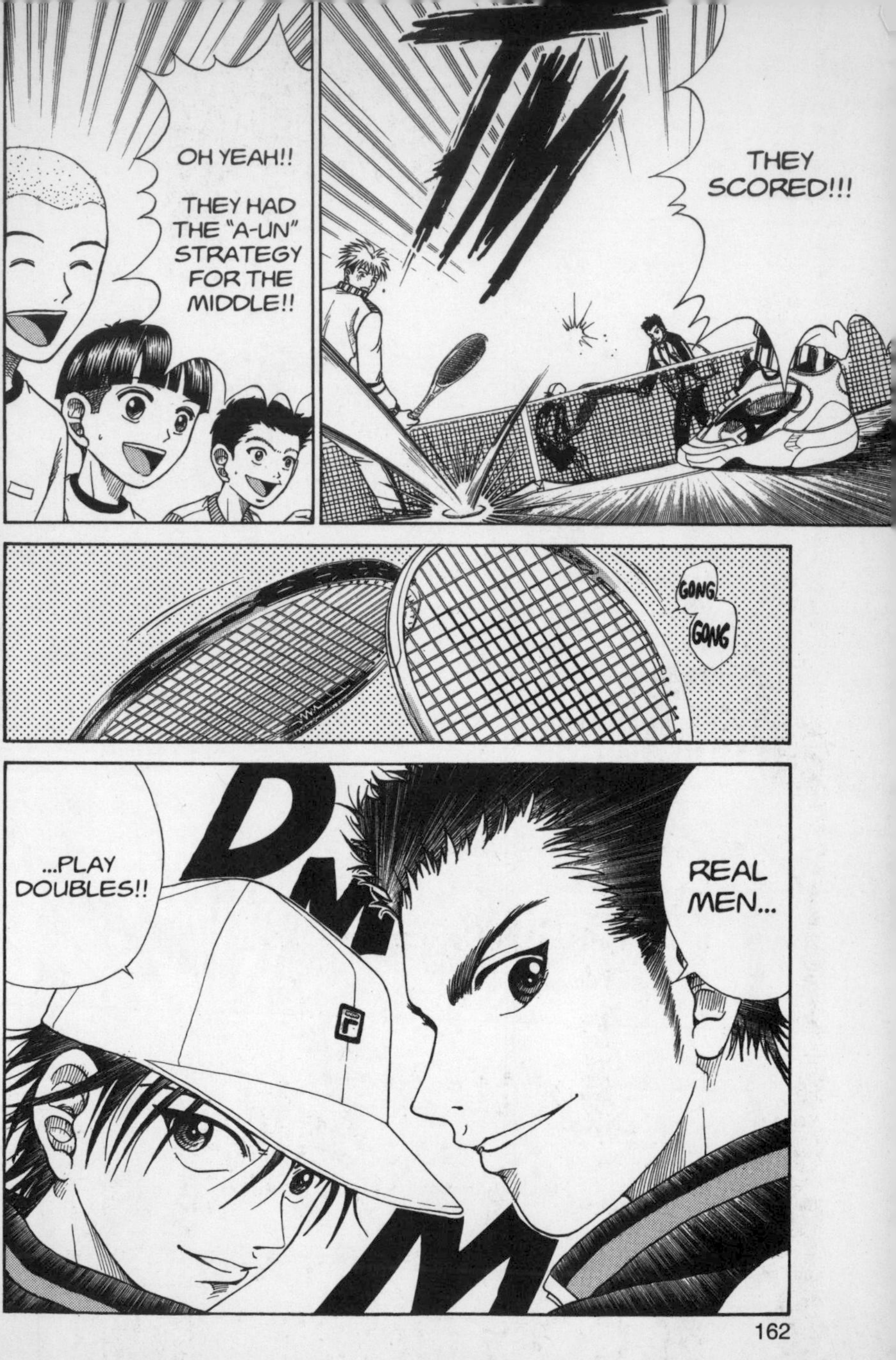
THEY SCORED!!!
OH YEAH!!
THEY HAD THE "A-UN" STRATEGY FOR THE MIDDLE!!
GONG
GONG
REAL MEN...
...PLAY DOUBLES!!

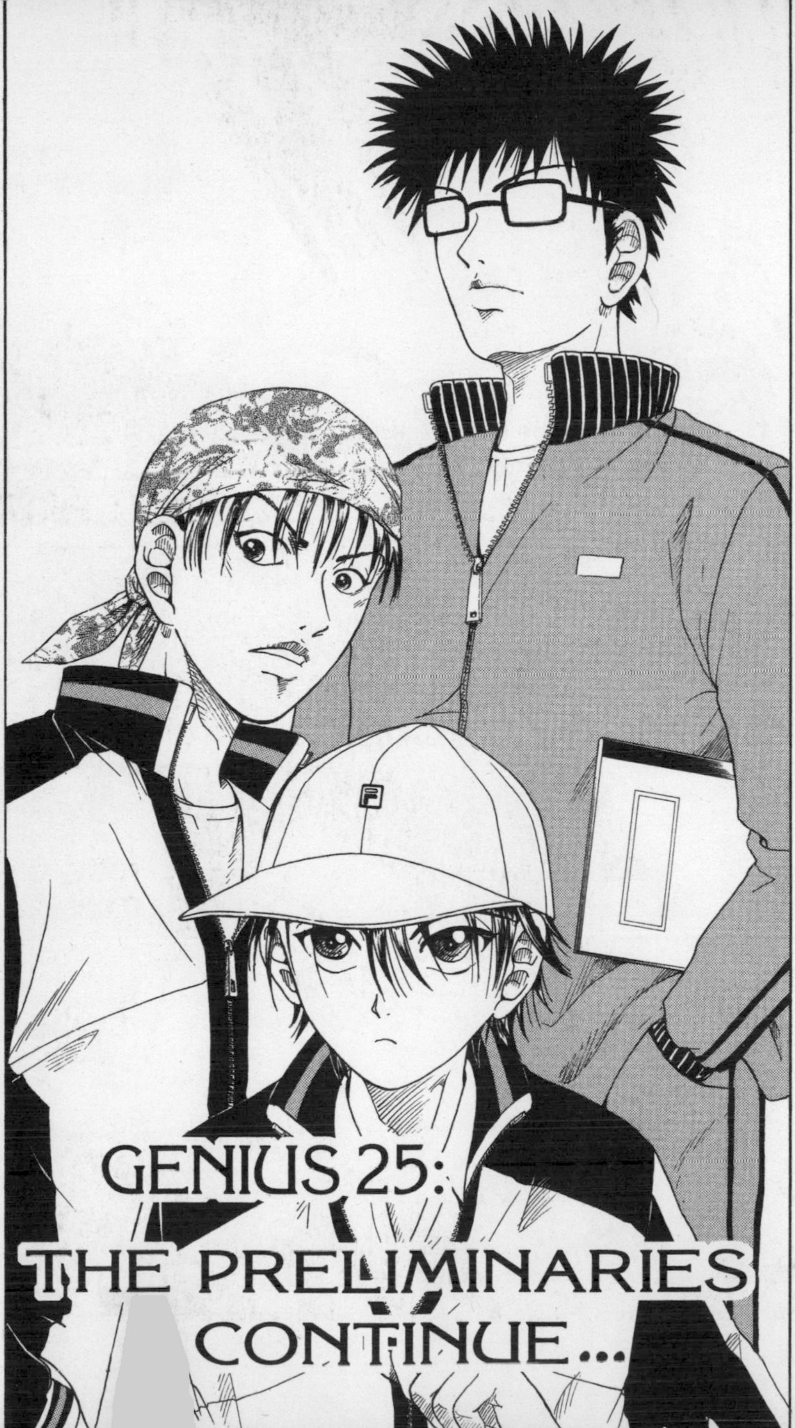
GENIUS 25:
THE PRELIMINARIES CONTINUE...

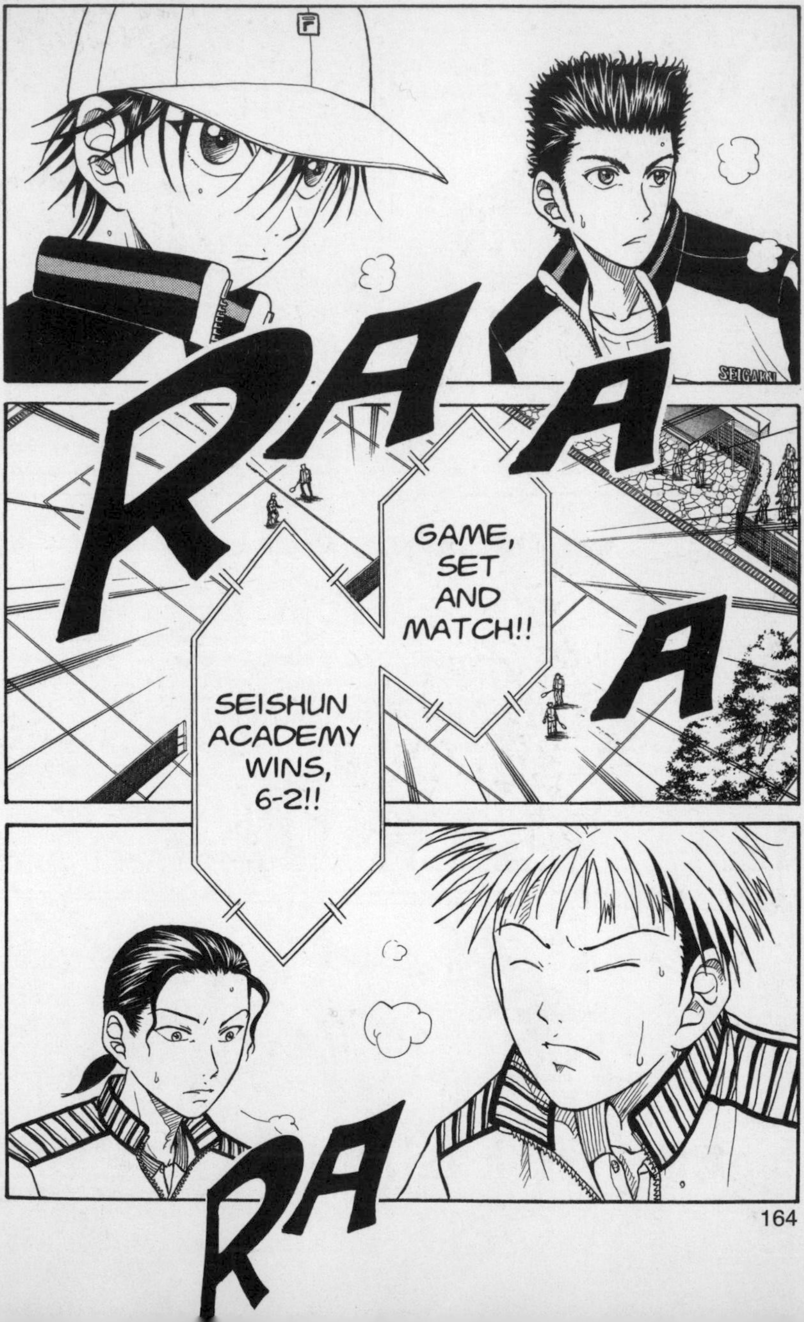
RAAAA
GAME, SET AND MATCH!!
SEISHUN ACADEMY WINS, 6-2!!
SEIGAKU
RA
RA

READ THIS WAY

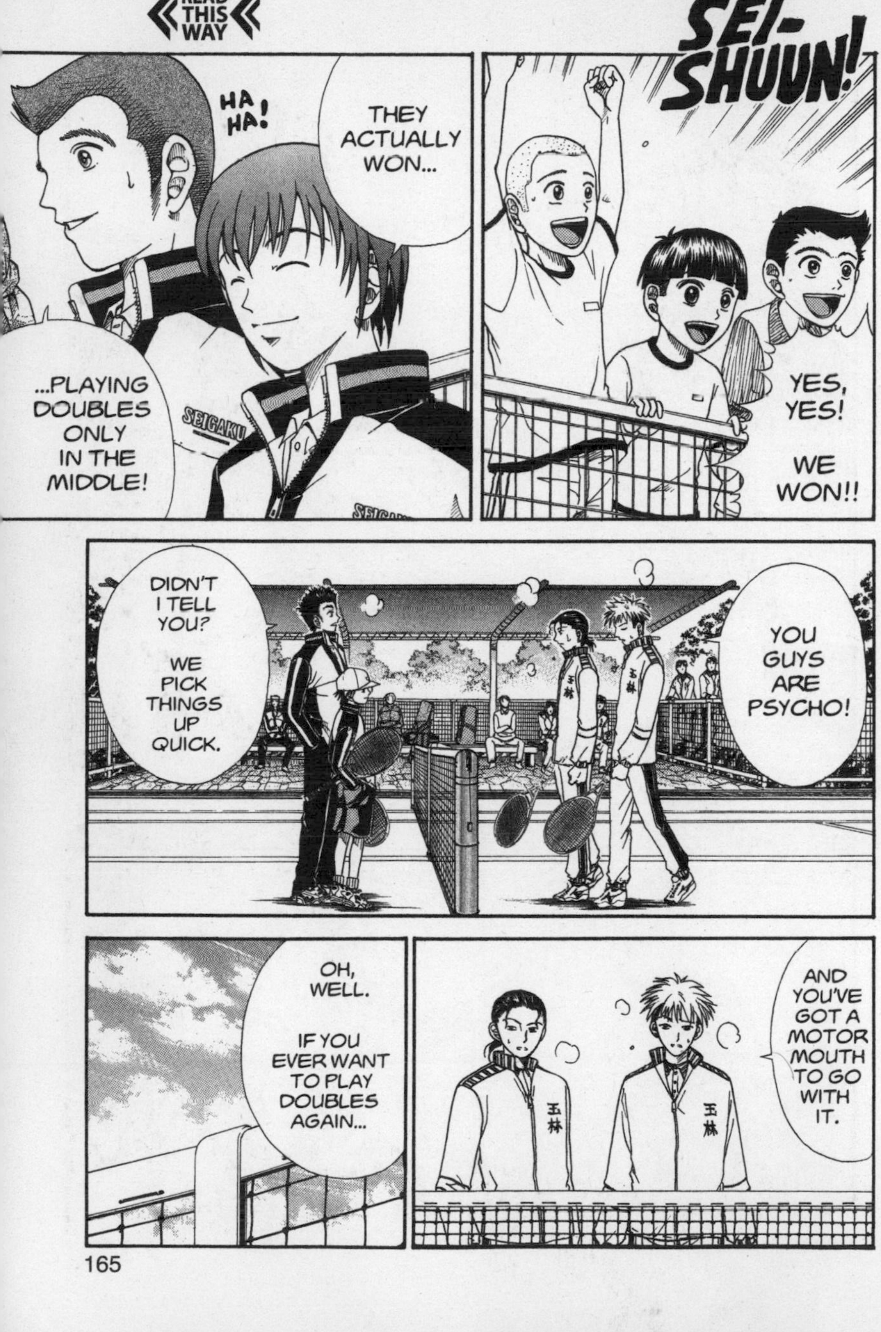
SEI-SHUUN!
YES, YES!
WE WON!!
THEY ACTUALLY WON...
HA HA!
SEIGAKU
...PLAYING DOUBLES ONLY IN THE MIDDLE!
YOU GUYS ARE PSYCHO!
DIDN'T I TELL YOU?
WE PICK THINGS UP QUICK.
AND YOU'VE GOT A MOTOR MOUTH TO GO WITH IT.
玉林
玉林
OH, WELL.
IF YOU EVER WANT TO PLAY DOUBLES AGAIN...

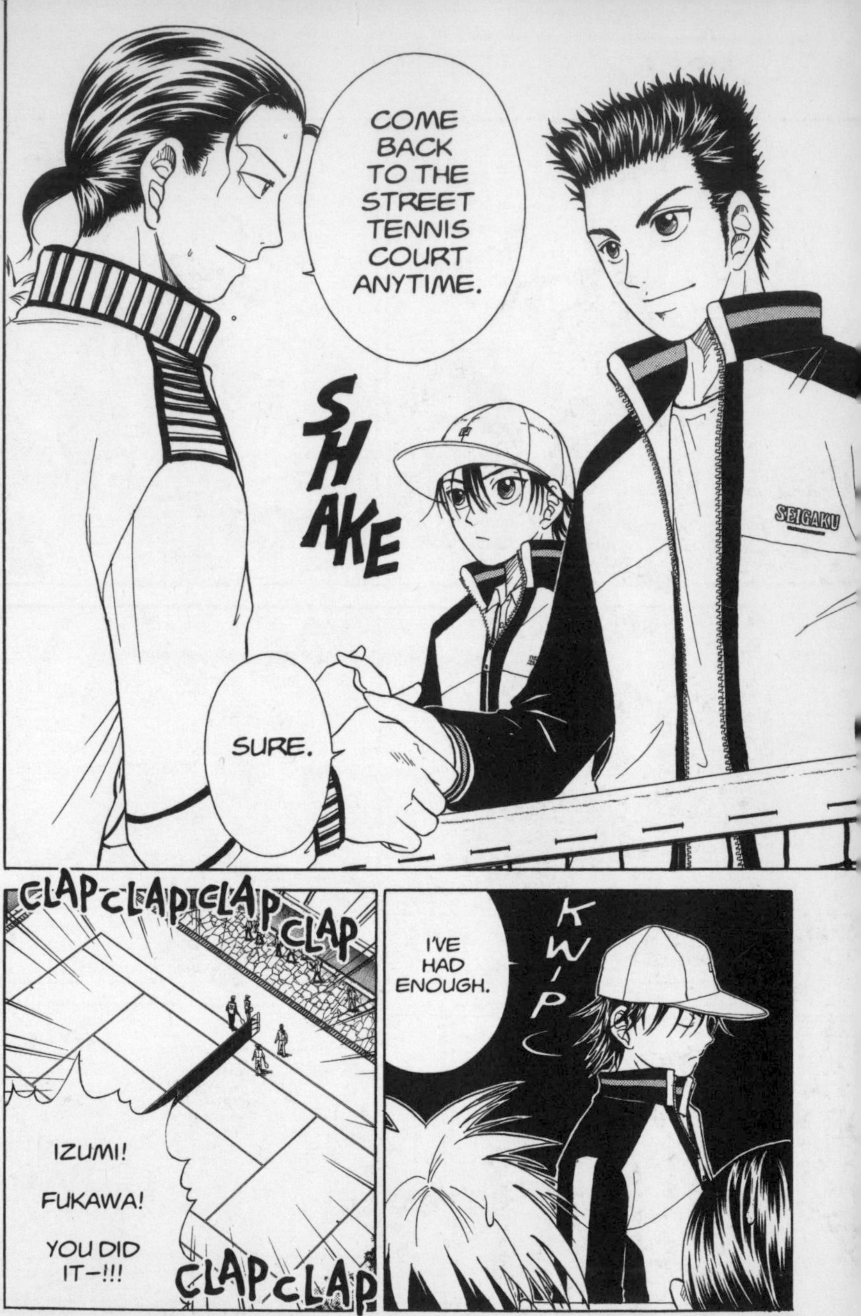
COME BACK TO THE STREET TENNIS COURT ANYTIME.
SHAKE
SURE.
KWIP
I'VE HAD ENOUGH.
CLAP CLAP CLAP CLAP CLAP
IZUMI!
FUKAWA!
YOU DID IT—!!!
CLAP CLAP

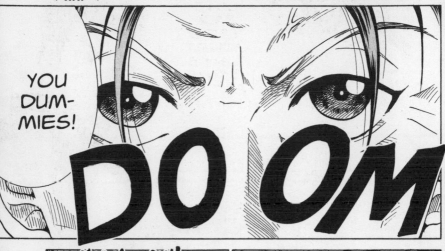

YOU DUMMIES!

DOOM

OWOW! OW!

YOU'RE JUST LUCKY YOU WON!

PINCH

OW!

OW!

OW!

PINCH

WAHAHAHA!

HEY, LOOK!

THE GUYS AT SEISHUN WON— BUT SHE'S MAKING 'EM SIT ON THEIR KNEES!

I'M NEVER PLAYING DOUBLES AGAIN...

GASP

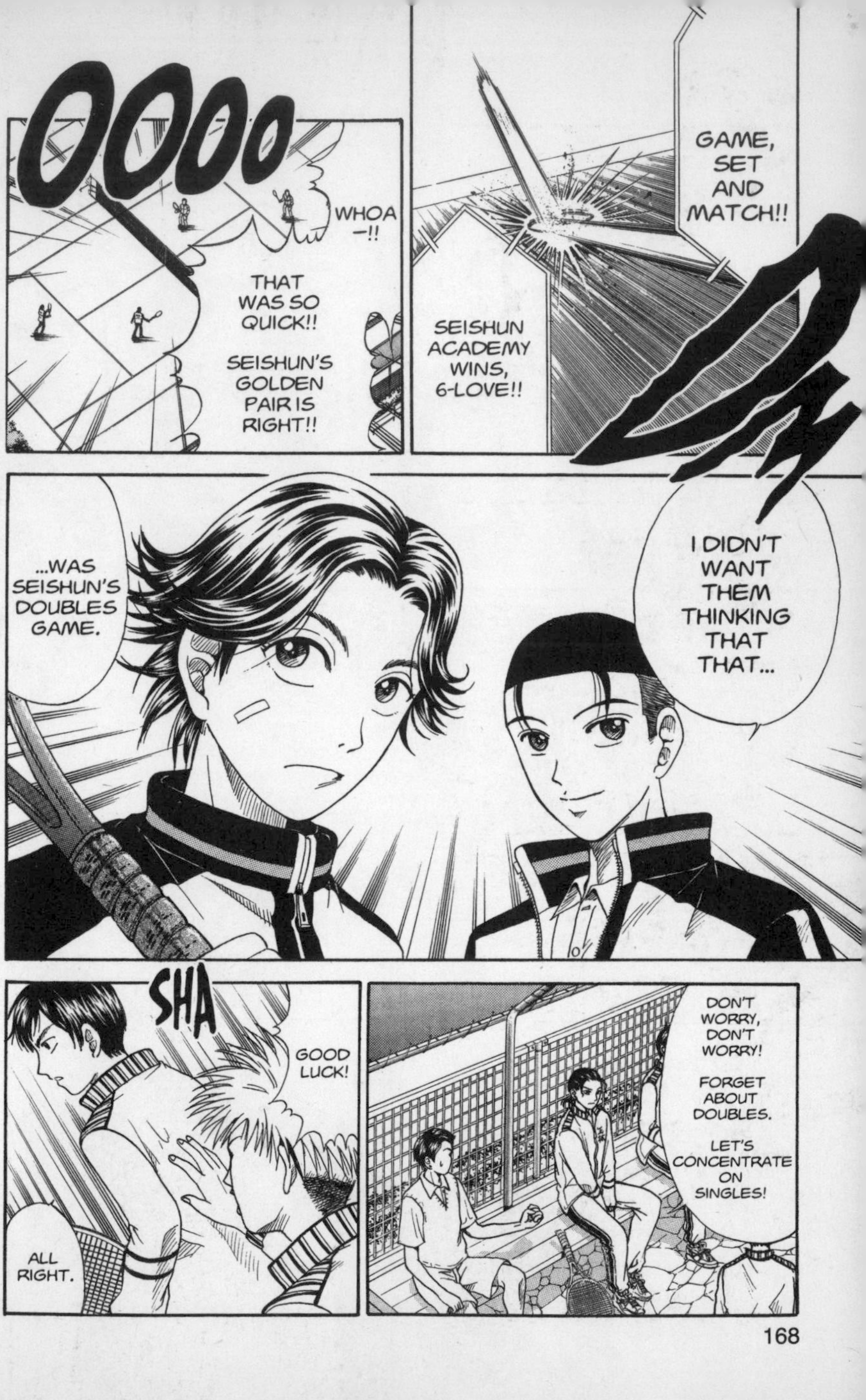
GAME, SET AND MATCH!!
SEISHUN ACADEMY WINS, 6-LOVE!!
DOM
OOOO
WHOA—!!
THAT WAS SO QUICK!!
SEISHUN'S GOLDEN PAIR IS RIGHT!!
I DIDN'T WANT THEM THINKING THAT THAT...
...WAS SEISHUN'S DOUBLES GAME.
DON'T WORRY, DON'T WORRY!
FORGET ABOUT DOUBLES.
LET'S CONCENTRATE ON SINGLES!
SHA
GOOD LUCK!
ALL RIGHT.

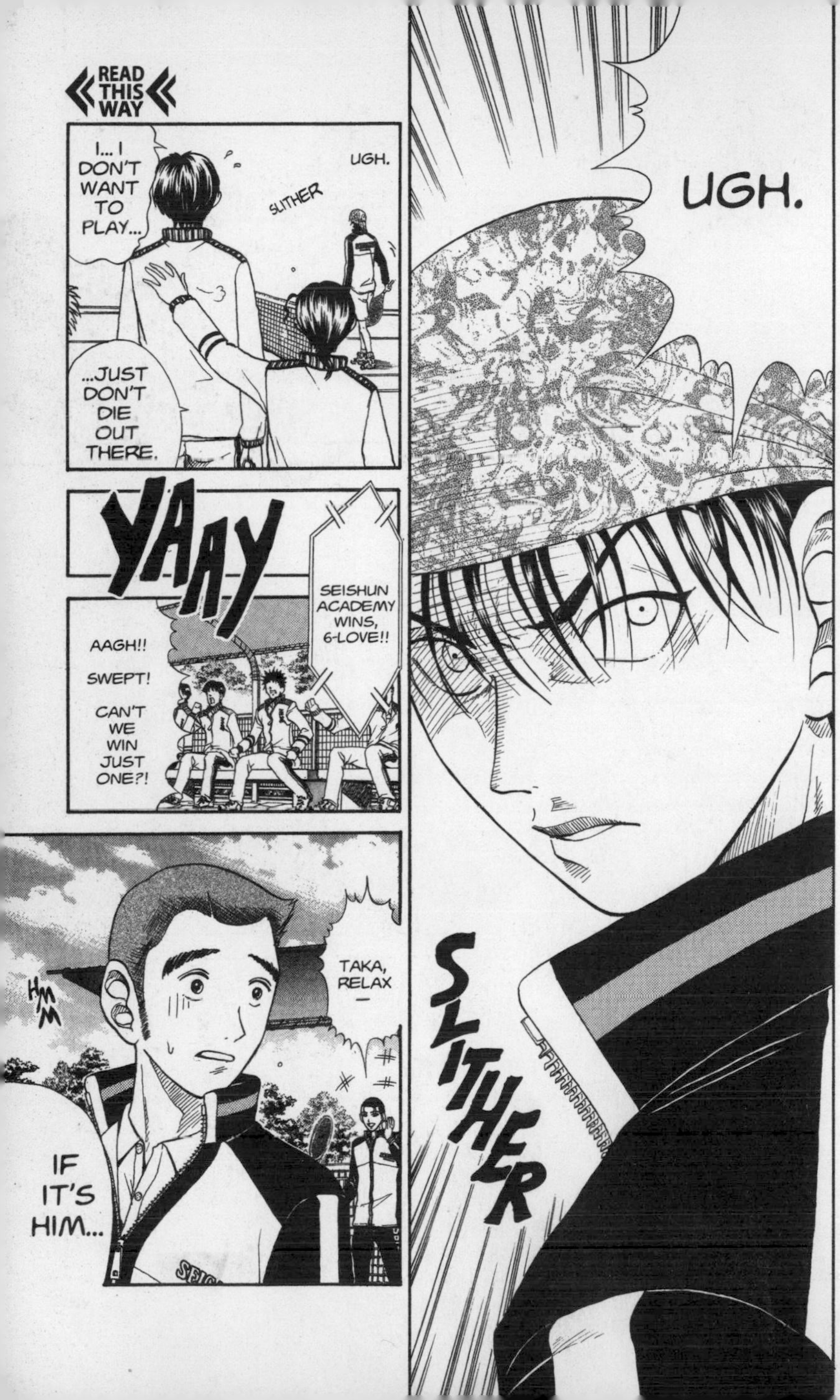
READ THIS WAY
UGH.
SLITHER
UGH.
SLITHER
I... I DON'T WANT TO PLAY...
...JUST DON'T DIE OUT THERE.
YAAY
SEISHUN ACADEMY WINS, 6-LOVE!!
AAGH!!
SWEPT!
CAN'T WE WIN JUST ONE?!
TAKA, RELAX —
HMM
IF IT'S HIM...

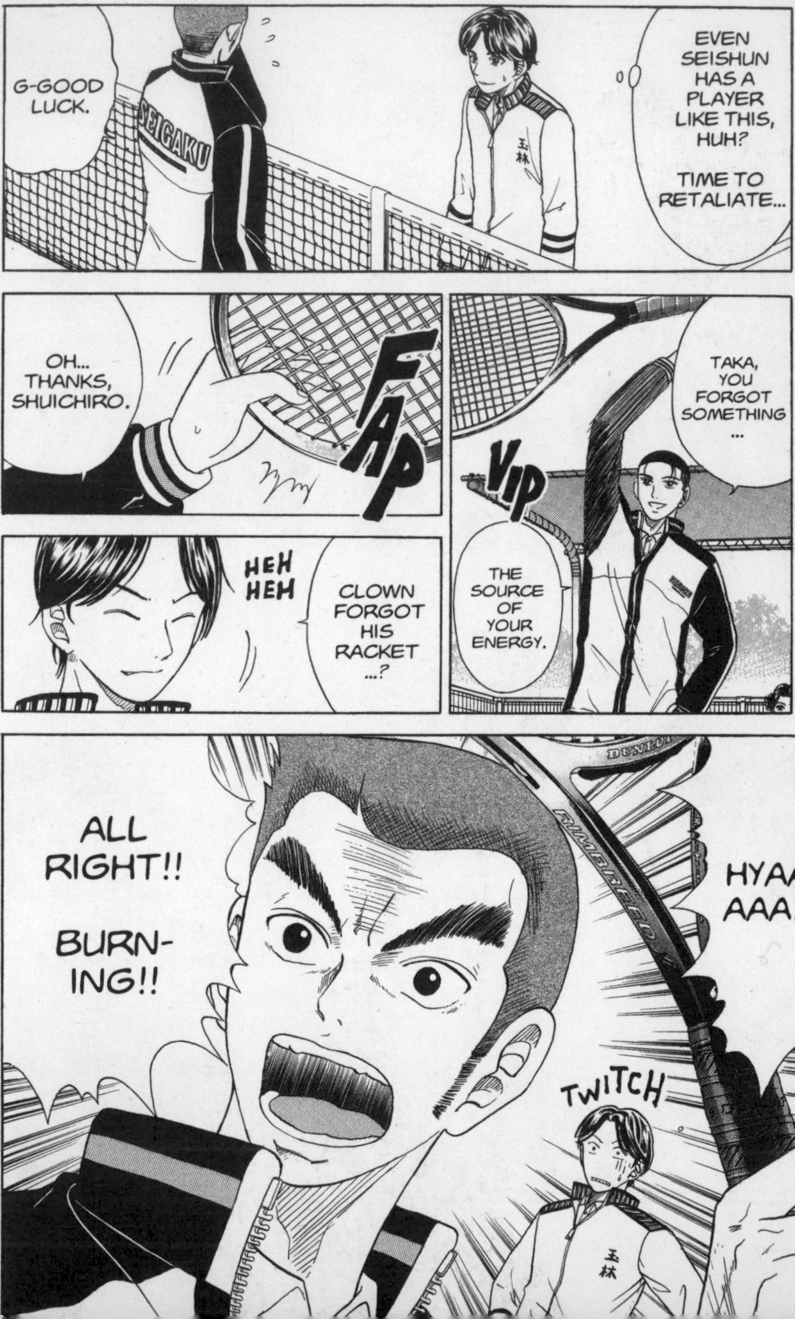
EVEN SEISHUN HAS A PLAYER LIKE THIS, HUH?
TIME TO RETALIATE...
G-GOOD LUCK.
TAKA, YOU FORGOT SOMETHING ...
VIP
THE SOURCE OF YOUR ENERGY.
OH... THANKS, SHUICHIRO.
FAP
CLOWN FORGOT HIS RACKET ...?
HEH HEH
HYAA AAA!!
ALL RIGHT!!
BURN-ING!!
TWITCH

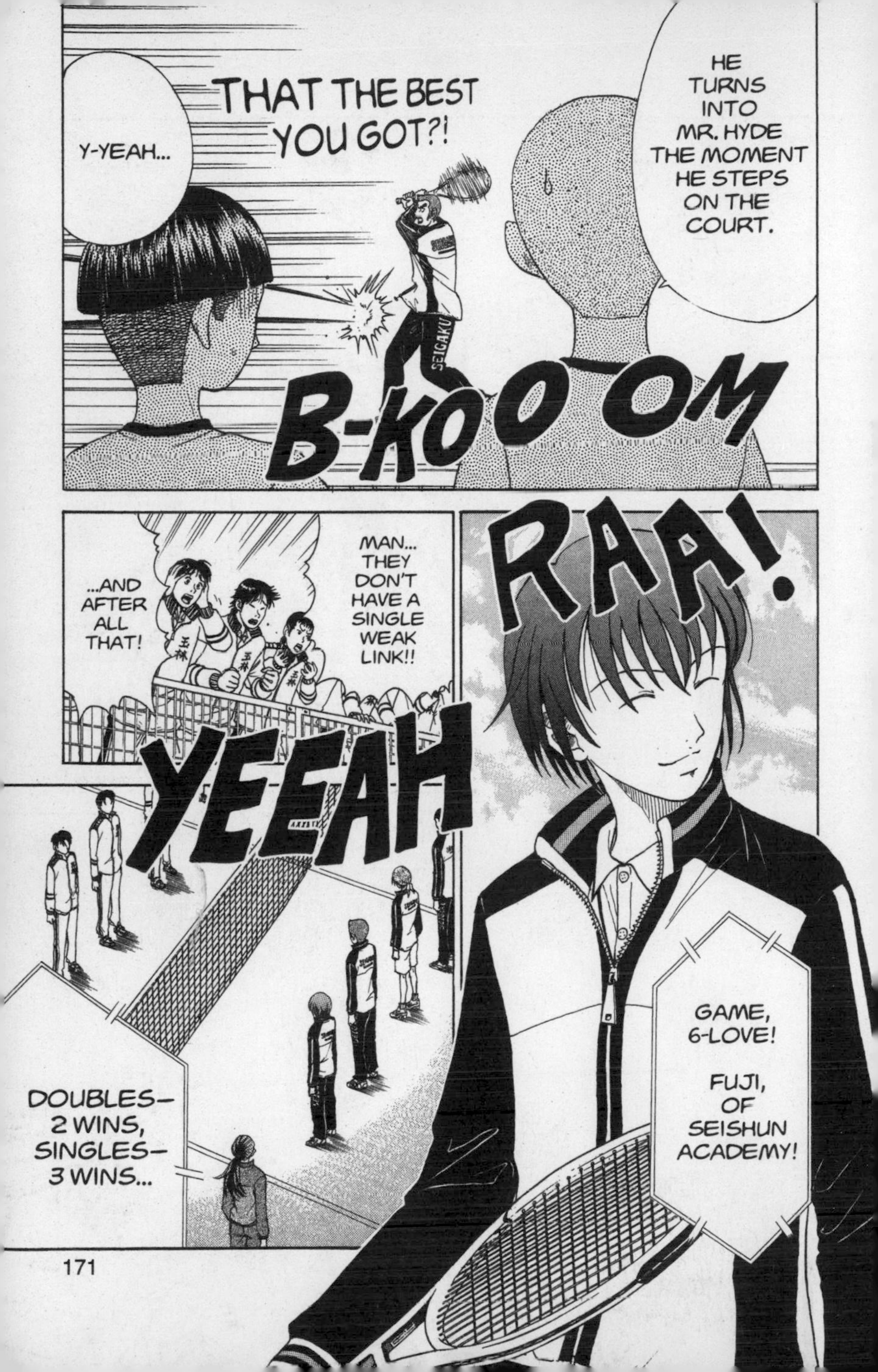

HE TURNS INTO MR. HYDE THE MOMENT HE STEPS ON THE COURT.
THAT THE BEST YOU GOT?!
Y-YEAH...
B-KOO-OM
RAA!
MAN... THEY DON'T HAVE A SINGLE WEAK LINK!!
...AND AFTER ALL THAT!
YEEAH
GAME, 6-LOVE!
FUJI, OF SEISHUN ACADEMY!
DOUBLES—2 WINS, SINGLES—3 WINS...

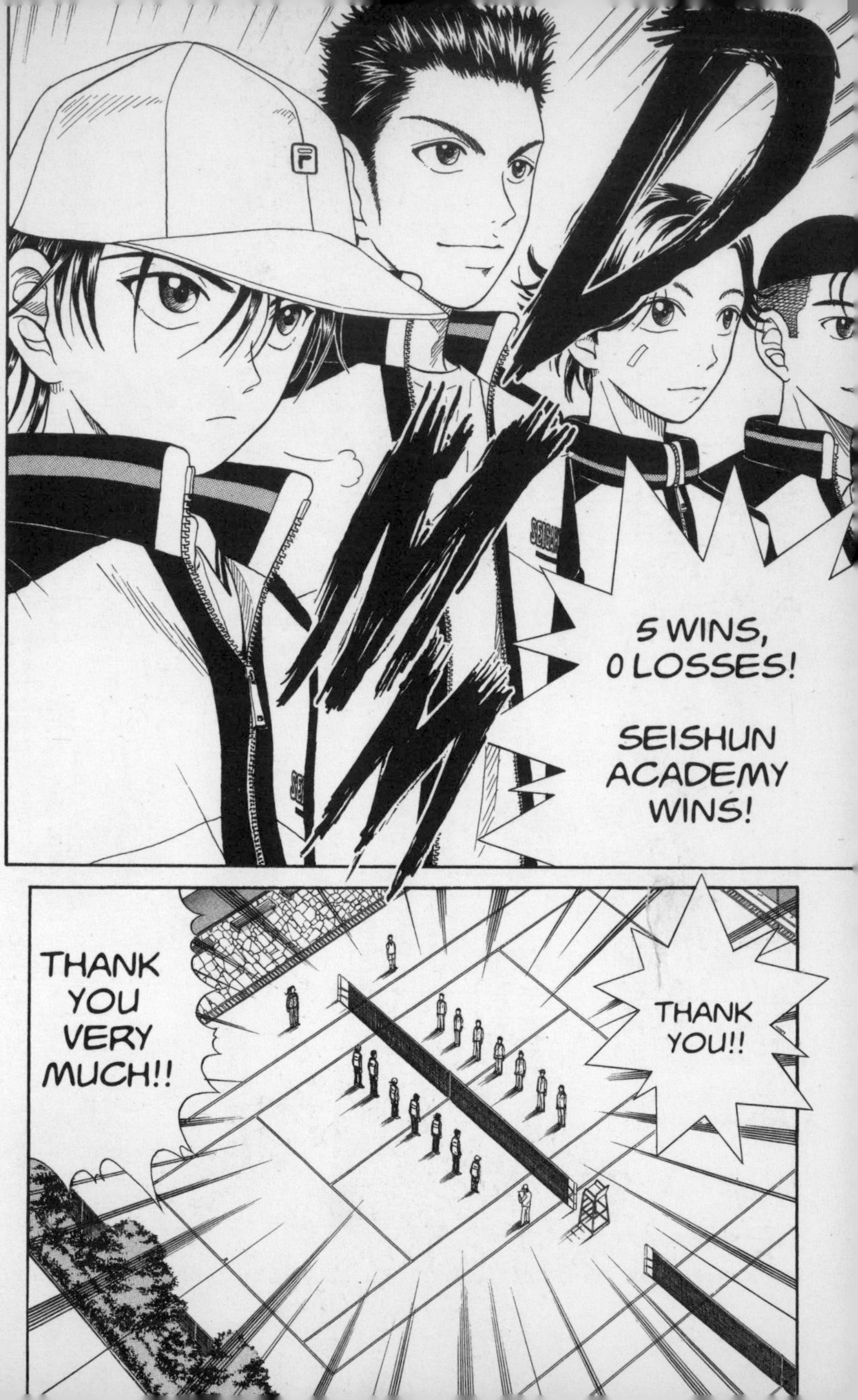
5 WINS, 0 LOSSES!
SEISHUN ACADEMY WINS!
THANK YOU!!
THANK YOU VERY MUCH!!

READ THIS WAY

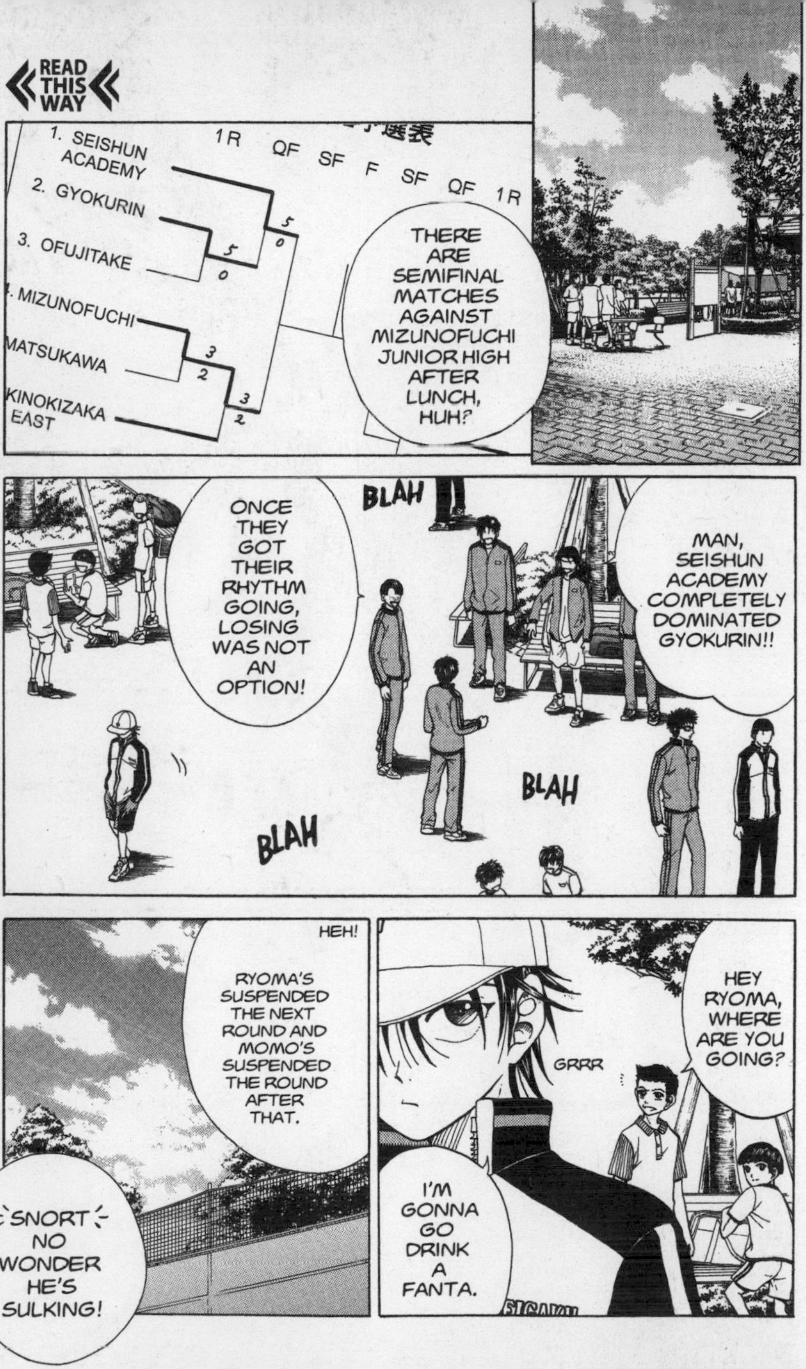
1R QF SF F SF QF 1R
1. SEISHUN ACADEMY
2. GYOKURIN
3. OFUJITAKE
MIZUNOFUCHI
MATSUKAWA
KINOKIZAKA EAST
5 0 5 0 3 2 3 2
THERE ARE SEMIFINAL MATCHES AGAINST MIZUNOFUCHI JUNIOR HIGH AFTER LUNCH, HUH?
MAN, SEISHUN ACADEMY COMPLETELY DOMINATED GYOKURIN!!
BLAH
ONCE THEY GOT THEIR RHYTHM GOING, LOSING WAS NOT AN OPTION!
BLAH
BLAH
HEY RYOMA, WHERE ARE YOU GOING?
GRRR
I'M GONNA GO DRINK A FANTA.
HEH!
RYOMA'S SUSPENDED THE NEXT ROUND AND MOMO'S SUSPENDED THE ROUND AFTER THAT.
SNORT NO WONDER HE'S SULKING!

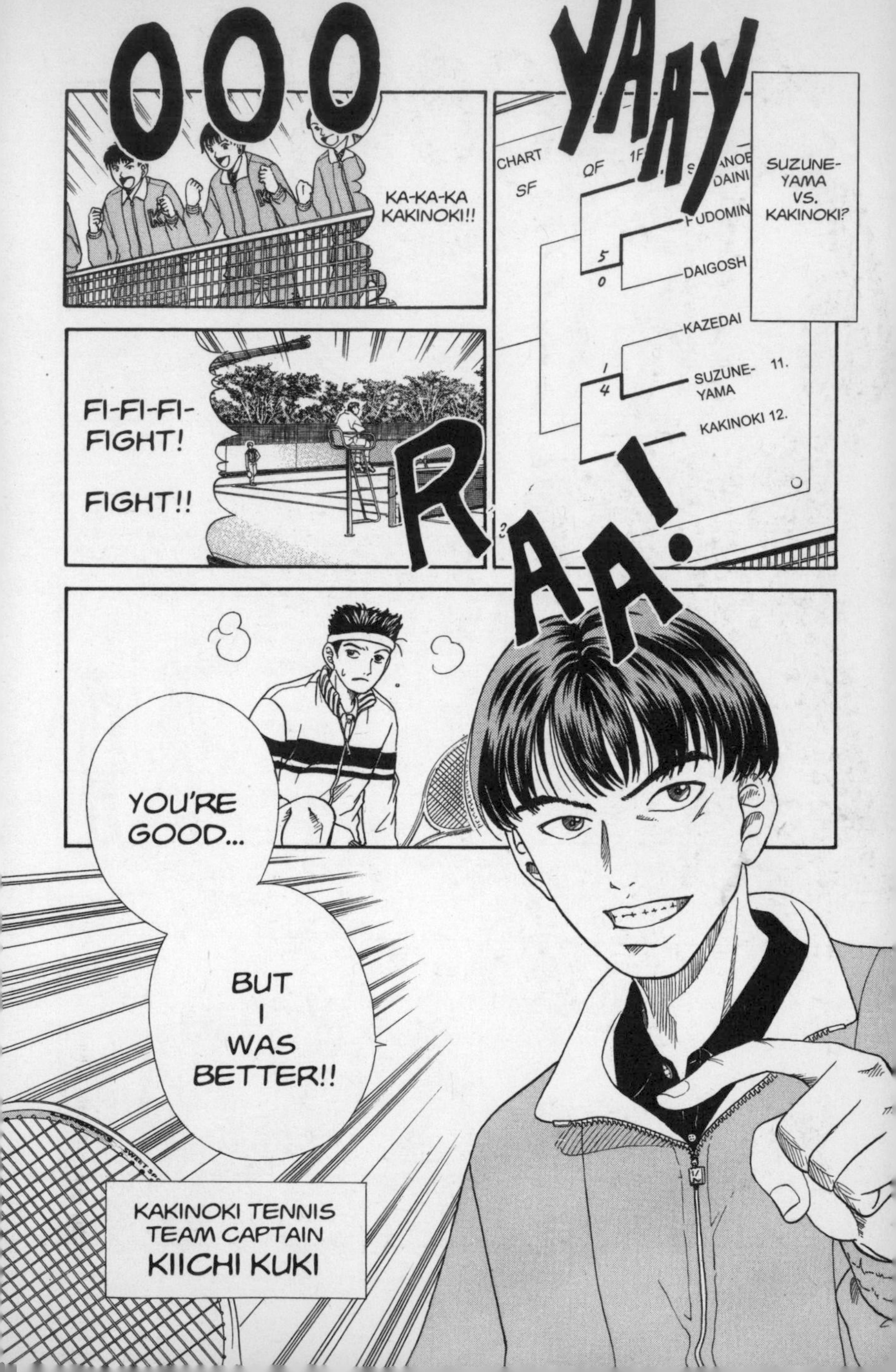
YAAY
SUZUNE-YAMA VS. KAKINOKI?
CHART
SF
QF
DAINI
DAIGOSH
5
0
KAZEDAI
1
4
SUZUNE-YAMA 11.
KAKINOKI 12.
OOO
KA-KA-KA KAKINOKI!!
FI-FI-FI-FIGHT!
FIGHT!!
RAA!
YOU'RE GOOD...
BUT I WAS BETTER!!
KAKINOKI TENNIS TEAM CAPTAIN KIICHI KUKI

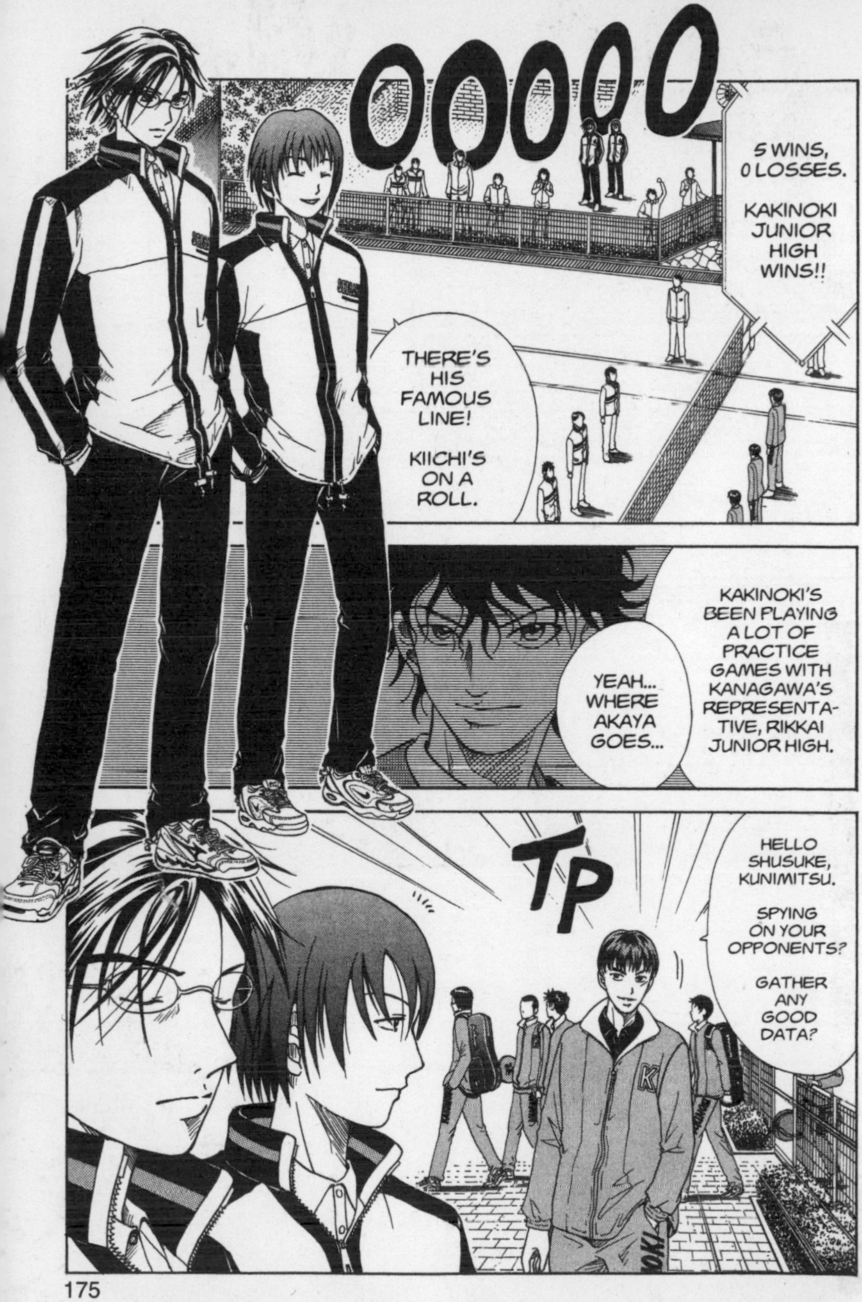
5 WINS, 0 LOSSES.
KAKINOKI JUNIOR HIGH WINS!!
OOOOO
THERE'S HIS FAMOUS LINE!
KIICHI'S ON A ROLL.
KAKINOKI'S BEEN PLAYING A LOT OF PRACTICE GAMES WITH KANAGAWA'S REPRESENTA-TIVE, RIKKAI JUNIOR HIGH.
YEAH... WHERE AKAYA GOES...
HELLO SHUSUKE, KUNIMITSU.
SPYING ON YOUR OPPONENTS?
GATHER ANY GOOD DATA?
TP

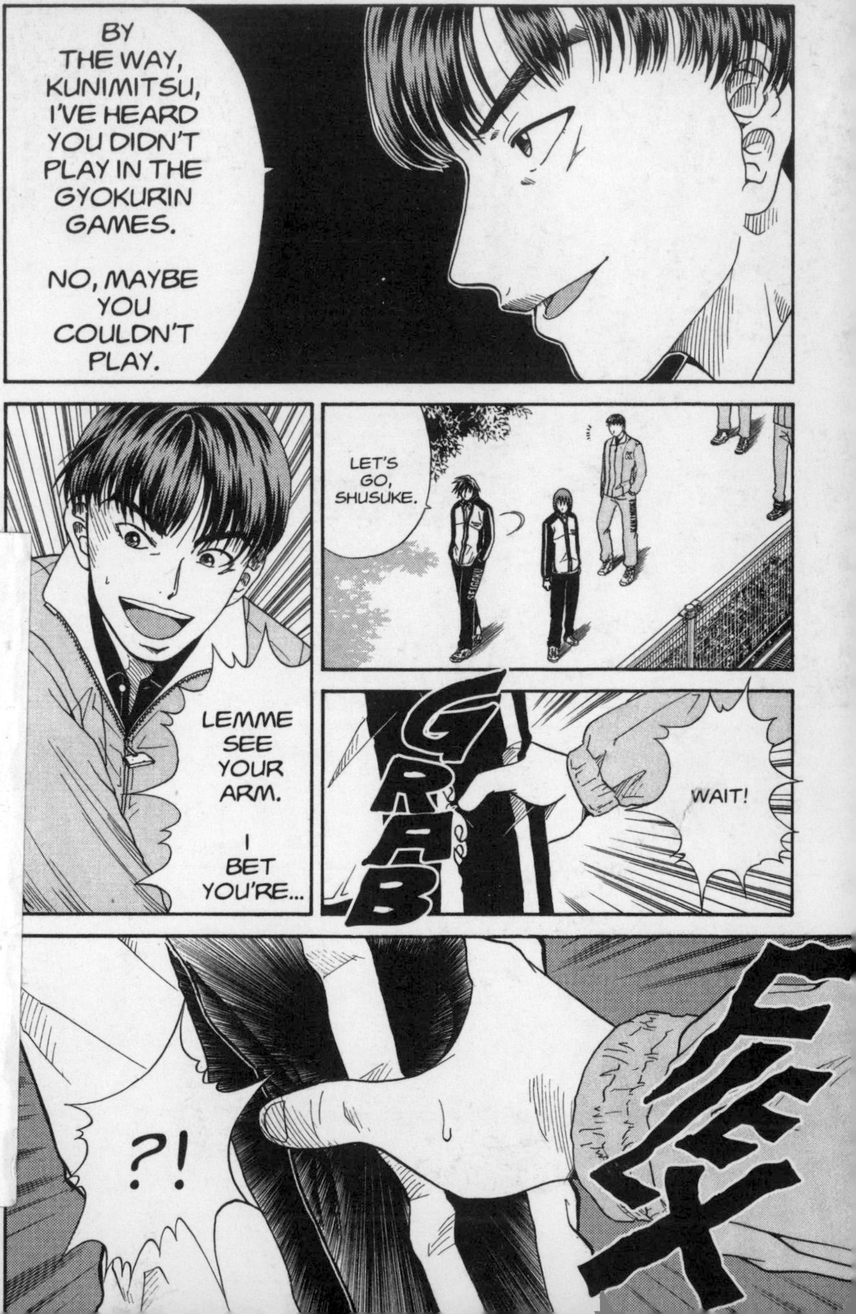
BY THE WAY, KUNIMITSU, I'VE HEARD YOU DIDN'T PLAY IN THE GYOKURIN GAMES.
NO, MAYBE YOU COULDN'T PLAY.
LET'S GO, SHUSUKE.
WAIT!
GRAB
LEMME SEE YOUR ARM.
I BET YOU'RE...
?!

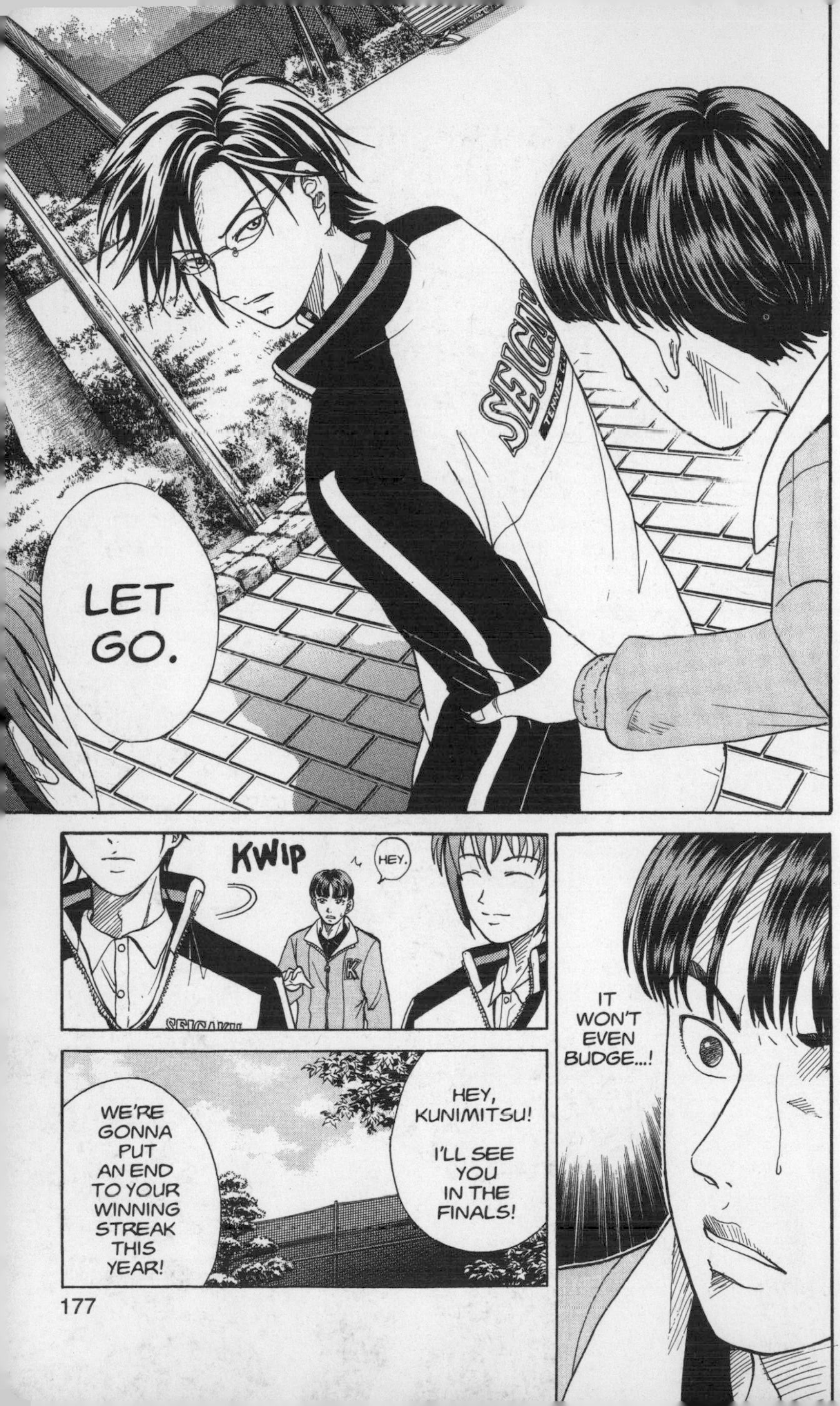
LET GO.
IT WON'T EVEN BUDGE...!
HEY.
KWIP
HEY, KUNIMITSU!
I'LL SEE YOU IN THE FINALS!
WE'RE GONNA PUT AN END TO YOUR WINNING STREAK THIS YEAR!

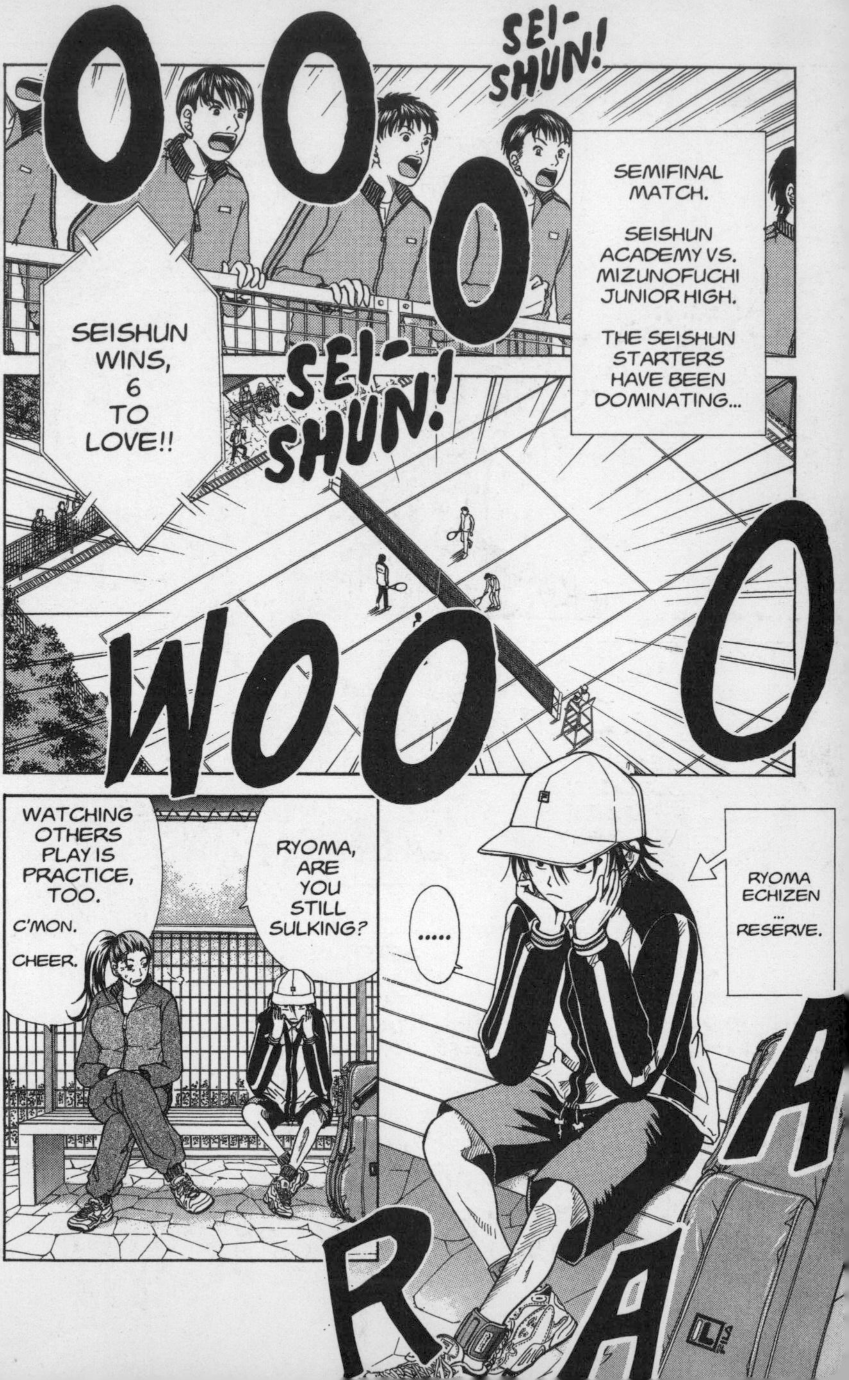
SEI-SHUN!
OOO
SEMIFINAL MATCH.
SEISHUN ACADEMY VS. MIZUNOFUCHI JUNIOR HIGH.
THE SEISHUN STARTERS HAVE BEEN DOMINATING...
SEI-SHUN!
SEISHUN WINS, 6 TO LOVE!!
WOOOO
RYOMA ECHIZEN ... RESERVE.
.....
RAAA
RYOMA, ARE YOU STILL SULKING?
WATCHING OTHERS PLAY IS PRACTICE, TOO.
C'MON.
CHEER.

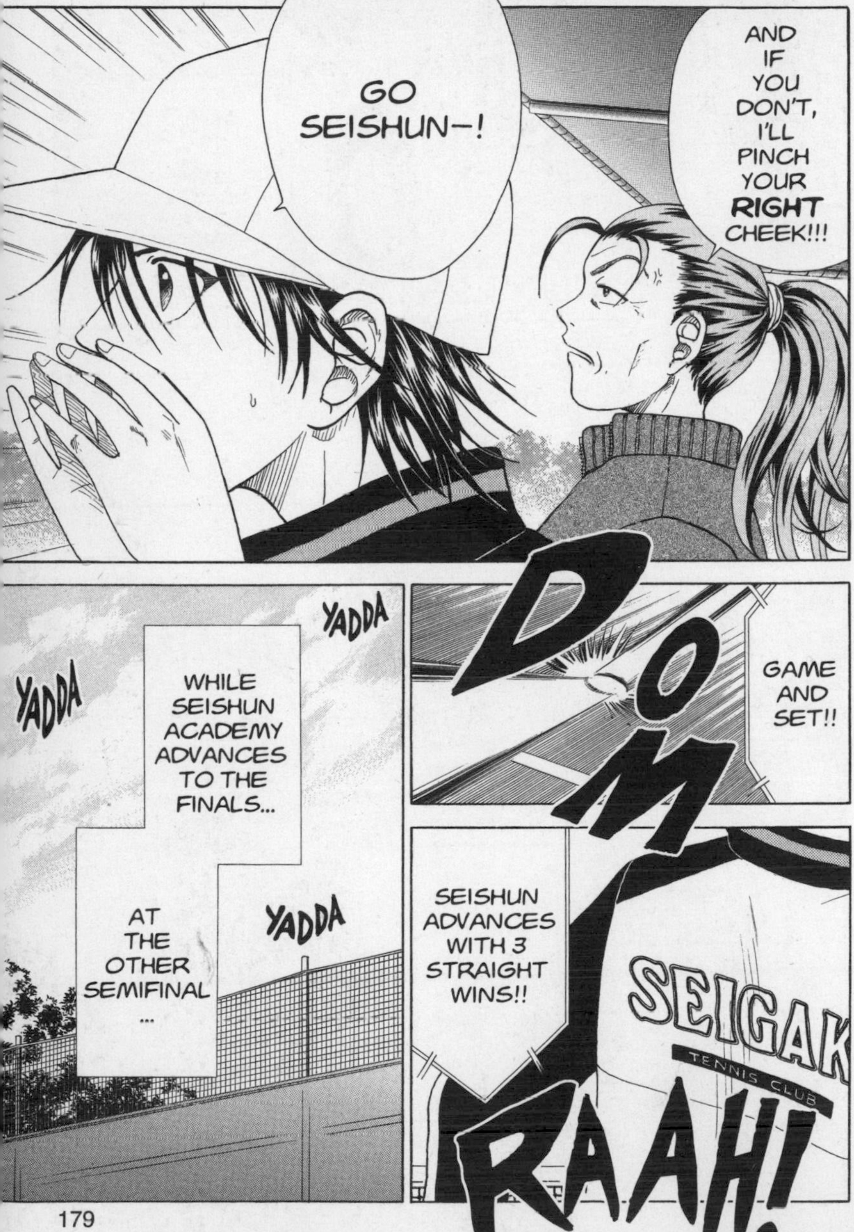
AND IF YOU DON'T, I'LL PINCH YOUR **RIGHT** CHEEK!!!
GO SEISHUN—!
DOM
GAME AND SET!!
SEISHUN ADVANCES WITH 3 STRAIGHT WINS!!
SEIGAK
TENNIS CLUB
RAAH!
YADDA
WHILE SEISHUN ACADEMY ADVANCES TO THE FINALS...
YADDA
YADDA
AT THE OTHER SEMIFINAL ...

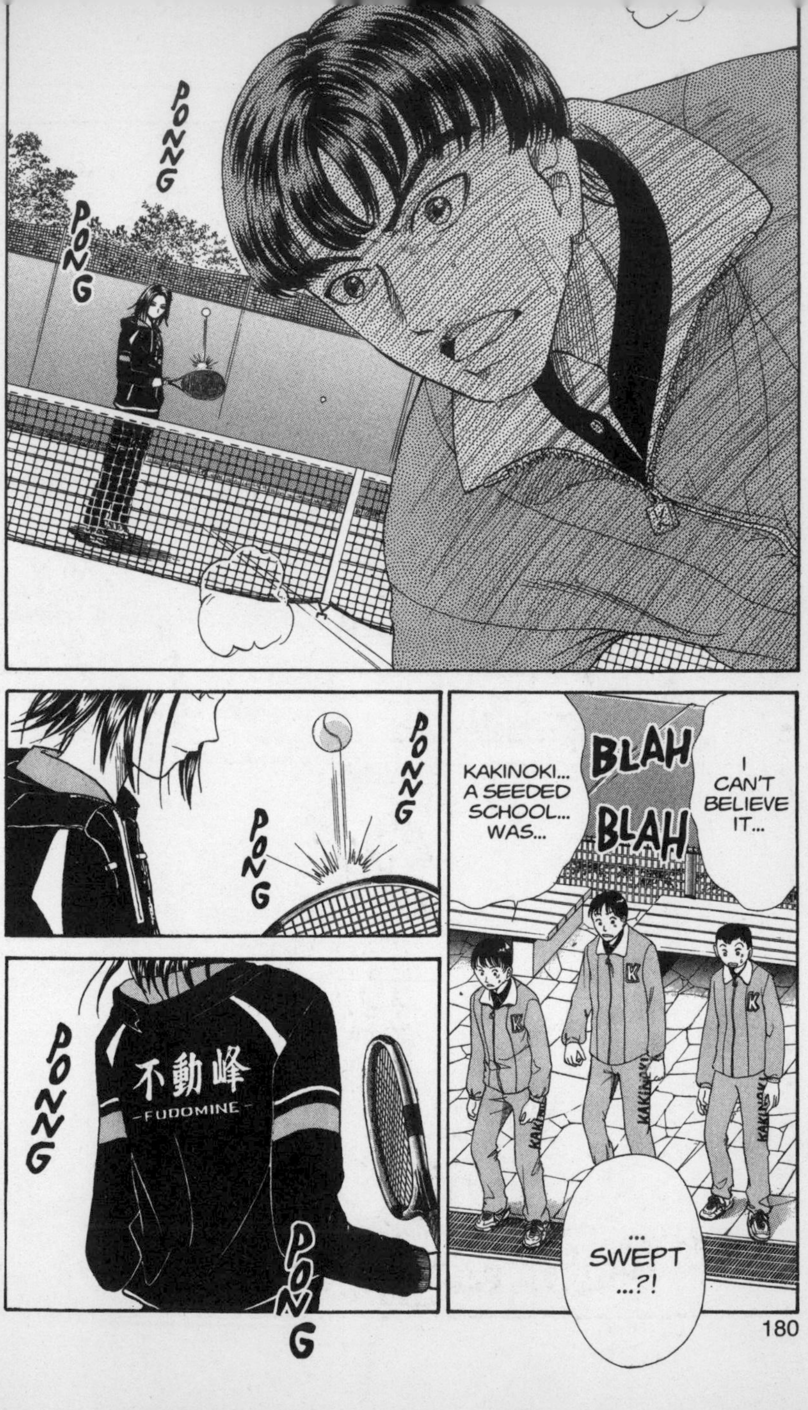
PONNG
PONG
I CAN'T BELIEVE IT...
BLAH
BLAH
KAKINOKI... A SEEDED SCHOOL... WAS...
... SWEPT ...?!
PONNG
PONG
不動峰
-FUDOMINE-
PONNG
PONG

READ THIS WAY

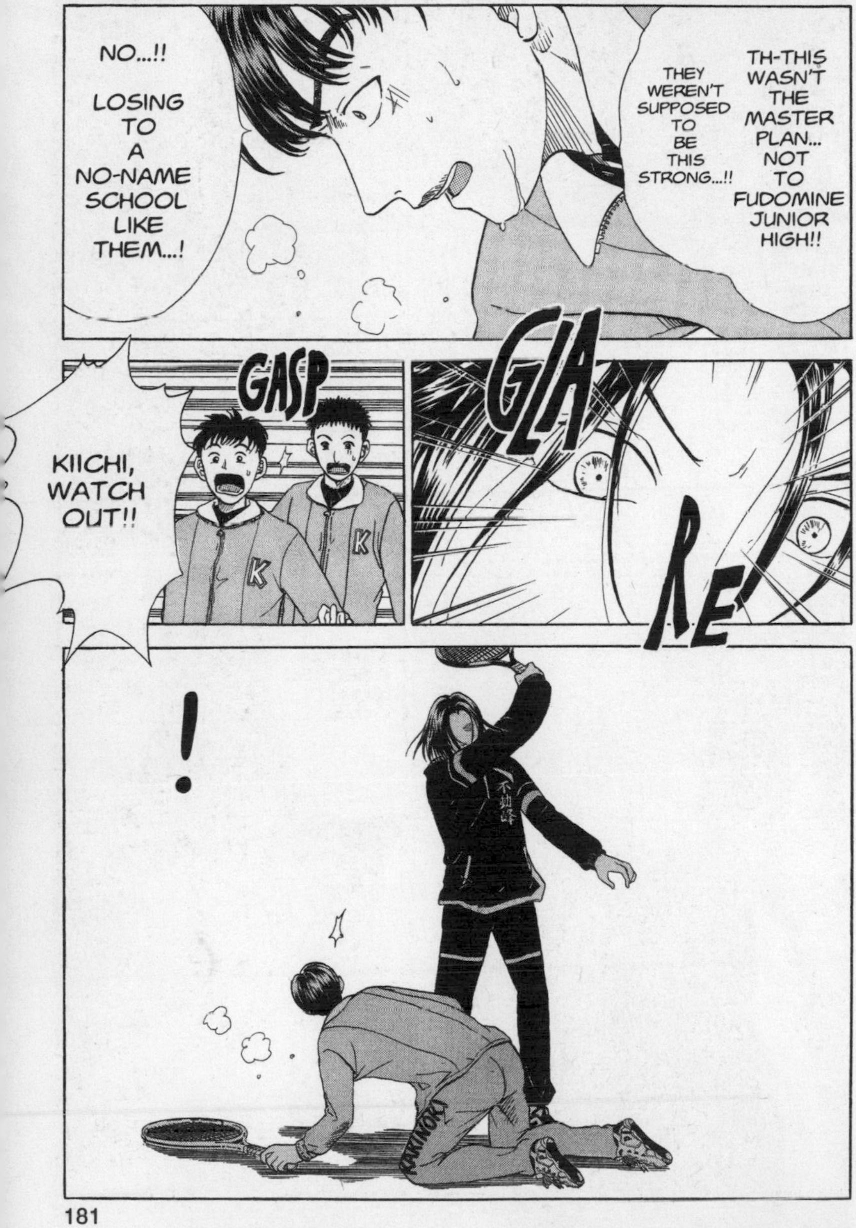
TH-THIS WASN'T THE MASTER PLAN... NOT TO FUDOMINE JUNIOR HIGH!!
THEY WEREN'T SUPPOSED TO BE THIS STRONG...!!
NO...!!
LOSING TO A NO-NAME SCHOOL LIKE THEM...!
GLARE
GASP
KIICHI, WATCH OUT!!
!
KAKINOKI

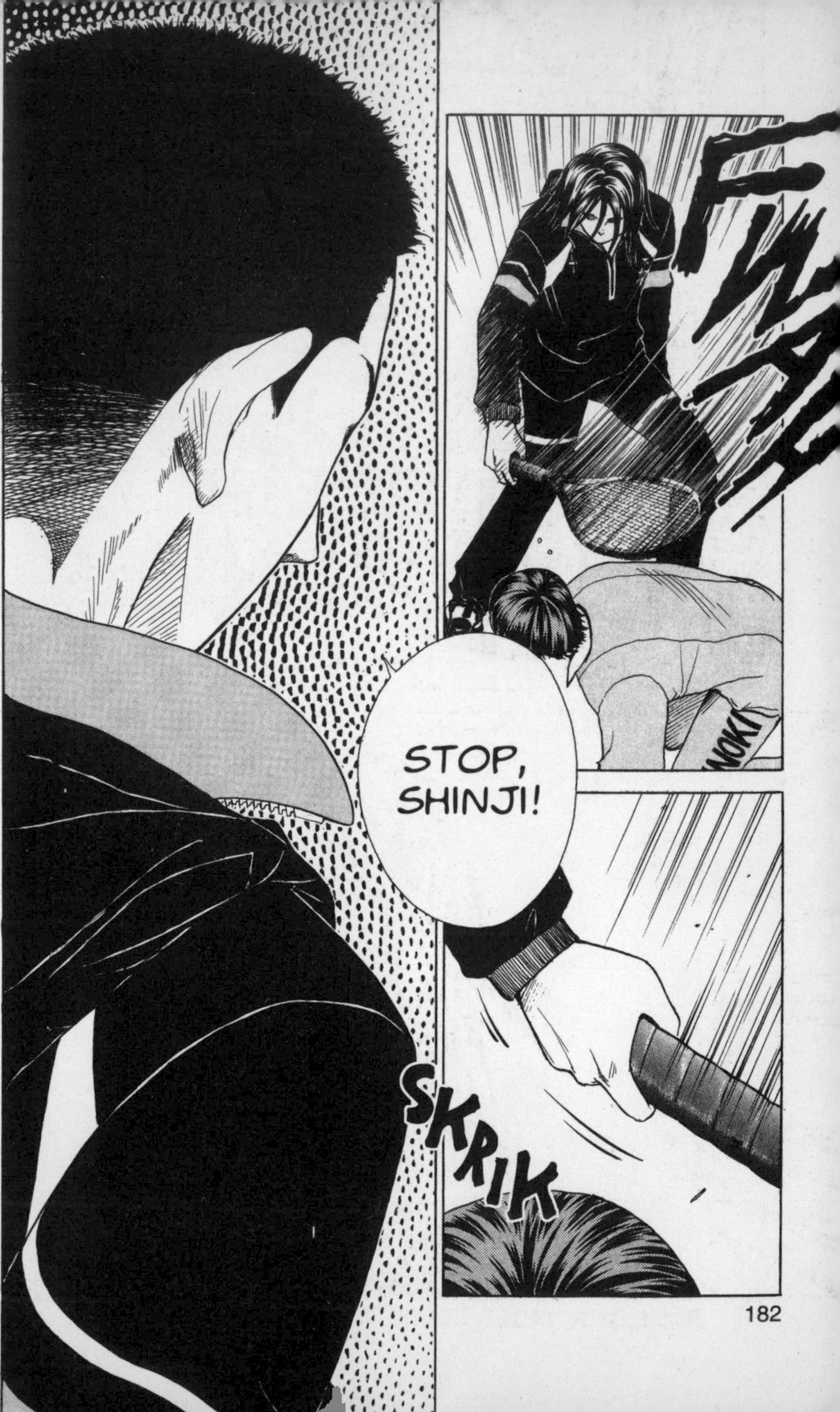
STOP, SHINJI!
SKRIK

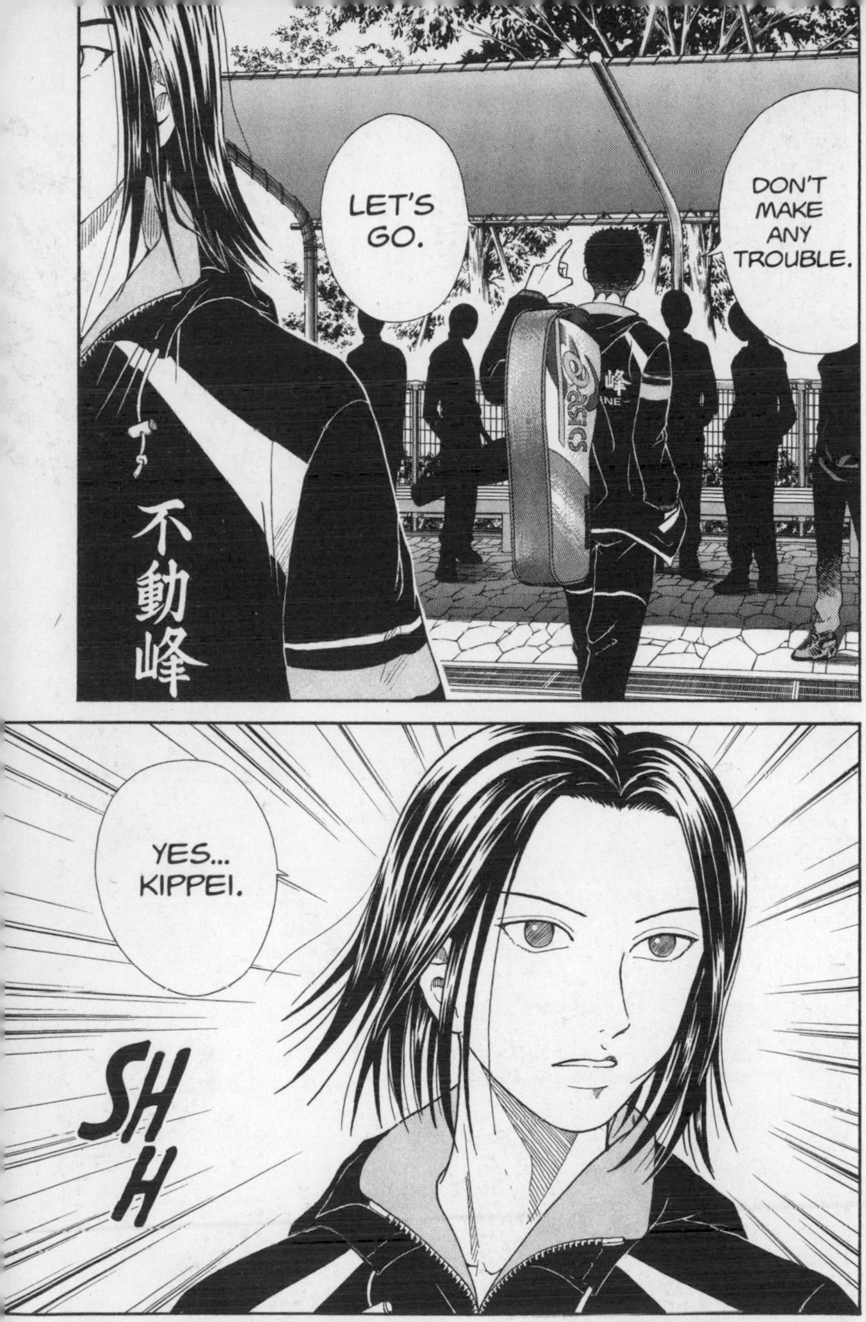
DON'T MAKE ANY TROUBLE.
LET'S GO.
不動峰
YES... KIPPEI.
SHH

 TO BE CONTINUED IN VOL. 4

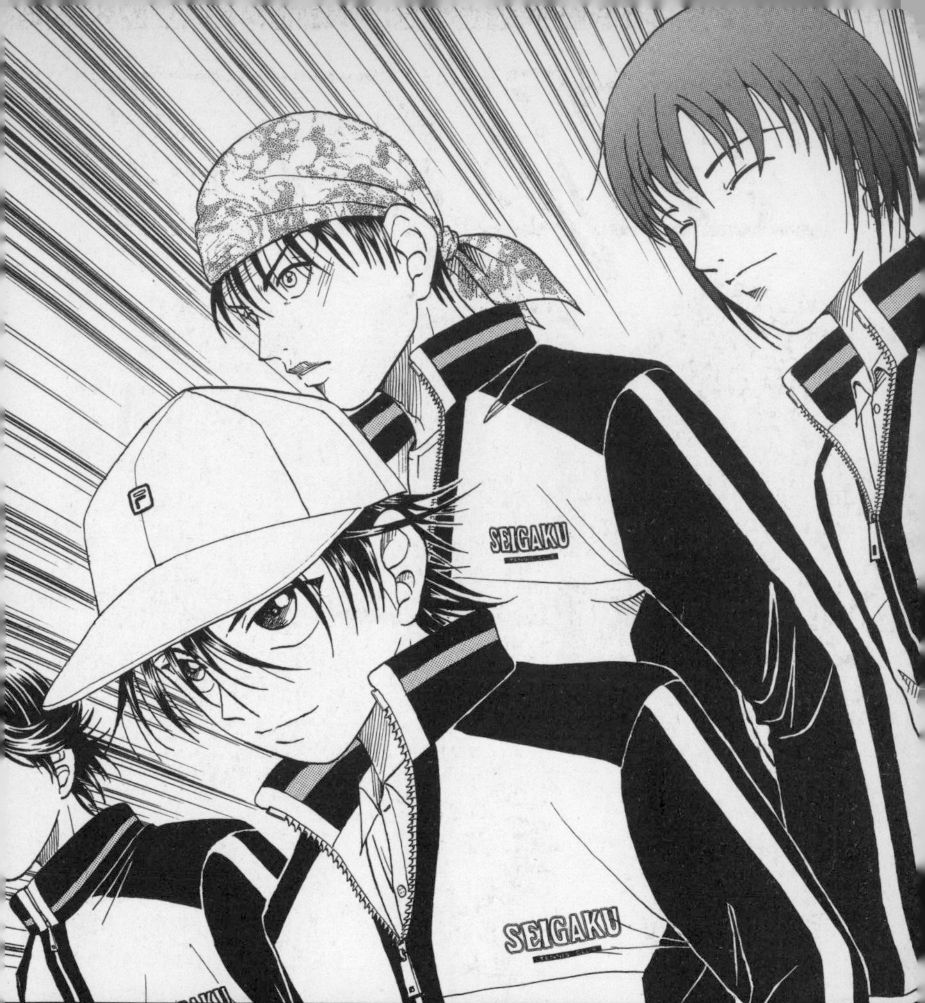

SEIGAKU
SEIGAKU

After coasting through Mizunofuchi Junior High, Seishun Academy tackles the unseeded Fudomine team, a rogue bunch of tennis players who were disqualified from the rookie games last year due to a fighting scandal. Frustrated with their school's team policy, these students rebelled and formed their own team. Find out in the next volume if Seishun Academy's players have the endurance, power and skills to vanquish the notorious Fudomine team in the District Preliminaries!

AVAILABLE NOW!

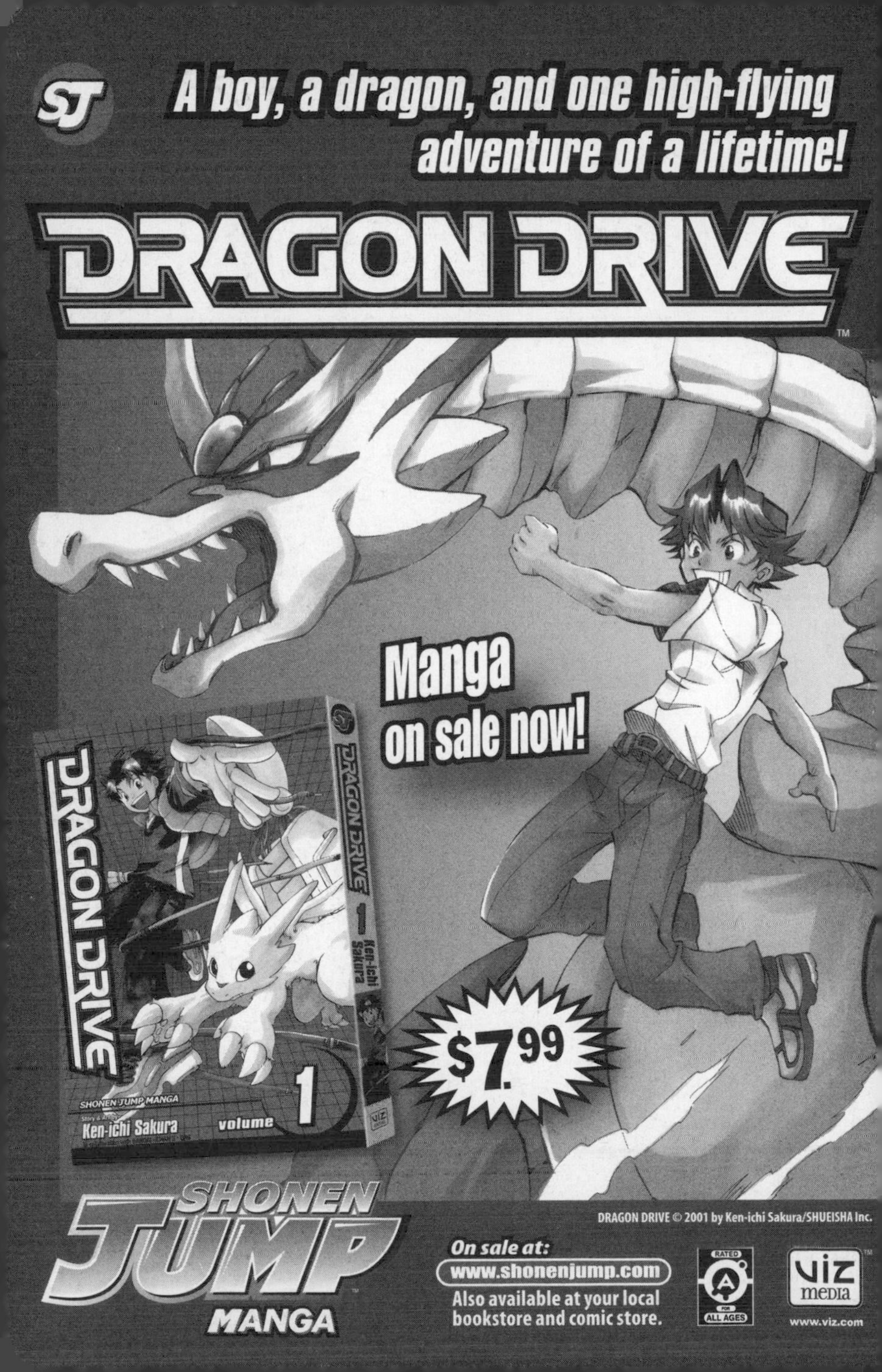

SJ
A boy, a dragon, and one high-flying adventure of a lifetime!
DRAGON DRIVE™
Manga on sale now!
SJ
DRAGON DRIVE
1
Ken-ichi Sakura
DRAGON DRIVE
SHONEN JUMP MANGA
Ken-ichi Sakura
volume 1
$7.99
SHONEN JUMP™ MANGA
DRAGON DRIVE © 2001 by Ken-ichi Sakura/SHUEISHA Inc.
On sale at:
www.shonenjump.com
Also available at your local bookstore and comic store.
RATED A FOR ALL AGES
VIZ media
www.viz.com

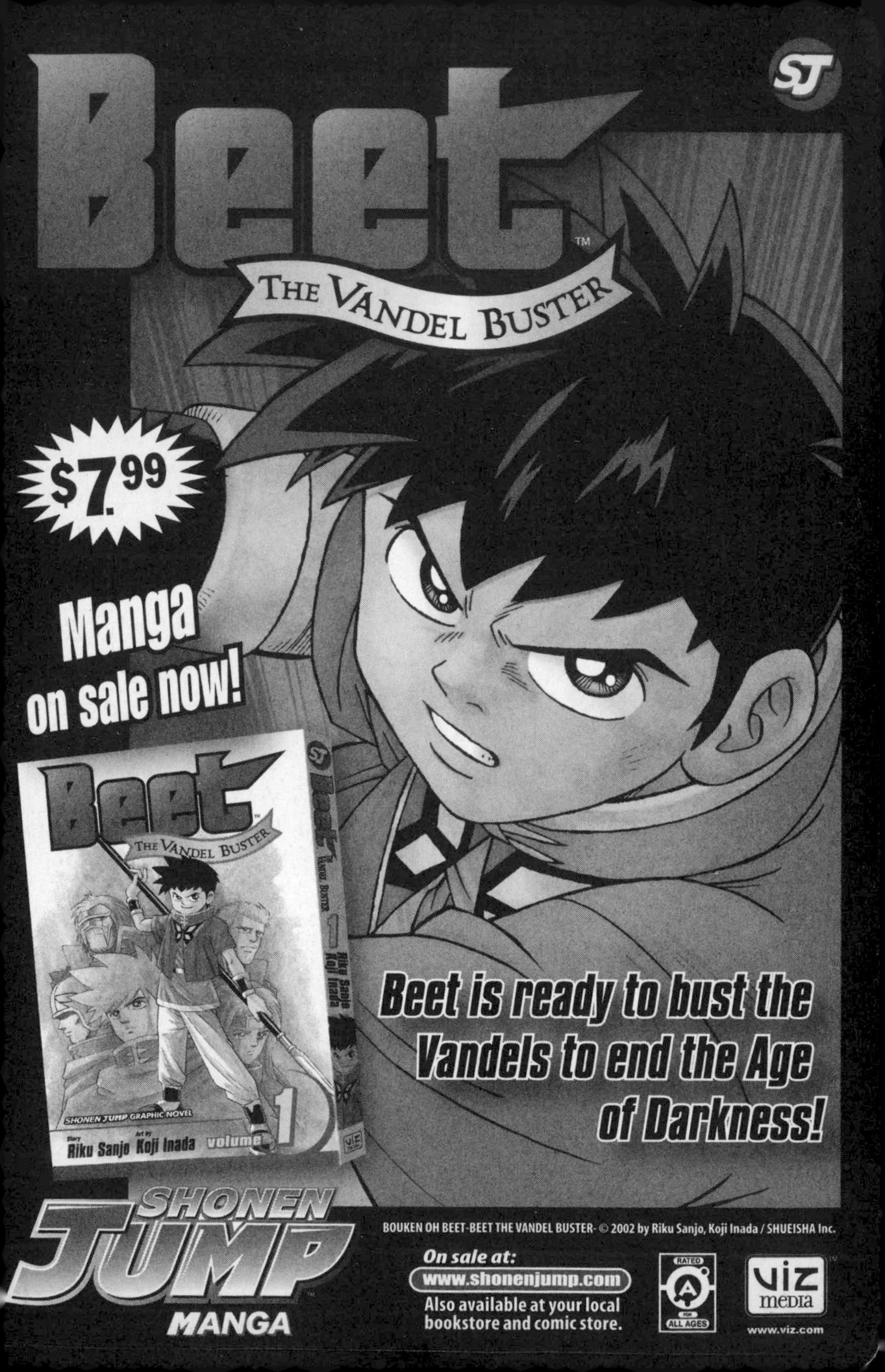
SJ
Beet™
THE VANDEL BUSTER
$7.99
Manga on sale now!
Beet is ready to bust the Vandels to end the Age of Darkness!
SJ
Beet™
THE VANDEL BUSTER
SHONEN JUMP GRAPHIC NOVEL
Story Riku Sanjo Art by Koji Inada volume 1
SHONEN JUMP MANGA
BOUKEN OH BEET-BEET THE VANDEL BUSTER- © 2002 by Riku Sanjo, Koji Inada / SHUEISHA Inc.
On sale at:
www.shonenjump.com
Also available at your local bookstore and comic store.
RATED A FOR ALL AGES
VIZ media
www.viz.com

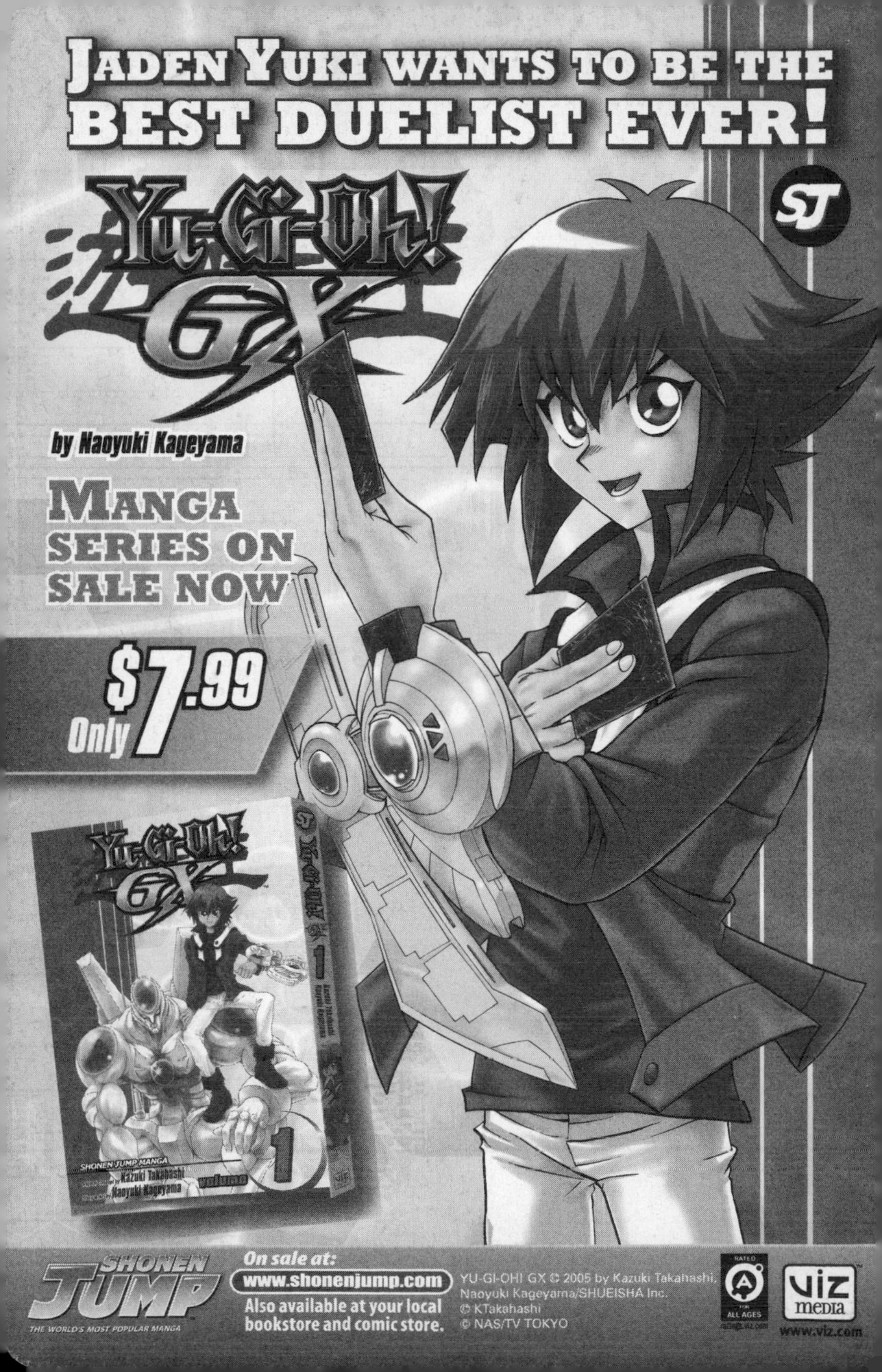
JADEN YUKI WANTS TO BE THE
BEST DUELIST EVER!
SJ
YU-GI-OH! GX
by Naoyuki Kageyama
MANGA
SERIES ON
SALE NOW
Only $7.99
YU-GI-OH! GX
1
SHONEN JUMP MANGA
Kazuki Takahashi
Naoyuki Kageyama
SHONEN JUMP
THE WORLD'S MOST POPULAR MANGA
On sale at:
www.shonenjump.com
Also available at your local bookstore and comic store.
YU-GI-OH! GX © 2005 by Kazuki Takahashi, Naoyuki Kageyama/SHUEISHA Inc.
© KTakahashi
© NAS/TV TOKYO
RATED A FOR ALL AGES
viz media
www.viz.com